Dreams and History

The interpretation of dreams from ancient Greece to modern psychoanalysis

Edited by Daniel Pick and Lyndal Roper

Routledge
Taylor & Francis Group

LONDON AND NEW YORK

First published 2004 by Routledge
27 Church Road, Hove, East Sussex BN3 2FA

Simultaneously published in the USA and Canada
by Routledge
711 Third Avenue, New York, NY 10017

Routledge is an imprint of the Taylor & Francis Group, an informa business

Transferred to Digital Printing 2011

Typeset in 10/12pt Times New Roman by
Graphicraft Limited, Hong Kong
Paperback cover design by Sandra Heath

British Library Cataloguing in Publication Data
A catalogue record for this book is available from the British Library

Library of Congress Cataloging-in-Publication Data
Dreams and history / [edited by] Daniel Pick and Lyndal Roper.—1st ed.
     p.   cm.
   Includes bibliographical references and index.
   ISBN 1-58391-282-7 (alk. paper) – ISBN 1-58391-283-5
(pbk.: alk. paper)
   1. Dreams–History.   2. Dream interpretation–History.
 I. Pick, Daniel. II. Roper, Lyndal.
BF1078.D735 2003
154.6'3'09–dc21

                                        2003006202

ISBN 978-1-58391-283-6 (pbk)

Publisher's Note
The publisher has gone to great lengths to ensure the quality of this reprint
but points out that some imperfections in the original may be apparent.

Dreams and History

Dreams are universal, but their perceived significance and conceptual framework change over time. *Dreams and History* provides fresh perspectives on the history of dreams and dream interpretation in western culture and thought.

Containing important new scholarship on Freud's *The Interpretation of Dreams*, and an exploration of subsequent psychoanalytical approaches, this collection celebrates and contextualizes Freud's landmark intellectual production, whilst placing it alongside very different traditions of thought. Drawing on recent work in psychoanalysis and history, anthropology and art history, literature and history of science, it also discusses controversial ideas about the role of the external world in the shaping of unconscious mental contents.

In accessible language it explores the causes, meanings and consequences of dreams, from Victorian anthropological exploration of ancient Greek sources to peasant interpretations of oneiric life in communist Russia, from medieval to modern dream narratives, from concepts of the dream in sixteenth-century England to visual images in nineteenth-century symbolist painting in France.

Dreams and History will fascinate those interested in psychoanalysis, art, literature and myth.

Daniel Pick is a psychoanalyst and Professor of Cultural History, Queen Mary, University of London.

Lyndal Roper is a fellow and tutor in History at Balliol College, Oxford.

Contents

List of figures

Contributors

Hans-Jürgen Bachorski was born in 1950 and studied in Hamburg and Berlin. He became professor of German medieval literature at the University of Potsdam and worked on the romance of the late middle ages and early modern period, on laughter and comedy, on the history of mentalities, and on the use of the 'medieval' in film. He died in 2001; his major study on the poetics of the late medieval and early modern novel is currently being prepared for publication.

Susan Budd is a member of the British Psychoanalytical Society. She was previously a lecturer in sociology at the London School of Economics. Her publications include *Sociologists and Religion* (1973) and *Varieties of Unbelief: Atheists and Agnostics in English Society, 1850–1960* (1977).

Laura Cameron is an assistant professor in Human Geography at Queen's University, Kingston, Ontario. She is the author of *Openings: A Meditation on History, Method and Sumas Lake* (1997): her work has appeared in *Histoire sociale/Social History, Native Studies Review, History Workshop Journal, Psychoanalysis and History, Radical History Review* and *Historical Geography*.

Patricia Crawford is professor of history at the University of Western Australia. Her most recent books are *Women in Early Modern England, 1550–1720*, with Sarah Mendelson (1999), and, with Laura Gowing, *Women's Worlds in Seventeenth-Century England: A Sourcebook* (1999). She is currently working on a book about parents and children in early modern England.

Jennifer Ford, an independent scholar based in Australia, works on Romanticism, poetry and history of medicine. Her book, *Coleridge and Dreaming*, was published in 1998.

John Forrester is a professor in the History and Philosophy of Sciences Department, Cambridge University. His publications include *Language and the Origins of Psychoanalysis* (1980) and *Truth Games: Lies, Money and Psychoanalysis* (1997). His new book, *The Freudian Century*, will be published by Penguin.

Ilse Grubrich-Simitis is a training analyst of the Frankfurt Psychoanalytical Institute and has written widely on Freud and the history of psychoanalysis. Her publications include *Back to Freud's Texts* (1996) and *Early Freud and Late Freud* (1997).

Rhodri Hayward is research fellow at the Wellcome Trust Centre for the History of Medicine at University College London. He is working on a history of psychiatry and general practice in twentieth-century Britain. He has published on the history of revivalism, psychiatry and neurology, and is completing a book on popular mysticism and the invention of the unconscious.

Stefanie Heraeus is an art historian. Her catalogue and commentary on the collection of paintings in the Staatliche Museen Kassel, Germany, *Spätbarock und Klassizismus*, appeared recently. She is the author of *Traumvorstellung und Bildidee – Surreale Strategien in der französischen Graphik des 19. Jahrhunderts* (1998) and also lectures in Göttingen and Kassel.

Edna O'Shaughnessy is a training analyst in the British Psychoanalytical Society, an editor of Melanie Klein and Roger Money-Kyrle's work, and an author of many influential papers on clinical technique. She is a trustee of the Melanie Klein Trust and a clinical supervisor in child psychotherapy at the Tavistock Clinic, London.

Maureen Perkins, research fellow at Curtin University of Technology, Perth, Western Australia, is the author of *Visions of the Future: Almanacs, Time and Cultural Change 1775–1870* (1996) and *The Reform of Time: Magic and Modernity* (2001). She is working on a history of stolen children in eighteenth- and nineteenth-century Britain.

Daniel Pick is professor of cultural history at Queen Mary, University of London, and a psychoanalyst. His work includes *Faces of Degeneration* (1989) and *Svengali's Web* (2000). He is completing a book on Garibaldi, Rome and nationalism in the nineteenth century.

Lyndal Roper is a fellow and tutor of Balliol College, Oxford. Her publications include *The Holy Household* (1989) and *Oedipus and the Devil* (1994). She is currently finishing a book on witchcraft in baroque Germany.

Hanna Segal was formerly Freud Professor at University College London, and President of the British Psychoanalytical Society. She is the author of many works on psychoanalysis, including *An Introduction to the Work of Melanie Klein* (1964) and *Dreams, Phantasy and Art* (1991).

Charles Stewart is reader in anthropology at University College London. His publications include *Demons and the Devil: Moral Imagination in*

Modern Greek Culture (1991). He is currently working on an historical and anthropological study of dreams in Greece.

Faith Wigzell is professor of Russian at the School of Slavonic and East European Studies, University College London. Her publications include *Reading Russian Fortunes* (1998).

Acknowledgements

Many of these essays first appeared in *History Workshop Journal*. Chapters 6, 7, 8, 10, 11 and 14 were published in Issue 48 (Autumn 1999); Chapters 4, 5, 9, 12 and 13 in Issue 49 (Spring 2000). Our thanks to the editors of *History Workshop Journal* and to Oxford University Press for permission and encouragement to publish this collection. The chapter by Ilse Grubrich-Simitis has also appeared in the journal *Psychoanalysis and History*, Volume 4, Number 2, Summer 2002 and we thank the editor for permission to republish it.

In developing this project, we received helpful advice and encouragement from Brenda Betteridge (Oxford University Press) and also from Susan Budd. Dave Moor, who was responsible for the original typesetting of the material, went beyond the call of duty in retrieving material we urgently required. Victoria Mihich has generously supplied the picture of Hanna Segal. We are also particularly grateful to John Forrester, Ruth Harris, Anna Davin, Margaret Hanbury, Irma Brenman Pick, Isobel Pick and Nick Stargardt for their helpful comments and suggestions. Several historians kindly supplied us with illuminating unpublished material, particularly, Joy Damousi, Willibald Steinmetz and Janine Rivière. We would also like to thank the executors of the late Hans-Jürgen Bachorski for providing information about his career.

Chapter 1

Introduction

Daniel Pick and Lyndal Roper

In the famous book that launched psychoanalysis in 1900, Freud set out a novel thesis about the scientific potential of dreams. Controversially and brilliantly, *The Interpretation of Dreams* drew upon – even as it profoundly recast – elements of folk-wisdom: belief in the psychic significance and the symbolic weight of even our most bizarre nocturnal visions. Freud observed differences in the way dreams had been understood across the ages – referring, for instance, to certain Victorian researches into ancient ideas – but he had other fish to fry, and thus declared that he would reluctantly have to leave these arcane matters aside.[1] His interest here was not primarily historical. This was not to be an archaeology of forgotten cultural beliefs but, rather, the foundation for a new psychology based on the concept of repression. Psychoanalysis was to be centred on the exploration of the unconscious: a domain of the mind, he later wrote, in which the dictates of time did not operate.[2] So much for history. Through the interpretation of dreams, Freud proposed to expose a fundamental psychic mystery and to reveal the dynamic nature of mental life itself, a dynamic that was itself partly unconscious.

Somewhat to the chagrin of historically minded readers, the dry tone of the early 'review' sections of *The Interpretation of Dreams* incline one to press 'fast-forward' (perhaps too fast) towards Freud's own lively material and arguments. His survey of all those time-bound Victorian predecessors has its points of interest – and its potential for arousing polemical debate as to principles of selection and exclusion – but it was clearly a preamble, presaging the cornucopia of ideas and examples that followed. The rich account of the author's process of dream analysis, the descriptions of condensation and displacement, the absorbing examples and remarkable theory of the mind offered in chapter seven of the book are generally remembered, whether appreciatively or critically; but what of the rest?

However captivating and universally significant Freud's psychological undertaking is judged to be, a myriad of historical questions soon reappear. Whilst some of these questions concern the genealogy of ideas, there are also many other varieties of historical speculation to which the text can give rise. The ramifications and implications of the dream book cannot be confined to its moment of historical composition; nor can its theses be seen as the predictable reflection of the career path or intellectual background of its author, yet nonetheless the personal, cultural, social and political contexts in which it was produced are all loudly present in the text itself.

Elements in Freud's dreams were drawn from and identifiable within nineteenth-century German culture and history, sometimes specifically within *fin-de-siècle* Vienna. In a particularly compressed sequence, for example, Freud finds references in his dream to an eminent and reactionary Austrian politician, Count Thun, a contemporary student-leader, Fischhof, and another 'leader of men', almost certainly the Austrian social democrat, Victor Adler. One scene seems to derive from the author's early student days and a heated political discussion in a German students' club on the relation of philosophy to the natural sciences, where the young Freud takes up a militantly materialist view. These recognizable contemporary political and autobiographical references are interspersed with allusions to Henry VIII, Zola's novels, Tennyson's poetry, and much besides.[3] But it is not simply the content of the dream book that reflects the culture and politics of the age. The whole approach itself is reminiscent of other methodologies and genres of writing evident at around the same time. As the historian Carlo Ginzburg has shown, it was not by chance that Freud was to compare his enterprise with that of a sleuth; for in the genre of the detective story, the emerging techniques of fingerprinting, the connoisseur's new methods of detecting fake paintings (via the scientific analysis of the minutiae of the work, for instance the 'signature' brushstrokes evident in the smallest physiognomic details of portraiture) and even the dream tradition of psychoanalysis itself, the pursuit of apparently small and easily overlooked 'clues' became the royal road to the uncovering of large truths about identity. Uncannily, such leads were being assiduously followed up in a variety of discreet disciplines at just this time: it was the age of 'Morelli, Freud and Sherlock Holmes'.[4]

As this suggests, our bill of fare includes the pre-history, the legacy and the methodological implications of Freud's dream book. The accounts by the psychoanalysts Susan Budd, Edna O'Shaugnessy and Hanna Segal all show how much the understanding of dreams in the consulting room has changed since 1900. Many psychoanalysts since Freud have pointed out that whereas the original focus was on the meaning of dreams, this was often at the expense of considering the process and function of its telling within the analytic session. Some now attribute as much, if not more, significance to the unconscious ways the dream is mobilized than to the symbolic content itself. As the French psychoanalyst J. B. Pontalis put it: 'It is not the dream's contents but the subject's "use" of it that reveals his true pathology.'[5]

At the same time as we explore this legacy, we insist that the earlier historical literature must not be seen either as leading ineluctably to our own psychoanalytically informed views, or as some mere preface we skim before arriving at Freud's own fascinating text. Freud famously remarked that 'Insight such as this falls to one's lot but once in a lifetime'.[6] More than a century since its publication, how far does historical research still support that view of the significance of this text within Freud's body of work and the wider claim by his biographer, Ernest Jones, that the main conclusions were 'entirely novel and unexpected'?[7] Contributions here ponder afresh the nature of dream theories in the period before and during Freud's career. Whilst not directly challenging Jones's assertion, Maureen Perkins's account of Victorian dream books, for instance, illuminates popular conceptions in the nineteenth century, exploring a tradition of dream interpretation that had so often been the special preserve of women.

Readers will discover in several of the essays how different was the role accorded to the supernatural in understandings of dreams before the twentieth century. Indeed, Freud's title itself echoes the long tradition of dream interpretation stretching back to the Greeks; for *Traumdeutung* is a possible translation of *Oneirocritica*, Artemidorus's famous second-century Christian era (CE) text on dreaming, which remained authoritative right up to the early modern period.[8] People in the medieval and early modern period often saw dreams as communications from God – or from the Devil. For the ancients, dreams were perhaps more like visitations. Dreams might predict the future or carry messages. So important was this apprehension that one group of sixteenth-century religious radicals from the region around Erlangen in Germany were known as the Dreamers: they believed that God might communicate with them directly through voices and visions. Disconcertingly, He advised them to enter new spiritual marriages and leave their old spouses, advice that was to set them at odds with their society. Because they conferred authority outside the structures of the church, dreams remained important for many Anabaptists and Protestant would-be prophets, just as they had been for medieval mystics, women in particular.[9] In times of religious and social upheaval, comprehension of dreams too has characteristically been 'on the move'. Dreams might point to other worlds of political possibility, conferring special authority on forces outside the established institutions and providing a visionary apprehension of how things might come to be.

Thinking our way backwards, then, allows us to ponder a cosmology in which spirituality played a central role and where the sphere of dreams was also the realm where the divine might intervene. Yet as Charles Stewart, Hans-Jürgen Bachorski and Patricia Crawford all show, the evidence of a secular approach to dream-interpretation in the modern age should not lead us to assume that men and women in the distant past only ever conceived of dreams as direct messages from supernatural powers. Some dreams were perceived to result from imbalances in the humours, or derived from what one took into the body, for instance, from the food one ate. This did not mean they were insignificant, for they could be used diagnostically to discover which humours predominated in the body, and where the cause of a physical disturbance might lie. These understandings of dreams were not purely physiological. Humoral medicine systematically linked the somatic and the psychological, and so reflecting on dreams involved thinking about an individual's character and disposition.

Catch-all theses about 'then' and 'now' fall foul of the evidence, and the reader of these pieces may well oscillate between perceptions of continuity and change in the history of the conception of the dream. In a survey of some seventeenth-century Englishmen's dreams, the historian Peter Burke observed that their manifest content concerned public life and religion, not sex, suggesting that early modern people's psychic lives were driven by very different forces than those of the Freudian epoch. The historian's role, then, might be to develop the possibilities of a cultural history of dream contents and of repression.[10] There is certainly much important work still to be done here, and historians have yet, for the most part, to take up Burke's challenge. But Crawford's discussion of dilemmas of womanhood in seventeenth-century England, for example, shows that there may be other uses of dreams for the historian too – a window, perhaps, through which to glimpse some of the private perceptions and deep conflicts of men and women in other epochs.

Hans-Jürgen Bachorski alerts us to the special status of dreams within medieval narratives. Moreover, in his close reading, we can see striking differences in psychological self-understanding emerging in each of the texts he considers. On occasion, dreams were indeed perceived to reflect the dreamer's inner conflicts, providing a potential route for insight. To this extent there may be more of a commonality between their view of dreams and our own than is often supposed. The seventeenth-century author Sir Thomas Browne commented on how 'consolations or discouragements may bee drawne from dreams, which intimately tell us ourselves'. While it may be true that even self-revelatory dreams were interpreted in the framework of the individual's path to salvation, such remarks show how dreams were also a way of reflecting upon one's own subjectivity.

Dreams may, Crawford suggests, offer a way into the psychic as well as the spiritual dilemmas of people in the past. They also force us to ponder the relation between reality, fantasy, and dream, because the boundaries between these categories of experience could be extremely fluid. Consider a Swiss journeyman who in 1667 attempted to commit suicide – a capital offence – on the incitement of the Devil. He told how Satan had appeared to him when he was alone in a trance-like state in the cold January snows, telling him to climb a nearby tree and hang himself with his trousers belt. Yet later in his interrogation he described a similar encounter as a dream; and gradually his entire narrative became an account of his dream, not of reality. Persuaded that he suffered from disturbances of fantasy, the authorities sent him off unpunished for convalescence.[11] Sometimes the ambiguity of dreams could be resolved the other way. One woman accused of witchcraft in the 1590s in Noördlingen in Southern Germany described a dream in which she split the skull of a newborn child from its head to its nose. We might see this as a terrifying vision of the potential for aggression a mother may feel towards her infant. But how was it seen at the time? Under the pressure of interrogation she transformed the dream into a 'real' encounter with the Devil and confessed to digging up, cooking and eating the bodies of dead children. Now she conceded she was a witch. The content of the dream and the witchcraft narrative were at core identical – perverted motherhood and unbearable destructiveness towards children.[12]

Even if either God or the Devil might send dreams, writers about dreaming were soon drawn to reflect on the nature of fantasy itself. After all, the Devil, as master of illusion, could always trick the senses; and from this apprehension, these writers moved to explore the particular character of dreaming. Jean Bodin, the famous sixteenth-century political theorist, also wrote a colloquium that debates the nature of dreams. His work on witchcraft, *De la démonomanie des sorciers*, includes an extraordinary passage of analysis, supposedly of the dream of a friend of his, but quite possibly his own.[13] Interestingly, Bodin, with a lively sense of the uncertainties of truth and the ambiguities of reality, demonstrated that he was also aware of the heavy responsibility judges bore for determining good and evil, and sentencing the guilty. He describes how his 'friend' is advised by an angel who visits him nightly and guides his actions, distinguishing right from wrong. This follows a passage where Bodin has been comparing the hierarchies of angels and devils. It is as if his friend's 'angel' provides him with the moral certainty that a judge condemning witches to death would need, and offers a parallel to the relation of the witch to the Devil. As with the Devil, so with angels; the medium of communication is the dream.

Attitudes to dreams were part of a whole package of conceptions of the body, the soul, morals and the nature of God; and they underwent a major transformation with the new understandings of the world developed by thinkers such as Hobbes or Descartes. If dream theory had remained fairly constant from the ancients to the Renaissance, with Artemidorus's *Oneirocritica*, printed in Latin in 1518 and disseminated in vernacular languages across Europe, still the authoritative manual of interpretation, dreams were nonetheless part of the simmering cauldron of debates about the divine and the diabolic, illusion and reality, which were eventually to contribute a great deal to the intellectual shifts of the Enlightenment.[14] For Hobbes, dreams could not be of divine or diabolic inspiration, nor could they even be explained by the humoral system of medicine.[15] Descartes supplied a theory of dreaming in natural, not supernatural, terms.[16]

It would be tempting to interpret this shift as progression, a major advance in understanding psychology that freed it from the shackles of religious modes of thought. Dreams were once understood to come from external sources and this idea gave way to the notion of an internal derivation and responsibility. Charles Stewart describes how, in Ancient Greece, the dream was 'seen'; gradually the idea emerged that one might 'have' a dream. Many of the essays here continue that story, showing how over time we have increasingly 'taken possession' of our own dreams. But before we subscribe entirely to such a narrative, it is worth pointing out that, as both Crawford and Bachorski show, the religious idiom did not necessarily make pre-modern people any less psychologically astute or less sophisticated about the functioning of what they, like Freud, termed 'the soul' (die Seele).[17]

Certainly, dreams had long played an important part in religious thought. In particular, they invaded the margins of demonological theory: commentators on witchcraft maintained that it was in dreams that devils came to men and stole their seed, which they then used when, in the shape of incubus devils, they had sex with female witches. The incubus is also the nightmare, and it was popularly believed that it pressed down on people whilst they were asleep, causing them nearly to suffocate.[18] By contrast, the sixteenth-century English writer Reginald Scot, who denied the reality of witchcraft, was just as contemptuous of dreams and dream interpretation. Many who believed in the real existence of demons and witches also took care to separate themselves from what they took to be the foolish beliefs of the common people, claiming that witches could not truly fly, but only dreamt that they did.

At the same time, we should not assume that such early modern debates about dreams were always desperately solemn or portentous affairs. In The Terrors of the Night (1594) for instance, Thomas Nashe provides a dizzying fantasia on the nature of dreams and manages to debunk them in vivid language that itself recalls the wandering, illogical and discursive character of dreaming. He dismisses dreams as 'nothing else but a bubbling scum or froth of the fancy, which the day hath left undigested', yet in a wonderful aside, which captures the pleasure of dreaming, he writes: 'He that dreams merrily is like a boy new breeched, who leaps and danceth for joy his pain is passed. But long that joy stays not with him, for presently after, his master, the day, seeing him so jocund and pleasant, comes and does as much for him again, whereby his hell is renewed.'[19]

A world away from Freud? In many ways, yes, but whilst Freud defined himself in opposition to earlier endeavours, even those of the immediately preceding period, he also drew significantly on work that went before. By exploring innovative and experimental studies of dreams in art history, the human sciences, fiction, religion and the occult before 1900, the Freudian revolution itself can be situated in new ways. Thus it is interesting to compare Freud's ideas with the dream theories of Samuel Taylor Coleridge, the accounts of the symbolic meanings that were presented in Victorian 'readers', the dream codes that flourished in Tsarist Russia, or again, with the ideas and images of the symbolist painter Redon (like Freud, a visitor to Paris, who drew in the latest fashionable ideas about hypnosis and hysteria circulating in the human sciences). The following chapters do not necessarily suggest that what is nearest to us in time is most culturally familiar; through illuminating a wealth of neglected sources, ideas and images, ranging from Classical Greece to the Middle Ages, from the early modern period, through romanticism to the twentieth century, we hope amply to have demonstrated that any account of the historical evolution of dream theory would necessarily be complex, variegated and inclined to double-back on itself.

Repeatedly, within the history of the developing 'interiorization' of the dream, we see more complex oscillations and movements, shifting 'viewpoints' within periods and sometimes within the same *oeuvre*. Thus Jennifer Ford shows how Coleridge seems to anticipate psychoanalysis, or at least to presage a growing interest in forces and features of psychic processes; at other times, however, he seems to rely on a quite different set of assumptions. Views about dreams as physiological processes jostled for attention in his work and thoughts with theories of the dream as spiritually inspired; if he seemed to hint at an intra-psychic mystery on the one side, he was also intrigued by the significance of animal magnetism on the other. In the eighteenth and nineteenth centuries, as Stefanie Heraeus puts it, we see various artistic moves towards the recognition of 'the radically subjective reality of dreams'. The examples of dream images she selects – Fuseli, Goya and Grandville – document a growing interest in the internal logic of dreaming, which was closely related to their dissatisfaction with established approaches to artistic representation.

To speak of history in terms of a simple progress of knowledge risks producing a number of distortions, not least a tendency to view the past teleologically. There is a tension in the story we are telling here: if we are less confident than all those ebullient nineteenth-century whigs, evolutionists and positivists who saw history as a gradual but ineluctable passage from primitive religion, through monotheism, and on, via metaphysics, to modern natural science and the triumph of reason, we also want to celebrate the achievement of the enlightenment and one of its heirs, Freud's psychoanalysis. It is tempting to conceive of our material in terms of straightforward 'stages' of oneiric theoretical development, but it might, on occasion, be as appropriate to think of an unsettled movement, back and forth, between intellectual positions: at one moment the dream may be construed as a phenomenon intruding from outside, with good and bad thoughts located in clearly defined *dramatis personae*; at other points, even in contemporaneous works or passages of the same text, the dream may be conceived quite differently, the narrator implying that, for all the manifold figures in the dream, it truly *all* belongs to the dreamer, each 'presence' to be integrated with – seen as a product of – the psychic life of the subject.

Of course, the moment we use a psychological model of increasing integration or of growing insight to describe cultural processes, problems emerge and the need for a cool historicist appraisal of the evidence is all the greater. As Charles Stewart observes, if we borrow definitions of psychosis drawn from current psychiatric manuals, we may have to define *everybody* in ancient Greece as round the bend; for all believed in what we would now consider to be a schizoid or persecutory order. Whilst it is unhelpful to see madness itself as chimœrical or as merely a cultural construct, yet we must be sensitive to the contingency of psychological concepts, attitudes and beliefs that shape our understanding and perception.[20]

***

There is – or ought to be – a creative tension between history and psychoanalysis, each calling the other's assumptions into question. These chapters frequently explore the contingency or universality of our most basic assumptions about dreams, and the conundrum of how we might read the dreams of the dead. Take a few examples of the potential historical and methodological dimensions of Freud's 'dream book' itself. Its cultural and scientific pre-history can be surveyed, its subsequent reception charted in a plethora of fields – from art to philosophy, anthropology to fiction, theatre to cinema.[21] We might pursue (to borrow terms from Bachorski's chapter), the private reservoir of meanings that dreams and their theorizations have involved for given individuals, whilst also tracing the changing social storehouse of images upon which such personal views and even unconscious fantasies also inevitably draw.

What might an historical assessment of the formation of *The Interpretation of Dreams* look like? Freud's secret intentions have themselves been subjected to an extraordinary degree of scrutiny and wild analysis. Using Freud's own book, we too might become detectives, seizing on examples in *The Interpretation of Dreams* itself. Some historians have indeed been tempted down this route, tracking the painful personal history that was masked in the names Freud used in his text; notoriously, for instance, behind his most celebrated dream figure, Irma. In 'the Dream of Irma's Injection' lay the name of a woman he knew, Emma Eckstein, the patient whose catastrophic operation on her nose, at the hands of Freud's friend Fliess, caused such acute pain, embarrassment and difficulty. Historical research can also be brought to bear in order to analyse the thicket of dream theories in the late nineteenth-century European human sciences that informed Freud's self-analysis of the 1890s; or to compare the influences he acknowledged with those that we suspect may have been present but unannounced.

Through analysis, as Freud then conceived it, the trajectory of the original 'dream work' was to be reversed. Freud urged us to make our way backwards; to retrieve, up to a point (it was only ever possible up to a point, as he acknowledged when he spoke of the impassable 'navel' of this hermeneutic process),[22] the ensemble of psychic bits and pieces, stories and fantasies that the subject cannot quite bear to recall, even within the privacy of sleep. The dream is a compromise formation. In short, the theory and exposition magnificently demonstrate the intricate inter-relationship of past and present, as well as of liberty and repression, knowing and disavowing, within the interior life of the subject. The dream of Irma's injection and all the other impressive instances offered in the book provide a stunning compression (or, as Freud would say, condensation and displacement), in which fragments of thought and fantasy, dreads and desires, materials distantly past and immediately present, are put back together again in an illusory narrative coherence, itself worked over in the 'secondary revisions' we make as we recount the dream to ourselves or others. Compare the brevity of the dream texts with the length of each ensuing analysis. The story that the dream appears to tell has to be deciphered, as it were transferred into long-hand, by the analyst and patient through the work of analysis; behind the dream, a bundle of dream thoughts. Words conflate a myriad of meanings, associations, and connections, multiplying into a bewildering and potentially limitless semantic field.

Part of the cultural history of *The Interpretation of Dreams* would have to include the vicissitudes of the book itself, which, as Ilse Grubrich-Simitis shows, went through various rewritings, expansions and then prunings as Freud developed his views about the nature of the psychoanalytic project. In a very real sense, the *Traumdeutung* remained an open text throughout Freud's life. More generally, the history of the reception of Freud's dream book tells us a great deal about social and cultural attitudes towards the mind, and of course to the author himself.[23] Any such assessment would have to consider how Freud's work inspired the outpourings of literary modernism and a plethora of innovative art forms and experiments that flowered in the last forty years of his life-time – not the least of which developments was of course surrealism, a movement near incomprehensible without specific reference to *The Interpretation of Dreams*.[24]

Not all assessments, of course, were favourable. Consider this remarkably insouciant review of *The Interpretation of Dreams* that appeared in *The Athenaeum* in 1913. The reviewer confidently predicted that 'Englishmen have little to learn about the manner of telling dreams, however deficient they may be in interpreting them' and concluded that Freud was exclusively preoccupied with the morbid rather than the healthy dreamer and betrayed in his tendency to introspection, the hallmarks of an 'Oriental heredity'. All in all, it seemed, there was nothing much for the English here and the whole book was swiftly dismissed:

His conclusions are sometimes far-fetched and fit the premises incompletely, whilst an atmosphere of sex pervades many parts of the book and renders it very unpleasant reading. The results he reaches are hardly commensurate with the labour expended, and reveal a seamy side of life in Vienna which might well have been left alone.[25]

But there were also more positive responses to Freud's work, even in sceptical England. During the First World War, the disturbing symptoms – and dreams – of so many shell-shocked army officers and privates caused a very significant reappraisal of 'the talking cure'. Such post-war re-evaluations took place in many countries. Freud was called upon to give his views to the War Office in Vienna, but the link between shell-shock and the changing institutional fortunes of psychoanalysis was perhaps most striking of all in Britain. One of the most important advocates of Freud's theory and form of therapy (albeit in suitably sanitised form) was W. H. R. Rivers, a doctor, psychologist and anthropologist, with a special interest in dreams. Rivers treated many shell-shocked soldiers during the war.[26]

In the 1920s, Britain was to witness a sustained endeavour (building on the war-time efforts of many such pioneers) to popularize Freud's work and to correct the endless misconceptions and misapprehensions that seemed to have arisen about his ideas and techniques. A full history of the diffusion of psychoanalysis in twentieth-century Britain remains to be written (nothing has been attempted here on quite the scale of Elizabeth Roudinesco's two-volume history of psychoanalysis in France), but books with titles such as *The Psychology of Self-Consciousness* (1923); *The Dream on the Anxiety Hypothesis* (1923); *Human Psychology as Seen through the Dream* (1924) – and there were many others – would no doubt need to be considered in any inventory of the reception of Freud and his theory of dreams in these inter-war years.[27]

A cultural historical survey of the reception of Freud's language of dreams after 1900 would include not only the work of psychoanalysts and serious-minded admirers and critics, but the weird, wild and sometimes wonderful expropriations of ideas that were made – myriad loose borrowings from the school of Freud as well as that of Jung, through cartoons, poems, films, essays, witticisms and anecdotes, and through the general babble of conversation about psychology, the new theories of dreams and the unconscious that has persisted across many decades. We may wish to investigate why the dream book was sometimes passed over or greeted in silence; but we should also register the opposite phenomenon – an increasing cacophony of admiration, consternation and complaint from many quarters, not least the pointed interest in Freud expressed by many of the period's most innovative novelists, essayists and poets.[28]

Various experiments and projects unfolded between the wars, attempting to link Freudianism with new sociological techniques. In Britain, for instance, the Mass Observation Movement (founded in 1937 by Charles Madge, Tom Harrison and Humphrey Jennings) sought to produce a new kind of ethnography of everyday life – assuming that individual psychic experience would, to a large degree, reflect a common social experience. Amongst its many initiatives was an endeavour to use dreams to interpret shared images and anxieties. Strikingly, however, the inquiry foundered: the dreams gathered did not seem to fit any clear pattern – there was no agreement that the evidence provided a clear collective form and it was gradually realized that there was a discrepancy between the idiosyncratic material submitted and the generalized theories of symbolism that motivated their collection in the first place. The idea of subsuming dreams in such a catalogue, rather than using them within a personal analysis, as a starting point for an inquiry into the unconscious of an individual dreamer, came unstuck.

Although such material may not provide the basis for a theory of the collective unconscious or a general symbolic code, the Mass Observation archive of dreams (held at Sussex University) may well have other uses for historians: for instance, enabling one to explore shifting popular attitudes to the role of dreams, and disclosing a striking persistence of belief that dreams are indeed prophetic. Take this example from an English woman correspondent who offered her dream to Mass Observation in 1939. If its deeper meaning for this individual dreamer is irretrievably lost, it evidences a certain conscious attitude towards the meaning of the dream and an appeal to the authority of dream books upon which the social or cultural historian might well be able to cast more light.

> I dreamt that Hitler was kissing me. I had a feeling of disgust as I saw his beady eyes and his small moustache, coming towards me, but my disgust didn't last. Later in the dream I thought he was making a fuss of my son who seemed like a little boy again of ten years old. He began to cry and I remembered that I had heard that Hitler had a reputation for liking boys and I was going to kill him. I then saw him as one of a crowd in a big railway station. I was grateful to find that it said in a dream book that all will be well if you dreamt an enemy was kissing you.[29]

In an extraordinary collection of German dreams from the Nazi era, Charlotte Beradt reports the case of a housewife who even appealed to dream books in her sleep. A bedside lamp had transmuted into a machine that brought to light all she said in bed. Terrified, she at first thought she would turn it off, but then she 'dashed over to see my girl friend, who had a dream book, and looked up "lamp" – lamp signified only "serious illness". For a moment I felt very relieved until it dawned on me that to be on the safe side people were using the word illness for arrest.'[30] The dreams Beradt assembles convey the terrible anxiety many people felt under fascism, and their self-censoring even in dreams – one man compiles a letter of protest but when he comes to post it, mails a blank sheet of paper instead.[31] A doctor describes a dream from 1934:

> It was about nine o'clock in the evening. My consultations were over, and I was just stretching out on the couch to relax with a book on Matthias Grünewald, when suddenly the walls of my room and then my apartment disappeared. I looked around and discovered to my horror that as far as the eye could see no apartment had walls any more. Then I heard a loudspeaker boom, 'According to the decree of the 17th of this month on the Abolition of Walls . . .'[32]

Just the previous day, the doctor had been reprimanded by the block warden for not hanging a flag at his window, and he had thought to himself, 'Not in *my* four walls' – a wish the dream had fulfilled with terrifying literalism. A world without walls – as Beradt points out, this is a powerful metaphor for the way fascism destroys privacy itself. Beradt's remarkable book selects all the evidently political content from the dreams for examination; and yet one might argue that what made Nazism so effective in colonizing the unconscious was that politics could not be separated from private life – from sexual fantasy for example. These individual conflicts also belong to 'history', but of a decidedly different kind, one whose contours cannot neatly be reconciled with those on the public, social, and political map.[33]

***

'A great body of dream literature and of fantasies of past ages is unexplored', lamented the distinguished American historian, Frank Manuel, thirty years ago.[34] At that time, despite some pioneering endeavours to consider the social and cultural context of dreams, historians had indeed mostly steered clear of the field, ceding dream life to psychologists, cultural theorists, artists, philosophers, anthropologists, psychoanalysts and, most recently, neurobiologists. But this one-time poverty of historical scrutiny has significantly changed. Any contemporary review of the historiography of dreams would reveal a transformation both in the available material and in the forms of inquiry that have been undertaken in recent decades.

None of the historical essays presented here sits comfortably with the old 'psychohistory' and 'psychobiography' tradition that developed principally in the United States in and beyond the 1950s, inspired above all by the work of the psychoanalyst Erik Erikson. We are now perhaps as wary of explanations of motivation and belief that rely on general theories about identity and its stages, or on any unqualified form of psychological determinism, as we had previously been sceptical about either biological or environmental determinisms. In a detailed investigation of the botanist, psychologist and analysand of Freud's, Sir Arthur Tansley, Laura Cameron and John Forrester show us how precise we need to be in establishing what we can and cannot know about the mind and motivation of the dead. They take up one particular dream upon which Tansley set great store. Their discussion and reconstruction shows what historians can indeed 'do' with the documentary evidence of dreams, even whilst remaining mindful of the methodological problems that surround such sources. Tansley's dream may be seen as exposing a conflict – between civilized sexual morality and the dictates of desire – but it may also be seen in his case to give expression to an existential conflict between his love of botany and of psychoanalysis. And of course these very broad-brush terms of reference would need to be explored and opened out much further. As Hanna Segal observes later, if we must be cautious about excessive certitude in the realm of psychobiography, we should not become so inhibited that we avoid speculation altogether. Here perhaps we might ponder the social, cultural, and psychological factors that *may* have produced for Tansley this kind of restless choice, this very particular structure of drive and frustration.

Tansley later expressed a sense of disappointment with his own analysis and yet it is hard not to be struck by the intensity of his admiration for Freud. Forrester and Cameron demonstrate how much we can determine, and how much we must acknowledge as obscure and imponderable in this record. Historians and psychoanalysts might debate the authors' principle of 'interpretative charity', according to which we accept (subject to their being no convincing counter-evidence) agents' own declarations of their motives as true. Despite this principle, Cameron and Forrester's account brings us back to the enormous hermeneutic uncertainties of dreams and of personal estimations of the importance of specific oneiric events in the destiny of individuals, to say nothing of the ambiguities of intention and interpretation evident in reported conversations, however 'wide awake' the participants. When Freud quizzed Tansley on the precise nature of the chair he had been given in Oxford – wondering how senior the post was – are we able to detect something of Freud's own unsatisfied longing for academic preferment, or rather Tansley's own sensitivity – and rivalry – with his one-time analyst?

Interestingly, even Freud himself, cavalier psychohistorian though he may sometimes have been, urged caution when invited to comment 'blind' on one of Descartes' dreams. How could he do this, Freud wondered, 'since working on dreams without being able to obtain from the dreamer himself any indications on the relations which might link them to one another or attach them to the external world . . . gives, as a general rule, only a meagre result.'[35] There is a nice irony here, for the dreams actually played a fateful role in Descartes' own intellectual development and his decision to pursue the path of philosophy. And it was the possibility that we might be dreaming that he used, in *The Meditations*, to develop his account of radical doubt as he arrived at the certainty of the *cogito*. Something of the commonality as well as the distance between Freud and earlier understandings of psychology can be glimpsed in Freud's response to the request that he interpret the dreams: he argued that Descartes's dreams came 'from above', that is, they were dreams that continued waking thoughts, so that Descartes might have arrived at the same intellectual destination by conscious means. Descartes, too, believed that these dreams came 'from above', that is, that they were divinely inspired, and he vowed to go on pilgrimage to Loretto in thanks.[36] Elsewhere Freud also famously insisted that psychoanalysis could not be conducted *in absentia*; it depended upon the existence not only of an analyst but also of an analysand; indeed, 'psycho-analytic intervention, therefore, absolutely requires a fairly long period of contact with the patient.'[37] In other words it is Freud himself, not only his latter-day opponents, who takes us to the heart of the problem of 'psychobiography'.

Whilst making no attempt to be encyclopaedic in range, we believe this collection richly demonstrates the diverse dilemmas of psychohistorical and cultural historical methodologies. If these articles are sometimes insistently historicist, at other points they intriguingly confront us with themes and preoccupations that appear to recur over the *longue durée*. Thus they provide a series of case studies for debating the limits of historicism and psychologism; for exploring the uses of psychoanalysis outside the clinical setting; for evaluating the advantages of modern dream theory in illuminating the historical past. How far need we – can we – think our way back to other ways of being and thinking, other forms of consciousness about consciousness, other cultural accounts of the meaning of waking or sleeping, dreaming or not-dreaming? And anyway, is it helpful to view dream discourses in these 'before' and 'after' terms – the history of our most intimately private life periodized around the imaginary year zero of 1900?

If Freud was jealous to protect and defend the fundamental insight of his book, he was also content to see it as a mere starting point, open to revision. The sense of the dream book as 'a work in progress' was surely important to the psychoanalytic enterprise itself: as Susan Budd points out, there have been remarkable changes and developments in psychoanalytic approaches to dreams (and much besides); and all this despite the severe concerns of some analysts, between the world wars, that the subject of dreams was disappearing from view.[38] Alongside various reflections, drawn largely from the British tradition, on changes in psychoanalytic theory and technique, we have included Ilse Grubrich-Simitis's rich study of the history of the revisions Freud made to successive editions of the book. She shows us how these shifts expressed Freud's own continuing conflict between the desire to make of his book something impersonal, objective and 'scientific' and the wish to free himself of the constraining protocols of the contemporary natural sciences. This account usefully prompts us to reflect on our own subjective investments in the history at stake in these pages. It would be difficult today, even should we so wish, to 'place' Freud's own landmark book neutrally in history; its provocative impact upon and diffuse influence within modern thought and therapy, culture and criticism has been so massive, its explanatory framework so pervasive, its logic so compelling (or, according to Freud's critics, so seductive),[39] that it is through the lens of the 'dream book' that we now tend to perceive much else in the history of psychology and the psychology of history. Even if much of the Victorian science in which Freud was steeped has now been stamped *passé*, it is by no means clear that acceptance of contemporary neuroscience entails the rejection of Freud's most important arguments or speculations about dreams: perhaps the contrary. Freud is still our contemporary in ways that, say, Charcot (the great Parisian neurologist whose work on hysteria was so greatly to interest Freud at the start of his career) is not. Even critics of psychoanalysis – of whom there is no shortage – usually take something of Freud's fundamental insights for granted.

The debate about the contingency or universality of dreams and their meanings is clearly part of a wider unsettled conversation within historiography. Historians now often seem to be divided between those who insist on the fundamental continuity of human nature over time, and those who want to show how far the self is historically contingent through and through. After the work of Michel Foucault, historians frequently pushed the idea of the contingency of the self to an extreme. This might give rise to the dizzying argument that dreams as well as waking thoughts are in fact informed and shaped by the ideas of psychoanalysis that they supposedly reflect. To borrow a phrase from Freud, *The Interpretation of Dreams* may have reshaped the very 'soul' that it seeks to explore. To pursue the Foucauldian line one might ask how this notion that we 'have' a 'psychology' came into being and how the model of the mind or self (or for that matter, of life or death, instinct or drive, Eros or Thanatos), was discursively constituted. What were the historical conditions that made possible the psychoanalytic account of dreams and the notion of interpretation as a 'royal road' to the unconscious? And with what cultural and political effects? The pursuit of such questions in the history of psychiatry, psychology and psychoanalysis, as well as medicine, biology, economics, criminology, and so forth, has produced some extremely sophisticated analyses of the way the most basic conceptual categories change over time; in the process, much that had seemed secure and natural has been called into question.[40]

Yet in recent years, we can also detect a certain dissatisfaction with such forms of approach to mind and subjectivity, and perhaps we can also glean, as the pendulum swings, an unapologetic reassertion of the values of an older humanism. Certainly the uses of historicism, Foucauldian or otherwise, have proved extremely illuminating and provocative, but they have also sometimes become not only shrill in tone, but defensive in function: a convenient denial of the inescapable truth of what we share across space and time; a basic humanity. But what does this entail? If there is an historically contingent discourse of dreams, there is also an age-old physiological and psychological phenomenon of dreaming that needs to be taken into account.

It is worth pausing before pursuing such questions further: for just because dream phenomena have been recorded across the ages, it does not necessarily mean that one can speak of a universal 'experience' of dreaming. The moment we move from the word 'phenomenon' to 'experience', the vexed debate between 'historicism' and 'psychologism' returns all the louder. Was the occurrence, or the retrospective feeling about the occurrence, really the same in ancient Greece, as in medieval Germany or in Soviet Russia? For Lucretius as for Bosch? For Artemidorus as for Freud? Susan Budd wonders whether dreams themselves have become shorter and more fragmentary in modern experience. Are they – were they ever – a singular human phenomenon? When that enthusiastic English follower of Freud's, Tansley, recounted his dreams 'over breakfast', are we in the same world of experience as those Russian dreamers who regaled their intimates with the night's symbolic residues at their morning tables? No doubt different readers will reach different conclusions about this 'commonality' as they tease out the particular and the general features in the following chapters.

Evidently, cultures encode dreams in different orders of symbolism: but deep down, it may not really matter that we could represent sexual thrust by a motorcycle in one society but not in another (to use Hanna Segal's pithy example). These may be merely superficial markers for a deeper shared process. Certainly new symbols appear over time and we might debate how significantly they inflect psychological experience. Wigzell records the introduction of new dream 'keys' in the codings of the nineteenth century: 'pineapple' began to appear as a significant sign in a Russian dream book that was translated from the French in 1839. Other terms can also be charted chronologically. Oranges, waltzes, artichokes, chocolate and planes made their entry into public dream texts at given moments. Wigzell also charts the appearance in dream books of the concept of the subversive, specifically of the Bolshevik agitator. Here there was a chance for certain Russian writers to make a clear political point or, as many may see it, to indicate their prescience; to dream of such agitators, readers were informed, signified loss of honour, deception, and unhappiness. Small wonder, as Wigzell observes, that politically incorrect dreambooks were to fall foul of the government censor in Russia after 1917.[41]

For Freud the apparent strangeness and obscurity of what we 'see' in dreams reflected mental conflict. The literal 'picture' seen in the dream was not the key issue – rather the picture was to be deciphered back into a less figurative realm of dream thoughts. For Freud, evidently, there was a profound commonality – the unconscious democratically ensnares us all, high or low, patrician or plebeian. He may have baulked at treatment for the socially or intellectually lowly, but from the 1880s onwards his writings continually probed and breached the 'cordon sanitaire' of ideas that the Victorian human sciences had so often established, between the degenerate and the healthy, fit and unfit, child and adult, man and woman, ancient and modern, primitive and sophisticated, mad and sane. Freud refused to confine his scrutiny to the mental life of those deemed primitive, degenerate or psychotic. Indeed, psychoanalysis was to implicate us all in its theory of dreams, sexuality and the unconscious. Even the concept of the patient was to be enormously extended through the offices of psychoanalysis. In due course every psychoanalytic practitioner was to be, first of all, a patient.

In conclusion, *Dreams and History* sets out from Freud's dream book, moving back as far as the ancient past and forward from 1900; it considers the kinds of challenge that psychoanalytic accounts of the dream pose to conventional historical studies of the past and *vice versa*. These contributions aim to rescue the dream records of women and men long dead from 'the condescension of posterity'; they consider dream accounts as historical documents, whilst pondering the enormous challenge that this form of material poses to historical understanding.

Above all, Freud shows how, in taking our dreams seriously, there could be no 'business as usual' for psychology, no impermeable frontiers in the understanding of 'character', 'will' or 'morality'. The history of the domestication, recuperation and sanitization of psychoanalysis in many of its institutional settings is another story, but the ambition was undeniable: no appeal to class, no barrier of morals, no border of the nation was to spare the blushes of the subject. Any number of certainties about the ego were now themselves revealed in their illusory and complacent aspect, a daydream of our 'selfhood' rudely interrupted by psychoanalysis and Freud's interpretation of dreams:

> One of my English friends put forward this thesis at a scientific meeting in America, whereupon a lady who was present remarked that that might be the case in Austria, but that she could assert as regards herself and her friends that *they* were altruistic even in their dreams. My friend although himself of English race, was obliged to contradict the lady emphatically on the ground of his personal experience in dream-analysis, and to declare that in their dreams high-minded American ladies were quite as egoistic as the Austrians.[42]

NOTES AND REFERENCES

1 The following passage was added to the dream book in 1914: 'It may be asked what view was taken of dreams in pre-historic times by primitive races of men and what effect dreams may have had upon the formation of their conceptions of the world and of the soul; and this is a subject of such great interest that it is only with much reluctance that I refrain from dealing with it in this connection. I must refer my readers to the standard works of Sir John Lubbock, Herbert Spencer, E. B. Tylor and others, and I will only add that we shall not be able to appreciate the wide range of these problems and speculations until we have dealt with the task that lies before us here – the interpretation of dreams.' *The Interpretation of Dreams*, 1900, The Standard Edition of the Complete Psychological Works of Sigmund Freud – henceforth SE – London, 1953, vol. 4, pp. 1–2.

2 See 'The Unconscious', 1915, SE 14, p. 187.
3 *The Interpretation of Dreams*, SE 4, pp. 208–219. For a detailed historical contextualization of this dream, see William J. McGrath, *Freud's Discovery of Psychoanalysis: The Politics of Hysteria*, Cornell University Press, 1986.
4 C. Ginzburg, 'Morelli, Freud and Sherlock Holmes: Clues and scientific methods', *History Workshop Journal* 9, 1980, pp. 5–36.
5 J. B. Pontalis, *Frontiers in Psychoanalysis: Between the Dream and Psychic Pain*, London, 1981, p. 29. See also J.-M. Quinodoz, '"Dreams that turn over a page": Integration dreams with paradoxical regressive content', *International Journal of Psychoanalysis* 80, 1999, pp. 225–238 (now also enlarged into a book of the same title, London 2002); cf. the chapter by Edna O'Shaughnessy in the present collection.
6 E. Jones, *Sigmund Freud: Life and Work*, London, 1953, 3 vols, vol. 3, p. 384.
7 Jones, vol. 3, p. 384.
8 P. Holland, '"The Interpretation of Dreams" in the Renaissance', in P. Brown (ed.), *Reading Dreams. The Interpretation of Dreams from Chaucer to Shakespeare*, Oxford and New York, 1999, p. 129.
9 C. P. Clasen, *Anabaptism. A Social History, 1525–1618*, Ithaca and London, 1972, pp. 130–132; G. H. Williams, *The Radical Reformation*, London, 1962, pp. 164 ff; R. Kagan, *Lucrecia's Dreams. Politics and Prophecy in Sixteenth-Century Spain*, Berkeley and Los Angeles, 1990.
10 'L'histoire sociale des reves', *Annales ESC* 28, 1973, pp. 329–342, p. 342.
11 Quoted in M. Weidhorn, *Dreams in Seventeenth-Century English Literature*, The Hague and Paris, 1970, p. 24.
12 Staatsarchiv Basel Stadt, Criminalia 4, Zauberei und abergläubige Künste 15, Stoffel Janz, 24 Jan–15 Feb 1667; Stadtarchiv Nördlingen, Hexenakten, Barbara Stecher, 5 Sept. 1590.
13 J. Bodin, *De la démonomanie des sorciers*, Paris, 1580, fo. 11 v; and see R. Scott, *On the Demon-Mania of Witches* (abridged), Toronto, 1995, p. 61. In his *Colloquium of the seven about Secrets of the Sublime*, representatives of different religions discuss dreams. See Holland, '"The Interpretation of Dreams" in the Renaissance', p. 137.
14 For an authoritative account of seventeenth-century attitudes to dreams and their relation to radical religion, see J. Rivière, '"The Distinction of Dreams": Dream-life, Belief and Reform in Seventeenth-century England', M. Phil. thesis, University of Queensland, 2002 and '"Visions of the Night": The Reform of Popular Dream Beliefs in Early Modern England', *Parergon* 20, no. 1, 2003, pp. 109–138.
15 *Leviathan*, 419; Weidhorn, p. 33.
16 J.-C. Schmitt, 'The liminality and centrality of dreams in the medieval West', in D. Shulman and G. G. Stroumsa (eds.), *Dream Cultures. Explorations in the Comparative History of Dreaming*, Oxford, 1999, p. 281.
17 Freud's *Totem and Taboo*, for example, was originally published in German in four parts under the title 'Über einige Übereinstimmungen im Seelenleben der Wilden und der Neurotiker'. This is translated in the Standard Edition as 'Some Points of Agreement between the Mental Lives of Savages and Neurotics' (SE 13, p. ix). See also I. Meyer-Palmedo and G. Fichtner (eds.), *Freud-Bibliographie mit Werkkondordanz*, Frankfurt am Main, 1989, p. 36.
18 S. Kruger, 'Medical and moral authority in the late medieval Dream', in P. Brown (ed.), *Reading Dreams. The Interpretation of Dreams from Chaucer to Shakespeare*, 1999, p. 59.
19 T. Nashe, 'The terrors of the night', in Nashe, *The Unfortunate Traveller and other Works*, ed. J. B. Stearne, London, 1972, pp. 218–219. Or consider the early modern demonologist Martin Del Rio, who discussed dreams at length, setting out a careful account of how their nature was determined by the humours and explaining why one kind of constitution inclined one to a certain sort of dream. But, as so often, the particular quality of dreaming ensnares the author, waylaying him into a more speculative and personal kind of writing. There follows a remarkable passage on anxious dreams, pointing out how dreams can have

internal and animate causes, and can be interpreted so as to free the dreamer from the anxiety expressed in the dream. Then comes a lengthy discussion of his friendship with the illustrious neo-stoicist, Justus Lipsius, and of their conversations about a woman who could foretell the future through dreams. This passage is a tribute to his dead friend and to friendship itself. The issue they debated was whether her dreams were of diabolic or divine origin.

20 For an interesting and influential reappraisal of such matters, see R. Porter, W. B. Bynum and M. Hunter (eds.), *The Anatomy of Madness*, London, 1985–7, 3 vols, vol. 1, editorial introduction.

21 To take the last example, note how Virginia Woolf celebrated cinema's potential capacity 'to connect with our "dream architecture"', to depict fantasies no matter 'how far fetched or insubstantial', to remind us of 'the savage' that still exists in us. 'We are peering over the edge of a cauldron in which fragments of all shapes and savours seem to simmer; now and again some vast form heaves itself up and seems about to haul itself out of chaos.' Cinema, she said, may seem stupid, but importantly, it intimates a 'secret language which we feel and see, but never speak'; 'cinema has within its grasp innumerable symbols for emotions that have so far failed to find expression.' See 'The cinema' (1926), *The Captain's Death Bed and Other Essays*, London, 1950, pp. 166–171. Cf. S. Heath, 'Cinema and psychoanalysis', in J. Bergstrom (ed.), *Endless Night, Cinema and Psychoanalysis, Parallel Histories*, Los Angeles, 1999, pp. 25–56, p. 30.

22 SE 5, p. 525.

23 Freud expressed considerable disappointment with the dream book's early reception. See for instance the preface to the second edition of 1909, where he remarked on the lacklustre responses, ill-informed critiques and sometimes deafening silence in professional circles, amongst psychiatric colleagues, professional philosophers or reviewers in the scientific press (SE 4, p. xxv). Various prominent historians have of course taken issue with Freud's recollection of his intellectual reception in Viennese medical and scientific circles.

24 See P. Collier and J. Davies (eds.), *Modernism and the European Unconscious*, London, 1990.

25 Anon., 'Two dream books' (review of Brill's English translation of the third edition of *The Interpretation of Dreams* and Reginald Hine's *Dreams and the Way of Dreams*), *The Athenaeum: Journal of Literature, Science, the Fine Arts, Music, and the Drama*, no. 4460, (13 April 1913), p. 424.

26 Rivers's mentors included the great neurologist John Hughlings Jackson. In 1901–2, Rivers travelled to study the Todas people in S.W. India, a journey that led to the publication of a famous study, *The Todas*, 1906. He was the author of many books including *Conflict and Dream*. See R. Slobodin, *Rivers*, Thrupp, 1997.

27 S. Raitt, *May Sinclair*, Oxford, 2000, p. 139. For France, see E. Roudinesco, *Histoire de psychanalyse en France: La bataille de cent ans*, Paris, 1986. For an important recent inquiry into the historical contexts of psychoanalysis in Britain, see R. Steiner, *'It's a New Kind of Diaspora': Explorations in the Sociopolitical and Cultural Context of Psychoanalysis*, London, 2000, and *Tradition, Change, Creativity: Repercussions of the New Diaspora on Aspects of British Psychoanalysis*, London, 2000.

28 A single example will have to suffice here, D. H. Lawrence's memorably written and remarkably ambivalent description of encountering the work of the Viennese professor:

> Suddenly, he [Freud] stepped out of the conscious into the unconscious, out of the everywhere into the nowhere, like some supreme explorer.
> He walks straight through the wall of sleep, and we hear him rumbling in the cavern of dreams. The impenetrable is not impenetrable, unconsciousness is not nothingness. It is sleep, that wall of darkness which limits our day. Walk bang into the wall, and behold the wall isn't there. It is the vast darkness of a cavern's mouth, the cavern of anterior darkness whence issues the stream of consciousness.

> With dilated hearts we watched Freud disappearing into the cavern of darkness which is sleep and unconsciousness to us, darkness which issues in the foam of all our day's consciousness. He was making for the origins. We watched his ideal candle flutter and go small. Then we waited, as men do wait, always expecting the wonder of wonders. He came back with dreams to sell.
>
> But sweet heaven, what merchandise! What dreams dear heart! What was there in the cave? Alas that we ever looked! Nothing but a huge slimey serpent of sex, and heaps of excrement, and a myriad repulsive little horrors spawned between sex and excrement.

(*Psychoanalysis and the Unconscious*, London, 1923, pp. 14–16. On Lawrence's relationship to Freud, see Collier and Davies op cit., ch. 3.)

29 Quoted in T. Miller, 'In the blitz of dreams: Mass Observation and the historical uses of dream reports', *New Formations* 44, 2001, 34–51, p. 45.

30 Charlotte Beradt, *The Third Reich of Dreams. The Nightmares of a Nation 1933–1939*, transl. Adriane Gottwald, with an essay by Bruno Bettelheim, Wellingborough, 1985 (German, 1966).

31 Bruno Bettelheim, 'An essay', in Beradt, p. 151.

32 Beradt, p. 21.

33 See Willibald Steinmetz, 'Träumen im Zeitalter der Extreme. Für eine historische Lektüre von Traumprotokollen', unpublished lecture, 2000.

34 F. Manuel 'The use and abuse of psychology in history', in *Freedom from History and Other Untimely Essays*, New York, 1972, ch. 2, p. 49.

35 In a letter of 1929, replying to Maxime Leroy (who had asked him to examine some of Descartes' dreams) Freud acknowledged his dismay. He goes on, nonetheless, to venture, tentatively, some brief remarks, based on the idea that the philosopher's dreams are 'dreams from above', i.e. formulations of ideas that could have been created just as well in a waking state as during the state of sleep and which have derived their content only in certain parts from mental states at comparatively deep level. Such a conveniently neat (and arbitrary) division of dreams into the immediately decipherable and the obscure, whilst perhaps intuitively convincing, seems puzzlingly at odds with accounts elsewhere of his dream theory in which there is no such quick 'let-out' clause for the historian/interpreter of dreams; SE 21, pp. 203–204.

36 P. Holland, '"The Interpretation of Dreams" in the Renaissance', in P. Brown, pp. 125–126.

37 '"Wild" psycho-analysis', SE 11, p. 226.

38 The psychoanalyst Ella Freeman Sharpe, for instance, drew attention to an apparent waning of interest in dreams within the psychoanalytic tradition during the 30s; see *Dream Analysis: A Practical Handbook for Psychoanalysts*, London [1937] 1961, p. 67. Cf. the following more recent observation on that view: 'the pendulum which [Sharpe] observed swinging away from psychoanalytic interest in dream interpretation in 1937 has never swung back'. S. Flanders (ed.), *The Dream Discourse Today*, London, 1993, p. 1.

39 A common criticism (after the work of Popper) has concerned the supposedly unfalsifiable nature of the enterprise – why *that* chain of associations and not another? Cf. the related argument about falsifiability, drawing on the work of the Italian philologist, Timpanaro, in Perry Anderson, 'Nocturnal inquiry: Carlo Ginzburg' [1991], *A Zone of Engagement*, London, 1992, ch. 10.

40 Amongst interesting recent work, inspired by Foucault, one might cite the important and densely illustrated study by Jonathan Crary that suggests how the very concept of concentrated attention may itself be a complex discourse fully elaborated in psychology and other fields in the late nineteenth century; see *Suspensions of Perception: Attention, Spectacle and Modern Culture*, Cambridge, MA, 1999. Shifting attitudes to dark, night and sleep, at the time of Freud's dream book, might also be pondered in relation to Wolfgang Schivelbusch's

fascinating inquiry, *Disenchanted Night: The Industrialisation of Light in the Nineteenth Century*, Berg, 1988.

41 Freud drew upon the Russian system for a different purpose altogether in *The Interpretation of Dreams*, namely to make an analogy with the nature of psychical censorship: 'This censorship acts exactly like the censorship of newspapers at the Russian frontier, which allows foreign journals to fall into the hands of the readers whom it is its business to protect only after a quantity of passages have been blacked out'. SE 5, p. 529.

42 'Thoughts for the times on war and death' [1915], SE 14, p. 286.

Chapter 2

How Freud wrote and revised his *Interpretation of Dreams*:
Conflicts around the subjective origins of the book of the century

Ilse Grubrich-Simitis
Translated by Arnold J. Pomerans

Sigmund Freud's centennial book, *The Interpretation of Dreams*, has recently seen its hundredth anniversary on the threshold of the twenty-first century. As its author himself has put it: 'Psychoanalysis may be said to have been born with the twentieth century; for the publication in which it emerged before the world as something new – my *Interpretation of Dreams* – bears the date "1900"'.[1]

It would take us too far afield were we to look, even in outline, at all the intellectual breakthroughs Freud made in this one book alone. Anyone reading the running heads in the first German edition attentively[2] will discover, in a kind of self-commentary by the author, a series of what may be called keywords, and will at the same time sense something, very directly, of the tone or flair of the great book. Time and again, Freud includes the titles of subsections in these running heads: 'Infantile material as a source of dreams', 'The work of condensation in dream-formation', 'Regression'. Other running heads mark out new terms: 'Secondary revision', 'Collective and composite figures', 'Day's residues'. Elsewhere, hypotheses are succinctly summarized: 'Unconscious wishes as the driving force of dreams', 'The abnormal processes are the primitive ones', 'The overestimation of consciousness'. Yet other running heads are used for additional emphasis, lending the text a musical touch. The only place in the book where the right-hand running head, which normally changes with every page, is continued over numerous pages – being, as it were, repeated as an unmistakable, continuous note – occurs in the second chapter: the dream of Irma's injection together with its analysis is presented under a single running head – 'The dream of Irma's injection' – which continues to the end of the chapter. Freud, as is well known, was convinced that on 24 July 1895 he had succeeded in discovering the wish-fulfilling function of dreaming in the analysis of his own dream about Irma. This second chapter then ends with the striking statement:

> For the moment I am satisfied with the achievement of this one piece of fresh knowledge. If we adopt the method of interpreting dreams I have indicated here, we shall find that dreams really have a meaning and are

far from being the expression of a fragmentary activity of the brain [. . .]. *When the work of interpretation has been completed, we perceive that a dream is the fulfilment of a wish.*[3]

In another key passage, namely in the context of typical dreams containing the death of 'loved relatives', Freud, while describing the oedipal constellation for the very first time in a published text, introduces a principal axis of the future theory of the neuroses, and also an indispensable basic configuration of psychical structure formation in general. And here the sequence of running heads has the effect of a drum-roll or of a staccato communication by a pioneer of child observation, which Freud unquestionably was at that time. I shall mention just three running heads in this passage about passion and hatred within the family that, in the then prevailing cultural climate, were considered to be downright scandalous: 'The child's hostile feelings towards its siblings', 'The child's idea of someone being "dead"', 'The child's sexual impulses towards its parents'. Finally, a running head in the theoretical seventh chapter – namely 'Primary and secondary process' – marks with extreme terseness one of the most important conceptual distinctions, effective to this day, which Freud introduced in his *Interpretation of Dreams*: primary and secondary process, those two distinct types of psychical functioning.

***

Above all, *The Interpretation of Dreams* presents a clinical method. It reflects Freud's ingeniously simple approach to the interpretation of dreams, namely to dismantle the manifest dream–content into its component elements, and then to elicit the dreamer's associations to each of these elements. As is well known, Freud exemplified this method above all with his *own* dreams. This brings us to my actual theme, though in what follows, I shall not be dwelling on the meandering interaction between self-analysis and the origins of *The Interpretation of Dreams* – or the genesis of psychoanalysis. There are numerous books on that subject, particularly Didier Anzieu's classical *L'auto-analyse de Freud et la découverte de la psychanalyse*.[4] My thesis is more concerned with a hitherto neglected aspect, namely the fact that Freud maintained a highly conflictual attitude to his magnum opus throughout his life. The fluctuations in this attitude can be gathered from the multifarious revisions he kept making to his book in a total of eight successive editions.[5] Incidentally, my thesis in no way contradicts the known fact that, although Freud admittedly subjected his dream book to uncompromising *formal* criticism, he always remained firmly convinced of the merit of its revolutionary *contents*.

The main reason for Freud's conflictual attitude seems to have been the self-analytic, that is, the subjective origin of most of the insights contained in his magnum opus. We must not forget that Freud never severed his ties with the positivistic approach inculcated in him during his training. However, while founding psychoanalysis as the paragon of a science of the human subject in his *Interpretation of Dreams*, he was constantly forced to ride roughshod over these ties. He had highlighted the dream as the central object of his study of man's inner world, so to speak as an *objective* object – objective, precisely because it is not under the dreamer's conscious control, but essentially generated by the dynamics of the unconscious. And it was the patient exploration of this objective object that led Freud to the discovery of *psychical reality* in the strict sense. In this magnum opus he used a telling metaphor, namely that interpreting dreams had served him as a 'window'[6] for this venture. But throughout his life, he seems to have feared that critics might use primarily epistemological arguments and the reproach that his studies had originally been based on a self-analytic procedure, to confound him by redefining dreams as subjective, quasi-fictitious contingencies: '*Träume sind Schäume*' – 'dreams are froth'.[7] That would have meant no less than the annihilation of his life's work.

On closer examination, the author's conflictual attitude can be seen to have influenced the very process of writing the book, a process involving a beneficial division of roles between Freud, who wanted to give full sway to his self-analytic rigour, and who said of himself that he had 'lost the feeling of shame required of an author',[8] and Wilhelm Fliess, representing the 'Other', whose task it was to protect the friend determined to expose his own dreams and their interpretation, that is, to commit a scandalous breach of the boundary between private and public life, which was still clearly demarcated in the then prevailing bourgeois culture. Freud not infrequently considered Fliess's interventions, generally dictated by motives of discretion, as being too drastic. In the course of 1898 these interventions in any case kept inhibiting Freud, indeed, they caused him to interrupt the writing process. They triggered off the work of mourning about what had to be suppressed, and tore holes in the emerging textual tissue. These repeated breaks in continuity seem, in fact, to have been partly responsible for a structural feature of *The Interpretation of Dreams*, one that also determined the fate of later revisions: the piecing together, the excisions, the shifting back and forth of material, the character of what, so to speak, remained an open book, a collective text, a patchwork.

On writing the preface to the first edition, however, Freud himself seems to have adopted Fliess's role to some extent, in that he had evidently reinternalized his conflict. He mentions the embarrassment caused by his attempt to illustrate his theoretical insights with his own dreams and by having to reveal the intimacies of his private life more 'than is normally necessary for any writer who is a man of science and not a poet'.[9] He also mentions the need for omissions and concealment to take the edge off at least some of his indiscretions. However, the explanation of why he nevertheless used his own instead of his patients' or other people's dream material sounds apologetic and hides what, at the time, were the predominantly self-analytic, that is, subjective origins of his insights. As if denying the innovative power of his centennial book, he insisted that he did not believe he had 'trespassed beyond the sphere of interest covered by neuropathology', because the dream struck him as being no more than 'the first member of a class of abnormal psychical phenomena',[10] such as hysterical phobias, obsessions and delusions. This classification sounds like a decided attempt to confirm the *objectivity* of his research object. Shortly before the publication of the first edition of *The Interpretation of Dreams*, Freud had thus plainly made the first of his attempts to distance himself from the self-analytic, that is, subjective origin of his magnum opus, something that he was to repeat, as we shall see, on subsequent occasions, admittedly in alternation with energetic gestures of reappropriation.

The first of these reappropriations already occurs in the second edition. It is well known that it took nine years before the no more than 600 copies of the first edition were sold and before Freud was able to prepare the second edition of 1909. Meanwhile he had experienced the enormous productivity of psychoanalytic thought embodied in the imposing sequence of major works he had published since, ranging from *The Psychopathology of Every-day Life* through the book on jokes and the *Three Essays on the Theory of Sexuality* to the presentation of the Dora case and the Gradiva study. This evidence of the explanatory power of psychoanalytic concepts, extending far beyond psychopathology, let alone neuropathology, when applied to countless cultural and everyday phenomena, now enabled Freud to add the following famous sentence near the end of the second edition: '*The interpretation of dreams is the royal road to a knowledge of the unconscious activities of the mind*'.[11] With it, he openly pressed the claim that he had founded a *general* psychology, embracing pathological as well as normal phenomena. At the time, he no longer seemed to fear that the self-analytic, that is, subjective origins of his insights and theories could be used to challenge their validity or, indeed, the worth of the dream as a research object. Not only did he include many further dreams of his own and add further intimate details to those already published in the first edition; in the preface to the second edition, he now stressed that it was precisely his own major specimen dreams that had proved to be particularly persistent during the process of revision, refusing, as it were, to be subjected to incisive changes. And here Freud added with self-assured emphasis that *The Interpretation of Dreams* was his most personal, quasi-autobiographical work, by stating: 'For this book has a further subjective significance for me personally [. . .]. It was, I found, a portion of my own self-analysis, my reaction to my father's death – that is to say, to the most important event, the most poignant loss, of a man's life. Having discovered that this was so, I felt unable to obliterate the traces of the experience'.[12]

Whereas Freud had therefore drawn his *Interpretation of Dreams* closer to himself, so to speak, in the intimate revision of 1909, he again pushed it away from himself in three distancing or objectifying ways in the preparatory work for the third edition of 1911, on which he started just one year later. First, his attention was now focused on the *theoretical* dimension of the book. In the restrained new preface Freud stressed the progress of his scientific knowledge and its effect on his *Interpretation of Dreams*: 'When I wrote it in 1899, my theory of sexuality was not yet in existence and the analysis of the more complicated forms of psycho-neurosis was only just beginning'[13] – as though this had not been the case as early as 1909. The inclusion of advances in the theory of sexuality and of psychoneuroses, gained mainly through clinical work with patients and exchanges of ideas with colleagues, that is, in more objective ways, is reflected in many passages of the third edition.

The second manner in which he relativized the self-analytic origins of his magnum opus was the resolute inclusion of contributions by his group of collaborators formed in 1902 – as if the empirical basis of his findings concerning his research object, the dream, could somehow be extended in this way, or as philosophers of science would put it, as if this kind of enumerative inductionism could, indeed, serve as proof. More clearly than in the 1909 revision, the authors of the material of countless new dream insertions are mentioned by name. From the third edition onwards, one can – certainly in the fifth and sixth chapters – observe a growing *orchestration* or a transition from solo voice to choir, which, as this expansion grew in yet later editions, could occasionally disintegrate into a babble of voices. In a sense Freud handed *The Interpretation of Dreams* over to his collaborators in the third edition, allowing it to become a *collective* work. Otto Rank began to establish himself as the most important quasi-co-author. And by emphasizing the significance of dream symbolism, Wilhelm Stekel provided Freud with a third way of turning away from the self-analytic, that is, subjective sources of *The Interpretation of Dreams*. The central importance was now increasingly assigned to the supra-individual, the typical, indeed, the stereotypical elements of the dream material, elements drawn from the phylogenetic roots of the dream language, and more suited to being interpreted independently of the associations of the individual dreamer. In other words, attention was now focused on the universal link, identical for every dreamer, between given symbols and what they symbolize.

The extent to which Freud, in fact, distanced himself from his dream book during the preparation of the third edition, even thinking of abandoning it altogether, can be gathered from his correspondence with C. G. Jung. Jung had complained in February 1911 that the persuasive power of the book was impaired by the fact that the unconscious mechanisms discovered by Freud were exemplified above all by his own dreams, and that he had been forced to interpret them incompletely for discretionary reasons.

Freud, who had, as we have seen, recognized and worried about this disadvantage from the outset, insisted in his reply that nothing could be done about it. However, he surprisingly suggested a way out: 'In the preface [to the third edition] that has already been written, I state that this book will not be re-issued, but will be replaced by a new and impersonal one, for which I shall collect material in the next three or four years with Rank's help. In this book I shall deal with dreams, presupposing or perhaps setting forth my findings concerning the theory of the neuroses, while Rank will follow out the literary and mythological implications'.[14] As we also know from the same correspondence, the publisher of *The Interpretation of Dreams*, Franz Deuticke, raised strong objections to this plan and so prevented the disappearance of the personal and intimate *Interpretation of Dreams* from the book market.

The next revision, made for the fourth edition of 1914, was the most thoroughgoing in scope and range, above all because Freud proceeded to restructure entire blocks of text in the copious Chapters V and VI, the better to contain the unwieldy form of *The Interpretation of Dreams* once again. However, as far as our theme is concerned, he stuck to the path he had embarked upon with the previous revision: he continued the *collectivization* of the book, inserting two voluminous articles by Rank between the sixth and seventh chapters, and scattering texts by his collaborators throughout the work. As a result, the threat that *The Interpretation of Dreams* might disintegrate increased once again. In his own supplements to the 1914 edition, Freud focused attention predominantly on the *theoretical* passages, much as he had done in 1911. If we study his important additions to the previously barely revised seventh chapter, we shall see that he was already attuning himself to the themes of the great metapsychological treatises with which he would be preoccupied a little later in 1915, that is, during the First World War: regression, pleasure principle and reality principle, the different meanings of the word 'unconscious', psychical vs. factual or material reality, etc. As a further method of moving away from the self-analytic, that is, subjective origins of his dream book, we may consider the countless additions drawn from the dream literature of various epochs and linguistic and cultural areas, which Freud included in the fourth edition: from Artemidorus of Daldis, to whom he attributed the most comprehensive work on dream interpretation in antiquity, down to modern oriental dream interpreters, and from the medieval mystics down to nineteenth-century philosophers. It is as if Freud had promised himself that the intensification of this dialogue with other authors across the centuries and millennia would provide further objectifying substantiation of his own findings.

And yet this revision, undertaken shortly before the outbreak of the First World War, includes an inconspicuous intervention through which the author reveals that he had nevertheless kept in touch with the self-analytic, that is, subjective origins of his magnum opus. Almost jocularly he points out that none of his findings had provoked such embittered denials, 'such amusing contortions – on the part of critics'[15] as his suggestion that childhood impulses towards incest persist in the unconscious, that is, his reference to the oedipal constellation, which he had at that time discovered essentially by self-analytic means but also by a deeper understanding of Sophocles' Oedipus drama, and which he had published already in the first edition of *The Interpretation of Dreams*. Yet, as if defiantly, he moved the Hamlet passage, that great variation on the Oedipus theme, previously printed as a footnote, to the centre of the main text in the fourth edition.

It was clearly the grim experiences of the First World War that persuaded Freud to add a supplement to the first post-war edition of the dream book, that is, to the fifth edition of 1919, in the relevant textual context: 'Later studies have shown that the "Oedipus complex", which was touched upon for the first time in the above paragraphs in *The Interpretation of Dreams*, throws a light of undreamt-of importance on the history of the human race [. . .]'.[16] Referring to *Totem and Taboo*, his previously published commentary on the prehistory of human aggression, however, Freud distanced himself once again from the sphere of the individual subject, and also from himself as the person in whom he had first observed and studied the oedipal impulses. Finally, the additions to the fifth edition reflect yet another distancing approach: here Freud begins with the *historicization* of his *Interpretation of Dreams*. For the first time, he states in the new preface that the attempt to bring *The Interpretation of Dreams* to the level of present-day psychoanalytic knowledge would 'destroy its historic character'; indeed, he wants to make the reader believe 'that after an existence of nearly twenty years it has accomplished its task'.[17]

In the said fifth edition, however, there are additional dreams and interpretations, war traces as it were, which, as if in a powerful counter-thrust, document a highly relevant reconciliation with the subjective origins of the dream book, indeed, a resumption of radical self-analysis. A case in point is the dream of the return of Freud's son Martin from the front, meant to illustrate the effect of a day's residue of distressing anticipation. There had been no news of his son for over a week. The manifest dream content represents the returning son not as someone who had 'fallen' (in battle) but as someone who had been climbing onto a basket to put something on a cupboard, and also as one who has a bandage round his head, that is, has been wounded. By association with a childhood accident of his own, Freud discovered in himself a concealed impulse: 'That serves you right'. And with truly merciless self-analysis, he was able to pinpoint the motive for this hostile affect, namely the envy felt for the young by one who had grown old, so that it was 'precisely the *strength* of the painful emotion which would have arisen if such a misfortune [that is, the son's death in battle] had really happened that caused that emotion to seek out a repressed wish-fulfilment of this kind in order to find some consolation'.[18]

Contrary to the expectation voiced in the preface to the fifth edition that the book had 'accomplished its task', the demand for it grew briskly during the early post-war years. However, Freud was not in a position to revise the sixth and seventh editions published in 1921 and 1922 respectively, because the publisher thought that he could not shoulder the costs. In 1923, Freud was diagnosed as having cancer. This persuaded his collaborators and friends to initiate a first complete edition of his works under the auspices of the Internationaler Psychoanalytischer Verlag, founded after the war: the *Gesammelte Schriften* (Collected Writings). In this editorial project, Freud decided to use a different, in a sense diachronic, presentation of his centennial book: in Volume II of the *Gesammelte Schriften* he presented *The Interpretation of Dreams* in the exact wording of the first edition. Here, we therefore find the most resolute *re-appropriation* of the dream book by its *single* author, Sigmund Freud, for in Volume II he freed his magnum opus rigorously from all additions under which the slimmer and more radical original version had increasingly been concealed.

Yet he did not simply slough off the material added in successive editions; instead he carefully preserved it in Volume III of the *Gesammelte Schriften* because he was still convinced that this rich material confirmed the status of the dream as a proper object of scientific research. In this third volume of 1925 he again added numerous new supplements of his own, including intimate details, for instance to his dreams about Rome, and above all a '*Zusatzkapitel*', an additional chapter running to several pages. That chapter ends with a discussion of the occult meaning of dreams – as if Freud had now deliberately set out to provoke a reproach he had apparently feared in the past: namely, that his dream research was guided by fantasy and speculation, and was therefore non-scientific. Although he had grown old and ill, he was still filled with the undiminished impetus of his intellectual independence, as he returned to the revolutionary stance of the primal *Interpretation of Dreams*: refreshingly unconcerned, he broaches such matters frowned upon in academic circles as telepathy, and comes up with several fascinating ideas, behind which the concept of projective identification can be clearly discerned. With this final chord, *The Interpretation of Dreams* may therefore be said to have remained an *open* book in the best sense of allowing for creative scientific curiosity.

In the eighth edition, published in 1930 – that is, in the last edition supervised by the author – this new questing finale was, however, suppressed, probably following an intervention by Ernest Jones, who had apparently pleaded for the omission of this additional chapter because, in his view, it might detract from the scientific respectability of psychoanalysis. In this last edition, again published by Franz Deuticke, the innovative bipartition of the material, thanks to which the original version of *The Interpretation of Dreams* had again been revealed, was also dropped in favour of another one-volume presentation, incorporating the supplements. This is the version with which we are accustomed to work today. Once again we see Freud attempting to distance himself from the book because, as he declared in 1930, he had come to consider it 'an historic document'.[19] And, in fact, this last edition contains no more than a very small number of new additions.

Yet there is one minimal revision by which no more than the *position* of a textual fragment is changed, but which nevertheless demonstrates that Freud tried to restore the link to the self-analytic, that is, subjective origins of his magnum opus for the last time. A passage that had been added as a footnote to the post-war revision of 1919 was now moved into the sharper light of the main text. I am referring to the passage mentioned earlier, with the dream about the return of his son from the front in which he, the father, worked out in remorseless self-analysis and presented in clearly recognizable form his envy of his son's youth, indeed his suppressed death wishes directed at his own child, as a complement, so to speak, to the murderous impulses of the son towards the father typical of the oedipal constellation. We might consider this lifting of a footnote into the main text as a kind of farewell gesture by Freud, as if he wanted to refer his readers, not least future ones, one last time to the royal road along which he had arrived at the insights contained in *The Interpretation of Dreams* at the end of the nineteenth century: radical self-exploration by the analysis of one's own dreams.

It was as if he were trying, by paradigmatically pinpointing through this seemingly minimal change of the position of a textual fragment, to outline once again the contours of the disenchanted image of man that had emerged during decades of psychoanalytic work, an image that he had been forced to discover in himself as well: one that, despite all civilizing efforts, was not very flattering, deeply tragic, and in any case torn by inescapable destructive ambivalence. In the *ugliness* of the discoveries Freud had made in the course of interpreting his own dreams, we can certainly identify another of the causes of his lifelong conflictual attitude to the subjective origins of *The Interpretation of Dreams*. The impulses and affects warded off included not only envy and death wishes towards one of his sons, but also a triumphant thirst for revenge against colleagues, a megalomaniacal pursuit of fame and glory, seduction wishes towards his eldest daughter, feelings of contempt for his father, exhibitionism, murderous rivalry directed at fraternal figures, etc. However, the main cause of Freud's conflictual attitude to his centennial book was evidently the break, due to the research method of self-analysis, with the positivistic epistemological tradition in which he had been brought up.

Freud's unconscious expressed the methodological paradox of his self-analytic procedure and the repulsive nature of his results in a vivid and highly condensed dream. 'Old Brücke must have set me some task; *strangely enough*, it related to a dissection of the lower part of my own body, my pelvis and legs, which I saw before me as though in the dissecting-room, but without noticing their absence in myself and also without a trace of any gruesome feeling. [...] The pelvis had been eviscerated [...]. Thick flesh-coloured protuberances (which, in the dream itself, made me think of haemorrhoids) could be seen'.[20] This is merely an extract from the long dream. And of Freud's multidimensional interpretation I shall here quote no more than that section in which he links the dream expressly with his self-analysis: 'The dissection meant the self-analysis which I was carrying out, as it were, in the publication of this present book about dreams – a process which had been so distressing to me in reality that I had postponed the printing of the finished manuscript for more than a year. A wish then arose that I might get over this feeling of distaste; hence it was that I had no gruesome feeling [. . .] in the dream'.[21] The fact that his 'physicalist' teacher Brücke, of all people, had given him instructions to proceed to the dissection of his own pelvis, and that this was done by the method characteristic of 'higher anatomy', could only mean a wish-fulfilling assurance that with his self-exploration Freud did not violate the procedural requirements of science.

***

The unwavering esteem in which Freud held the findings he had published in *The Interpretation of Dreams* is reflected not least in the persistence with which, throughout his life, he continued along his royal road to a knowledge of the unconscious – and this not only in the form of the revisions that he made in successive editions of his magnum opus, but also in the long series of separate texts on dreams and interpretation of dreams that he produced after 1900, beginning with the brief study entitled 'A Premonitory Dream Fulfilled',[22] written shortly after the publication of *The Interpretation of Dreams*, and ending with the dream chapter included in 1938 in *An Outline of Psycho-Analysis*.[23]

It is certainly no accident that Freud should have begun his *New Introductory Lectures on Psycho-Analysis* with a 'Revision of the theory of dreams', once more giving a succinct account of the scope and depth of the insights into the dynamics and mechanisms of unconscious thought during sleep that he had gained at the turn of the century. In the end, he admittedly altered his formula that a dream is the fulfilment of a wish to 'a dream is an *attempt* at the fulfilment of a wish'[24] – evidently in order to meet objections to the wish-fulfilment theory that had emerged, above all, during the treatment of severely traumatized patients. Such patients, Freud argued, were regularly thrown back into the most unpleasurable traumatic situation by their dreams – which leads to sleep-disturbing generation of anxiety; in their case one might well say that the function of the dream fails. Although Freud did not yet go on to describe the compulsive urge of traumatized patients to persist with coping and curative attempts in their dreams, he was broaching topics in these passages that, starting with Sándor Ferenczi's concept of the 'traumatolytic function'[25] of dreams, are at the centre of modern psychoanalytic dream research conducted in connection with trauma research. These topics, moreover, had bothered Freud from an early stage like irritating foreign bodies, not least during the revisions of his *Interpretation of Dreams*. One such topic, for instance, was the extent to which traumas suffered in early childhood, and since veiled by amnesia, recur in dreams and may be recognized and dealt with along this path.

In that same introductory lecture written at the beginning of the thirties, Freud regretfully diagnosed a clear decline of interest in dreams. Psychoanalysts behaved as if nothing new could be added to the study of dreams. Hence the prognosis for the future development of his method of dream interpretation, in his view, looked bleak. What is certain is that there have been important further developments since his day. Above all, work with psychotic and borderline patients, and especially greater familiarity with their thinking disorders, have led to a far-reaching expansion of our understanding of the development and significance of the symbolization process, here used in the primary, wider sense of the capacity to form psychical representations – with varied repercussions on the present-day psychoanalytic conception of dreams and of dreaming. Thus, to mention but one example, Jean-Michel Quinodoz in his work on ' "Dreams that Turn Over a Page" ',[26] has recently shown how seemingly regressive dreams, regardless of their anxiety-inducing primitive manifest content, can be understood, interpreted and worked through as the first signs of progress on the road from projective identification to introjection, or to the integration of hitherto unrepresentable aspects of the dreamer's personality.

Perhaps we can say, however, that Freud's prognosis was not entirely mistaken, inasmuch as work on dreams in the therapeutic process no longer holds the highly privileged position he attached to it at the turn of the nineteenth century, and insofar as interest in dream symbolism in the narrower, that is, in Stekel's sense, has in fact been waning. However, in clinical work, dreams are nowadays carefully examined for traumatic elements in the patient's life history that are not accessible to conscious memory. Moreover, we connect dreams much more closely than was customary in Freud's day with the patient's momentary inner state, for instance with his prevailing defence level, and in general with the current phase of the analytic process, that is, with the context of a particular session or of the adjoining sessions. And above all, we nowadays link dreams as closely as possible to the ongoing transference and counter-transference processes, which are not only reflected in but also impelled and shaped further by the occurrence, recounting and working through of each specific dream. Recently dreams have been considered to be the intersubjective creations of the analytic pair, and should be interpreted accordingly.[27]

Needless to say, later contributions to dream interpretation are not necessarily better than earlier ones simply because they are more recent. The fact that the potential of *The Interpretation of Dreams*, now over a hundred years old, to instigate future dream research is far from exhausted, seems lately to have been realized, especially by neuroscientists.[28] Moreover, we can still learn a great deal from Freud's observational acumen and committed search for the deeper understanding of the fabric of *individual* dreams with their highly complex pictorial grammar, created by the dreamer in his nocturnal isolation from external reality. It is precisely because of the self-analytic origins of *The Interpretation of Dreams* that the transference and counter-transference aspects of dreams were inevitably left underexposed at the time. What may strike us today as a one-dimensional approach nevertheless focused Freud's stupendous observational powers on the dream as an artfully constructed *monadic* sign phenomenon, and hence enabled him to take seriously and study assiduously, in a semiotic and almost structuralist sense, the manifest as well as the latent content, much as an exegete treats 'Holy Writ'[29] – a simile used by Freud himself in his dream book. Seen in this light, *The Interpretation of Dreams*, with its myriad details culled from the actual texts of dreams, embodies a degree of differentiation that seems nowadays to be increasingly forgotten.

There is yet another lesson we can learn from rereading Freud's dream book. Although, as I have pointed out, the self-analytic, that is, subjective origins of many of his insights, and the divergence of his method of investigation from established academic procedures admittedly troubled Freud – in the 1925 revision he expressly advised caution regarding spontaneous symbol translations by means of intuition and clearly distanced himself from Wilhelm Stekel's 'peculiar gift for the direct understanding' of symbols, adding that the resulting findings 'have no claim to [scientific] credibility'[30] – he was nevertheless prepared to cross the traditional boundaries whenever he felt that this was necessary. Only in this way, with his *Interpretation of Dreams*, did he succeed in wresting a stretch of virgin territory for the human sciences 'from popular beliefs and mysticism'.[31]

However, even when committing his *Interpretation of Dreams* to paper, Freud was aware, to a greater extent than we seem to be today, that work with the unconscious goes – and will always go – against the grain, that its 'strangeness' and genuine 'uncanniness' will not diminish, and that anyone working in this field will, for that very reason, never be able to acquire the degree of unquestioned academic respectability granted to scientists engaged in areas of research far removed from the unconscious. Without his willingness to remain an outsider, however, Freud would hardly have reached the conclusion at the very end of his *Interpretation of Dreams* with which he first guided us into the realm of unconscious psychical life. To quote him for the last time: 'The unconscious is the larger sphere, which includes within it the smaller sphere of the conscious. [. . .] The unconscious is the true psychical reality; *in its innermost nature it is as much unknown to us as the reality of the external world, and it is as incompletely presented by the data of consciousness as is the external world by the communications of our sense organs*'.[32] What he wanted to stress by that pronouncement was, not least, that anyone working in this field must – regardless of the precision of his thought, the acuity of his well-trained perceptual apparatus and his conjectural caution – be blessed with an un-shakeable tolerance of obscurity, uncertainty and ambiguity, because this triad is an indispensable part of even the most disciplined dealings with the unconscious. The lesson we can learn from rereading Freud's book is ultimately a warning, namely that the adaptation of psychoanalysis to conventional criteria of scientific rigour can ultimately be attained only at the price of a gradual distancing from the realm of the deep unconscious, and of renouncing the highest degree of differentiation in the application of the clinical method. Viewed in this light, *The Interpretation of Dreams* bears testimony to Freud's imposing and persistent refusal to bow to such external and, as I have tried to show, also internal pressure to conform.

We live in a time that, by all appearances, is trying to rid itself of psycho-analysis. Our discipline is under constant attack. Above all it is accused of being 'non-scientific'. Instead of eagerly submitting to standard proof or reliability criteria, or seeking protection by adaptation to other established dis-ciplines, we should go on the offensive and insist that the material generated by our highly specific clinical method during the everyday collaboration of analysts and analysands provides the unique and highly specific subject matter for an entirely novel epistemological debate, based not on the traditional dichotomy of subjectivity and objectivity, but on their *interrelationship*. It is precisely this interrelationship that develops in the 'potential space' of the psychoanalytic situation – particularly through creative use of projective identification – in the to and fro of transference and counter-transference, con-tinually oscillating between reality and fantasy/illusion.[33] It may well turn out that in the exploration of the unconscious, which for much of the time does not operate via sensory perception, the wide-awake registration of the finest subjective motions within the sphere of transference and counter-transference is the indispensable prerequisite of an approximation of objectivity in this realm, or as André Green has put it, of an 'objectivation of subjectivity'.[34] The resulting debate may well prove to be no less illuminating and stimulating for epistemology than it would be for psychoanalysis. In other words, such a debate might well produce quite new criteria for evidence, proof, reliability etc., more suited to our enormously complex research object and our inter-active clinical method and to interdisciplinary dialogues on such matters.[35] But this is another and extremely complex topic. However, what can be said in conclusion is that such efforts would be entirely in keeping, notwithstand-ing his conflictual attitude, with the great cultural heritage Freud founded, on the threshold of the twentieth century, with his *Interpretation of Dreams*.

NOTES AND REFERENCES

Earlier versions of parts of this chapter were presented at the English-speaking Weekend Conference of The British Psychoanalytical Society, October 2000, London and at the 42nd Conference of The International Psychoanalytical Association, July 2001, Nice.

1 Freud, 'A short account of psycho-analysis' (1924), SE 19, p. 191.

2 They have regrettably been omitted from the *Standard Edition*.

3 Freud, *The Interpretation of Dreams* (1900), SE 4, p. 121.

4 Paris (1988 [1959]).

5 See Ilse Grubrich-Simitis, 'Metamorphoses of *The Interpretation of Dreams*' in *International Journal of Psychoanalysis* 81, 2000 [1999], pp. 1155–1183.

6 Freud, *The Interpretation of Dreams* (1900), SE 4, p. 219.

7 Ibid., p. 133.

8 Freud, *The Complete Letters of Sigmund Freud to Wilhelm Fliess 1887–1904*, J. M. Masson (transl. and ed.). Cambridge, MA, 1985, p. 315.

9 Freud, *The Interpretation of Dreams* (1900), SE 4, p. xxiv.

10 Ibid., p. xxiii.

11 Ibid., SE 5, p. 608.

12 Ibid., SE 4, p. xxvi.

13 Ibid., p. xxvii.

14 Freud and C. G. Jung, *The Freud/Jung Letters: The Correspondence between Sigmund Freud and C. G. Jung*, W. McGuire (ed.), R. Mannheim and R. F. C. Hull (transl.), Princeton, NJ, 1974, p. 395.

15 Freud, *The Interpretation of Dreams* (1900), SE 4, p. 263, note 2.

16 Ibid.

17 Ibid., p. xxix.

18 Ibid., SE 5, p. 560.

19 Ibid., SE 4, p. xxxi.

20 Ibid., SE 5, p. 452.

21 Ibid., pp. 477f.

22 Freud, 'A premonitory dream fulfilled' (1941[1889]), SE 5, pp. 623–625.

23 Freud, *An Outline of Psycho-Analysis* (1940[1938]), SE 23, pp. 144–207.

24 Freud, *New Introductory Lectures on Psycho-Analysis* (1933), SE 22, p. 29.

25 S. Ferenczi, *Final Contributions to the Problems and Methods of Psychoanalysis*, M. Balint (ed.), E. Mosbacher and others (transl.), London, 1955, p. 240 (reprinted London, 1980).

26 J.-M. Quinodoz, ' "Dreams that turn over a page" ', in *International Journal of Psychoanalysis* 80, 1999, pp. 225–238.

27 See, for instance, T. H. Ogden, *Reverie and Interpretation*, Northvale, NJ, and London, 1997.

28 See, for instance, M. Solms, 'The interpretation of dreams and the neurosciences', in *Psychoanalysis and History* 3, 2001[1999], pp. 79–91.

29 Freud, *The Interpretation of Dreams* (1900), SE 5, p. 514.

30 Ibid., p. 350.

31 Freud, *New Introductory Lectures on Psycho-Analysis* (1933), SE 22, p. 7.

32 Freud, *The Interpretation of Dreams* (1900), SE 5, p. 612f.

33 See G. Adler, 'Transitional phenomena, projective identification, and the essential ambiguity of the psychoanalytic situation', *Psychoanalytic Quarterly* 58, 1989, pp. 81–104.

34 A. Green, comment on W. S. Poland, 'The analyst's witnessing and otherness', in *Journal of the American Psychoanalytic Association* 48, 2000, p. 60.

35 See H. Shevrin, 'Is psychoanalysis one science, two sciences, or no science at all? A discourse among friendly antagonists'. See also the commentaries on that article in the *Journal of the American Psychoanalytic Association* 43, 1995, pp. 963–1049. See further U. Dreher, 'Was sollte man bedenken, wenn man Übertragung messen will?', in *Zeitschrift für psychoanalytische Theorie und Praxis* 14, 1999, pp. 260–283, and the interviews with P. Fonagy, R. Zak de Goldstein and G. O. Gabbard in *International Psychoanalysis* (IPA Newsletter) 8, 1999, No. 2.

Chapter 3

Dreams and desires in ancient and early Christian thought

Charles Stewart

Freud considered the ancient Greeks to have been a relatively unrepressed people. In their literature, art and mythology the Greeks, he thought, could directly contemplate the fulfilment of the 'primeval wishes of our childhood'.[1] After classical antiquity, however, a 'secular advance of repression in the emotional life of mankind' led Western civilization into its current predicament.[2] Whereas childhood fantasy could be expressed in the *Oedipus Rex*, by the time of Shakespeare's *Hamlet* the same fantasy had to be repressed. Oedipus was tragic, whereas Hamlet was neurotic.

As an anthropologist I have learned to suspect accounts of 'unrepressed societies' for the simple reason that they usually turn out to be unreliable. A case in point is Margaret Mead's *Coming of Age in Samoa* (1928), which contended that because the Samoans led a life of sexual freedom they did not confront any 'adolescent crisis' as American youth did.[3] Samoan sexual arrangements, Mead argued, presented a lesson that American society would do well to heed. Some fifty years later, however, Derek Freeman pointed out that most of the girls Mead studied were, in fact, Christian and thus somewhat familiar with the concept of guilt. At least half of them were virgins at marriage – female virginity was, apparently, a value – and furthermore, Freeman presented shocking stories of rape and manual defloration.[4] In another study of a supposedly unrepressed people, Kilton Stewart reported that the Senoi of Malaysia were able to control their dreams and steer them to fulfilling conclusions – erotic dreams included.[5] Subsequent visitors to the Senoi have not encountered this lucid dreaming practice and most now consider that it was Stewart's fanciful creation.[6]

These examples suggest that stories of unrepressed, non-neurotic primitives are more rooted in modern Western romantic fantasy than in reality. A generalized, negative feeling in Western societies that 'we' are repressed has, I think, supported the production of these ethnographic allegories.[7] As the literary theorist Marianna Torgovnick put it, 'The West seems to need the primitive as a precondition and a supplement to its sense of self'.[8] Similar stories of non-repressed ancient societies arguably derive from the same motivation to locate a happier, utopia-dwelling 'other' for use as a counterpoint to our own self-perception as repressed. The 'primitive' and the ancient potentially teach the same lesson.

REPRESSION AND SUPPRESSION

In what follows I use the evidence of erotic dreams in order to reconsider the question of ancient repression. Should these dreams themselves be considered symptoms of (earlier) repression? Were the strategies that pagan and early Christian societies devised to cope with them repressive? In order to address these questions it is necessary to consider what we might understand 'repression' to mean. The best place to start is with Freud, who introduced the concept to psychoanalysis from whence it has diffused into the everyday vocabulary of modern Western society.

The main features of repression that emerge from Freud's writings are as follows:[9]

1   With the exception of certain phylogenetic elements inherited at birth, repression creates and structures the unconscious; the two are virtually synonymous.
2   Freud used repression to refer to a variety of modes of defence against unwanted ideas. In his later writing he recategorized repression as but one type of defence.
3   Repression (*Verdrängung*) occurs unconsciously by contrast with suppression (*Unterdrückung*), which occurs consciously and results in the material in question either being eliminated altogether or transferred to the preconscious.[10]
4   There are two types of repression: *primal repression*, in which a mental representation of an instinctual desire is denied access to consciousness, and *repression proper*, in which already conscious material becomes repressed because of contact with repressed ideas/instincts.
5   The repressed dynamically attempts to return. It makes itself apparent, if not always known or recognized, in the form of neuroses, behavioural slips, dreams and jokes.

This summary of the complicated senses of repression in Freud's conceptual system should make it apparent that its meaning is not the same as 'repression' in everyday speech. In English, people do use 'repression' to refer to the intrapsychic activity of barring a thought or impulse, but they tend to think of it as something that someone does intentionally or wilfully. The terms repression and suppression are, furthermore, virtually synonymous in their most frequent application – reference to political domination or control. Freud's uncanny effect has been to change the overtones of ordinary words, thus making it seem that everyone is thinking within his very particular system of thought when, in fact, they are disregarding some significant conceptual distinctions.[11] Ordinary speakers (lay people, non-specialists) basically grasp the idea of the unconscious and the return of the repressed as dysfunctional symptoms, but they do not, I think, comprehend the phylogenetic component of the unconscious, nor do they think of repression as necessarily occurring unconsciously.

Freud's opponents have argued that the idea of unconscious repression, and indeed of 'the unconscious' itself, are untenable ideas since they cannot be observed and because they pose epistemological paradoxes. How can one know something and yet not be aware of knowing it? How can one repress something of which one is unaware? How can one do this repressing unconsciously?[12] These objections do not, in my view, demolish psychoanalysis, which, in addressing the area of human irrationality, must venture formulations that model this irrationality. In clinical practice, furthermore, the psychoanalyst receives numerous clues for inferring repression including dialogical interaction with, and observation of, the patient.

More worrying is the place that Freud allotted to the individual inheritance of species-evolved elements of thought. The biologist Ernst Haeckel's idea that ontogeny replicated phylogeny, although widely subscribed to in the latter part of the nineteenth century when Freud studied medicine (and biology), came to be rejected in the early twentieth century.[13] Even though his colleagues urged him to get rid of the idea of ancestral memories, Freud's psychological thought retained this particular biological idea.[14]

Freud's supposition of phyletic origins for certain desires and complexes meant that his formulations would be universally true. The origins for both the Oedipus complex and religious ideas of God, for example, were explained as resulting from the inherited memory of a phase in human evolution. At a very speculative – practically mythical – point in prehistory, the young males of the human group rose up in sexual frustration and slew their father, who had hoarded all the attractive females. Immediately overcome by guilt they instituted the worship of the father (God, religion) and forbade themselves sex with closely related females (incest taboo).[15] The insistence on universalism led early psychoanalysts to dismiss the anthropologist Bronislaw Malinowski's suggestion that the Oedipus complex could take a distinctive form in the Trobriand Islands (Melanesia) involving aggressive impulses against the mother's brother and desire for categorical sisters.[16] The unwillingness of psychoanalysts to allow that deep emotional attachments could be conditioned by socialization in a matrilineal society, in which the role of the father in reproduction was not understood, made anthropologists sceptical about psychoanalysis.

According to Freud's theory, dreams potentially communicated forbidden wishes and desires from the unconscious. The oedipal wish would not, according to Freud's model, receive direct expression as such. One would not see oneself lying with one's mother, but would rather see certain displacements, condensations and symbols that could be interpreted as representing this. In the middle of Sophocles' *Oedipus Rex* Oedipus reports his uneasiness over having dreamt of sleeping with his mother.[17] Jocasta attempts to defuse his mounting anxiety by pointing out that many men have dreamt of sleeping with their mothers. The dream is insignificant and one does best to ignore it. Freud cites this passage and accepts that people in his day also have the same dream, but that it causes revulsion.[18] This concession seems to contradict his general position.

The oedipal dream should not be dreamable at all in literal form, certainly not in latter-day societies that had accumulated the heavy load of repression supposed by Freud. The Greeks could have this manifest dream precisely because, in his view, they were relatively unrepressed. Yet even this position clashes with his subsequently developed contention that oedipal desire and its repression were part of human phylogenetic history, a species memory arrived at through the prehistoric evolution of the earliest social rules. Such developments would have well pre-dated the Greeks, who should not, therefore, have been exempt from this complex and its repression.[19] Yet not only did the ancients have manifest oedipal dreams, the majority of these dreams were given auspicious meanings.[20]

Perhaps the earliest such dream we know of comes from an Egyptian papyrus dating back to the second millennium BCE (Before Common Era, i.e. BC). A dream of sleeping with one's mother meant that the dreamer's clansmen would support him.[21] Numerous oedipal dreams span Graeco-Roman antiquity. One can begin with the Greek traitor, Hippias, who interpreted his dream of sleeping with his mother as presaging his return to Athens and his recovery of power.[22] Caesar reportedly had a similar dream of sex with his mother that foretold the success of his campaign across the Rubicon.[23] These dreams are capped by Artemidorus, a second-century Common Era (CE, i.e., AD) professional dream interpreter, who devoted considerable space to explicating dreams of sex with one's mother in every conceivable position.[24] Artemidorus explained why this dream meant good fortune for public figures: '[J]ust as a man who follows the precepts of Aphrodite when he makes love completely governs the body of his obedient and willing partner, the dreamer will control all of the affairs of the city'.[25]

Krauss's original (1881) German translation of Artemidorus, which Freud read, excluded all of the passages on sexual dreams, including the one cited above, because they were deemed scandalous in his time.[26] Freud himself similarly avoided discussing dreams with manifest sexual content in *The Interpretation of Dreams*. Paradoxically, the volume that sensitized the world to the latent sexual content of dreams managed not to include analysis of a single erotic dream.[27]

The frequent occurrence and auspicious treatment of oedipal dreams in antiquity tells us that such dreams were not repressed, but this observation does not necessarily vindicate Freud's theory of ancient innocence. Rather, the evidence prompts us to study how particular historical societies determined which desires were permissible, literally and/or symbolically, and how these views gave rise to conscious strategies of suppression. Indigenous theories about erotic dreams and how to manage them are much easier to study than the operation of repression. Suppression does, nonetheless, take us into the domain of psychoanalysis and it may be the case that documented strategies of suppression do lead, over time, to the establishment of unconscious, embodied modes of repressive practice. By studying ancient suppression, then, it might be possible to develop a historical, as opposed to a mythico-biological, account of the unconscious repression posited by Freud.

DREAM AND DESIRE IN ANTIQUITY

The earliest erotic dreams are known from Mesopotamian and Egyptian dream books, or collections of omens, which give us very little more than the dream motif and its interpretation. They exemplify a 'dream key' approach. Each dream is reduced to certain symbols or motifs that have only one, or a few, determinate and usually prophetic meanings. One is free to wonder if a given ancient dream of sex really was an erotic dream (involving sexual arousal) or whether it merely symbolized other considerations, such as prospective political or economic success. The evidence of dream books only takes us a short distance along the way to understanding how ancient people related to their dreams of sexual desire.

What is needed is some evidence of people's emotional involvement in particular dreams and/or some indication of whether they thought certain dreams were morally good or evil. In the Christian period, as we shall see, the idiom of evil demons, which stirred up emotions, offers this kind of insight into personal psychology. In earlier Graeco-Roman antiquity demons were conceived otherwise, as cosmological forces located above the earth who sent dreams, but whose involvement implied no moral or psychological significance. Demons in ancient Greece were a necessary correlate of dreaming, but they did not account for the individual's psychological response to his/her dreams, indeed, as extrinsic forces they precluded the whole idea of individual responsibility for the production of dreams.[28]

The change to considering erotic dreams as more squarely indicative of individual desire and psychological disposition began in early Christianity consequent upon the pollination of earlier Hellenic demonology with the Hebrew idea of *yetser ha-ra*, 'evil inclination'.[29] Before considering the early Christian view of the person that emerged from this fusion, I present a brief examination of ancient Mesopotamian and then ancient Greek ideas about erotic dreams. The surviving body of Babylonian magical incantations and exorcisms yields a demonology that allows us to see that certain bodily desires were viewed as negative and fearful. These ideas may not necessarily be direct antecedents to the later notion of *yetser ha-ra* but they are, perhaps, the earliest point at which we can document a negative socio-religious evaluation of erotic dreams.

Mesopotamian demons were fundamentally bad; their actions and effects on humans were frightening. The Ala-demon is described in one incantation as 'the evil Ala who, on the couch at night, spills (semen) from a man in his sleep'.[30] Another text describes a maiden ghost (*ardat lilî*), the spirit of a virgin who died without ever experiencing sex, and who was thought to return at night to satisfy herself with men while they were sleeping.[31] The experience of having an erotic dream, or a wet dream, would thus appear to have been viewed negatively and this might have caused such dreams to be experienced as embarrassing, or as productive of anxiety.

Consider the following dream omen: 'If a man has sex at night and in his dream he is smeared with his own semen, he will suffer a loss'.[32] The Assyriologist Mark Geller has contended that this scenario is 'bad' because it is excessive to first have sex and then also have a nocturnal emission. The Mesopotamian dread of nocturnal emissions thus differed from the Hebrew fear that the demons could take semen released in sleep and use it to spawn offspring. Perhaps, however, the crux of the inauspiciousness was pollution – the fact of being smeared with one's own semen rendering one socially or ritually impure. If so, then the Mesopotamian emphasis would coincide with other prominent Hebrew traditions recorded in the book of Leviticus.[33]

Geller has further argued that the Mesopotamian conception of demons as motivators of erotic feelings could be an example of the projection or displacement of feelings that people could not face directly and which they wanted to disavow. The fear with which they were viewed can be taken as a neurotic symptom arising from the power of the feelings and difficulty in keeping them under control. Nocturnal emissions and erotic dream imagery were a return of the repressed; a conversion of disallowed desire into symptom. On Geller's view, then, the Mesopotamians were no strangers to repression. They had become repressed at an earlier point in time and certain of their erotic dreams were anxious, neurotic symptoms of this repression.

The possibility remains, however, that the symbols and interpretations of dream books – and the erotic dreams cited above come from similar books of omens – are purely arbitrary semiotic equations, rather than moral indicators. The omen cited above could be 'inauspicious' within a divinatory code of symbols, but this did not necessarily mean that the actions described were 'bad' morally, religiously, medically or on any other social grounds. In an Ancient Egyptian dream book, for example, we read that if a man sees himself in a dream 'eating excrement, [this is] good; [it means] eating his possessions in his house'. Or, if he sees himself 'having intercourse with a cow: good, passing a happy day in his house'.[34] Although auspicious for divinatory purposes, it is unlikely that the activities seen in either dream were socially approved. Erotic dreams in dream books or omen collections may not tell us much about individual erotic desire or morality.[35]

One must wonder also about the applicability of psychoanalytic concepts such as 'projection' or 'displacement' to a society that did not suppose an integrated human subject ideally responsible for his/her own thoughts and actions. For the ancients, as well as for numerous societies around the world today, spirits pre-exist the individual. As the anthropologist Vincent Crapanzano has pointed out in relation to spirit possession, cultural context is crucial: possession differs from a psychosis such as paranoia in that the whole society is convinced of the 'persecutory order'.[36] If a people normally deem desires and emotions to originate outside the body–mind, and not to be under the control of an integrated consciousness, then they can always potentially be judged neurotic or psychotic in the terms of contemporary Western psychology. That terms like 'neurotic' or 'repressed' are diagnostic labels for pathological conditions that modern psychotherapies aim to remove make their application to these societies very problematic.

Certainly in the Homeric world and well into the Greek classical period, the organs for thinking and feeling were distributed throughout the body – in the chest, liver, and heart as well as the head. These organs could receive messages directly from the gods beyond the control of individual will or power of reason. Dreams, in this period, were thought to be created and sent by the gods to be visualized in the sleeping minds of humans. From Homeric times up until the present-day the way to say 'I had a dream' in the Greek language is 'I saw a dream'. This usage was bound up with ideas that what one saw in dreams were 'images' (*eidola*), simulacra, of real objects or persons.[37] In Book Two of the *Iliad*, for example, the image of Nestor appeared to the sleeping Agamemnon instructing him to attack the Trojans. Once a dream vision was seen, the primary task was to determine if the message was true. Were the gods urging one to act in a way that would be beneficial or catastrophic? Dreams had little to do with individual moral life or psychological states.

In the classical period opinions about the god-sent nature and predictive value of dreams began to divide, as can be seen in Herodotus' account of a dream that repeatedly came to the Persian ruler Xerxes.[38] This dream urged him to wage war against the Greeks even though he had resolved not to attack. His adviser, Artabanus, cautioned him not to heed the dream. Dreams, he said, are just things that you have seen during the day and which float before your eyes at night. There's no need to take them seriously.[39]

This episode indicates the conceptual shift to a new sense of the person as the origin of emotions, thoughts and feelings (although in the end, Artabanus is made to recant his opinion and accept the prophetic power of dreams). The classicist E. R. Dodds and others have termed this a transition from a shame to a guilt culture, where one assumes responsibility for one's actions rather than attributing them to exterior forces.[40] Changes in the Greek conception of the soul (*psukhe*), culminating with Plato, located it in the interior of the person, thus grounding the sense of a deep, interior reality.[41] Although dream interpreters continued to cater to the broad populace, which thought that dreams contained divinatory messages (perhaps sent by the gods), philosophers and doctors produced more physiological and psychological explanations of dreams.[42]

Where Aristotle supplied a resolutely physical account of dreams as a type of cognition, Plato understood dreams as being more closely involved with individual character and ethics. He focused on dreams as a facet of his overall study of politics, since he considered that the credentials to govern others were first developed and proved in relation to oneself. Success in business, politics or athletics was predicated on self-mastery.[43] In Plato's view the *psukhe*, which we might today term the 'self', was comprised of three parts: the rational mind (*nous*), high spirits (*thumos*, e.g. anger, joy, courage) and the appetitive desires (*epithumia*, for food, drink, sex).[44] Self-mastery involved regulating these three components and integrating them under the command of reason. One recommended technique involved forging a strategic alliance between reason and high spirits so that the appetitive desires were overpowered. The education of the young through dancing and verse recitation exemplified this approach by bringing the two higher parts of the soul together – 'fostering the one [reason] with fair words and teachings and relaxing and soothing and making gentle the other [high spirits] by harmony and rhythm'.[45]

Dreams were likewise produced by an interaction between the different parts of the soul, which were distributed hierarchically in the body: reason in the head, the spirits around the heart, and the appetites Plato conceptualized as a savage beast at its trough near the navel.[46] Left to its own devices the appetitive part of the soul would pay no heed to reason, but instead spend its time 'bewitched . . . both day and night by images and phantasms' (*hypo de eidolon kai phantasmaton*).[47] In order to remedy this, God set the liver in the region of the midriff so that it could relay messages from the intellect and occasionally whip the appetitive desires into line by releasing bitter bile until any debauchery ceased. Nothing like a bout of hepatitis for curtailing one's drinking proclivities. When suitably calmed the liver would then switch to exuding a pleasing sweetness and the appetitive soul could occupy itself with divining during sleep.[48]

All humans, according to Plato, possessed the ability to control their appetites but not all of them exercised it. The happy and wise democratic man was such because of his success in living a moderate life whereas the tyrant was a slave to his appetites.[49] In any case, sleep presented a dangerous moment for all men. While reason slumbered, the way was open for the savage part of the soul to break free and express itself, especially if the person had just indulged in excessive eating and drinking.

I'm sure you're aware of how in these circumstances nothing is too outrageous: a person acts as if he were totally lacking in moral principle and unhampered by intelligence. In his dreams, he doesn't stop at trying to have sex with his mother and with anyone or anything else – man, beast, or god.[50]

Plato's idea that basic desires, the products of instinctive drives, emerged and sought expression in dreams anticipated one of Freud's fundamental contentions.

Plato considered 'lawless desires' (*paranomoi/anomoi epithumiai*) to be basic to all, yet the wise man could bring them under control and even eliminate them entirely by moderation. Such a man would derive the prophetic benefits from dreams described in the *Timaeus*, but even this person would normally have to turn to a professional diviner, a quasi-holy man, whose intellect would be calm enough to decipher the messages of the frenzied lower soul. Only exceptional philosophers like Socrates were able to balance intellect and appetite so as to interpret their own dreams successfully. Such a philosopher occupied the extreme opposite social position to the tyrant who was entirely involved with his uncontrollable passions.[51]

The two sexes were assumed to have very different structures of desire with attendant political, social and ethical consequences. Where men could overcome or at least moderate their responses to desires by internal mental effort, women were conceived to be fundamentally helpless victims of their insatiable sexual appetites.[52] A man who failed to moderate himself was feminized; female gender offered a metaphor for incontinence, passivity and lack of self-control. According to ancient medical thought, female physiology precluded reason being exercised by women in the same way as by men. This was because the womb, the seat of her sexual appetite, was not under a woman's conscious control. It could move around in her body, even up to the head, where it could 'stifle those organs in which consciousness was thought to lie'.[53] Thus women had no chance to succeed or fail in the fundamentally ethical arena of relating to their own sexual desire. They were denied the possibility of acting as moral agents.[54]

***

Sexuality was apparently easy for the Greeks to contemplate. A glance at any coffee-table book on Greek erotic art suggests as much. An anonymous classical Athenian observed that all humans were driven by three desires. The desire for food and drink he considered to be present from birth while the desire for sex arose only later, but it was 'the fiercest desire and the most despotic, urging men most powerfully to all kinds of lunacy'.[55] To make the point that the need for sexual gratification was no less normal than that for food and drink, Diogenes the Cynic simply masturbated when the prostitute he had booked was late in arriving. He sent her away with the words, 'My hand was faster than you in celebrating the bridal night'.[56]

These sorts of stories indicate that sexual desire was conceived as a real and powerful force with which humans had to reckon. We may also note a difference in the ways that the Athenian's three main desires might be satisfied. Sexual desire might be assuaged by the contemplation of images alone – at least momentarily – while the imagination of food or water will not substitute for actually eating or drinking. As Diogenes put it: 'If only one could satisfy one's hunger by rubbing one's stomach'.[57]

MODERATION

The recommended attitude to the desires in classical Greece can be characterized as one of moderation (sophrosune), 'nothing in excess' (meden agan). We have seen this idea referred to in Plato's picture of the democrat. The medical tradition and schools of philosophy such as Stoicism also elaborated and continued to develop this ideal. For those practising moderation, sex was not problematic so long as one kept the whole body in balance. Indulgence of the appetites was negotiable according to the age and gender of a person and the season of the year. Imbalances could be corrected by medically prescribed diet and exercise regimens. Sex was only worrisome if it took uncontrollable forms such as satyriasis (a goading itch, as if one had ingested an aphrodisiac), priapism (unrelievable sexual tension), dorsal consumption, and even gonorrhoea.[58] Nocturnal emissions and unusual feelings of lust could be symptoms of the onset of epilepsy or madness (mania), both of which, like orgasm, were characterized by uncontrolled 'shuddering spasms'.[59]

For Soranus, nocturnal emissions were a variant of gonorrhoea and in a survey of acute and chronic diseases Caelius Aurelianus did, indeed, contrast the two.[60] Gonorrhoea could occur at any time, without imagery, while nocturnal emissions occurred only during sleep and as a consequence of imagining sexual intercourse through 'unreal images' (inanibus visis).[61] Unlike gonorrhoea, nocturnal emissions did not necessarily constitute an illness according to Caelius. They simply resulted from desire, which could arise either through regular sexual practice or through prolonged continence.

The implication that people might be able to respond differently to unreal figments of the imagination resonates with Stoic ideas developed during the last three centuries before the Christian era (BCE). Chrysippus emphasized the difference between impressions (phantasiai) resulting from the perception of real physical objects, and figments (phantasmata) produced by the imagination and occurring especially 'in people who are melancholic and mad'.[62] According to the Stoics, appetite, fear, distress and pleasure comprised primary passions – states not produced, but only suffered by the mind.[63] The term '*pathos*' in Greek could mean 'emotion, passion' as well as a passive 'suffering'. Active control or passive submission to the emotions was precisely the issue. The early Stoics held that all emotions were the results of judgements, and thus could be modified, and their goal was to reach a state of *apatheia* (impassivity) in which one had eradicated uncontrolled emotional responses entirely, and thus eliminated passive suffering from one's life.[64] This achieved, one could be happy, while those who neglected actively to confront the passions were, in latter-day terms, pathetic.

Clearly the Stoics had moved one step beyond earlier Greek philosophical ideas of moderation. The kernel of Aristotle's ideas that in dreams people received images that they were not able to judge is still discernible, but much elaborated.[65] Now total extirpation of the passions was the appropriate goal for the wise man.[66] Thus we can see that even before widespread conversion to Christianity control of bodily desires and impulses was problematic for some ancient thinkers, and erotic dreams formed one of the battle lines. The doctors and the philosophers concurred that nocturnal emissions and nightmares were potentially worrisome if they were the result of chronic submission to fantasy. A sign of spiritual progress and strength of the soul would be the ability to resist, or never incur, the assault of images that could cause erotic dreams.

DEMONIC DREAMS

Early Christian preachers such as Justin Martyr assimilated all of the pagan gods to 'demons' under the control of the Devil.[67] Granted that pagan Hellenes thought that demons sent dreams, Christians were counselled to distrust them as possibly satanic. Dreams came to be placed squarely on the negative side of a morally polarized universe, and at the First Council of Ancyra (314 CE) the Church banned dream interpretation altogether.[68]

Beginning with Tertullian, the Church Fathers entertained a tripartite classification of dreams as coming variously from God, the Devil or the soul.[69] Early ascetic theories of human nature and psychology reveal how monks understood demons to inspire erotic dreams. For example, Evagrius, who became a monk in Egypt around 382 CE, considered that sinful passions could be instigated by the senses, by memories or by demons – all of which were closely intertwined.[70] Monks constructed for themselves an environment of sensory deprivation designed to prevent the passions being stimulated by everyday perceptions of objects or people. As the demons could not easily make inroads through quotidian experiences in this austere environment, they sought instead to coax the monks into thinking corrupting thoughts (*logismoi*).

Demons got purchase on monks by activating in them memories of their pre-monastic lives. On Evagrius' view, memories – first registered by the physical senses, particularly sight and touch – remained connected to the emotional state in which they were initially received.[71] Demons could manipulate an individual's previously acquired, emotionally charged representations to excite the passions, and set sinful thoughts in train. Thus evil thoughts were simultaneously exogenous and endogenous; exterior demons activated what was already internally there. Evagrius' ascetic practice called for continuous, critical introspection in order to identify demon-inspired thoughts and prevent them from progressing. He conceded that disturbing thoughts would inevitably occur, even in the course of monastic life – such thoughts were part of the human condition. But sin set in only if one mentally entertained such a thought for too long. As Evagrius expressed it: 'It is not up to us whether evil thoughts might trouble the soul or leave it in peace. What does depend on us is whether they linger or not, and whether they set the passions in motion or not'.[72] The goal was inner stillness, which Evagrius referred to by the familiar Stoic term, *apatheia*.

Like Plato, Evagrius divided the person into three parts: (1) the quasi-divine intellect (*logistikon*); (2) the soul (*psukhe*), which was subdivided into two parts, the high-spirited *thumikon*, and the sensual *epithumikon*; (3) the body.[73] Evagrius named eight primary demons – the model for what would become the 'seven deadly sins' in Western Christianity. Each of these demons normally attacked only one of the two vulnerable parts of the soul. Predictably the demon of fornication (*porneia*) attacked the sensual part of the soul. According to Evagrius it 'compels one to desire "remarkable" bodies; it violently attacks those living in abstinence in order to cause them to quit, convinced they will amount to nothing. And, soiling the soul, it inclines it to "those acts" [obscene acts]. It causes monks to speak and hear things, as if some object were visible and present'.[74]

As these passages show, the battle with demons spilled over into the realm of dreams and delusion, where the power of the will to resist demons was weakest. The cornerstone of Evagrius' system of ascetic practice was the continual internal monitoring of one's own thoughts – the 'hermeneutics of the self' as Foucault put it.[75] Spiritual progress rested on the ability to discern and avoid reacting to demonic thoughts or bodily stirrings. Eventually the verbal confession of one's inmost thoughts and feelings to a more experienced elder also became part of monastic practice. Within the monastic community spiritual progress hinged on fighting and winning these battles with erotic dreams, and the prospect of this continuing struggle no doubt provoked a certain amount of anxiety, since failure could stymie one's progress as a monk.[76]

Within ascetic 'anthropology' – as patristic theories of human nature and psychology are known – dreams were the ultimate diagnostic of the condition of the self. How much passion still lurked inside one? How strong or

weak was one's will, even in sleep, to resist demonic incursions and mani-
pulations? While some of the earliest Church Fathers held that it was
possible to eradicate sensual thoughts completely through spiritual exercises, opinion increasingly held that certain bodily 'movements', including
sexual arousal, were not entirely controllable.[77] Nocturnal emissions might
be pardonable so long as they were merely that: simple seminal discharges
unaccompanied by imagery or passion, and certainly not involving any
pleasure or consent of the will.[78] The distinction between nocturnal emission
and erotic dream was thus crucially significant for the monks.

John Cassian, a disciple of Evagrius, who brought monasticism from
Egypt to Gaul, held that there were six steps on the way to spiritual purity:
(1) the monk does not give in to the assaults of the flesh while awake; (2) his
spirit does not entertain erotic thoughts; (3) the sight of women stirs no
response; on to the sixth step where 'the seduction of feminine phantoms
(*fantasmata feminarum*) cause no illusions, even in sleep . . . this would be
an indication of a cupidity still located in the marrow.'[79] Dreams potentially
represented the last unruled part of the self and the goal of ascetic practice
was to colonize even this dark recess with the force of the will. If the dream
did not occur just as one wanted it, then it was necessary proactively and
preventively to 're-make' it. As Freud put it, confidently referring to the
suppressive power of reason: 'Where id was, there ego shall be'.[80]

CONCLUSION

This has been a necessarily abbreviated tour of ancient ideas about desire,
the impact of desire on dreams, and the strategies devised for regulating
this impact. It should be enough, however, to allow us to decide whether the
ancient Greeks were unrepressed. Certainly even the free male citizens who
had the luxurious choice of practising *sophrosune* were not entirely free.
Those who ate too greedily or engaged in sex insatiably came in for ridicule,
if not scorn.[81] The desires were conceived as formidably real impulses that
one needed to be strong and active in resisting.

After surveying the ancient Greeks' ideas about suppression, Michel
Foucault concluded that they were not repressed. He considered the
Greeks' 'aesthetics of existence' and their practice of 'care for the self' to be
expressions of liberty and independence.[82] He thus (accidentally) concurred with Freud on the absence of repression in ancient Greek society.
He did, however, consider early Christian ideas of continence (*enkrateia*)
to be continuous with classical conceptions of moderation. Guilt, sin and
damnation may not have troubled the ancient Greeks, but they did have
other reasons to worry about becoming victims of their desires. They
were concerned with an overall balance of desires and expenditures in an
ideally stable economy of moderation. Clearly everyday social rules and

informal popular opinions prompted the ancient Greeks occasionally to suppress desires.

Thus far I have argued for an analytical separation between suppression and repression, a distinction that Freud also drew. The verdict would thus seem to be that the Greeks may have suppressed, but they were not repressed. Yet, even if conscious suppression can be differentiated from repression, the activity of suppression may nonetheless give rise to signal anxieties and neuroses. My understanding of suppression thus differs from that of Freud, who supposed that suppression banished ideas altogether rather than consigning them to the unconscious where they could fester and then return. The suppression of the ancient Greeks might have had consequences very similar to those associated with repression.

A last glance at one of those apparently 'unrepressed' societies considered at the outset of this chapter illuminates precisely this point. The Mehinaku of Amazonia, as studied by Thomas Gregor, place no moral bar in the way of having sex and they do, indeed, engage in lots of pre- and extra-marital sexual activity, thus giving the appearance of being sexually 'free'.[83] Yet Gregor found that men exhibit considerable anxiety about sex because they think that it saps their strength. Wrestlers, in particular, avoid sexual activity in preparation for their matches. The successful wrestler is said to crush his prey like an anaconda. At the same time many men view sexual intercourse as comparable to defeat in wrestling. In sex, it is the woman who crushes her prey.[84]

Gregor also provides details about erotic dreams among the Mehinaku that might suggest something about erotic dreams among the ancient Greeks in the absence of historical sources. He found that 35% of his sample of men's dreams involved overt sexual activity and that fully half of these were perceived as disturbing. It might well be that the ancient Greeks similarly had an incipient dread of erotic dreams arising from their concerns with physiological depletion, the disruption of moderation, the loss of self-control, or folk stories such as those in circulation among the Mehinaku. If so, these ideas did not convert into a discourse of dread – at least not one that has survived in the historical record.

The early Christians, as we saw from the writings of Evagrius and Cassian, did develop an account that demonized erotic dreams on moral grounds. The monastics and their followers submitted to a generalized set of rules that took no account of differences in age, class or gender, or season of the year. They sought to extirpate their passions, or else sublimate them into a worship of God that would give them salvation in the world to come. My point is that whether desire and sexuality were conceived of as moral or aesthetic issues they could still lead to anxiety and neurosis so long as there was some stricture against them. Foucault has argued that the imposition of restrictions produced volumes of public discourse that violated the silence normally associated with repression. At the same time, however, he recognized that rules not only fostered desires, but also suppressed them.[85] Proliferating discourses of sex were ongoing paradoxes; they contradicted the secrecy of repression, while actively increasing the social and personal reality of this repression.

The ancient Greeks were not without rules, although they seemed to have had fewer and less pressing strictures governing their desires than the Christians. Both groups were, nonetheless, engaging in techniques and practices (*askeseis*) of the self. Although Christian asceticism fundamentally involved renunciation, it was also, for many of its adherents, a practice of freedom, an act of self-making, as recent studies of the monastic movement are at pains to argue.[86] The ancient Greeks were, thus, not alone in practising an aesthetics of existence.

Where does all of this leave our thinking on repression? The search for unrepressed societies must be approached cautiously as a potentially ethnocentric exercise underwritten by the nagging worry that we are ourselves repressed but shouldn't be. If the people under study are aware of, and able to articulate, what they are doing, then we are actually studying suppression. Such a focus on how a given people conceive of the need to regulate their appetitive desires, and the practices they follow in order to do this, places the basic psychological issue of 'repression' in a domain where historians and anthropologists can confidently study it. Freud's idea that repression occurred unconsciously makes it much more difficult to identify convincingly, especially in historical retrospect. Psychotherapists working with patients in the present will always have more ability to identify the classic Freudian form of repression.

My purpose has not been to deny the operation of repression or the existence of unconscious impulses but rather to demonstrate the confusion surrounding the concept of repression in the social sciences and to offer a way of approaching repression via suppression. Repression may yet be one of Freud's most fruitful ideas for historical research if we can see it as emerging from the embodiment of suppressive strategies, themselves deriving from changing social ideas of self-regulation. This suggestion places the development of repression in 'real' historical time rather than in speculative evolutionary prehistory, or entirely in the early childhood formation of the superego.[87]

Freud presumed that repression necessarily accumulated in a linear fashion with the steady accretion of rules in a 'civilization process'. This quantitative account of repression depends on a progressivist, hierarchical view of Western civilization in relation to other more 'primitive' forms of life. High and low degrees of repression should, in theory, be discoverable in all sorts of societies, Western or non-Western, ancient or modern, because suppression is a situation that societies arrange for themselves according to internal rules and ideas. Some ideas, furthermore, may simply drop out. Ancient medical ideas of dorsal consumption or gonorrhoea no longer make sense.

They have not contributed to a linear accumulation making for more suppression today.

It is not the rules alone, or their number, that give rise to unconscious repression, but rather their internalization through practice. The earliest monks were self-conscious about their practice and sought to elaborate and transmit their skills. It was after their ascetic practices and modes of thought became routinized over the centuries amongst the Christian laity – embedded in a received morality, renewed in every generation by teaching and notions of sin and confession – that we can see a fully embodied and hence more automatic form of suppression i.e. repression taking shape. The sociologist Norbert Elias has termed this the passage from sociogenesis to psychogenesis.[88] Such passages from the social to the psychological are diachronic processes, which may occur in a few days or months, or over decades and centuries. The study of this transition remains a conceptual challenge requiring the synthesis of anthropological, historical and psychological approaches.

NOTES AND REFERENCES

1 Freud, *The Interpretation of Dreams* (1900), SE 4, p. 262. See also G. Sissa, 'Interpreting the implicit: Georges Devereux and the Greek myths', in S. Heald and A. Deluz (eds.), *Anthropology and Psychoanalysis: An Encounter Through Culture*, London, 1994, p. 31.

2 Freud, SE 4, p. 264.

3 M. Mead, *Coming of Age in Samoa: A Psychological Study of Primitive Youth for Western Civilisation*, New York, 1961 [1928].

4 D. Freeman, *Margaret Mead and Samoa*, Cambridge, MA, 1983, p. 246.

5 K. Stewart, 'Dream theory in Malaysia', in Charles Tart (ed.), *Altered States of Consciousness*, New York, 1969, p. 163.

6 G. W. Domhoff, *The Mystique of Dreams: A Search for Utopia Through Senoi Dream Theory*, Berkeley, CA, 1985, p. 62.

7 J. Clifford, 'On ethnographic allegory', in J. Clifford and G. Marcus (eds.), *Writing Culture*, Berkeley, CA, 1986.

8 M. Torgovnick, *Gone Primitive*, Chicago, 1990, p. 246.

9 This summary draws particularly on Freud's papers: 'Repression' (1915; SE 14, pp. 58–143), 'The unconscious' (1915; SE 14, pp. 166–204), 'The ego and the id' (1923; SE 19, pp. 12–59), and 'Inhibitions, symptoms, anxiety' (1926; SE 20, pp. 77–175). During the fifty years in which he wrote, Freud himself used a vast array of terms to refer to repression. Anna Freud attempted to systematize the psychoanalytic vocabulary of terms for repression in her *The Ego and the Mechanisms of Defense*, New York, 1966 [1936].

10 Freud already drew a distinction between these two terms in 1900 (SE 5, p. 606): '[I] have omitted to state whether I attribute different meanings to the words "repressed" and "suppressed". It should have been clear, however, that the latter lays more stress than the former upon the fact of attachment to the unconscious'. He apparently has the same opposition in mind in the opening paragraph of his essay on 'Repression' (p. 146) and he returns to it in his late work *The Future of an Illusion* (SE 21, p. 43). See also J. Laplanche and J.-B. Pontalis, *The Language of Psychoanalysis* (transl. D. Nicholson-Smith), London, 1973, 438f.

11 Freud initially adapted the term *Verdrängung*, meaning literally 'displacement', from the sphere of hydraulics. For German speakers today it is distinct from the term for 'suppression',

Unterdrückung, which has primarily political connotations. In everyday German speech people do often speak about intentionally 'repressing' a thought. I thank Gabriele vom Bruck and Burkhard Schnepel for their advice on questions of German usage.

12 For a summary of these critiques see M. Billig, *Freudian Repression: Conversation Creating the Unconscious*, Cambridge, 1999, p. 25.

13 S. J. Gould, *Ontogeny and Phylogeny*, Cambridge, MA, 1977, especially pp. 155ff., for the influence of Haeckel's biogeneticism on Freud.

14 F. Sulloway (*Freud: Biologist of the Mind*, p. 391) contends that Freud's thinking became more, rather than less, biological over time.

15 Freud, *Totem and Taboo* (1913), SE 13. Freud revalidated this evolutionary idea in his late work, *Moses and Monotheism* (1939), SE 23, p. 132.

16 B. Malinowski, *Sex and Repression in Savage Society*, Cleveland, OH, 1965[1927]; E. Jones, 'Mother-right and the sexual ignorance of savages', in his *Psycho-Myth, Psycho-History*, New York, 1974, p. 169.

17 Sophocles, *Oedipus the King* (980), in D. Grene (transl.), *Sophocles I*, Chicago, 1970.

18 Freud, SE 4, p. 264.

19 As Freud wrote in a later footnote (1920) to his 'Three essays on the theory of sexuality' (1905; SE 7, p. 226): 'Every new arrival on this planet is faced by the task of mastering the Oedipus complex; anyone who fails to do so becomes a victim of neurosis'.

20 C. Grottanelli, 'On the mantic meaning of incestuous dreams', in D. Shulman and G. Stroumsa (eds.), *Dream Cultures: Explorations in the Comparative History of Dreaming*, Oxford, 1999, pp. 143–166.

21 Egyptian Dream Book, British Museum Papyrus 10686 (ca. 2000 BCE), in N. Lewis, *The Interpretation of Dreams and Portents*, Toronto, 1976, p. 8.

22 Herodotus, *History*, 6.107.

23 Plutarch, *Life of Caesar*, 32.6.

24 Artemidorus, *Oneirocritica*, 1.79.

25 Artemidorus, *Oneirocritica*, 1.79. R. J. White (transl.), *The Interpretation of Dreams: Oneirocritica*, Torrance, CA, 1990, p. 83. In some cases the dream of sex with the mother was not auspicious. Artemidorus suggests (*Oneirocritica*, 1.79) that it could also lead to jealous conflict with the father, in cases where the father was still living.

26 F. S. Krauss, *Symbolik der Träume*, Vienna, 1881. Freud was also aware that Krauss later published the omitted passages as: 'Erotische Träume und ihre Symbolik', *Anthropophyteia* 9, 1912.

27 L. Wittgenstein ('Conversations on Freud; Excerpt from 1932–3 lectures', in R. Wollheim and J. Hopkins (eds.), *Philosophical Essays on Freud*, Cambridge, 1982, p. 5) did not fail to see this omission of sexual dreams. Freud wrote in a footnote (*Interpretation*, pp. 606f., fn. 2 – the same footnote quoted above in note 10) that he did not avoid consideration of overtly sexual dreams out of modesty, but rather because: '[A]n explanation of sexual dreams would involve me deeply in the still unsolved problems of perversion and bisexuality; and I accordingly reserve this material for another occasion'.

28 Although Aristotle ruled out the possibility that dreams were produced and sent by gods, he paradoxically declared that they were 'demonic' (*On Divination Through Sleep*, 463b.14). By this he apparently meant that they were 'natural', that is, governed by rules of probability and chance. If one had enough 'prophetic' dreams, some were bound to seem to foretell subsequent events. See D. Gallop, *Aristotle on Sleep and Dreams*, Peterborough, Ontario, 1990, pp. 39ff.

29 See P. Brown, 'Bodies and minds: Sexuality and renunciation in early Christianity', in D. M. Halperin, J. J. Winkler and F. I. Zeitlin (eds.), *Before Sexuality: The Construction of Erotic Experience in the Ancient World*, Princeton, NJ, 1990, p. 481; A. Guillaumont, 'Introduction', in P. Géhin, C. Guillaumont and A. Guillaumont (eds.), *Évagre le Pontique, Sur les pensées*, Paris, 1998, p. 27.

30 M. Geller, 'Freud, magic and Mesopotamia: How the magic works', *Folklore* 108, 1997, p. 1.

31 Ibid., p. 3.
32 Ibid., p. 6.
33 According to Leviticus, sexual intercourse rendered both the man and woman unclean until evening (Lev. 15:18), while an emission of semen by the man alone also rendered him impure till evening (Lev. 15:16). A soldier who suffered a nocturnal emission should leave the encampment until after he had washed and the sun had gone down (Deut. 23:11–12). See D. Brakke, 'The problematization of nocturnal emissions in early Christian Syria, Egypt and Gaul', *Journal of Early Christian Studies* 3, 1995, p. 422; H. Eilberg-Schwartz, *The Savage in Judaism*, Bloomington, IL, 1990.
34 Egyptian Dream Book, British Museum Papyrus 10686 (ca. 2000 BCE), in Lewis, *Dreams and Portents*, p. 7.
35 J. Bottéro, *Mesopotamia: Writing, Reasoning and the Gods* (transl. Z. Bahrani and M. van de Mieroop), Chicago, 1992, p. 117. For a study, and translation, of Mesopotamian erotic dream omens, see A. K. Guinan, 'Auguries of hegemony: The sex omens of Mesopotamia', in M. Wyke (ed.), *Gender and the Body in the Ancient Mediterranean*, Oxford, 1998.
36 V. Crapanzano, 'Introduction', in V. Crapanzano and V. Garrison (eds.), *Case Studies in Spirit Possession*, New York, 1977, p. 13. See also V. Crapanzano, *Tuhami*, Chicago, 1980, p. 15.
37 Epicurean philosophers held that dreams were produced by images (*eidola*) emanating from physical objects and which assumed chance, sometimes bizarre, conglomerations in the air and permeated the mind of the sleeper where they appeared as dreams. See G. Björck, 'ONAP IΔEIN: De la perception de rêve chez les anciens', *Eranos* 44, 1946, p. 313; E. R. Dodds, 'Supernormal phenomena in classical antiquity', in his *The Ancient Concept of Progress and Other Essays*, Oxford, 1973, p. 161.
38 Herodotus, *History*, 7.12ff.
39 Herodotus, *History*, 7.16.
40 E. R. Dodds. *The Greeks and the Irrational*, Berkeley, CA, 1951.
41 J.-P. Vernant, 'Psuche: Simulacrum of the body or image of the divine?', in his *Mortals and Immortals: Collected Essays*, Princeton, NJ, 1991, p. 190.
42 The most prominent examples would be Aristotle's tracts *On Dreams* and *On Divination through Sleep* (Gallop, *Aristotle*) and the Hippocratic chapter *On Dreams (Regimen IV)* (G. Lloyd, ed., *Hippocratic Writings*, London, 1978).
43 Plato, *Republic* 443d.
44 Plato, *Republic* 441a.
45 Plato, *Republic*, 441e.
46 Plato, *Timaeus*, 71e.
47 Plato, *Timaeus*, 71a (transl. R. Bury), Cambridge, MA, 1942.
48 Plato, *Timaeus*, 71d. See E. Vegléris, 'Platon et le rêve de la nuit', *Ktema* 7, 1982, p. 63.
49 Plato, *Republic*, 571a.
50 Plato, *Republic*, 571c (transl. R. Waterfield), Oxford, 1994, p. 313.
51 Vegléris, 'Platon', p. 65.
52 L. Dean-Jones, 'The politics of pleasure: Female sexual appetite in the Hippocratic corpus', *Helios* 19, 1992.
53 Ibid., p. 78.
54 Ibid., p. 86.
55 Plato, *Laws*, 6.783ab, cited in J. Davidson, *Courtesans and Fishcakes: The Consuming Passions of Classical Athens*, London, 1997, p. 160.
56 Galen, *Affected Parts*, K419, in R. Siegel (transl.), *Galen. On the Affected Parts*, Basel, 1976, p. 185.
57 Plutarch, *Moralia*, 1044b, cited in Davidson, *Courtesans*, p. 180. Freud made the same observation (*Introductory Lectures on Psychoanalysis*, 1916; SE 15, p. 134): 'Since it is characteristic of the sexual instinct to be a degree less dependent on its object than hunger and thirst, the satisfaction in dream emission can be a real one'.

58 Dorsal consumption (*phthisis notias*), was considered a disease of the marrow causing involuntary loss of seed via nocturnal emissions and other outlets. See Hippocrates, *On Diseases* 2.51 and *On Seed*, where erotic dreams of the dorsal consumption sort are considered to prefigure insanity. On involuntary, pathological forms of sexuality generally, see Caelius Aurelianus, *On Chronic Diseases*, 5.6ff.

59 Caelius Aurelianus, *On Chronic Diseases*, 5.7.81. See J. Pigeaud, 'Le rêve érotique dans l'antiquité gréco-romaine: l'oneirogmos', *Littérature, Médecine, Société* 3, 1981, p. 10.

60 Soranus, *Gynaecology*, 3.45. The 5th-century CE author Caelius Aurelianus' *On Acute Diseases* and *On Chronic Diseases* are thought largely to be Latin translations of Greek texts by the early 2nd-century CE medical writer, Soranus.

61 Caelius Aurelianus, *On Chronic Diseases*, 5.7.82.

62 Chrysippus, in Aëtius, *Placita*, 4.12.1–5, in A. A. Long and D. N. Sedley, *The Hellenistic Philosophers*, Cambridge, 1987, p. 237.

63 Stobaeus, 2.88,8–90,6, in Long and Sedley, *Hellenistic Philosophers*, p. 411.

64 Seneca (1st century CE) later modified the Stoic position to hold that there were certain 'first movements' such as shuddering when splashed with cold water, or experiencing sexual arousal (*On Anger*, 2.1–3) that could never be subject to mental control and thus were not passions, but rather just a physical 'impulse of the body' (*corporis pulsus*). I thank Richard Sorabji for his observations drawn upon here (personal communication). See also his *Emotion and Peace of Mind: From Stoic Agitation to Christian Temptation*, Oxford, 2000.

65 Aristotle, *On Dreams*, 461b29.

66 M. Nussbaum, *The Therapy of Desire: Theory and Practice in Hellenistic Ethics*, Princeton, NJ, 1994, p. 390.

67 E. Pagels, *Adam, Eve and the Serpent*, New York, 1988, p. 42.

68 J. Le Goff, 'Christianity and dreams (second to seventh centuries)', *The Medieval Imagination*, Chicago, 1988, p. 211.

69 Tertullian, *On the Soul*, 47.

70 F. Refoulé, 'Rêve et vie spirituelle d'après Évagre le Pontique', *La vie spirituelle* (Suppl. no. 59), 1961, p. 501.

71 Evagrius, *Praktikos*, 34; Evagrius, *On Evil Thoughts (Peri Logismon)*, 2.

72 Evagrius, *Praktikos*, 6.

73 Evagrius, *Praktikos*, 89; Refoulé, 'Rêve', p. 486.

74 Evagrius, *Praktikos*, 8. Antoine Guillaumont and Claire Guillaumont (ed./trans.), *Évagre le Pontique. Traité Pratique, ou Le Moine*, vol. 2 (*Sources Chrétiennes* 171), Paris, 1971.

75 M. Foucault, 'About the beginning of the hermeneutics of the self', in his *Religion and Culture* (texts edited and selected by J. Carrette), Manchester, 1999, pp. 158–181.

76 See D. Elliott, 'Pollution, illusion and masculine disarray: Nocturnal emission and the sexuality of the clergy', in her *Fallen Bodies: Pollution, Sexuality and Demonology*, Philadelphia, 1999; Brakke, 'Problematization'. The ideas introduced by Evagrius, and developed by subsequent writers, still inform monastic practice today. A recent ethnographic study of a monastery on Mt. Athos (M. Sarris, 'Some fundamental organizing concepts in a Greek monastic community on Mt. Athos', unpublished PhD thesis, London School of Economics, 2000) reveals that the struggle with erotic 'images' (*parastaseis*) still threatens spiritual progress. Before the rite of tonsure representing transition to senior monk status, the candidate keeps an all-night vigil so as to protect against any erotic dream that would cancel the ritual. Monks refrain from daily communion after a nocturnal emission, an abstention apparent to the whole community of monks assembled in the monastery chapel. The formulaic phrase spoken by a monk to the Abbott to excuse himself from communion on account of a nocturnal emission is: 'Last night I suffered (*epatha*)'. This verb is clearly continuous with the ancient and early Christian vocabulary (sc. *pathos, apatheia*) applied to these matters.

77 Refoulé, 'Rêve', pp. 489ff.

78 Brakke, 'Problematization', p. 440; Elliott, 'Pollution', p. 17.

79 John Cassian, *Conferences*, 12.7.

80 Freud, *New Introductory Lectures on Psychoanalysis* (1933), SE 22, p. 80.

81 Davidson, *Courtesans* (see Note 55).

82 M. Foucault, *The Use of Pleasure: The History of Sexuality*, vol. 2, New York, 1985, p. 253; M. Foucault, 'The ethic of the care for self as a practice of freedom', in J. Bernauer and D. Rasmussen (eds.), *The Final Foucault*, Cambridge, MA, 1987, p. 5.

83 T. Gregor, *Anxious Pleasures: The Sexual Lives of an Amazonian People*, Chicago, 1985, p. 7.

84 Ibid., p. 155.

85 M. Foucault, *The History of Sexuality: An Introduction*, vol. 1., New York, pp. 33, 81.

86 R. Valantasis, 'Constructions of power in asceticism', *Journal of the American Academy of Religion* 63, 1995; K. Ware, 'The way of the ascetics: Negative or affirmative?', in V. Wimbush and R. Valantasis (eds.), *Asceticism*, New York, 1995.

87 Freud posited the formation of the super-ego as occurring in early childhood and mainly involving the internalization of the parents ('Ego and Id', p. 35). Melanie Klein considered the formation of the super-ego to begin earlier, and to continue to develop later and to involve a broader and more varied introjection of rules and objects. This more open-ended conception of the super-ego might offer a needed bridge to history and society. See R. D. Hinshelwood, *A Dictionary of Kleinian Thought*, London, 1989, p. 98.

88 N. Elias, *The Civilizing Process: Sociogenetic and Psychogenetic Investigations* (transl. E. Jephcott, rev. edition), Oxford, 2000, p. xi.

Chapter 4

Interpreting dreams in medieval literature

Hans-Jürgen Bachorski
(Translated by Pamela E. Selwyn)

> The dream is a little hidden door in the innermost and most secret
> recesses of the soul . . .
> C. G. Jung, *The Meaning of Psychology for Modern Man*[1]

DREAM WEAVE, NARRATIVE WEAVE

Among the many shocks with which the modern age has confronted the
subject is the ominous insight that it is by no means the master of its own
self. There is, however, at least one consolation: thanks to Freud's *Interpretation of Dreams* (1900),[2] dreams are no longer considered visionary
manifestations in which higher powers articulate themselves, but rather as
a specific 'organisation of [the individual's] thoughts'.[3] To be sure, they
appear at first as a kind of bewildering picture-puzzle but, once deciphered,
they prove to be a perfectly plausible 'organisation of thoughts, or a discourse expressing one or more wishes'.[4] The individual knows more about
him or herself in the dreaming than in the waking state, it appears, which
also explains why dreams are 'so strange and so difficult: for we have learned
from experience that they are invariably seeking to express something that
the ego does not know and does not understand'.[5]

This coexistence of the waking ego, which understands less, and the dream
ego, which understands more, may be bearable and even productive in the
case of real human beings. Matters are necessarily quite different when it
comes to dreams in literature, that is, 'dreams that have never been dreamt
at all'.[6] Here the competition between the non-knowing and the knowing
self is multiplied by the complex nesting of speaking subjects in the text:
a literary figure recounts a dream, which is recounted by a narrator, who is
in turn a function of the implicit author, who may ultimately be the product of a real author's work. Between which of the many minds is the
dream-work taking place? Whose unconscious is asserting itself against the
internal censor in the displacements and condensations of the dream?[7] About

which of the speaking/narrating subjects' economy of drives does the dream inform us?[8]

I will approach the problem of dreams and what they mean in literature by considering three contrasting uses of dreams in medieval German literature, in the *Nibelungenlied* (about 1200), the *Parzival* of Wolfram von Eschenbach (about 1220), and *Gabriotto und Reinhart* by Jörg Wickram (1551). In each text, the connection between the speaking subject of the text and the dream is different, and the extent to which psychoanalytic ideas might illumine the text is different too.[9] Who is dreaming here of falcons, thunderstorms and dragons, of bloody faces and skewered maidens? And, if the dream text contains something that the dreamer does not quite know, but which nobody else can know either, who in a literary text knows the origins of the picture-puzzle that emerges in dream-work? Where does the dream text get its material, the individual pictures for the puzzle? Finally: if the dream represents a 'little hidden door in the innermost and most secret recesses part of the soul', into whose soul are we looking in the dreams recounted in medieval romances?

THE NARRATOR SPEAKS IN DREAMS

Kriemhild's maidenly dream is, if you will, the very first of her many deeds recounted in the *Nibelungenlied*. In the midst of the joys of court life, the high honour in which she lives

> . . . Kriemhild dreamt,
> she reared a falcon, strong, handsome and wild,
> but that two eagles rent it while she perforce looked on,
> the most grievous thing that could ever befall her.[10]

This grim dream image of the death of the beautiful falcon, like the suffering it unleashes, comes quite suddenly, since up until then the text mentions only a life of courtly pleasures, of which Kriemhild is the radiant centre – 'none was her enemy', the narrator expressly tells us (p. 17). The dreamer does not understand her dream; she needs help to interpret it. This task is performed by her mother Ute – and by the narrator. Ute deciphers one dream element, the falcon, when she declares: 'the falcon you are rearing is a noble man who, unless God preserve him, will soon be taken from you' (p. 18).[11] Kriemhild reacts as one must to such grim dreams: she vows henceforth to avoid love altogether, in order to escape the misfortune it brings (p. 18). Determined as this sounds, the narrator as the second interpreter immediately contradicts her with equal determination, for no one can escape the fate foreseen in a dream:

Yet the time came when she was wed with honour to a very brave warrior, to that same falcon whom she had seen in the dream which her mother had interpreted for her. What terrible vengeance she took on her nearest kinsmen for slaying him in days to come! For his one life there died many a mother's child (p. 19).[12]

This commentary and the further course of events allow the character's dream and the narrative prediction to blend seamlessly together: the narrator's speech is identical to the dream. The linguistic expression 'dream' proves to be speech inserted from outside, which retains no surplus beyond the narrative function, and offers no further insight into the character's conscious mind.[13]

This also applies later to Kriemhild's second and third dreams, shortly before the death of Siegfried, when, in quite similar images, she once again imagines the same constellation in which the beloved object is slain by two overpowering opponents: 'I dreamt last night . . . that two boars chased you over the heath and the flowers were dyed with blood!' (p. 124),[14] she relates, and then immediately doubles the motif: 'Last night I had a sinister dream of how two mountains fell upon you and hid you from my sight' (p. 125).[15] The only difference is that in the dream configuration Siegfried no longer appears displaced as a noble animal, but rather has been 'unburied'. Where Kriemhild earlier dreamt of a falcon, strong, handsome and wild, she now speaks of death overtaking Siegfried. What remains, however, is the threat to her beloved from two aggressors. In contrast to this clairvoyance, which lays bare the future, Siegfried's answers, with which he marches off to his death despite Kriemhild's fears, are helpless attempts at ostensibly rational arguments against her nightmares. And so what must happen, happens.

The results of Hagen's firm contradiction of the dream that Kriemhild's mother Ute has before the warriors ride off to Etzel's court are no different. Her vision, in which she anticipates the final catastrophe, will also prove 'true' in the sense of Kriemhild's dreams:

'Stay at home, good warriors', noble Ute implored her sons. 'Last night I had a dreadful dream that all the birds of this land were dead.' (p. 190)[16]

Once again, as in Kriemhild's first dream, we find the displacement of the noblemen in the image of the birds, although in this case it is a matter not of a single hero, but of the death of all: here there are no longer hunter and hunted birds, but only a terrible final tableau littered with corpses. Everybody – Hagen, Ute, and the narrator – knows that this is a genuine prediction. Hagen's contrary response no longer questions the truth of the dream – quite the reverse. Rather, he insists on knightly honour, which demands unerring action despite the grimly inauspicious prospects: 'Those who set store by dreams cannot rightly know where their whole honour lies', interposes Hagen (p. 190).[17]

The dreams recounted in the *Nibelungenlied* reveal a constellation typical of dream descriptions in medieval literature. The content and imagery of dreams appear scarcely motivated by day residues, that is, by the waking experience of the figures. Similarly, they are not related to the specific consciousness of the figures. Instead, their sole function is to present a direct preview of the future. In this they differ fundamentally from the form of dream known to modernity since Freud, in which 'the latent dream content' consists of 'day's residues, childhood memories, bodily impressions . . . etc.', which are 'distorted' in dream-work.[18] Here, instead, they belong primarily to the narrator's discourse, and are identical to his epic prognostications, which insert into the events of the plot a wealth of utterances such as 'In the land of the Burgundians there grew up a maiden of high lineage . . . [who caused] many knights to lose their lives' (p. 17). For that reason the interpretation of such dreams is easy, since they are quite simple to decipher: the birds of prey are noblemen, and the death of the falcon refers to the death of one of them. The imagery of the dreams follows conventional patterns and established symbols. They use material that has been drawn not from an individual ('private') reservoir, but from the social storehouse of images.[19] The brief plot, reduced to a single event, is anything but obscure; we are struck, rather, by its logical structure (which is certainly not the case for the material that Freud used to develop his method of interpreting dreams). It is unsuitable for the reconstruction of a collective, let alone an individual unconscious; at most it represents an element of narrative strategy in the early and high medieval romance. This was to change in later texts, however.

THE *MODUS DICENDI* OF DREAMS

Before proceeding to an interpretation of these other dreams, let us consider the traits that help mark a text as a 'dream'. When a sequence within a text begins with a phrase such as 'she dreamt the following' or 'she had a heavy dream', a shift in the type of text follows. Just as literary texts, for example, may involve a 'fictionality pact', which calls upon the reader to regard certain events and narrative strategies as possible, but by no means everything in the account as true, other signals serve to establish the horizon of a specific genre. The expression 'once upon a time' at the beginning of a story, for example, not only promises that what follows will be a fairy-tale, but also functions as an abbreviated installation of a system of rules that determines what can happen or be said in the text – and what must not occur or be said.[20] Such 'textual type markers' can take the most various forms; what interests us here, however, is which rules a dream marker sets for the text that follows.[21]

First of all, there is the heightened complexity of the dream content and of its form of speech as compared to waking, controlled speech: 'It is only rarely that a dream represents or, as we might say, "stages", a single thought: there are usually a number of them, a tissue of thoughts'.[22] This tissue does not, however, follow the principles of narrative succession or logical structure. On the contrary, in this kind of text we accept the suspension of logic as perfectly normal, since 'It is as though psychological activity had been transported from the brain of a reasonable man into that of a fool'.[23] In this 'foolish' brain the usual logical connections (as regards chronological order, spatial organization, causal relationships, etc.) have been suspended, while new idiosyncratic relations are formed between the individual building-blocks: 'They can represent foreground and background, digressions and illustrations, conditions, chains of evidence and counter-arguments. When the whole mass of these dream-thoughts is brought under the pressure of the dream-work, and its elements are turned about, broken into fragments and jammed together – almost like pack-ice',[24] it must consequently be equally acceptable for dream texts to hover in a certain obscurity, for although 'the dream is the product of our own psychic activity', the 'finished dream strikes us as something alien to us'.[25]

This 'feeling that dreams are extraneous to our minds'[26] is a function, not least, of the strategy of pictorializing complex subject-matter and abstract concepts, which operates in dreams.

> The direction taken by the displacement usually results in a colourless and abstract expression in the dream-thought being exchanged for a pictorial and concrete one . . . A thing that is pictorial is, from the point of view of a dream, a thing that is *capable of being represented* . . . But not only representability, but the interests of condensation and the censorship as well, can be the gainers from this exchange. A dream-thought is unusable so long as it is expressed in an abstract form; but when once it has been transformed into pictorial language, contrasts and identifications of the kind which the dream-work requires, and which it creates if they are not already present, can be established more easily than before between the new form of expression and the remainder of the material underlying the dream. This is so because in every language concrete terms, in consequence of the history of their development, are richer in associations than conceptual ones.[27]

Because of their capacity to dissolve logical connections, their obscurity and pictorialization, dream texts require translation. The directly visible – the manifest content – and what is hidden underneath – the latent content of dreams[28]

> are presented to us like two versions of the same subject-matter in different languages. Or, more properly, the dream content seems like a

transcript of the dream-thoughts into another mode of expression, whose characters and syntactic laws it is our business to discover by comparing the original and the translation.[29]

The work of interpreting dreams is thus inverse 'dream-work', in which the 'distortion'[30] is reversed by following established rules of translation. After all, what is true of all dreams (in a literary context) is that they cannot simply be ignored as insignificant. Despite historical differences in the assumed relationship between the dream text and the dreamer (looking into the future / processing waking experience / wish fulfilment), the belief that dreams always have significance for the dreaming subject remains a constant.

A BEWILDERED HERO AND HIS DAYDREAM

Wolfram's *Parzival*[31] contains two dreams, which – compared to the type of the epic prognosticating dream – have an enormous surplus that shifts them from the narrator's discourse into the individual conscious minds of the figures, while at the same time articulating their unconscious. Thus the actual hero of this romance falls into a deep dream, even if it is a daydream in this case, a dream that does not fly by in sleep, but rather seizes him while awake, tearing him away from his usual conscious activity.[32] I refer here to the famous episode of the drops of blood at the beginning of Book Six. King Arthur's best falcon, which had flown away from its master, tries to capture a goose, which manages to escape, but 'from its wound three [red] tears of blood fell upon the snow' (p. 148).[33] The sight of the three drops of blood on the snow casts Parzival into a somnolent state ('he sat motionless . . . as though asleep': p. 148),[34] in which he can scarcely react to the practical demands of life as a knight, but spins the picture of blood in the snow into an intense dream image:

> When he saw the tears of blood on the white, white snow he asked
> himself 'Who has set his hand to these fresh colours?
> Condwiramurs, these tints may truly be likened to your complexion!
> . . .
> Condwiramurs, here lies your bright image!
> The snow lending its white to the blood,
> The blood reddening snow –
> Condwiramurs! Your fair person is reflected here, I'll not excuse you
>   the comparison!'
> The hero set two tears against her cheeks, the third against her chin.
> . . .
> For the Queen of Belrepeire was mirrored in these colours, her
>   presence bereft him of all awareness (p. 148).[35]

Unlike Kriemhild's dreams, this vision does not foretell the future, but instead invokes the hero's (repressed) past: the recollection of the woman he left behind motivates the displacement of what Parzival really sees on a memorial image pregnant with meaning. Thus for Parzival, the goose's blood falls not in drops but in tears (*zäher*). The associative link is first established by the red and white of blood and snow, which points to Condwiramurs; and tears stand out on her cheeks and chin. The repeated invocations of the chromatic contrast between red and white contains a sort of leitmotif, which describes both Condwiramurs alone and Parzival-Condwiramurs as a couple. Thus during their very first encounter the text mentions that both of their mouths are red (p. 103), and Condwiramurs is described as 'like a rose still moist, with the sweet dew revealing from the bud its pristine glory of white and red' (p. 104).[36] Shortly thereafter she appears before 'the one they called "The Red Knight"' (p. 98) in a white silken shift (p. 106). Tears flow in streams, while during the chaste wedding-night the sheet is sullied by no other colour, remaining pure and gleaming white (p. 110). Both the colours and the motif of tears link the lovers as leitmotifs, and one of the elements alone easily suffices to place the hero in a dream state and to connect him with what is absent and yet so present to him.

In order to grasp fully the explosive nature and the density of meaning of this passage in Wolfram's version of the story, it is necessary to turn to Chrétien's account, in his late twelfth-century *Perceval*.[37] The differences are significant. They begin with a detail that appears at first to be merely incidental. Chrétien sets the encounter between Perceval and King Arthur's court amidst snowy meadows and bitter cold without further comment.[38] In Wolfram's account, in contrast, the snow falls especially for this scene and quite unseasonably. To ensure that no reader overlooks this symbolic arrangement, the narrator comments ironically on his highly significant action, which severely violates the usual topoi:

A heavy snow had descended on him during the night. Yet according to what I heard it was not the time for snow. All that was ever told of Arthur, the man of the merry month of May, happened at Whitsun or at blossom-time in Spring. Think of all the gentle breezes they waft at him! Thus the tale is of contrasting colours here, it is chequered with that of snow (p. 147).[39]

Wolfram's snow is not simply there, but is spread out with care, rather like a parchment waiting to be written upon.[40] While both versions arrange the material for Perceval's/Parzival's later daydream, only Wolfram accentuates the total artificiality of this dream element. The motif of the falcon undergoes a further displacement, with the falcon hunting the goose and wounding it in such a way that its wounds produce the writing against a white background. While Chrétien has the bird of prey swoop out of the sky on to the wild geese before Perceval's eyes, Wolfram has already closely associated the falcon with his hero: not only is it a falcon from Arthur's court – and the best one at that – that has flown away, but 'that night she lodged near Parzival where the forest was known to neither, and both were freezing cold' (p. 148).[41] Further vivid commonalities between birds of prey and knights also come to mind.[42] Although they are composed of the same material, the images that Perceval and Parzival see before them in the snow are ultimately quite different. Perceval sees (drops of) blood and snow, and this colour combination of red and white evokes for him the shining presence of his beloved.

> The goose was caught in the throat; three drops of blood gushed from the wound and flowed on to the white snow like the hint of red that nature lends to a visage. [Perceval] leaned on his lance to observe this resemblance, for blood and snow together recalled to him the high colour of his beloved; and so he became lost in the thought that the red of her face shone out among the white like the three drops of blood on the white snow. In his enraptured gazing he thought he saw before him the face of his beautiful beloved in all its freshness. All morning Perceval stared transfixed at the drops.[43]

Chrétien speaks here neither of sorrow nor of tears on a face but only of a smiling, lively visage, as Eric Rohmer portrayed it so movingly in his Perceval film. Perceval's rapt contemplation may thus be attributed to the physical and aesthetic attraction of his beloved, whom he forms in his dream from a tiny scrap of real material. Although it proceeds from the same details, the image of snow and blood that appears to Wolfram's Parzival creates a completely different dream image and association. To be sure, here, too, the chain of associations begins with the contrast of the colour red on a white background, which evokes the appearance of Condwiramurs.[44] But then we notice that Wolfram, unlike Chrétien, does not speak of drops of blood (*goutes de sanc*) but rather quite consistently of tears of blood (*drî bluotes zäher rôt* (stanza 282, verse 21), similarly, 'two tears against her cheeks, the third against her chin').[45] This reinterpretation of the drops of blood as tears of blood,[46] however, opens up quite another semantic and emotional field than the aesthetic one established by Chrétien. For Wolfram's hero, Condwiramurs's true attraction lies in the consciousness of sadness and pain. In his dream he condenses the positive feeling of intense affection with the negative emotion of the tears, which are as much of a leitmotif for Condwiramurs as for the other women in this romance: Herzeloyde, Sigune and Jeschute.

However much one tries, Parzival's daydream cannot be related to any future event, and memory alone also cannot explain the deep distress that grips him. It would also be insufficient to seek the meaning of this sequence solely in the wish fulfilment that the daydream offers (that is, organizing the presence of the beloved temporarily and imaginarily through the displacement and condensation of the material of reality), for it is the tear-soaked image of the three 'tears' that is truly puzzling and in need of interpretation.[47] This exact reading of the signs 'snow' and 'blood', so carefully arranged by the narrator, is by no means the only possible one, as Perceval's vision shows. The wild associations that seize Parzival were thus doubtless deliberately motivated. To this extent they are not primarily determined by Parzival's point of view, although they are conveyed in a wonderfully vivid manner. They result primarily from the point of view of the German narrator, who after all had already changed the *goutes de sanc* of the earlier text into *bluotes zäher*. This intentional translation of the French model opens up the possibility of bringing together Parzival's conscious mind, as it is revealed in the dream, with the narrator's ideological project as it constitutes the entire romance.

HERZELOYDE'S TERRIBLE DREAM-WORK

Herzeloyde also dreams. We will recall that Herzeloyde had won over Gahmuret, who is now – as so often – far away on a knightly journey. The text explicitly mentions her great love and intense longing for him, which is followed by a dream:

> One noonday the lady lay in a [nightmarish] sleep, [when she was shaken by] a dreadful vision. It seemed to her as though a shooting star swept her to the upper air where a host of fiery thunderbolts assailed her, flying at her all together so that her long tresses hissed and crackled with sparks. The thunder pealed with loud claps and [spurt out] tears of fire. As she came to herself again a griffin[48] snatched at her right hand – whereat all was changed for her! For now she marvelled at how she was mothering a serpent which then rent her womb and how a dragon sucked at her breasts and flew swiftly away and vanished from her sight! It had torn her heart from her body! Such terrors had [her eyes] to behold! (p. 62)[49]

This is a terrifying dream, and one can vividly imagine Herzeloyde lying at first as if paralysed, then kicking and 'writhing, moaning, and wailing in her sleep' in torment and fear (p. 62),[50] so that she has to be wakened in order to come to herself. In contrast to the *Nibelungenlied*, the narrative provides no interpretation of her dream, nor any account of a third dream. The narrator adds only a brief commentary, which does not decipher the dream, but simply concludes: 'Sorrows to come are on their way to her' (*ir nâhent komendiu herzenleit*). All in all, the dream seems embedded in the narrative with curious awkwardness. At first (in an earlier, 'simpler' version, as it were) it appears as if a gloomy epic prognostication by the narrator, which addresses the reverse of her fortune into misfortune, had been appended to the account of Herzeloyde's happy life as a queen.[51] In the midst of this rather rational speech the narrator sets down a clearly separate narrative sequence: Herzeloyde's dream. Nevertheless, he does not assign the dream the function of epic prognostication, since the narrator has already assumed this role just prior to the account of the dream, commenting 'the blade of her contentment then snapped at the very hilt. . . . But such is the way of the world: joy today and grief tomorrow' (p. 62).[52] This dream, too, undeniably foretells later events (in the immediate and more distant future),[53] yet its significance is by no means limited to this.[54] For this reason, the passage contains no concrete interpretation or translation of the (encoded) dream text into an open prediction of the future: even Herzeloyde's advanced pregnancy is mentioned only immediately after the dream and the account of Gahmuret's death (pp. 65–66).[55]

Even if this section of Parzival does not interpret the dream, it has found competent interpreters. I quote only two of them – Trevrizent and Klaus Speckenbach – since their readings appear to stand for those of many others. Much later in the romance, Trevrizent returns to Parzival's departure, which tore Herzeloyde's heart in two. He not only judges this deed of the 'silly simpleton' (tumber tor) as part of the complex guilt that the hero had taken upon himself, but also interprets Herzeloyde's dream – if highly selectively, for he restricts himself to its second part:

> No sooner had you left your mother than she died. . . . You were the Beast she suckled, the Dragon that flew away from her. It had come upon her as she slept, sweet lady, before giving birth to you (p. 243).[56]

The omniscient narrator is speaking through Trevrizent here, of course, and both formulate an interpretation of the dream that fits easily into the moral argumentation used here to lend meaning to Parzival's life-story up until this point by reading it exclusively as the tale of a sinner. And from the perspective of this interpretation, Herzeloyde appears as the purely passive object of the acts of others. Trevrizent's reading is not, however, wholly convincing. It not only remains completely unclear how he learned of the content of the dream, but it is also difficult to know why his interpretation – the mere utterance of a character – should contain the truth about Herzeloyde's strange dream images. Nevertheless, his reading has shaped the interpretation of a good segment of modern scholars.[57] Thus Speckenbach's analysis,[58] for example, rests on two basic ideas. On the one hand, he consistently reads all elements of the dream in an exclusively allegorical manner,[59] without explaining his reasons. It is also unclear why he so timidly avoids categories such as displacement and condensation, which Freud's *Interpretation of Dreams* has placed at our disposal, and which might help us to solve the riddle of the secret writing of dreams.[60] Because of this strategy of avoidance he leaves the dream text wholly in the hands of the narrator: for only he can devise allegories, and only he can articulate concepts within a moral-theological framework. He does not even consider Herzeloyde's conscious mind as the possible author of this text. On the other hand, Speckenbach's reading is based on a deeply moralistic construction, and he incessantly mentions guilt. As a specific *modus dicendi* ['mode of speaking'],[61] at least, the dream recognizes no such moral dimension: instead of engaging in moral reflection, bodies collide hard in dreams, while value judgements are wholly absent.[62]

Let us free Herzeloyde's dream from the allegorical captivity in which it is usually held (most maliciously in the moralistic assertion – which does not take Wolfram very seriously – that what Herzeloyde sees in the dream is God's judgement on her sinful life).[63] Our aim, instead, is to open the dream to a reading that resists the moral logic of the rules of 'allegory': a psychoanalytic reading.[64] In a first step, the reading of Herzeloyde's dream is constructed on a methodological error:[65] we are supposed to believe that Herzeloyde actually dreamt and recounted her dream just as we read it in *Parzival*.[66] To treat the literary figures 'in all their mental manifestations and activities' as if they were 'real people and not the author's creations'[67] obviously contradicts any reflective treatment of fictional texts, but it may facilitate the 'decoding of the picture-puzzle'. Nonetheless, the dream text is naturally not a linguistic expression of Herzeloyde's, but rather – as is the case with the textual type-marker for dreams – of the narrator or the implicit author.[68] Thus we might consider how this overlapping of different speakers and their voices within a single utterance[69] should be interpreted.[70]

Quite unlike Kriemhild's dream, which belongs wholly to the narrator's discourse and draws its material solely from the later course of events, but not from the experiences of the character, Herzeloyde's dream, which is not logically constructed, but rich in complex imagery,[71] is scarcely exhausted by such a speech act on the part of the narrator. Her – 'completely egoistic'[72] – dream is motivated by the love described immediately beforehand in the text and by her yearning for the absent Gahmuret: what she desires here is clearly closeness, not distance. With this the narrative immediately preceding the dream not only lays the groundwork for what Herzeloyde dreams, but also provides the material for the specific form of work.[73] Awake, Herzeloyde is as aware of her deep love for Gahmuret as she is intensely pained by his absence (pp. 103,15ff).[74] This ambivalent emotional state constitutes the humus for the dream, and thus the course of events follows 'the everyday experience that people's thoughts and feelings are continued in sleep'.[75] To this extent what we find here represents 'day's residues', which transport into the dream Herzeloyde's desires and worries: her deep longing for Gahmuret as well as her anxiety – until this point not yet explicitly addressed – over his absence. The dream text, however, provides a substantial surplus in comparison both to Herzeloyde's state of mind,[76] as described up to this point, and to the accustomed procedure of epic prognostication.

In the dream, Gahmuret and Parzival, her beloved and her son, appear as identical and inseparable; both function equally as the object of her affective phantasies.[77] This identification between the two, which is permissible in the dream, is also explicitly expressed later in the waking state: shortly thereafter Herzeloyde says of the now-dead Gahmuret: 'I am his mother and his bride' (p. 65),[78] and phantasizes about her newborn son: 'It was as though her prayers had restored Gahmuret to her arms' (p. 65).[79] Herzeloyde's fears and desires – also, and particularly, in their extreme erotic and sexual intensity – thus relate to both men equally – or, to put it the other way around: her affects have such power and dynamism that the central difference between husband and son becomes a matter of no concern, and both appear as appropriate objects of desire.[80]

The displacement extends so far that the dream does not, however, mention the actual men Gahmuret and Parzival. The dreaming subject is confronted instead with something referred to as a griffin (*grif*),[81] worm, or dragon (*trache*). This figuration of both as dragons represents a superimposition of a positively connoted aristocratic element (of strength and fighting power, which forms the *tertium comparationis* – third point of comparison – between the beast of prey and noble heroes)[82] on to a terrifying image (springing from the connotations of destruction and the devil).[83] This ambivalent figuration of the absent beloved, which inextricably confuses love and hate, describes Herzeloyde's inner attitude towards the object of her desire more precisely than her official discourse (and than the 'official' discourse of the text). This ambivalence clearly returns to a basic problem of feudalism when it underlines the contradictory function of violence as a force that at once produces society and honour and destroys them. It would be difficult to find a better image for this aporia, which is so constitutive of feudalism, than the strong, aggressive and deadly predator.[84] It is surprising here that in Herzeloyde's dream this contradiction is regarded as an intrinsic one rather than as a neat dichotomy between friends and enemies. It is disconcerting that the contradiction, associated with Herzeloyde's men, is allowed to appear in connection with the main characters who give the romance its perspective; and it is shocking that the negative, destructive moment of noble identity appears to be so strong. Here, too, a displacement occurs, though: 'Herzeloyde would have every reason to hate the true author of her misfortune. In fact, however, she suffers in a dream and the hatred is directed against herself'.[85]

As evidenced by the imagery chosen in the dream, Herzeloyde's feelings towards the noblemen closest to her (unlike those that would have been permitted in the waking state) are highly contradictory but, anxiety-laden as they are, they appear to be more negative than positive.[86] This negative dimension in the actions of the beloved person becomes all too clear if we follow in detail the horrible animal that represents him and its effect upon the dreamer. Something stronger than Herzeloyde's own desire snatches at her hand; the worm rends her womb, the dragon sucks at her breasts and in the end suddenly departs, tearing the heart from her body (p. 62): injuries, physical pain and sorrow are imagined here. It makes sense to interpret these injuries as sorrow over the death of Gahmuret, and the pain of abandonment, which will ultimately destroy her.[87] These aggressive attacks and the destruction of her body appear to reach well beyond her previous experience of the courtly and well-mannered Gahmuret, and also seem far more threatening than what she might expect of her unborn and innocent son:[88] Parzival, too, appears here as a destructive dragon.[89] Thus while in the waking state Gahmuret and Parzival are described in purely positive terms, the dream permits an ambivalent, negative view of these characters as well. In so doing, it abruptly shifts the violence that is otherwise always delegated to external forces into the heart of the courtly idyll; the struggle for a stable ideological-system boundary between the positive and the negative capitulates before the condensations of the dreaming consciousness.

Herzeloyde is mourning her absent husband. In the dream, this psychic pain appears largely as bodily harm, injuries that take her to the threshold of death: her belly rent, the heart torn from her body. What is striking, though, is that the damage caused by the aggressor does not merely follow the logic of annihilation. It is oriented instead towards an erotically and sexually organized topography of her body: coming to from a state of cosmic inner conflict, she is seized by the right hand and carried away;[90] her breast, always a part of the erotic phantasma, is attacked;[91] her womb is rent and with it her vulva.[92] Tellingly, the chosen phrasing (the serpent that rent her womb) leaves open whether she was torn from the inside out – the later act of birth – or from the outside in – the experienced act of coitus:[93] the fact that both can be associated as the destructive acts of a male monster further underlines the status of this curious dream as genuine 'dreamwork' in the Freudian sense. The male principle of sexual action is imagined and revealed here from what was conceived of as the female perspective. These shocking images are diametrically opposed to courtly love (*minne*) as previously described in the interactions between Herzeloyde and Gahmuret. Yet the dream offers an unmistakable glimpse of exactly what slumbers behind the discourse of courtly love: sexuality. At the same time, we witness the triumph of the element to which generalized love was intended to form the sublimated counter-pole: violence.[94] In the most concise ideological and aesthetic programme of the suspension of contradictions, as pursued in Wolfram's romance, we thus find articulated the violence of sexuality, its destructive power, which ultimately even feudal society could not erase.[95]

Up until now, such a decoding of the dream content has followed a cultural-historical trail, which can refer to the various analyses of feudal society, its fundamental contradictions and psychosocial dynamics.[96] But where might an interpretation take us that went beyond a reconstruction of the collective historical consciousness and collective repressions and obsessions[97] to attempt a psychoanalytic examination of the individual consciousness (Herzeloyde's?)?[98]

As a conclusion to his *Interpretation of Dreams*, Freud notes that the dream should be interpreted 'as a wish of the dreamer's represented as fulfilled'.[99] What is important about this thesis is, on the one hand, the idea – formulated in distinction to earlier theories – that dreams refer directly and exclusively to the dreamer and his or her consciousness, wishes and feelings. On the other hand, this assessment of the dream does not refer the interpreter to a real future, which can be seen, but rather to an imaginary wish fulfilment in the here and now of the dream, and it is not surprising, given Freud's basic assumptions about the psychic economy of the individual, that he assumes these wishes to be primarily erotic in nature. The wish fulfilled in the dream is not merely plagued by its non-fulfilment in waking reality, but also collides with the censor during the dream, which forces it to formulate a picture-puzzle in dream-work, which – like all puzzles – at once conceals and reveals.

What, then, does Herzeloyde's dream tell us about her wishes and desires? First of all, it fulfils the desire for very intense contact with a beloved male person. It appears quite unimportant here whether this person is her husband or her son, since the two are uninhibitedly phantasized as one. The reality of ideal courtly society, however, did not generally permit this presence of the noble heroes at court, with their wives. In two romances, Hartmann von Aue elucidates the good military reasons for the absence of knights and rulers from their lands and thus their wives. It is also well known that sons were torn from the mother-child dyad at an early age to be educated according to feudal-noble principles at foreign courts. Clearly, however – if we follow Herzeloyde's dream – the practice of protracted male absence was by no means consistent with women's wishes. The specific identity of the longed-for man seems to be of secondary importance here: Gahmuret and Parzival are melded into a single figure in the dream – an equivalence that continues in the grotesque, sexually charged scenes before and after Parzival's birth and reaches a highpoint in the narrator's repetition of the dream rhyme *ammel/wamme* (nurse/womb) after the birth.[100] In this context the two stages of the dream also take on meaning. Both images relegate Herzeloyde to a certain no-man's-land: she is removed from her surroundings and then immediately pulled away again, and in both cases she presents a picture of misery (but heaven at least weeps, thus acknowledging the validity of her wishes). In the dream, the court lady Herzeloyde is thus reduced to the lonely ego torn from its accustomed social moorings.[101] Only – or precisely – in this wished-for no-man's-land, though, does she imagine the sexual events. Later, Herzeloyde actually fulfils the wish already realized in her dream, when she moves with her dearly loved Parzival (whom she phantasizes as Gahmuret's alter ego) to a social non-place, where she cultivates an intimate twosome with the object of her desire until social reality intervenes to destroy her wishes.

Let us return to the image of the body presented in Herzeloyde's dream. Her overwhelming 'ascension' does not lack a certain orgiastic dimension; her body is shaken through and through, shivering, while the elements rage and shower: fear-pleasure and pleasure-fear meld inextricably. After this dramatic conflict of the dreaming ego, pulled violently back and forth between celestial forces in the first half of the dream, the transition to the second image is marked by the verse: 'ir lîp si dâ nâch wider vant'. This might be interpreted as 'she came to herself again', but there is also a second variant, that 'she found her body again'. Unlike the first part of the dream, in which only her wild plaits appear as a concrete element of her corporeality (while the cosmos itself appears to be a living body), the focus is now on various parts of the body, tellingly enough some of those very parts that play an important role in the erotic context: hand, womb, breasts, heart, eyes. The order of these details in the dream text also departs quite strikingly from the usual direction of the gaze wandering over the body of the beautiful lady in courtly literature. Instead of following the topos of the praise of beauty from top to bottom, from the hair to the feet, here the bodily sensations are described from bottom to top: her hand is snatched before her womb is rent; she feels her breasts before her heart is torn out, and only at the end does the text refer to her eyes. The centre of this female dream-ego is the middle of her body; all dreaming proceeds from her womb: only at the end does she open her eyes – in terror. Herzeloyde dreams here of a radical sexualization of her body, sensations and wishes. The narrative of the dream images gives voice to female desire.[102] Her profound horror at such a wild phantasy articulates itself not in her dream-text, however, but only in the narrator's commentary.

Thus the psychoanalytic notion that the dream – in whatever censored form – is the fulfilment of an erotic wish may provide another approach to Herzeloyde's dream than the pious phantasma of the eternal 'guilt complex', which, like the obsessive notion of the romance's moral tendency, has occupied the minds of scholars. We still need to interpret the deep fear and horror that Herzeloyde experiences in this dream (at least according to the narrator, who uses words such as 'dreadful' and 'anguish'). If, however, we apply Freud's idea that the excessive fear in the anxiety dream results not from the horrors dreamt of but from the repression of 'a sexual affect, a libidinal feeling',[103] to a new reading of Herzeloyde's dream, the focus shifts once again. I have already mentioned the sexual connotations of the injuries Herzeloyde suffers in her dream; to this extent, a reference to the libido present in the dream does not appear to be a 'wild analysis'. In the dream Herzeloyde accepts the sexual assaults, and indeed even imagines them as having taken place, while her everyday life is marked more by their absence. What is dominant in this constellation of imaginary sexuality, however, is not joy or satisfaction, but rather enormous anguish and sorrow (p. 62). This virtually panic-stricken fear (of the dreamer?), however, points to an equally strong potential for both libido and the compulsion to repress. The longings expressed here appear to be impermissible, and in the dream are still subject to a censorship that not merely hinders their practical realization, but also forces their dreamt fulfilment into displacement.

Herzeloyde's dream, formed of the day's residues of longing and fear for Gahmuret, thus contains the most varied layers of meaning, in which insights, valuations and wishes for which she cannot find words in the waking state overlap: the emotionally and erotically charged equation of husband and son; the revelation of a deep ambivalence in her perception of the aggressivity of the noble hero; the close ties between sexuality and violence; the sexual affects and libidinous sensations expressed as fearful trembling. Thus Herzeloyde's dream-text appears to be a highly consistent result of her very individual dream-work, in which the day's residues and wishes combine in such a way that they escape the control of the inner censor (the super-ego) and come to vivid expression. But naturally it is not Herzeloyde, but rather the narrator, who recounts this, like everything else.

And so the experiment, in which the dream of a literary figure is read as if it were that of a real person, reaches its conclusion – or rather, the framework formed by the narrator's discourse. Whose conscious mind and whose unconscious does this dream-text articulate, then? This question can hardly be answered with certainty, particularly for Herzeloyde. For the character Herzeloyde, the text establishes a difference between the conscious and the unconscious, and this difference forces the images and wishes into the dream, through whose work they become describable for her in the first place. Her unconscious, however, corresponds to the ideological project pursued by the narrator of *Parzival*: to draw our attention to the fundamental aporia of court society, which turns every joy into suffering. The images of Herzeloyde's dream, her unconscious, express the narrator's highly conscious scepticism regarding the programmatic ideals of an only tenuously civilized warrior society, in which, under the veneer of refined *courtoisie*, untamed physical violence continues to determine all behaviour. In the dream sequences of the *Nibelungenlied*, the narrator makes Kriemhild his mouthpiece for the epic function of prognostication. In Herzeloyde's dream in *Parzival*, the narrator makes himself the amplifier for the world-view and state of mind of one of his characters, which however correlates quite well with his own point of view.[104]

WICKRAM'S MASCULINE DREAMS AND THE NAVEL
OF THE DREAM

Viewed against this background, the relationship of the various conceivable speakers in a dream recounted by Jörg Wickram in his *Gabriotto und Reinhart* in the mid-sixteenth century (1551) proves far more complicated.[105] The two title characters fall in love with two ladies, but are separated from them by unfortunate circumstances. Like Parzival, Reinhart is then suddenly cast by a rather arbitrary sign (in this case, a rose) into a state of recollection and sorrow, worry and longing for his absent beloved, as well as into extensive ruminations. In this state he goes to sleep, only to fall into a heavy dream:

> He thought he saw his most beloved maiden . . . and the two maidens spoke of him and Gabriotto/as Gernier came to them with a sorrowful visage/carrying a great chain in each hand and with weeping eyes spoke to the two maidens/'Oh, you chaste and noble maidens/I regret/that I must carry out this my office upon you'/and thereupon took a sharp cutting sword/and stabbed the two maidens through their noble hearts/ but he did no harm to their lives/although they suffered great pain afterwards Gernier the old knight took the chain/and bound the two maidens together to a large column/and firmly locked them together with a padlock/and spoke thus/'no man has the power to undo this lock and fetter/except my son Gabriotto and his companion Reinhart'/but so this might be all the more certainly prevented/he brought two hounds . . . / so that anyone trying to loosen their bonds/would be run off by the dogs/after which Gernier, in tears, left the maidens in suffering and pain/sitting with the cruel hounds/and they spent their time in bitter lamenting.[106]

Strangely enough, scholars have interpreted this dream, too, as a reference to the hero's future fate,[107] while remaining completely blind to its latent text. Only quite recently has Christine Pfau offered a captivating interpretation from a psychoanalytic perspective. I will outline her reading briefly before proceeding to my search for the speaking subject. Even if this dream resists 'anything that approaches an unambiguous semantics', its 'pictorial language' still unfolds 'a space drenched in violence, fear and danger; an imagery that departs radically from the positively connoted relationships and emotional dispositions of the characters within the events of the plot'. This violent undercurrent is inextricably mixed up with an expressive sexual charge in the individual images and actions: thus the 'stabbing, bondage and locking . . . refer to a farther reaching semantics of the dream-material: contrary to anatomical wisdom, a stab wound to the heart by no means results in death, but instead merely in "great pain"'.[108] This practical absurdity[109] of Gernier's action facilitates the discovery of the subtext within the image: the maidens' keeper deflowers them both. In the representation of the father, the ego phantasizes itself in the role of both guardian and transgressor,[110] who, in a form of compromise, both preserves and ignores social boundaries. The commanding male sexual deed is also figured here in the image of killing, and thus placed within a completely different frame of reference than that otherwise assigned to it in this romance. Instead of discipline and order within the bonds of matrimony, as consistently propagated by Wickram's romances, uninhibited sexual desire rules here, as dreamlike as it is violent. 'This warlike detour lends the corporeality of love an absoluteness and insistence which the literary enterprise as a whole disavows.'[111] A warlike detour, but – it must be added here – also the detour of a dream, which then permits both, the detour and the objective.

But who in *Gabriotto und Reinhart* dreams in such a way that the text's programmatic intentions appear completely undermined? As awkwardly as the dream itself is inserted into the plot, the subject to whom these dream images can be attributed remains obscure. While in the *Nibelungenlied* the narrator delegates a narrative act, prognostication, to Kriemhild's dream, the narrator of *Parzival* impressively uses his figures' dreams to pursue his ideological project in another *modus dicendi*, which determines the entire romance. If in the first case one can proceed from an identification between the character and the narrator, in the second there is a relatively large overlap. Nevertheless, Herzeloyde's dream is her own dream, since it processes her fears and wishes in a specific and individualized way.

It is doubtless to Reinhart, too, with his very individual desires and inhibitions, that we must assign the dream-work that produces the obscure image of the virgins who are painfully penetrated but not killed: his small but recognizable day's residue, his displaced fulfilment of wishes whose realization in the waking state was as impermissible as its mere articulation. This sequence lends the figure a contradictory dimension that would otherwise be wholly absent. At the same time, however, Reinhart's dream text itself relates to the narrator's ideological project like a dream-text: here, and here alone – clearly motivated by the licences provided by the textual type of the dream – do his wild eroticized phantasies escape the authority of the censor, which represents the internalized moral and didactic drive-regulating programme of the Protestant ethic.[112] In Reinhart's sexualized dream the narrator's unconscious wins out over his ideological intentions. Of course it is not the narrator who dreams, but rather his figure. Nonetheless, the character's dream does not (merely) express his own unconscious but also needs and phantasies that are programmatically excluded from the manifest level of the romance.[113] Once again one notices an overlap and general agreement between the discourse of the narrator and the character. But why does the narrator speak a text in this sequence that he really shouldn't, and why does he suddenly permit images and desires that transcend his ideological concept? I suspect that the power of the censor has been suspended here by a shift to the textual type of the 'dream'. Reinhart's 'hard and difficult dream' opens up and demands a different *modus dicendi* from the text in which it is embedded. In the production of this textual type particular linguistic rules prevail, such as the suspension of logic, illustration, displacement, condensation, obscurity, the necessity of translation, etc. In conceptualizing such obscure images, which are in need of translation, however, the consciousness of the waking narrator appears to undergo exactly the same process that he tries to demonstrate by using the consciousness of the sleeping hero: his inner censor is also suspended, and the repressed becomes representable.

At this point it may be both necessary and legitimate to relate the narrator, and his self-revelation in the hero's narrated dream, to a further figure in the literary game: the author, or at least to the implicit author, who cannot, to be sure, be understood as the historical individual 'Jörg Wickram', but as the 'sum of all textual functions'.[114] For him, too, we may assert that his ideological project consists in the positive illustration of marriage, which is not merely the 'goal of successful social integration', but also, in its chaste nature, a model of disciplined life that shuns all 'disorderly love'.[115] In *Gabriotto und Reinhart* the wealth of key words such as *züchtig* (chaste, modest, virtuous) signals the importance of this concept; in Wickram's work this is otherwise normally formulated in paratexts.[116] To this extent all three figures in the triad – implicit author, narrator and hero – move equally in a psychosocial milieu that is geared towards a massive repression of the drives and demands a high degree of self-discipline – as programmatically formulated by the Protestant ethic.[117] This pressure demands the partly conscious and partly unconscious negation of sexuality and the erotic in both real life and literature, and it appears to have been internalized unquestioningly by the characters.[118]

This lack of opposition and programmatic rigidity can only be maintained on the surface of the text, however. In the midst of the obstinate 'blindness' of the manifest text, the latent text allows – as is always possible at certain points – ambivalence or even opposing desires to emerge. Thus long before the advent of the 'psychological novel',[119] in the romances and novels of the early modern period we already find an outcry of the repressed. This has consequences for the ideological project of the early modern period, which in the face of such incursions appears as a 'brittle and far less successful juggling of love, sexuality and marriage than we might expect in view of the relentless steering towards marriage'. On the other hand, the very text sequences that are marked as dreams function 'as a strategy for the occupation of an "inner space" that not merely reflects or depicts the outside world, but also individually modifies it'.[120]

On the one hand, as Jung puts it, 'Dreams . . . do not deceive, they do not lie, they do not distort or disguise, but naively announce what they are and what they mean. They are irritating and misleading only because we do not understand them. They employ no artifices in order to conceal something, but inform us of their content as plainly as possible in their own way'.[121] On the other hand, however, in Reinhart's/Wickram's dream the interpretation does encounter a scarcely surmountable barrier, not least because the act of interpretation by the dreaming subject is absent, indeed, the actual dreaming subject is difficult to locate. Of course, Freud himself already recognized the limits of dream interpretation:

> There is often a passage in even the most thoroughly interpreted dream which has to be left obscure; this is because we become aware during the work of interpretation that at that point there is a tangle of dream-thoughts which cannot be unravelled. . . . This is the dream's navel, the spot where it reaches down into the unknown.[122]

THE DREAM – A LITERARY ARTIFICE

Precisely this scepticism towards the capacity of dream interpretation demands some final reflections on the legitimacy of a psychoanalytic approach to the literary dreams of another epoch. What seems central to me here is not the often-discussed question[123] of whether psychoanalysis has anything at all to tell us about pre-bourgeois culture.[124] Agostino Paravicini Bagliani and Giorgio Stabile have noted a specific medieval way of dealing with the dream: it always requires 'interpretation, because it has symbolic character; it points to another reality. This view of the dream is the result of that typically medieval notion of the symbolic nature and legibility of the world: all manifestations in this world are the language of God made visible'.[125] If we wished to reformulate this assertion for the modern period, we would retain much of the same language, but with certain significant shifts of emphasis: 'The dream always requires interpretation, because it has symbolic character; it points to another reality. This view of the dream is the result of a notion of the symbolic nature and legibility of the world: all manifestations in this dream-world are the language of the unconscious made visible'. According to this view, the historical process should be regarded from the perspective of how the shift from one model of treating dreams to the other was organized.[126] I agree with Jacques Le Goff's assessment that it is 'promising to consider culture in the light of its obsessions and repressions, examining both individual and collective mechanisms of censorship'.[127] For within 'a given culture people tend to dream particular kinds of dreams', while the typical 'stresses, anxieties and conflicts vary from one culture to another'.[128] The dreams that have come down to us in medieval texts provide ample evidence of this,[129] particularly when they begin to create an individual interior space and thereby to differentiate individual from societal phantasmas. How we understand sequences that recount dreams within a fictional text is an equally controversial issue. Steven R. Fischer takes an extreme position, preferring to restrict the interpretation solely to the literary constructedness of these dreams: 'The dream in the Middle High German epic is essentially a literary device'.[130] Following this premise, he proceeds to distinguish between various types of dreams:

> The *somnium*, based upon the discrepancy between the *genus literale* and *genus allegoricum*, enables the author to transcend epic temporal limitations to contrapose his hero with a tragic fate. . . . The *oraculum* allows the author to guide the hero toward a justified resolution through a form of authorial self-objectification. An approximate inverse, the *insomnium*, permits the author to externalize his protagonist's sentiments. The *visio*, like the *somnium*, enables the author to contrapose his hero with a future event, but with the significant difference that here the hero understands and makes use of the revelation to solve a problem.[131]

Fischer's reflections on the function of dream narratives in a literary setting encourage us to define more precisely the relationship between narrative strategy and the respective psychological dimensions in each of the examples presented here. What particularly interests me is the relationship between the discourse of the narrator and that of the character, which overlap in a variety of hybrid constructions. I distinguish among three possible constellations.

The narrator dominates the discourse of the dreaming figure. What Fischer refers to as the purely literary dimension of the dream in medieval literature applies only to this mode of deploying the speech pattern 'dream', which I have explained using the example of Kriemhild's dreams. The intended narrative function of epic prognostication determines this sequence completely, while no opening of an interior space, in which an individual or collective psychic constellation might be recognizable, occurs. Text and character are consistently dominated by the omniscient epic narrator.

The consciousness of the narrator speaks through the unconscious of the dreaming figure. Herzeloyde's dream, in particular, demonstrates how under the heading 'dreaming' – despite the potential for an allegorical decoding of the individual images – a dimension of her thought and feeling becomes portrayable that the character's conscious mind could not have expressed, even if it was quite consistent with the figure's psychic nature. Conceptually speaking, however, the figure's unconscious, as it is revealed in the dream, forms part of the discourse of the narrator, who has conceived his entire romance as not merely an intellectually, but also an emotionally and psychically motivated protest against the idealized ruling ideology and mentality of the courtly feudal nobility.[132] If *Parzival* continues to fascinate us today, however, it is because this scepticism towards the ideal is articulated not in the dry diction of the lecturer, but rather with laborious intensity in the language of a hurt and confused individual, who knows, yet does not know, who desires, yet is forbidden to desire, and who comes to him/herself only in dreams.

The narrator's unconscious expresses itself in the unconscious of the dreaming figure. It is Reinhart who dreams in Wickram's romance: his unconscious phantasizes a dreamlike fulfilment of all those desires that his conscious mind and the law so clearly condemn. Hero and narrator are agreed in this conscious affirmation of societal norms, which had recently begun to set such tight limits on the desires of the body, for the entire romance consistently sings the praises of modern social and self-discipline. In Wickram's manifest text we find not a single departure from, not a single doubt or resistance to the propagated norm – unless we choose to interpret the impudent invocation of proper behaviour and the stubborn resistance to all forms of disorder in Wickram's romances themselves as a superficially negated articulation of an improperly rejected deeper desire.[133] Only the decision to make the character dream opens up the possibility of imagining the repressed, at least in obscure images. But just as the character and the narrator are identical in their idolatry of the law, so the unconscious of each is transparent to that of the other.[134] Only in Reinhart's dream does the narrator – or should we already be speaking of an implicit author?[135] – permit himself to affirm the forbidden: the realization of 'burning love' in the sexual act. And only in the dream can both admit that it is terribly painful, but by no means fatal. The displacement of narration into the textual type of the dream suspends the narrator's self-control and the repressed creeps into the text.[136] Even more than in Herzeloyde's dream the point is reached here at which the literary text no longer appears as a self-controlled discourse, but rather a playground of the uncontrollable, an articulation of the unconscious, a notebook of the collective repressions and obsessions of that epoch as they were manifested in the individual.

Taking these various constellations into account, we cannot help but agree with Herman Braet's lovely notion that 'enclosed in the sphere of dreams, literature dreams only of itself'.[137] After all, these medieval dreams that were never dreamt also represent their own, quite beautiful form of literary discourse: '"There lies in dreams a marvellous poetry, an apt allegory, an incomparable humour, a rare irony"'.[138]

NOTES AND REFERENCES

1 C. G. Jung, 'The meaning of psychology for modern man', in *The Collected Works of C. G. Jung*, vol. 10: *Civilization in Transition* (2nd edn.), Princeton, NJ, 1970, p. 144.
2 Freud, *The Interpretation of Dreams*, SE 4 and 5.
3 On the theories of dreams current in the Middle Ages, see S. R. Fischer, *The Dream in the Middle High German Epic: Introduction to the Study of the Dream as a Literary Device in the Younger Contemporaries of Gottfried and Wolfram*, Berne, 1978, pp. 17ff. On the modern scientific literature on dreams, see Freud, *Interpretation*, SE 4.

4 J. Laplanche and J.-B. Pontalis, *The Language of Psycho-Analysis* (transl. Donald Nicholson-Smith), New York and London, 1973, p. 235.

5 C. G. Jung, 'Analytical psychology and education', in Jung, *The Development of Personality: Papers on Child Psychology, Education and Related Subjects* (transl. R. F. C. Hull), Princeton, NJ, 1981, pp. 63–132, 103.

6 Freud, 'Delusions and dreams in Jensen's *Gradiva*' (transl. J. Strachey), in Freud, *Psychological Writings and Letters* (ed. S. L. Gilman), New York, 1995, p. 193 (henceforth Freud, 'Delusions'). The reinforced negation in this context clearly refers to Freud's unconscious uneasiness with the interpretation of dreams in a literary text (rather than in relation to the account of an analysand) that he undertakes here. See also the cautious phrasing in P. Burke, 'The cultural history of dreams' in his *Varieties of Cultural History*, Cambridge, 1997, pp. 23–42, 28:

> Historians need to bear constantly in mind the fact that they do not have access to the dream itself but at best to a written record, modified by the preconscious or conscious mind in the course of recollection and writing . . . Historians also need to remember that unlike psychoanalysts they do not have access to the associations of the dreamer to the incidents of the dream, associations which enable analysts to avoid a mechanical decoding.

7 Following the summary definition offered by Laplanche and Pontalis in their entry 'Unconscious, subj. and adj.' (*Language of Psycho-Analysis*, p. 474), I understand (the) unconscious as 'all those contents that are not present in the field of consciousness at a given moment', and a system that 'comprises the repressed contents which have been denied access to the preconscious-conscious system by the operation of repression'.

8 In asking this question, the reflections that follow enter the precarious ground between psychoanalysis, literary intepretation and historical anthropology. Freud's *Interpretation of Dreams*, like his other works, is certainly not an exercise in literary criticism, but he does engage in hermeneutic work with texts, whose obscure meaning he seeks to understand, just as literary scholarship cannot stop at the description of the obvious contents of texts if it wishes to do more than merely repeat what someone else has already written better. Finally, the related disciplines meet in their interest in reconstructing historical forms of consciousness and their individual and collective repressions and obsessions.

9 For an extensive list and interpretation of dreams in Middle High German literature see Fischer, *Dream*.

10 *The Nibelungenlied* (transl. A. T. Hatto), London, 1969, p. 18. All page numbers in the text refer to this English edition.

> troumte Kriemhilde,
> wie si zöge einen valken, starc, scoen und wilde,
> den ir zwêne arn erkrummen. Daz si daz muoste sehen,
> ir enkunde in dirre werlde leider nimmer geschehen.
> (*Das* Nibelungenlied *nach der Ausgabe von*
> *Karl Bartsch*, Vollständiger Text
> (ed. Helmut de Boor), Berlin, 1972, verse 13)

11 der valke, den du ziuhest, daz ist ein edel man.
in welle got behüeten, du muost in sciere vloren hân
(*Das Nibelungenlied*, verse 14)

12 sît wart si mit ren eins vil küenen recken wîp.
Der was der selbe valke, den si in ir troume sach,
den ir besciet ir muoter. wie sêre si daz rach
an ir næhsten mâgen, die in sluogen sint!
durch sîn eines sterben starp vil maneger muoter kint.
(*Das Nibelungenlied*, verses 18–19)

13 This applies to the dream elements in this text, while an interpretation of the motif of the falcon and its implications for the collective unconscious of court society more generally could be quite promising.

14   . . . mir troumte hînte leide, wie iuch zwei wildiu swîn
        jageten über heide, dâ wurden bluomen rôt
                    (*Das Nibelungenlied*, verse 921)

15   mir troumte hînte leide, wie ob dir zetal
        vielen zwêne berge: ine gesach dich nimmer mê
                    (*Das Nibelungenlied*, verse 924)

16   Dô sprach zuo z'ir kinden diu edel Uote:
        'ir soldet hie belîben, helde guote.
        mir ist getroumet hînte von angestlîcher nôt,
        wie allez daz gefügele in disem lande wære tôt'
                    (*Das Nibelungenlied*, verse 1,509)

17   'Swer sich an troume wendet', sprach dô Hagene,
        'der enweiz der rehten mære niht ze sagene,
        wenn ez im ze êren volleclîchen stê . . .'
                    (*Das Nibelungenlied*, verse 1,510)

18 Laplanche and Pontalis, *Language of Psycho-Analysis*, pp. 235 and 124.
19 On this see also Burke, 'Cultural history of dreams'.
20 A logic of genre developed in this way generally functions perfectly and determines the reader's 'horizon of expectations' – and even the process of genre destruction or parody always presupposes an understanding of the signals and the meeting of certain expectations.
21 At this point I will pass over the (quite significant) differences in the rules governing types of texts between medieval and modern texts and concentrate, from a systematic perspective, on the commonalities.
22 Freud, 'Delusions', p. 237.
23 Freud, *Interpretation*, SE 4, p. 55, quoting G. T. Fechner (1889).
24 Freud, *Interpretation*, SE 4, p. 312.
25 Freud, *Interpretation*, SE 4, p. 48.
26 Freud, *Interpretation*, SE 4, p. 48.
27 Freud, *Interpretation*, SE 5, pp. 339ff.
28 Laplanche and Pontalis, *Language of Psycho-Analysis*, p. 235: 'Latent content: Group of meanings revealed upon the completion of an analysis of the unconscious – particularly a dream'.
29 Freud, *Interpretation*, SE 4, p. 277.
30 Laplanche and Pontalis, *Language of Psycho-Analysis*, p. 124.
31 Where not otherwise indicated, references to the German *Parzival* in the notes (with stanza numbers) are to W. von Eschenbach, *Parzival* (transl. Wolfgang Spiewok), 2 vols, Stuttgart, 1981. The English translation cited in the body of the text (with page numbers) is W. von Eschenbach, *Parzival* (transl. A. T. Hatto), London, 1980. Occasional small alterations or additions to Hatto's translations have been placed in brackets in the text.
32 With the exception of the noctural anxiety dream at the Gral castle, of whose content the text mentions little: *Parzival*, p. 130.

33   Ûz ir wunden ûf den snê
        vielen drî bluotes zäher rôt
                    (stanza 282, verse 10)

34 'sus hielt er als er sliefe' (stanza 283, verse 23). The question of whether Parzival is actually dreaming here may be answered in the affirmative with reference to J. Le Goff's remark

that, from the medieval viewpoint, 'Everything seen by a sleeping person belongs to the sphere of the dream' ('Dreams in the culture and collective psychology of the medieval West', in his *Time, Work and Culture in the Middle Ages* (transl. Arthur Goldhammer), Chicago and London, 1980, pp. 201–204, n. 24, p. 349; see also Fritz Schalk, 'Somnium und verwandte Wörter im Romanischen', in *Festschrift: Exempla romanischer Wortgeschichte*, Frankfurt, 1966, pp. 295–337); and the formulation 'as though asleep' would then set up this connection. The statement that 'her presence bereft him of all awareness' underlines this reading.

35 do er die bluotes zäher sach
   ûf dem snê (der was al wîz),
   dô dâhte er 'wer hât sînen vlîz
   gewant an dise varwe clâr?
   Cundwîer âmûrs, sich mac vür wâr
   disiu varwe dir gelîchen. . . .
   Cundwîr âmûrs, hie lît dîn schîn.
   sît der snê dem bluote wîze bôt,
   und ez den snê sus machet rôt,
   Cundwîr âmûrs,
   dem glîchet sich dîn bêâ curs:
   des enbistu niht erlazen'.
   des heldes ougen mâzen,
   als ez dort was ergangen,
   zwên zaher an ir wangen,
   den dritten an ir kinne.
   . . .
   dirre varwe truoc gelîchen lîp
   von Pelrapeire die künegin:
   diu zucte im wizzenlîchen sin
     (*Parzival*, stanzas 282–283)

36 als von dem süezen touwe
   diu rôse ûz ir bälgelîn
   blecket niuwen werden schîn,
   der beidiu wîz ist unde rôt
     (*Parzival*, stanza 188)

37 *Perceval* is quoted with verse numbers according to the bilingual Old French/German edition, C. de Troyes, *Le Roman de Perceval ou Le Conte du Graal* (transl. and ed. F. Olef-Krafft), Stuttgart, 1991.

 For a comparison between the two versions of Parzival, see also Walter Haug, 'Die Symbolstruktur des höfischen Epos und ihre Auflösung bei Wolfram von Eschenbach', in his *Strukturen als Schlüssel zur Welt. Kleine Schriften zur Erzählliteratur des Mittelalters*, Tübingen, 1990, pp. 483–512, 496ff. Haug not only gives a brief summary of the differences between the two texts, but also touches on various points of the interpretation presented here.

38 Au matin ot molt bien negié
   Et froide estoit molt la contree.
     (*Parceval*, verses 4,162–163)

39 von snêwe was ein niuwe leis
   des nahtes vaste üf in gesnît.
   ez enwas iedoch niht snêwes zît,
   ist ez als ichz vernomen hân.

Artûs der meienbaere man,
swaz man ie von dem gesprach,
ze einen pfinxten daz geschach,
oder in des meien bluomenzît.
waz man im süezes luftes gît!
diz maere ist hie vast undersniten,
ez parriert sich mit snêwes siten
(*Parzival*, stanza 281)

40 That is the reason why it disappears as soon as the 'text' has been written and read. Compare the subsequent festivities at Arthur's court, which take place on a 'flowery mead' (p. 161).

41   da in bêden was der walt unkunt
und dâ si bêde sêre vrôs
(*Parzival*, stanza 282)

42 Despite the objections of B. Jessing ('Die Blutstropfenepisode. Ein Versuch zu Wolframs Parzival', in D. Lindemann, B. Volkmann and K. P. Wegera (eds.), *bickelwort und wildiu maere. Festschrift für Eberhard Nellmann zum 65. Geb.*, Göppingen 1995, pp. 120–143, 124–125 and 134–135), let us recall that even the positive heroes of the romance were seized, at the sight of a woman, by an involuntary compulsion to pursue the 'prey'. In fact, this very metaphor is used, for example in the description of Gahmuret's reaction to his first glimpse of Herzeloyde: 'The radiance shed by the Queen brought his leg down smartly into position, he strained like a falcon that has sighted its quarry' (p. 43). The narrator also emphasizes the potent aggression exuded by Parzival, despite his somnambulous absence, when, in full panache and with upraised lance, he looks 'ready to joust' (p. 149).

43   La jante fu navree el col,
Si sainna trois goutes de sanc
Qui espandirent sor le blanc,
Si sambla natural color.
. . . [Perceval] s'apoia desor sa lance
Por esgarder cele samblance;
Que li sanz et la nois ensamble
La fresche color li resamble
Qui ert en la face s'amie,
Si pense tant que il s'oblie,
Qu'autresi estoit en son vis
Li vermels sor le blanc assis
Com ces trois goutes de sanc furent,
Qui sor le blance noif parurent.
En l'esgarder que il faisoit,
Li ert avis, tant li plaisoit,
Qu'il veïst la color novele
De la face s'amie bele.
Perchevax sor les goutes muse,
Tote la matinee i use. . . .
(*Perceval*, verses 4,186ff.)

44 Here, too, the use of the colour red as a leitmotif also evokes a significant isotopy: on the one hand Parzival's warrior name (the *Red* Knight), earned with Ither's armour, a characterization that bears an indelible 'stain of blood and sin' (D. Welz, 'Episoden der Entfremdung in Wolframs Parzival. Herzeloydentragödie und Blutstropfenszene im Verständigungsrahmen einer psychoanalytischen Sozialisationstheorie', *Acta Germanica* 9, 1976, pp. 47–110, 77); and on the other the 'macabre "thing-symbol"' (G. J. Lewis, 'Die unheilige Herzeloyde. Ein ikonoklastischer Versuch, *Journal of English and German*

Philology, 1975, pp. 465–485, 470) of the love between Gahmuret and Herzeloyde: her white silken shift, which he exposes in battle to bloody sword-blows and which she wears symbolically on her bare skin (or wishes to wear reddened by his blood, pp. 61, 65).

45   zwên zaher an ir wangen,
        den dritten an ir kinne
        (*Parzival*, stanza 282, verse 24)

46 Spiewok's modern German translation consistently erases this particular accentuation of Wolfram's, speaking only of *Blutstropfen* (drops of blood), while D. Kühn (Frankfurt, 1986) translates *Tränen aus Blut* (tears of blood), but then *Tropfen für Wangen und Kinn* (drops for cheeks and chin). Only P. Knecht (Frankfurt, 1993) translates both passages correctly as *Blutstränen* and *Tränen auf ihren Wangen*. Hatto's English translation speaks first of tears, and then of drops.

47 When Jessing interprets the three drops of blood as 'the new, significant Other', that is respectively, 'God', 'the Trinity' and 'the Holy Family', then 'a binding frame of reference for an actual, moral, allegorical and anagogical world-view', which 'should be the measure of all things in the text' appears to apply less for medieval literature than for the modern interpreter: 'Die Blutstropfenepisode', pp. 127, 140ff.

48 An alternative translation would be 'something snatched' at her hand.

49   Diu frouwe umb einen mitten tac
        eins angestlîchen slâfes pflac.
        ir kom ein vorhtlîcher schric.
        si dûhte wie ein sternen blic
        si gein den lüften vuorte,
        dâ si mit creften ruorte
        manc fiurîn donerstrâle.
        die vlugen al zemâle
        gein ir: dô sungelt unde sanc
        von gänstern ir zöpfe lanc.
        mit crache gap der doner duz:
        brinnende zäher was sîn guz.
        ir lîp si dâ nâch wider vant,
        dô zucte ein grîfe ir zeswen hant:
        daz wart ir verkêrt hie mite.
        si dûhte wunderlîcher site,
        wie si wære eins wurmes amme,
        der sît zervuorte ir wamme,
        und wie ein trache ir brüste süge,
        und daz der gâhes von ir vlüge,
        sô daz si in nimmer mêr gesach.
        daz herze er ir ûz dem lîbe brach:
        die vorhte muosen ir ougen sehen
        (*Parzival*, stanza 103f.)

50 Herzeloyde 'cries out her unconscious anguish': Fischer, *Dream*, p. 115.

51 One can test this thesis by leaving out the dream sequence and proceeding directly to the verse that follows.

52   dô brast ir vröuden clinge
        mitten ime hefte enzwei.
        . . .
        alsus vert diu mennischeit,
        hiute vröude, morgen leit
        (*Parzival*, stanza 103)

53 'It displays three distinct divisions which reveal or characterize Gahmuret's death, Parzival's birth and fatal apostasy, and Herzeloyde's death.' This also locates Parzival within the ideological conflicts of the novel, however. 'The dream not only symbolically introduces the hero, but also immediately places him into the polemic situation which characterizes his dilemma throughout the epic': Fischer, *Dream*, pp. 117ff.

54 This is also what distinguishes it from Kriemhild's dream of the falcon, in which the course of events is anticipated, as well as from Parzival's day-dream, which has no connection whatsoever to the future.

55 If, as Artemidorus held, pregnant women often dream of dragons (see A. T. Hatto, 'Herzeloyde's dragon-dream', *German Life and Letters* 22, 1968–9, pp. 16–31, 21), Herzeloyde's dream would be the first indication of her pregnancy, which has not been mentioned up to this point.

56   . . . dô du von ir schiede, zehant si starp.
         du waere daz tier daz si dâ souc,
         unt der trache der von ir dâ vlouc.
         ez widervuor in slâfe ir gar,
         ê daz diu süeze dich gebar
                 (*Parzival*, stanza 476)

57 On this see R. Rosskopf, *Der Traum Herzeloydes und der rote Ritter*, Göppingen, 1972; K. Speckenbach, 'Von den Träumen. Über den Traum in Theorie und Dichtung', in H. Rücker and K. O. Seidel (eds.), *sagen mit sinne. Festschrift Marie-Luise Dittrich zum 65. Geburtstag*, Göppingen, 1976, pp. 169–204, etc. D. Welz's outstanding essay, 'Episoden der Entfremdung', takes a very different approach, although despite programmatic references to psychoanalytic method he undertakes no interpretation of Parzival's and Herzeloyde's dreams.

58 Speckenbach, '*Von den Träumen*'.

59 Freud already sneered at a particular method of dream interpretation, which

> considers the content of the dream as a whole and seeks to replace it by another content which is intelligible and in certain respects analogous to the original one. This is '*symbolic*' dream-interpreting; and it inevitably breaks down when faced by dreams which are not merely unintelligible but also confused. . . . Most of the artificial dreams constructed by imaginative writers are designed for a symbolic interpretation of this sort: they reproduce the writer's thoughts under a disguise which is regarded as harmonizing with the recognized characteristics of dreams (*Interpretation*, SE 4, p. 97).

60 The allegorizing interpretation of dreams in medieval texts recalls Freud's critical portrayal of the theory of Artemidorus: 'It might be described as a decoding method, since it treats dreams as a kind of cryptography in which each sign can be translated into another sign having a known meaning, in accordance with a fixed key', *Interpretation*, SE 4, p. 98. The only difference is that in allegoresis, the signs being translated into signs of well-known moral meaning are not obscure, but rather universally familiar ones that have been conventionalized in their didactic function.

61 I borrow this term from H. R. Jauss (*Alterität und Modernität der mittelalterlichen Literatur. Gesammelte Aufsätze 1956–1976*, Munich, 1977), who uses it to refer to genre-specific forms of speech; but for dreams one could also use descriptions such as *modus cogitandi* [mode of thinking] or – in light of the suspension of particular channels of thinking – *modus operandi* [mode of acting], alongside *modus dicendi*.

62 In addition, what is at stake here is not a dream dreamt by Parzival, that is, by the person who according to Trevrizent and Speckenbach's interpretation should feel morally responsible, but rather one dreamt by Herzeloyde, who in both interpretations is an innocent victim. It remains unclear, however, how guilt and the moral dimension might be communicated with the perspective of the dreamers.

63 Rosskopf sees this sin in her marriage to Gahmuret: *Der Traum Herzeloydes*, p. 29. See also his allegorizing attempts to establish a typological connection between Eve and Herzeloyde, or Herzeloyde and the whore of Babylon, using the image of the worm or serpent (pp. 80ff) or later (pp. 130ff) to interpret Herzeloyde as Mary (because she does penance?) and Parzival as Jesus (who then rides off as an evil dragon?).

64 S. R. Fischer apodictically excludes such a method for the objects of his study: 'Psychological methodology is invalid in the study of the dream in medieval literature. Whereas in Freudian oneiromancy the "manifest dream content" is eliminated to reach the "latent dream thoughts" of the psyche, in medieval literature ... the dream is the conscious manipulation of a purely literary form. The "manifest dream content" alone provides a valid basis for interpretation' (*Dream*, p. 12). Aside from the incorrect assertion that Freud eliminates the manifest dream content, the decision to take into account the literary context, the entire structure of the text and also of the genre, is doubtless an important suggestion for reading dreams in medieval texts. Fischer does not, however, explain why we should refrain from looking for the latent dream content.

65 On the pros and cons of this methodology, see W. Schönau, *Einführung in die psychoanalytische Literaturwissenschaft*, Stuttgart, 1991, especially pp. 102ff.

66 Not to mention the mistake, reminiscent of 'wild analyses', that it is the analyst who is doing the interpretation here, and not the analysand, whose assessments of his or her own material were the only valid ones, as we will recall.

67 Freud, 'Delusions', p. 222.

68 My use of these terms follows U. Eco, '"*Lector in Fabula*": Pragmatic strategy in a metanarrative text', in *The Role of the Reader: Explorations in the Semiotics of Texts*, Bloomington, 1984, pp. 200–260. See also J. Schutte, *Einführung in die Literaturinterpretation*, Stuttgart, 1985.

69 On this see M. Bakhtin, *Die Aesthetik des Wortes* (ed. Rainer Grübel), Frankfurt, 1979; and 'Towards the aesthetic of the word' (partial translation by Kenneth R. Brostrom), in *Dispositio* 4:11–12, 1979, pp. 299–315.

70 There is also a linguistic trace of this notion in the dream-text itself. The formulation 'si dûhte' and the subjunctives that follow are used twice (stanza 103, verse 28 and stanza 104, verse 10) to emphasize that it is a matter not of 'objective reality' but rather of 'inner reality'. Both content and language temporarily leave the latter behind when the narrator states 'she came to herself again' (p. 62) ('ir lîp si dâ nâch wider vant', stanza 104, verse 7). On the whole, this brief sequence thus offers multiple and highly confusing shifts of perspective.

71 'Herzeloyde's dream appears to be actually a synthesis of Revelations Book 12, medieval imagery, dream topoi, and poetic imagination': Fischer, *Dream*, p. 117. How exactly we might imagine the snatched and tormented Herzeloyde (or what kind of depiction the text might have had in mind in describing her) can be gleaned from Taddeo di Bartolo's 1396 representation of Hell in the fresco of the punishment of Luxuria in San Gimignano: a wild shower of fire rains down on the naked female figure, while she is pulled aloft by her hair and a monstrous demon and serpent attack her vulva.

72 Freud, *Interpretation*, SE 4, p. 267, on anxiety dreams.

73 When Herzeloyde weathers the fiery storm, the loss of her right hand and the pain of birth and lactation, is abandoned and finally loses her heart, this may indeed represent mere passive experience in the dream, which then erupts into a scream, as Fischer asserts (*Dream*, p. 122). This view places far too little value on the active work of dreaming, however.

74 The ultimately deadly longing for an absent spouse, whom undeniable battle-lust drove to distant lands (pp. 39ff), is found doubled in the fate of Gahmuret's first, abandoned wife, Belacane, who 'died pining for the love she had lost in him' (p. 373). ('durch minne ein sterben nâch im kôs/dô sie minne an im verlôs', stanza 750). Conversely, Gahmuret threatens to leave Herzeloyde secretly as well if she tries to hinder his adventuring (p. 59).

75 Freud, 'Delusions', p. 194.

76 Freud, 'Delusions', p. 194.

77 This affective dimension of the image does not contradict the chosen religious imagery, as D. Welz has aptly noted: 'In her own way Herzeloyde discovered the earthly family as the secret of the heavenly one, when, using the typology as a mode of thought, she applies the Trinity metaphor of the Holy Family to herself and her family circumstances . . .': 'Episoden der Entfremdung', p. 71.

78 'ich . . . bin sîn muoter und sîn wîp . . .' (*Parzival*, stanza 109).

79 'sî dûht, si hete Gahmureten/wider an ir arm erbeten' (*Parzival*, stanza 113).

80 Following a phrase of Wapnewski's, Welz speaks here of a 'saving madness', which imagines the son as a replacement for the lost love-object: 'Episoden der Entfremdung', p. 69.

81 *Grif* or *Greif* in one version of the verse, would then be a third synonym for what is referred to as a lindworm and a dragon (*Drache*). In both readings, the dream portrays an alien force that affects the dreaming ego, whether impersonally as a *Griff* (grip) or personified as a *Greif* (griffin). On this see also Hans Hesse, 'Herzeloydens Traum', in *Germanisch-Romanistische Monatsschrift* 43, 1962, pp. 306–309.

82 See A. T. Hatto, 'Herzeloyde's dragon-dream', *German Life and Letters* 22, 1968–9, pp. 16–31, 18ff, which illustrates both the positively connotated association of the nobleman and his authority with the dragon (for example the dragon as a symbol of Utherpendragon and Arthur in Geoffrey of Monmouth) and the tradition of the image going back as far as Artemidorus, *Oeneirokritika*.

83 Speckenbach, '*Von den Träumen*', pp. 183ff. For examples of a negative reading of the image of the dragon see also Rosskopf, *Der Traum Herzeloydes*, p. 25 and throughout. He describes it as symbolizing an unquenchable thirst to possess and hoard gold and precious gems as well as the compulsion to attack people and rob them.

84 See the fundamental study by H. Fischer and P.-G. Völker, 'Konrad von Würzburg: Heinrich von Kempten. Individuum und feudale Anarchie', in D. Richter (ed.), *Literatur im Feudalismus*, Stuttgart, 1975. On the ideological acuity of the animal epic, with its representation of the nobility as a collection of beasts of prey, see W. Röcke, 'Fuchsjagd und höfischer Friede. Das niederdeutsche Tierepos Reynke de vos von 1498', in H. Wenzel (ed.), *Adelsherrschaft und Literatur*, Berne, 1980, pp. 287–338.

85 Welz, 'Episoden der Entfremdung', p. 57. G. J. Lewis points to another example of the ambivalent superimposition of deep love and raging aggression (Herzeloyde kills the birds whose song makes Parzival both cheerful and sad): here, too, the ambivalence of the feelings appears to be translated into a powerful image ('Die unheilige Herzeloyde', p. 478).

86 Lewis misunderstands this painful ambivalence, offering a patronizing and banal attack on the 'repulsive' and unnatural mother, whom she describes as malicious and egotistical. According to her view, the requirements of successful socialization ('. . . it has always been the duty of a mother to raise her son to be a man able to cope with life . . .': 'Die unheilige Herzeloyde', p. 482) in feudal society meant the good mother was the one who best prepared sons for the trade of murder and an early death.

87 Thus H. Brackert reads *Parzival* as a romance about 'women's suffering', which is repeatedly treated in the most vivid situations and images. Herzeloyde's dream vividly condenses this experience of suffering. See Brackert's 'der lac an riterschefte tot. Parzival und das Leid der Frauen', in R. Krüger and J. Kuolt (eds.), *Ist zwivel herzen nachgebur. Günther Schweikle zum 60. Geburtstag*, Stuttgart, 1989, pp. 143–163.

88 Hatto, who interprets this dream as a prognostication, considers the destruction of Herzeloyde's body by Parzival's *large size* to be highly significant: 'For a big-boned boy who caused his mother severe pangs; for one who was to be a great warrior; for a son who was destined to be the lord of a great empire that was to stretch as far as the lands of Prester John, albeit a spiritual empire, like that of the Babe in the Apocalypse . . .' ('Herzeloyde's dragon-dream', p. 27).

89 This ambivalent view of the hero sometimes moves out of Herzeloyde's dream into the discourse of other characters, as when Orilus refers to Parzival as a dragon (stanza 80).

90 An alternative reading might be that she is bitten by a griffin in the hand that she reaches out to her beloved. See note 81.

91 To what extent the female breast was also an erotic phantasma in the Middle Ages is a matter for debate (for strong arguments against this view, see C. W. Bynum, 'The female body and religious practice in the later Middle Ages', in her *Fragmentation and Redemption. Essays on Gender and the Human Body in Medieval Religion*, New York, 1991, pp. 181–238). It would doubtless be equally wrong, however, to reduce it primarily to the function of nursing, since the suckling of noble infants by the mother was a scandalous exception in Wolfram's day, and one that required special justification. (See *Parzival*, stanza 65; and Karl Bertau, 'Regina lactans. Versuch über den dichterischen Ursprung der Pietà bei Wolfram', in his *Wolfram von Eschenbach. Neun Versuche über Subjektivität und Ursprünglichkeit in der Geschichte*, Munich, 1983, pp. 259–285.)

92 The word used in the original, *wamme*, often translated neutrally as belly or gender-specifically as womb, also meant vulva, as the entry in Grimm's dictionary shows.

93 This makes sense not only because of the equation of son with husband – which is subsequently made in the waking state as well. The placement of the figures (the monster approaches Herzeloyde rather than coming out of her body) and the order of the events (first it nurses at her breast, and then it rends her womb) is ambiguous throughout and resists clear explication as an anticipation of the birth traumata.

94 The overdetermined dream-text may, to be sure, have been motivated by the fear of the pain of childbirth, but at the same time its also makes a statement about the experience of coitus from a female perspective (see note 42 on the violent metaphor of the falcon sighting its quarry, which is used in a highly vivid manner to represent a male erotic-sexual impulse (*Parzival*, p. 43). In this point, at least, however, Herzeloyde's dream contains a surplus, a knowledge of the unknown, which is no longer contained within the consciousness of the narrator, and to this extent already approaches what is described below for *Gabriotto und Reinhart*. What is more, like all dreams – if they are not exhausted by epic prognostication – this one also contains a residue that resists interpretation.

95 Further examples of this concept of sexuality in Parzival are Parzival's 'courtly' rape of Jeschute or the death of Schionatulander, which Sigune sent him to for the sake of love.

96 In particular see N. Elias, *The Civilizing Process* (transl. Edmund Jephcott), Oxford and Cambridge, MA, 1994.

97 See the formulations in Le Goff, 'Dreams in the culture', p. 202.

98 Such an approach doubtless encounters as much calm approval among psychoanalysts as discomfort among medievalists, since, in the light of the fundamental social differences in a pre-bourgeois society and the socialization of children in a manner wholly unlike that of the modern nuclear family, one cannot assume that individuals had the same psychic dispositions. Nevertheless, Herzeloyde's dream (or what Wolfram imagined and marked as a dream in *Parzival*) can scarcely be understood any other way, indeed it cries out for such an interpretation.

99 Freud, 'Delusions', p. 193. He had expressed a similar view earlier: 'we perceive that a dream is the fulfilment of a wish', *Interpretation*, SE 4, p. 121.

100 *Parzival*, stanza 113.

101 This goes so far that her plaits fly loose: married women, in contrast, wore their hair under a bonnet. The order of things and the sexes literally unravels.

102 I use desire (*Begehren*) here in the traditional Freudian sense to refer to an 'instinctual impulse' that is located in the unconscious and which – since it is subject to the censor – can only manifest itself in more-or-less coded form.

103 Freud, 'Delusions', p. 238.

104 I cannot resolve the tension here. What is particularly striking in the light of gender studies is the distinction between the clear and emphatically male narrator figuration in Parzival and this dream text, which is just as clearly articulated from a female perspective. It is difficult to understand how this subtle shift from a male to a female perspective is possible.

The particular achievement of this sequence in Wolfram's text consists in the fact that such a dual shift (male/female narrator-ego; controlled narrator text/uncontrolled dream-text) opens up a new potential for unprotected speech in a language of desire.

105 It is more complicated, of course, only if one is coming from the simple model of the visionary dream dominant in the Middle Ages. It is simpler, however, when seen from the viewpoint of Freud's model of dream-interpretation: here a form of dream corresponding to the basic structural assumptions of modern theory, which can be analysed with its help, would be given literary form for the first time.

106 'ihn gedaucht wie er sein aller liebste junckfraw . . . seh/unnd die beyden junckfrawen von im unnd Gabriotto redten/in dem Gernier mit trawigen angesicht zuo in kaem/in yeder hand ein große kettin truog/mit weynenden augen zuo den beyden junckfrawen sprach/"O ir züchtigen und edlen junckfrawen/mir ist leydt/das ich diß mein ampt an euch vollbringen muoß"/damit ein scharpff schneydent schwert nam/die beyden junckfrawen durch ire edlen hertzen stach/aber ihnen an ihrem leben nit schaden bracht/wiewol sye grossen schmertzen davon erlitten/demnach Gernier der alt ritter die Kettin nam/die beyden junckfrawen zuosamen an ein grosse seulen binden thett/mit einem Mahlenschlossz hart zuosamen verschloss/also sprach/"dises schlossz und band nymandts macht hatt auff zuo loesen/dann mein Son Gabriotto und Reinhart sein gesell"/damit aber diß dest sicherer verhuet würd/legt er die beyden hund . . . zuo in/damit so yemandts sye von solchen banden loeßen wollt/das sye von den hunden abgetriben würden/demnach Gernier mit weynenden augen von in gieng, die junckfrawen also in leiden unnd schmertzen behafft/bei den grausamen hunden sitzen ließ/die mit jaemerlicher klag ir zeit vertriben.'

The markers for the beginning of the dream text are completely obvious here, and the day's residue is also clearly described: 'With such thoughts was Reinhart occupied the whole evening, until he went to bed/and fell asleep with such thoughts. And thus a heavy and hard dream came to him.' ('Mit solchen gedancken Reinhart den gantzen abent vertreiben thet, so lang das man zuo bett gieng/in solchen gedancken entschlieff. Desshalben im ein schwerer unnd harter traum zuostund.') Both quotations from J. Wickram, *Gabriotto und Reinhart*, in *Sämtliche Werke* (ed. H.-G. Roloff), vol. II, Berlin, 1967, p. 150 (transl. P. E. Selwyn).

107 See, in contrast, C. Pfau, 'Drei Arten von Liebe zu träumen. Zur Traumsemantik in zwei Prosaromanen Jörg Wickrams', *Zeitschrift für Germanistik*, 1998, pp. 282–301. 'It is scarcely to be understood as a concrete allegorical prognostication for the later peripeteia; none of the images are invoked in the subsequent narrative, and no day's-reproduction enters into it' (p. 295).

108 Ibid. pp. 295ff.

109 The image of the throat run through by a sword that is still capable of speaking points to the corresponding motif of legend in the Life of Saint Lucy, for example.

110 'The "patriarchal right", which Gernier claims in his action, is accorded to him in the dream in the form of a violent defloration. In the subtext, however, this phantasy is the wish of the protagonist Reinhart. . . . In this way the protection of chastity becomes its destruction, and desire and prohibition become inextricably superimposed in the image of the destructive protector' (Pfau, 'Drei Arten', p. 297).

111 Ibid., p. 298.

112 Alongside M. Weber, *The Protestant Ethic and the Spirit of Capitalism* (transl. T. Parsons, ed. A. Giddens), London and New York, 1992, see especially E. Fromm, *The Fear of Freedom*, London, 1942, and Elias, *Civilizing Process*.

113 On the virtually fanatical propaganda for marriage not just in Wickram but in sixteenth-century writings more generally, see the publications of the Berlin research project: M. E. Müller (ed.), *Eheglück und Liebesjoch. Bilder von Liebe, Ehe und Familie in der deutschen Literatur des 15. und 16. Jahrhunderts*, Weinheim and Basle, 1988; and H.-J. Bachorski (ed.), *Ordnung und Lust. Bilder von Liebe, Ehe und Sexualität in der Literatur des Späten Mittelalters und der Frühen Neuzeit*, Trier, 1991, as well as the list of didactic texts on

marriage in E. Kartschoke (ed.), *Repertorium deutschsprachiger Ehelehren der frühen Neuzeit. Handschriften und Drucke der Staatsbibliothek zu Berlin* (compiled by W. Behrend, S. Franke, U. Gaebel and E. Hauck, Berlin, 1996).

114 On this category see Eco, '"*Lector in Fabula*"'.

115 J.-D. Müller, 'Jörg Wickram zu Liebe und Ehe', in H. Wunder and C. Vanja (eds.), *Wandel der Geschlechterbeziehungen zu Beginn der Neuzeit*, Frankfurt, 1991, pp. 27–43, 29; see also his 'Frühbürgerliche Privatheit und altständische Gemeinschaft', *Internationales Archiv für Sozialgeschichte der deutschen Literatur*, Sonderheft 1, 1980, pp. 1–32.

116 This is probably clearest in the introduction to his 1554 *Knabenspiegel*.

117 Alongside Max Weber, *The Protestant Ethic and the Spirit of Capitalism*, transl. Talcott Parsons, ed. Anthony Giddens, London and New York, 1992, see especially E. Fromm, *The Fear of Freedom*, London 1942, and Elias, *Civilizing Process*.

118 In view not only of Elias's theory of civilization, but also of the literary material from the Middle Ages and the early modern era, it seems to me that we must assume for this long period of time not one uniform process of drive-regulation, but two phases (which, however, varied greatly as to individual effects and social scope) associated with the spreading influence of the court and of Protestantism.

119 Freud, 'Creative writers and day-dreaming', SE 9, pp. 143–153, 150:

> It has struck me in many of what are known as 'psychological' novels only one person – once again the hero – is described from within. The author sits inside his mind, as it were, and looks at the other characters from outside. The psychological novel in general no doubt owes its special nature to the inclination of the modern writer to split up his ego, by self-observation, into many part-egos, and, in consequence, to personify the conflicting currents of his own mental life in several heroes.

> In the case of the interpreted passage from *Gabriotto und Reinhart*, it appears that 'the writer' is looking at himself from inside through the other characters.

120 Pfau, 'Drei Arten', p. 301.

121 Jung, 'Analytical psychology and education', p. 103.

122 Freud, *Interpretation*, SE 5, p. 525.

123 See the review of the literature by W. Maaz, 'Psychologie und Mediävistik. Geschichte und Tendenzen der Forschung', in T. Kornbichler (ed.), *Klio und Psyche*, Pfaffenweiler, 1990, pp. 49–72.

124 L. Roper has discussed for the early modern period the fundamental question of how far sources from the pre-modern and pre-bourgeois period can be interpreted using a theory that all too obviously bears the marks of its emergence in bourgeois turn-of-the-century Vienna. *Oedipus and the Devil: Witchcraft, Sexuality and Religion in Early Modern Europe*, London and New York, 1994, pp. 1–34. See also Burke, 'Cultural history of dreams' and the literature cited there.

125 A. P. Bagliani and G. Stabile (eds.), *Träume im Mittelalter. Ikonologische Studien*, Stuttgart and Zurich, 1989.

126 How and when this imagery etc. in dreams changed historically, and when a different model became dominant, is controversial and in need of systematic investigation. Le Goff ('Dreams in the culture', p. 203) cites an increase as early as the twelfth century in 'neutral' dreams, that is, dreams rooted in human physiology, at the expense of those inspired by God or the devil. Burke formulates a similar idea, but attributes a definitive shift in dream imagery from public to private symbols to the period since the seventeenth century. Burke, 'Cultural history of dreams', p. 42.

127 Le Goff, 'Dreams in the culture', p. 202.

128 Burke, 'Cultural history of dreams', pp. 25, 27.

129 That Freud's thesis of imaginary wish-fulfilment in dreams is not too far-fetched and can apply quite well to medieval texts is made abundantly clear by the example of the fabliau *Le Sohait des Vez* (The Dream of the Cocks) by J. Bodel, written in the second half of the

twelfth century (although the censor does not seem very powerful in this case, and as a result the dream-work, and the necessity of any elaborate translation of the manifest into latent dream content, is rather minimal). A husband returns from a two-month absence, only to fall into a deep sleep despite his wife's more than warm welcome. Frustrated, she curses him and then has a vivid dream about a fair at which there is nothing to buy but balls and cocks (*coilles et viz*), large and small, singly and by the dozen. Naturally, the lady purchases the largest and lustiest *vit* – only to make do upon awakening with her husband's pitiful one. Jean Bodel, 'Le Sohait des Vez', in L. Rossi and R. Straub (eds.), *Fabliaux érotiques. Textes de jongleurs des XIIe et XIIIe siècles*, Paris, 1992, pp. 137–153.

130 Fischer, *Dream*, p. 155.

131 Ibid. For a systematic differentiation of medieval texts that fall under the categories of *somnium* and *visio*, see W. Haubrichs, 'Offenbarung und Allegorese. Formen und Funktionen von Vision und Traum in frühen Legenden', in W. Haug (ed.), *Formen und Funktionen der Allegorie*, Stuttgart, 1979, pp. 243–264, 244–245. Haubrichs proposes thematic-semantic criteria (to recognize or foresee something), structural-syntagmatic criteria (to conceal or openly announce the truth/the future) and functional-pragmatic criteria (mantic or psychosomatic origin? deception, illusion or revelation?).

132 I refer the reader once again to the essays by H. Brackert and K. Bertau cited above.

133 The deadly results of 'burning love' that are invoked in the very title of *Gabriotto und Reinhart* might encourage us to do so.

134 This construction conceives of the relationship between the psyche of the literary figures and that of their creator differently to the way that Freud's formulation suggests when he remarks ('Delusions', p. 222) that he has treated the characters 'in all their mental manifestations and activities, as though they were real people and not the author's creations, as though the author's mind were an absolutely transparent medium and not a refractive or obscuring one'.

135 In the sense of the reflections cited above (n. 68), the 'narrator' may be understood as the authority who recounts the plot of the romance, while the 'implicit author' refers to the sum of all textual functions, including, among others, the conceptualization of the narrative authority. To this extent something appears to happen to the implicit author here that his other narrative and ideological strategies not merely do not provide for, but also systematically resist.

136 A literary text contains many gateways for the repressed into the controlled discourse: metaphors, plays on words, slips, etc. On this, see H.-J. Bachorski, 'Der treu Eckart in Venusberg. Namenspiele und Triebverdrängung in Fischarts Geschichtklitterung', in T. Kornbichler and W. Maaz (eds.), *Variationen der Liebe. Historische Psychologie der Geschlechterbeziehung*, Tübingen, 1995, pp. 202–233. The only remedy might be to lock them with padlocks and install fierce hounds 'so that anyone trying to loosen their bonds/ would be run off by the dogs'.

137 'Enfermée dans la sphère du songe, la littérature ne rêve qu'elle-même', H. Braet, 'Rêve, réalité, écriture. Du référentiel – la sui-référence', in T. Gregory (ed.), *I Sogni nel Medioevo*, Rome, 1985, pp. 11–24, 23.

138 Freud, *Interpretation*, SE 4, p. 62, quoting F. W. Hildebrandt (1875).

Chapter 5

Women's dreams in early modern England

Patricia Crawford

Figure 5.1 Anne Bathurst, pictured in 1707, enjoyed dreams of her oneness with God. Courtesy of the Bodleian Library, Oxford.

Over the centuries, dreamers in different historical contexts have wrestled with questions about the meaning of their own dreams and those of other people. This chapter focuses on the dreams of early modern women, and raises questions about how we as historians can use their recounted dreams to gain insights into their lives. For many years I have been interested in exploring the potential of different kinds of sources for understanding women's lives and have been collecting records of their dreams. Here I will focus on dreams that were linked with sleep, that women labelled as dreams, and that were not products of their waking minds. Thus some visions will be included, but day-dreams will be excluded, although women's fantasies are a fascinating subject in their own right.[1]

Like all other surviving evidence, dream stories are puzzling and incomplete. Dreams tantalize us by seeming at one moment to be obvious, at another totally opaque. Several filters have come between us and the dream itself (which could, of course, be a total invention). If told in good faith, then we know that the dreamer has struggled to recall the fragmentary and puzzling images, to place what may have been simultaneous into a narrative sequence, and to translate fragments into words. In other words, accounts of women's dreams have been shaped by memory, language and narrative form. Details may have been forgotten or deliberately suppressed, and the recorder, whether the dreamer herself or another, may have further altered some elements in an attempt to construct a meaningful narrative. Rather than regret the vanished dream, or lament the imperfections of the surviving records, we should consider what these sources offer us.[2] I am interested here in dreams as sources of self-knowledge and in how early modern women used their dream narratives for various purposes, constructing meanings that were sometimes personal and at other times public. Further, some of Freud's insights may prove helpful in allowing us to see how certain themes of human development can be glimpsed as they are worked through in a different historical context.

The dreams selected for discussion here reveal women as historical agents, actively shaping the meanings in their lives, and offering these interpretations to others. They tell us that women thought deeply about emotional relationships with others, especially their families, their husbands and their children, and that many were preoccupied with their religious and spiritual states. Although none of this is new information, it documents from yet another source that we should be careful in making generalizations about the lack of emotional attachments in the family in early modern times. Dream records show that wives and mothers were intensely involved in emotional relationships with others and with the physical, material and spiritual welfare of their children. These records of dreams provide us with some access to women's inner lives.

We cannot interpret evidence about women's use of their dreams without engaging with our own understandings of human behaviour and the inner life. Here some general concepts from psychoanalysis may prove useful. Initially, I suspected that Freud's explanations of the meaning of dreams would provide no assistance, because the meaning seemed so often to lie in events in the individual's life history to which we as historians had no or only very limited access. Furthermore, the Freudian paradigm of dream interpretation seemed ahistorical, taking insufficient account of historical difference. Psychoanalysis itself seemed to depend upon a different notion of selfhood from that common in medieval and early modern times. Stephen Greenblatt, for instance, argues that individual subjectivity in the sixteenth century may have depended more on relations with others than it did at the end of the nineteenth century. Thus he suggests that the peasant Arnaud du Tilh, who took on the identity of Martin Guerre, was able to do so because concepts of owning an individual identity were established not by the individual himself but by evidence as judged in court about his place in society.[3]

While I reject the idea that dreams can be interpreted in a transhistorical way, some of Freud's concepts may help us understand some of the similarities, as well as the apparent differences, between early modern people and ourselves. For example, Freud's theory, that dreaming may involve a longing for the early state of union with the mother that the infant experiences, offers us an insight into the extraordinarily rich dreaming life of Anne Bathurst, a widow who was a member of the mystical Philadelphia Society active in London in the 1690s. Night after night she recorded in folio volumes her visions of oneness with the divine. These are the terms in which Bathurst wrote of her union with God in 1693:

> The word divine multiplies in me & fills me, taking away my herts life into it. . . . O, a fountain seal'd, breasts full of consolation. I am as pent milk in the breast, ready to be poured forth & dilated into Thee, from whom my fullness flows with such fulness and plenitude & pleas'd when eas'd.[4]

Here the dreamer as a lactating mother is at one with the divine, as her milk flows, and her breasts are relieved. Her dream is expressive of women's experience of being physically possessed, and of lactation as a mystical fusion, in which nurturer and nurtured were one, and her search for wholeness has been satisfied. Bathurst's dream seems sexual in the sense that her body is the source of pleasure. Her language is strongly gendered and full of sexed body imagery: her dream is very specifically grounded in the female bodily experience of lactation. Furthermore, Bathurst dreams not as a child seeking her mother, but as a mother satisfying her child. Nevertheless, although the dream speaks of a female experience available to women across time, the story of the dream takes a twentieth-century reader into a different historical world, one in which religion was of overpowering importance. The brief discussion of women's dreams that follows gives some account both of historical and of some possible unconscious meanings.

While an early modern writer could speak of dreams as 'the naked and natural thoughts of our souls',[5] and Freud would speak of the interpretation of dreams as 'the royal road to the unconscious', several historians in the late twentieth century have been intrigued by their interpretative possibilities. For the early modern period, Alan Macfarlane, a pioneer of historical anthropology, analysed the dreams that an Essex clergyman, Ralph Josselin, recorded in his diary. Josselin regarded dreams both as predictions of the future and as a guide to self-knowledge.[6] The historian Peter Burke compared the dreams of four early modern men in public office with those of a generalized group of people in the USA in the 1950s, concluding that people in the past were more concerned about politics.[7] This methodology now seems seriously flawed; also, it ignored questions of gender. There have been attempts to analyse early modern dreams in Freudian terms, but as Charles Carlton pointed out, to interpret Archbishop Laud's dream of losing a tooth as a fear of castration seems crudely reductive.[8] Keith Thomas's brief discussion offers the most valuable general understanding of the learned and popular context in which early modern dreams were understood.[9] More recently, gender has figured in the discussion of prophetic dreams. Richard Kagan has used 400 or so dreams of a young Spanish woman, Lucrecia de León, which survived in the Inquisition records, for a fascinating study of prophetic dreams and their political significance in the time of Philip II.[10]

In early modern times, there was both a learned and a popular lore for the interpretation of dreams in which the gender of the dreamer was a factor. Although by the nineteenth century the world of dreams was sometimes dismissed as a feminine world, where reason, a masculine quality, was absent, early modern people did not generally view women's dreams as a sign of female inferiority.[11] Recognizing that women might have special access to the supernatural through dreams, ministers, physicians, justices and male relatives might all record and seek the meaning of women's dreams.

As Thomas has pointed out, opinions were divided about the origins and meaning of dreams.[12] Learned men debated whether they originated from bodily disorders or the supernatural. Like Dame Pardelote in Chaucer's *Nun's Priest's Tale*, many attributed dreams to physical causes, such as rich suppers and strange sleeping postures. Some physicians thought it worthwhile to ask their patients about their dreams.[13] 'Frightful dreams' might cast people into illness, as the Jacobean Richard Napier recorded, when he was consulted by several women who had terrifying dreams and were mentally disturbed after childbirth.[14] On the other hand, contemporaries knew that some people liked to dream, and even recorded recipes 'to cause marvelous dreames'.[15] Popular sayings reflected a variety of attitudes: all dreams were lies; only those after midnight were true; and 'Dreams go by contraries'.[16] People were interested in dreams. The work of the second-century oneirocritic Artemidorus was immensely popular in early modern times. His book, which explained the meaning of various elements of a dream, was reprinted in English twenty-four times before 1724, although some were sceptical of his theories, deeming them no better than the speculations of 'every weatherwise old wife'.[17] Other dream books included that of Thomas Hill, first published in 1576.[18] More interestingly, some saw dreams as revelatory of the inner being: 'They say dreames declare a mans Temperament', mused Ralph Josselin, as he recollected a shameful dream of his passionate anger.[19]

Contemporaries were often hard pressed to determine the differences between dreams, waking dreams, visions and prophecies. Visionary insights might be perceived as dreams, and the nature of prophecies was complex.[20] Some prophetic dreams were recounted over and over in the context of God's providential care of his people. John Aubrey repeated a story told by John Foxe of how a deacon saved a congregation of 300 Protestants in Mary Tudor's reign by acting upon a providential warning in his dream.[21] During the 1640s and 1650s, when the unnatural conflicts and events were taken as signs of the apocalypse, Mary Pope observed that the dreams which people recounted to their neighbours were frequently given more credit than the Bible.[22]

If contemporaries decided that a dream was of supernatural origin, then the next question was whether it was divine or demonic. If the dream seemed curious, rather than serious, people did not bother too much. But if dreams related to public policies, to monarchs, or to nations, then the source did matter, and to determine whether or not the dream came from God or the Devil, the social status, age and the gender of the dreamer all came into question. Aubrey recorded the dreams of 'persons worthy of Belief' as he thought them remarkable or divine.[23] Adolescent women whose dreams boded ill for the monarch would find themselves in trouble, as did Elizabeth Barton, a young woman who prophesied in rhyming couplets against the marriage of Henry VIII to Anne Boleyn.[24] During the Interregnum, the Fifth Monarchist Anna Trapnel, who prophesied while in a twelve-day trance that the political regime of Oliver Cromwell was a threat to the saints, was imprisoned in Bridewell and cross-examined by the Council of State.[25] The more a dream related to contested political issues, the more likely the dreamer was to be in trouble, irrespective of her social status. Lady Eleanor Davies, for example, who prophesied the death of the Duke of Buckingham, was imprisoned in the Tower.[26]

Men's reactions to their wives' dreams varied. James I was undeterred from a proposed journey by a premonitory dream of his wife's, but the clergyman Ralph Josselin recorded two of his wife's dreams in his diary, together with his own and those of his children. Jane's first dream in 1654 was that they were familiar with the Lord Protector; her second, a few days later, was a complex apocalyptic dream of blazing lights and stars warning of the need to be ready for Christ's second coming. Ralph noted Jane's struggles to interpret her dream: the detail in the dream of flowers from a root 'shee thought of the roote of Jesse, but there were two of them.' Jane feared and trembled, but remembered Christ's mercy. A day later Ralph recorded that Jane was still pondering her dream, observing that they should be ready for Christ's coming.[27]

What did women think of their dreams? Some women believed that their dreams offered an insight into the meaning of their lives. They might record a dream, ponder it over the years, and settle upon an interpretation only retrospectively. A late seventeenth-century gentlewoman, Elizabeth Freke, recorded that she dreamt of falling off a long ladder in her garden. Her dream foretold that she would survive, but 'Live Miserably Till I dyed'. In her autobiography she concluded that her dream was a true prognostic, thereby enhancing her own prophetic status. However, we might suggest that she selected a dream whose symbolism offered her the opportunity to pass a judgement upon her life, in which her sorrows came largely from her unhappy relations with her adult son and heir.[28] Some women shared the widespread view that dreams were a key to self-knowledge, 'whereby', as Sir Thomas Browne observed, 'we may more sensibly understand ourselves'.[29] In 1695, when Mary Mollineux, a Quaker, lay dying, she told the bystanders that she 'had such a Dream, as I have seldom had; *it is an Emblem of my Life*'. She was going beside a broad river. She crossed with difficulties of various kinds until she came to the final breach: 'How shall I get over this Breach? But yet she went on, and passed through it, and it was fair on the other side; and she awakened'. Because she recounted the dream to her husband as a significant parable, he thought that all could learn from it.[30] Mary Mollineux found that the visual images of her dream symbolically represented the meaning of her existence. Through dream metaphors, she represented her life as a passage through dangers to a better, fairer state. Her life-story became the archetype of the Christian soul's journey to God, bearing public witness to her assurance of salvation. Interestingly, in her dream-story of her salvation, gender was comparatively insignificant.

Mary Mollineux's dream was for public knowledge, but other women recorded their dreams for private musing in diaries and autobiographies. Some recounted only a single dream, others many. Katharine Austin, a young London widow, noted several dreams. In 1665, seven years after her husband died, she had a dream that 'ran in my mind divers days afterwards'. She concluded that it was a premonition of a plot to ruin her, an interpretation confirmed when she was summoned to a meeting in the same room, with the same disposition of furniture as she had seen in her dream. At the time, she was engaged in a complex legal struggle with her in-laws in which her own marriage settlement was an issue. Musing upon the common observation that in dreams 'a wedding foretells a burying', she rejected conventional dream lore, concluding instead that 'the business was a wedding, for it was a contract, a confederacy'. Austin found comfort and courage in reworking the dream's details in her waking mind: later she added to her notes that her muff, which she left behind in her dream and returned to collect, was a sign 'I was to be lapped warm'.[31] The gentlewoman Alice Thornton recorded several dreams in her diary, one of which gave her a sign of God's providential care. She dreamt of the bailiff's arrival, and claimed that she was prepared when he appeared the next day. The dream's authenticity and Thornton's own prophetic status were validated by subsequent events.[32]

Dreaming might give access to inner healing power, which was recounted in terms of the special providence of God towards the dreamer. Susannah Arch was cured of leprosy and scurf in her dream. A 1695 pamphlet told of how she pleaded with God, and saw a man standing by her, who laid on his hand, saying 'I will be thou clean'. When she awoke, Susannah perceived that she had been dreaming. Although she grew worse, she was convinced that she would be whole. The pamphlet declared her cure a miracle.[33] Similarly, Joseph Hall's mother dreamed that her troublesome fits would cease. Disconsolate on waking, a minister persuaded her 'that dream was no other than divine'. Hall recorded his mother's dream as a premonition from God.[34]

Many early modern women's dreams focused on their childbearing and relationships with their children. Pregnant women dreamt of their children's futures. Since childbearing was crucial for wives, particularly among the elite, such dreams of mothers-to-be about their progeny were noted by their families. One famous dream was Lady Seymour's, of a nest with nine finches in it. Contemporaries merrily retold this dream which they viewed as prefiguring how many children she would have by the Earl of Winchelsea, whose family name was Finch.[35] Similarly, Aubrey recorded the dream of Archbishop Abbott's mother, who dreamed when she was with child that if she should eat 'a jack' (a small fish), 'her Son in her Belly should be a *Great Man*'.[36] Such dreams could even enhance a woman's reputation for godliness. Pregnant with her second child, Lady Russell had 'a strange kind of divining dream or vision' that this child would be her sole heir. Anne Clifford, who recorded her mother's dream, explained that she had set it down 'because undoubtedly, whilst she lived here in the world, her spirit had more converse with heaven and heavenly contemplation than with terrene and earthly matters'.[37]

Mothers' dreams could be part of family lore, an inheritance to their children, and also a way of inserting themselves into family narratives. Lucy Hutchinson recounted how her mother, pregnant with Lucy, 'dreamt that she was walking in the garden with my father, and that a starre came downe into her hand'. A dream of a daughter's fame was unusual. Perhaps Lucy's mother feared immodesty in offering such a prognostic, for in this case, Lucy's father was the dream's interpreter: the dream 'signified she should have a daughter of some extraordinary eminency'. Lucy's observation on the family tale was that this vain prophecy 'wrought as farre as it could its own accomplishment', a modest way of alluding to her achievements and fame.[38]

Recounting her dream might provide a woman with an opportunity of speaking about a particular subject, a means by which a mother might convey a special message to her child. In 1710 Lady Wentworth wrote to her son of her dreaming life: 'Thees thre nights I have been much happyer then in the days, for I have dreamt I have been with you'.[39] Some of women's most vivid and disturbing dreams were of the deaths of children.[40] Alice Thornton had a frightening dream of lying in childbed with a white sheet spread, which was sprinkled with drops. Her aunt, seeking to reassure her, declared that such dreams were not to be regarded, no doubt echoing the widespread belief that 'dreams go by contraries'.[41] Yet Alice 'kept it in my mind till my child died'.[42] In 1639 Lady Eleanor Davies, a woman whom many recognized as a prophet, recorded a horrible dream from her imprisonment in the Tower. She dreamt of a child's head cut off and women trying to comfort the 'head that cryed'. Subsequently, Lady Eleanor received her daughter Lucy's letter about the death of a child.[43]

A dream might provide a way for a woman to negotiate a family conflict. A Nonconformist daughter, Agnes Beaumont, who was at odds with her father over her attendance at John Bunyan's congregation, had many dreams before her father died, some of which she believed were from God. She dreamed of a tree falling down, which she could not pick up, and implied that the tree was her father whose death was determined.[44] Her sense that God was overseeing her life enabled her to resolve her unhappy situation of being a disobedient daughter; God, who directed that she should attend the separatist congregation, sent her a dream which showed that the fate of her father was in His hands. We might argue that through her dreaming she was able to come to terms with her own unresolved guilt for her defiance of her father.

Dreams confronted women with their own violent emotions and fears. Around 1650 a married woman dreamt of being so angry with her husband's drinking companion that she murdered him. Her own dreaming state provided the answer to the temptation, for into her dreaming mind came the text 'Vengeance is mine, saith the lord'.[45] She interpreted her dream as a salutary warning. Vavasor Powell, who was said to be a great observer of dreams,[46] published this one as a sign that God intervened in daily life. In 1700 Susanna Blandford, a Quaker who was unhappy at some of the divisions within the movement, published 'this Prophetical Dream, which I had many years ago, when I had no thought or suspicion of what is since come to pass'. In her dream, she was with Christian friends, some of whom changed into cruel enemies, who set two or three 'Nasty Dogs at me'. Blandford felt their teeth, but noted they had no power to bite her.[47] Similarly, in the early 1690s the Lord responded to Joan Whitrowe, a defector from the Quakers, who was worried about Queen Mary. Whitrowe dreamt that the Queen was on the ground, with her servants on top of her: 'I was given to understand, she was under them, and them over her; and therefore could not do what her Pious Heart was Inclined to'. For a period of over six months, Whitrowe enjoyed 'Visions and Revelations' night and day and was 'in Unity with the whole of creation'.[48]

Emotional insights might come from dreams. In the reign of Elizabeth, Lady Magdalen, Viscountess Montague, found that the fines imposed for her Catholicism were ruining her family, so that she fell into 'an extreme, and continuall griefe and affliction of mind'. God, however, had compassion upon her, as she told her confessor, 'For in a dreame (as she particularly related unto me) it was clearly and manifestly demonstrated unto her, what she should do to be freed of her inward grief'. After she performed the pious action as directed, she was immediately calmed, and declared that 'she had learned that God worketh all things for our good'.[49]

A dream could justify a woman in a course of action she knew that her contemporaries would think questionable. Since a good woman was ideally silent, publishing a book or speaking out were not usually approved. Nevertheless, in her publication of 1611 reflecting upon the passion of Christ, Aemilia Lanyer explained 'to the doubtfull [hesitating] Reader' that they should 'know for certaine, that it [the title] was delivered unto me in sleepe many yeares before I had any intent to write in this maner'. The dream, she wrote, went out of her memory till she wrote of the passion of Christ 'and thinking it a significant token, that I was appointed to performe this Worke, I gave the very same words I received in sleepe as the fittest title I could devise for this Booke, *Salve Deus Rex Iudeorum*' (Hail, O God, King of the Jews). Lanyer's collection of poems included 'Eve's apology in defence of women'.[50]

Catholic Englishwomen as well as Protestants found in their dreams justifications of unorthodox actions. In 1624, when the English Benedictine convent of nuns at Ghent was in financial trouble, a lay sister, Catherine Matlock, had a dream of how the nuns might survive by making and selling silk flowers. Although enclosure made such economic activity questionable, in the dream she was instructed in how to make the flowers by an old man in a garden, whom she identified as St Augustine, her patron. Augustine told her 'that to fullfil her earnest wish and Desire, he would teach her ho[w] to Imprint those leaves in Silk work, Instantly Derecting her in all perticulars. Awaking therefore she retain'd this in memory, And the next day printed them as we See in practice to this Day amongst us, teaching all her art in this kind the revend Dames of the quire'. The nuns worked in shifts, selling the flowers for up to £30 per consignment to a local merchant.[51]

Accounts of religious dreams were more likely to survive than any others, for they were both more common and more highly valued.[52] Religious dreams ranged from the simple didactic, which warned women to amend their lives, to complex and even mystical dreams in which the dreamer was at one with the divine. A preacher recounted a maid-servant's warning dream for its obvious moral message. The young woman fell asleep in church, and imagined herself walking, when two ways presented themselves to her, one leading by a great fire, and the other by the church: 'she awakened with this application of her dream, she had been wont to sleep much at Church, and if she did not amend that fault, she must expect no other but hell fire'.[53] Margaret Grey, who became a Benedictine nun at Ghent in 1631, received her vocation in a dream. Enjoying a life of pleasure in her youth, her dream showed her a list of sins she had forgotten to confess. She did not immediately abandon her old ways, but one night when she was dancing, God called her to the cloister. This time, she acted, 'making no Delay, having her former vision, or Dream as she called it afresh represented to her memory, she presently prepared for her Journey and Came to Ghent'.[54]

Vivid dreams confirmed a woman's sense that Christ was really present with her. Sometimes the dream's content was both physical and symbolic. An anonymous woman's conversion narrative told of her slumber 'in which Christ seemed to appear to me, with his breast open, and Blood issuing out as Water from a Fountain'. She awoke and found soul and body refreshed as with a rich cordial.[55] Sara Wight, a member of a separatist congregation in the 1640s, had a terrifying dream or vision in which she was rescued by 'one like the appearance of a man. He came, and took me in his armes'.[56] Interesting, too, is the sensuous quality of the recollections. In January 1680 Anne Bathurst, a later seventeenth-century prophet linked with the visionary Jane Lead, saw Christ in a dream or vision 'in a figure like a Man, wth his legs of white beryl-stone'.[57] Mary Pennington, a Quaker, later in her life recorded an early dream of Christ as 'a fresh lovely youth, clad in grey cloth (at which time I had not heard of a Quaker or their habit) very plain and neat'.[58]

Sometimes the dream was so graphic it seemed to the dreamer a vision, in the sense of a divine foretelling, and enhanced the woman's status with others. The Reverend R. Roach, another follower of the visionary Jane Lead, recorded the example of a woman at Utrecht who dreamt that the glow-worms she had gathered on a fan would go out. The dreamer 'expostulated with my self wether it might not be a Dream but the plainness of ye Object convinced me I was awake that it must be a Reall Vision'. She interpreted her dream as a sign that the religious leader Jane Lead would soon die, and the world would be darkened.[59]

The sexual dreams of Lady Magdalen Montague, an Elizabethan Catholic, seem so unfamiliar in their conceptualization of desire as to make Freud seem both spot-on and irrelevant. According to her confessor, Lady Magdalen, having vowed herself to widowhood after her husband's death, never felt the 'rebellion of the flesh' which provoked her mind to lust. If the enemy did suggest something to her soul 'whereto her flesh did not allure her', she rejected it from her waking mind and spat; but if she was asleep, when reason had no power to aid her, 'yet did her body so strive and labour to expell that filthy suggestion, that it awakened her mind, after which the victory was easy'.[60] To interpret Lady Magdalen's dream of sexual temptation as revealing the workings of a psyche free from trammels of conscious will seems misguided, because body, mind and soul are clearly understood by contemporaries in a different relationship from that defined by Descartes later and on which so much psychoanalytic thought depends. Yet why, we might ask, was she dreaming of sex if not tempted?

Dreams can offer access to some of the more difficult historical questions about the respective roles of ideology and physical and material circumstances in shaping individual consciousness. I would argue that if women shared a similar cultural world to men, they experienced it differently. To substantiate this from a comparative analysis of the dreams of men and women is beyond the scope of this chapter. Briefly, I would suggest that some of women's dreams reflect their specific experiences of birth and lactation; and that the social restrictions upon their having a public voice means that dream stories had a more significant role in their daily lives, because they could present themselves as a medium for a message, a prophetic voice, or a visionary. Dreams were of more *use* to women than they were to men.

What would we have if dreams were our only source about women's lives? At the most basic level, we could take recorded dreams as fragments of evidence about lives and thoughts, reflecting women's concerns and preoccupations. In my view these dream narratives demonstrate how far religious belief and language were at the core of women's being. We can see in this evidence the extent to which women were preoccupied with life, death, sickness, salvation and wholeness. We could say that dreams gave a woman access to her own knowledge that had not yet emerged into her waking consciousness, although we know that she would speak of this in terms of divine guidance. Because of gendered social prohibitions, such knowledge could not easily emerge in other ways.

Ultimately dream stories provided women with an opportunity to experience their wishes and fears. As an avenue to self-knowledge, dreams offered ideas to ponder, actions to contemplate and imaginings that extended women's daily lives. For us as historians, dreams offer a continuing puzzle over their emblematic or symbolic meaning. Dreams offer insights about the sameness and differences between early modern people and ourselves, and another way into questions about how individuals and society relate to each other.

NOTES AND REFERENCES

My thanks to Laura Gowing, Sara Mendelson, Philippa Maddern and Lyndal Roper, for many conversations about early modern women; to Barbara Todd and Claire Walker, who contributed to my collection of dreams; to Jane Long, Maureen Perkins, Laura and Lyndal for comments on drafts; and to the London Women's History Group for their suggestions.

 1 M. Cavendish, for example, wrote prose fictions in which she was the central heroine, loved and admired by all; S. H. Mendelson, *The Mental World of Stuart Women: Three Studies*, Brighton, 1987, pp. 34–61.
 2 See N. Z. Davis, *Fiction in the Archives. Pardon Tales and Their Tellers in Sixteenth-Century France*, Stanford, CA, 1987, pp. 1–6.
 3 S. R. F. Price, 'The future of dreams: From Freud to Artemidorus', *Past and Present* 113, 1986, pp. 3–37; S. J. Greenblatt, 'Psychoanalysis and Renaissance culture', in his *Learning to Curse: Essays in Early Modern Culture*, London, 1990, pp. 131–145.
 4 Anne Bathurst, Bodleian Library, Oxford, MS Rawlinson D 1263, f. 1.
 5 O. Feltham, *Resolves*, London, 1709, p. 125.
 6 A. Macfarlane, *The Family Life of Ralph Josselin: A Seventeenth-Century Clergyman*, Cambridge, 1970, pp. 183–187.

7 P. Burke, 'L'histoire sociale des rêves', *Annales* 28, 1973, pp. 329–42; C. S. Hall, 'What people dream about', *Scientific American* May 1951, pp. 60–63.
8 C. Carlton, 'The dream life of Archbishop Laud', *History Today* 36, 1986, pp. 9–15.
9 K. V. Thomas, *Religion and the Decline of Magic: Studies in Popular Beliefs in Sixteenth and Seventeenth Century England*, London, 1971, pp. 128–132.
10 R. L. Kagan, *Lucretia's Dreams: Politics and Prophecy in Sixteenth-Century Spain*, Berkeley, CA, 1990.
11 M. Perkins, 'The meaning of dream books', in this volume.
12 Thomas, *Religion and the Decline of Magic*, pp. 128–132.
13 Levinus Lemnius, *The Secret Miracles of Nature*, London, 1658, pp. 140–141.
14 Notebooks of Richard Napier, in P. Crawford and L. Gowing, *Women's Worlds in England, 1580–1720: A Sourcebook*, London, 1999, section 10, 'Mental worlds', pp. 277–278.
15 Folger Shakespeare Library, Washington, MS V. a. 140 (1587), f. 12v.
16 M. P. Tilley, *A Dictionary of the Proverbs in England in the Sixteenth and Seventeenth Centuries*, Ann Arbor, MI, 1950, D585–591.
17 Price, 'The Future of Dreams', p. 32; T. Nashe quoted in M. Weidhorn, *Dreams in Seventeenth-Century English Literature*, The Hague, 1970, p. 41.
18 T. Hill, *The Most Pleasaunt Arte of the Interpretation of Dreames*, London, 1576, included over 100 dreams, and was reprinted several times.
19 *The Diary of Ralph Josselin 1616–1683* (ed. A. Macfarlane), London, 1976, p. 20 (12 Sept. 1644).
20 Thomas, *Religion and the Decline of Magic*, pp. 128–132; P. Mack, *Visionary Women. Ecstatic Prophecy in Seventeenth-Century England*, Berkeley, CA, 1992, p. 375 and throughout.
21 J. Aubrey, *Miscellanies*, London, 1696, pp. 49–50.
22 Mary Pope, *Heare, heare, heare, heare, A Word or a Message from heaven*, London (Jan.) 1649, p. 31.
23 Aubrey, *Miscellanies*, p. 45.
24 P. Crawford, *Women and Religion in England 1500–1720*, London, 1993, pp. 28–29; S. L. Jansen, *Dangerous Talk and Strange Behaviour: Women and Popular Resistance to the Reforms of Henry VIII*, London, 1996, pp. 41–56; D. Watt, *Secretaries of God: Women Prophets in Late Medieval and Early Modern England*, Cambridge, 1997, pp. 51–80.
25 A. Trapnel, *The Cry of a Stone*, London (1655), pp. 13–14; *Anna Trapnels Report and Plea. Or, a Narrative of her Journey from London into Cornwall*, London, 1654.
26 Quoted in E. S. Cope, *Handmaid of the Holy Spirit: Never Soe Mad a Ladie*, Ann Arbor, MI, 1992, p. 22.
27 Thomas, *Religion and the Decline of Magic*, p. 128; *Diary of Ralph Josselin*, pp. 333–334.
28 *Mrs Elizabeth Freke her Diary*, Cork, 1913, p. 55.
29 Sir Thomas Browne, *On Dreams*, Norwich, 1929, pp. 9–10. Thomas Tryon regarded dreams in infancy as meaningful; *Memoirs of the Life of Mr Thomas Tryon*, London, 1705, p. 9.
30 M. Mollineux, *Fruits of Retirement*, London, 1702, sig. B 2.
31 'Katherine Austien', ed. B. Todd, in V. Frith (ed.), *Women and History: Voices of Early Modern England*, Toronto, 1995, pp. 229–230, 232–233. Austin's manuscript is in the British Library, Additional MS 4454.
32 *The Autobiography of Mrs Alice Thornton* (ed. C. Jackson), Surtees Society, 62 (1875), pp. 136–137.
33 *A relation of the miraculous cure of Susannah Arch*, London, 1695, p. 14.
34 J. Hall, *Works* (ed. P. Wynter), Oxford, 1863, vol. 1, p. xxi.
35 J. Aubrey, *Miscellanies* (2nd edn), London, 1721, p. 59.
36 Ibid., p. 58.
37 *Lives of Lady Anne Clifford, Pembroke and Montgomery (1590–1676) and of her parents summarized by her self* (ed. J. P. Gibson), Roxburghe Club, 1916, p. 24.

38 *Memoirs of the Life of Colonel Hutchinson* (ed. James Sutherland), Oxford, 1973, p. 287.
39 J. J. Cartwright (ed.), *The Wentworth Papers, 1705–1739*, London, 1823, p. 148.
40 Women did also dream of fires and murders. Richard Baxter noted that his wife Margaret's dreams of fires and murders 'workt half as dangerously on her as realities'; S. Clark, *A Collection of the Lives of Ten Eminent Divines*, London, 1662, p. 190.
41 Tilley, *Proverbs*, D 585.
42 Thornton, *Autobiography*, p. 123.
43 Quoted in Cope, *Handmaid of the Holy Spirit*, p. 22.
44 *The Narrative of the Persecution of Agnes Beaumont in 1674* (ed. G. B. Harrison), London, 1929, pp. 8–10.
45 V. Powell, *Spiritual Experiences of Sundry Believers*, London, [6 Jan.] 1653, pp. 168–170.
46 Aubrey, *Miscellanies*, 1721, p. 66.
47 S[usanna] B[landford], *A Small Treatise Writ by One of the True Christian Faith*, London, 1700, pp. 4–5.
48 J. Whitrowe, *Faithful Warnings*, London, 1697, pp. 20–22, 70–80.
49 R. Smith, *The Life of the Most Honourable and Virtuous Lady, the La. Magdalen, Viscountesse Montague*, London, 1627, p. 34.
50 A. Lanyer, *Salve Deus Rex Iudaeorum. Containing, the Passion of Christ*, London, 1611, sig.[Ii v.].
51 'Obituary notices of the English Benedictine nuns of Ghent in Flanders . . . , 1627–1811', *Miscellanea XI, Catholic Record Society* 19, London, 1917, pp. 50–51. Thanks to Claire Walker for this reference.
52 S. Mendelson, 'Stuart women's diaries and occasional memoirs', in M. Prior (ed.), *Women in English Society, 1500–1800*, London, 1985, p. 185.
53 J. Angier, *An Helpe to Better Hearts*, 1647, in E. Axon (ed.), *Oliver Heywood's Life of John Angier of Denton*, Chetham Society, 97, 1937, p. 150.
54 'Obituary notices of the English Benedictine nuns', pp. 25–26.
55 *Conversion exemplified*, London, 1669, p. 19.
56 S. Wight, *The exceeding riches of grace, advanced by the spirit of grace in an empty nothing creature*, London, 1647, p. 149.
57 Anne Bathurst, Writings, Bodleian Library, MS Rawlinson D 1262, f. 66.
58 M. Penington, *A brief account of my exercises from my childhood*, Philadelphia, 1848, p. 9.
59 Papers of Reverend R. Roach, Bodleian Library, MS Rawlinson D 833, ff. 90–90v.
60 Smith, *Life of Magdalen, Viscountess Montague*, pp. 20–21.

Chapter 6

Samuel Taylor Coleridge and 'The pains of sleep'

Jennifer Ford

> ... the night's dismay
> Saddened and stunned the coming day.
> Sleep, the wide blessing, seemed to me
> Distemper's worst calamity.
> The third night, when my own loud scream
> Had waked me from the fiendish dream,
> O'ercome with sufferings strange and wild,
> I wept as I had been a child.
> Coleridge, 'The Pains of Sleep'

The poet Samuel Taylor Coleridge (1772–1834) frequently wrote on the subject of dreams and dreaming. His three greatest poems, *The Rime of Ancient Mariner*, 'Kubla Khan', and 'Christabel', all have dreams as a thematic concern. He was a vivid and prolific dreamer who carefully recorded, analysed and discussed the distinct features, possible causes and meanings of his dreams. He turned to a wide range of British, German and French writers, discussing the subject with friends who were poets, scientists, doctors and philosophers; he read both contemporary and ancient dream writers; and he gave a lecture (in March 1818) on the related topics of dreams, witchcraft and mesmerism. He also planned to write an 'entire work' on the subject but never arranged his copious fragmentary writings into one volume. Some of his major thoughts on dreams are expressed in his poetry, notably in the small volume entitled *Christabel*, published in 1816, which included the dream-vision poem, 'Kubla Khan', the unfinished 'Christabel' and the short poem on nightmares, 'The Pains of Sleep'. All three poems reveal key ideas on Coleridge's thinking on dreams and dreaming. However, it was in *'The Pains of Sleep'* that he most poignantly articulated how a 'fiendish crowd/Of shapes and thoughts' so tortured him in his dreams that he feared to fall asleep each night.[1] This poem, written in 1803 but not published until 1816, expresses Coleridge's views on the origin of dreams:

that the dreamer's body acts and is acted upon in intricate ways during dreaming states, and that dreams are caused by external creatures that enter the dreamer's mind.

While borrowing and learning from his contemporaries, Coleridge also undertook personal study and analysed his own experiences to create his particular approach to dreaming phenomena. Coleridge's approach to his dreams was representative of his age but also influenced by his own intelligence and independent scholarship. Despite his considerable reading and experience of dreaming phenomena, Coleridge never claimed that he had developed a general explanatory theory.[2] His opinions on dreaming changed and shifted in emphasis over the course of his lifetime: as new scientific trends emerged (such as animal magnetism), or new medical theories were debated, so too did Coleridge's study of dreams broaden to consider their possible impact on his understanding. That such wide-ranging fields of intellectual inquiry had relevance for understanding dreams perhaps seems odd in the early twenty-first century: however, in the eighteenth century dreams were considered variously as philosophical occurrences, as links to literary inspiration, as physical events, and as portents of divine significance and personal meaning. New ways of understanding the world were highly relevant to probing the dark mysteries of somnial activity. Even complex linguistic pursuits apparently provided Coleridge with greater ability to analyse what he believed to be the many differing languages of his dreams.[3]

Coleridge was often frustrated by the continual perplexity of his dreams and he never claimed that he had solved their riddles. In 1827, at the age of fifty-seven, he wrote to a friend that he had resolved the mysteries of natural philosophy but was unable to 'solve the problem' of his own dreams. Despite considering the causes of his dreams over many years, he was incapable, he concluded 'of explaining any one Figure of all the numberless Personages of this Shadowy world'.[4] Part of the perplexity of dreams is that the experience is quintessentially private. To write, record and discuss dreams is to remain captive within their internal, uncertain frameworks. Coleridge faced this problem as he attempted to analyse and record his own dreams objectively whilst being aware of their inescapably subjective nature. Hints of his struggles to understand dreams emerge in some of his poetry; however, it is the explorations in his private diary writings and fragmentary essays that best reveal his intellectual independence and his ability to draw from diverse and often contrary approaches to dreams.[5]

The importance of dreams in Romantic poetry and philosophy has often been noted.[6] Dreams were frequently seen as embodying imaginative power. Potentially visionary mediums, dreams were utilized in a number of major poems as dramatic devices or to hint at a future ominous event. Dreams had featured heavily in earlier poetry, especially during the middle ages; and although their use had declined by the second half of the eighteenth century, several major writers still included dreams within their oeuvre.[7] Coleridge was perceived by his contemporaries as a poet with a special and significant knowledge of dreams: his disposition was described by one observer as 'more abstract and dreamy' than any other of his generation.[8] To many of the second generation of Romantic poets, Coleridge was 'a good-natured wizard, very fond of earth, but able to conjure his aetherialities about him in the twinkling of an eye'.[9] Thomas De Quincey described him as a poet, a philosopher, an opium-eater, a prolific dreamer: a man whose poetry was 'shrouded in mystery – supernatural – like the "ancient Mariner" – *awfully sublime*'.[10] In short, Coleridge was a poet doubly blessed: his intimate knowledge of the theory and experience of dreams indicated his poetic prowess, and he also *looked* as though he was a great dreamer.[11]

In the late eighteenth and early nineteenth century divergent opinions as to the origin and meaning of dreams proliferated in an astounding array of medical, philosophical and poetical writings. Dreams and dreaming were topics that attracted intense scrutiny and vibrant conversational exchange. At Coleridge's Thursday evening dinners, during the years he lived with Dr and Mrs John Gillman on the fringes of London in Highgate (1816–34), the dreams of guests would be discussed in detail as well as dreams attributed to the famous and dreams described in novels and treatises.[12] It was widely believed that dreams revealed the powers of the imagination and that dreaming was a form of poetic inspiration.[13] Others argued that dreams were entirely attributable to the dreamer's physical or psychological constitution. Some authors steadfastly maintained a belief in the prophetic and divine nature of dreams,[14] or proclaimed that the only useful thing about them was that they might 'serve to exercise the faculties and improve the temper of the mind'.[15] Dreams were classified: the 'nightmare' (or *incubus*) was described in one of the earliest British dream treatises as a dream caused by 'difficult respiration, a violent oppression of the breast, and a total privation of voluntary motion'.[16] The bewildering nature of dreams and dreaming was no closer to being explained but, increasingly, it was the process of dreaming that fascinated those who wrote on the topic. What was discussed and debated in Coleridge's circles and their counterparts at the time was not the interpretation of dreams but their origins and their particularities, such as the persons or events encountered.

The mechanical and associationistic explanations of dreams offered, for instance, by John Locke (1632–1704), David Hartley (1705–57) or George Berkeley (1685–1753) came increasingly to be perceived as unsatisfactory and in need of challenge. Interest in the forces and features of psychic life was growing, along with thinking that pointed towards the early twentieth-century identification of the 'unconscious' mind, especially the notion that there are parts of consciousness and of identity that are unknown, hidden and dynamic.[17] The development of empiricism, primarily through the works of Immanuel Kant (1724–1804) and David Hume (1711–1776), also cast significant doubts on whether the five senses could ensure an accurate perception of the world outside the self, or indeed even of the self.[18] A major component of this scepticism took the form of various speculations into the nature and origins of dreams and into broader questions about the nature of fundamental life processes including sleeping, waking, digestion and disease. A startling array of treatises and scholarly dissertations on dreaming appeared, in medical as often as in philosophical texts. Physicians throughout the eighteenth and early nineteenth centuries (unlike their late twentieth-century equivalents) often included discussion of nightmares, dreams and visions in their wider treatises, as part of the broad domain of medical inquiry, not as a specialized discipline.[19]

Medical works that contained discussions of dreams usually paid close attention to bodily processes and the possible links between those processes and psychological or intellectual states. The physician William Buchan (1729–1805), for example, cited heavy meals too close to bedtime as a cause of bad dreams:

> That light suppers cause sound sleep is true even to a proverb. Many persons, if they exceed the least at that meal, are sure to have uneasy nights: and, if they fall asleep, the load and oppression on their stomach and spirits occasion frightful dreams, broken and disturbed repose, the night-mare, &c. Were the same persons to go to bed with a light supper, or sit up till that meal was pretty well digested, they would enjoy sound sleep, and rise refreshed and cheerful.[20]

This explanation emphasizes the role of the body's digestive processes, rather than the dreamer's psyche or self, as an influence on strange and wonderful or terrifying images and feelings experienced during sleep. The remedy for nightmares and other manifestations of 'disturbed repose' is simple: a light supper must be eaten, so that the contents of the meal can be thoroughly digested before sleeping. Such ideas were not exclusive to physicians. Thomas Hobbes (1588–1679) had already much earlier observed that dreams could be generated from sensations of appetite or aversion to pain, and that 'cold doth in the same manner generate fear in those that sleep, and causeth them to dream of ghosts, and to have phantasms of horror and danger'.[21] The philosopher David Hartley (1705–57) argued that the body's position in sleep 'suggests such ideas, amongst those that have been lately impressed, as are most suitable to the various kinds and degrees of pleasant and painful vibrations excited in the stomach, brain, or some other part'.[22] For the physician Erasmus Darwin (1731–1802) in the 1790s, the cause of dreams lay in the workings of the arterial and glandular systems, and the internal senses of hunger, thirst and lust. Nightmares were caused by indigestion. All of these physiological systems 'are not only occasionally excited in our sleep, but their irritative motions are succeeded by their usual sensation, and make a part of the farrago of our dreams'.[23] In his *Elements of the Philosophy of the Human Soul* (1791), Dugald Stewart (1753–1828) argued that the will, or volition, was suspended in sleep and that the powers of association were most strongly evident in processes of dreaming, while the celebrated surgeon, John Hunter (1728–93), claimed that dreams are 'always independent of the relative connexion between body and mind'. This 'perfect' independence allowed the mind to 'distinguish perfectly what is sensation and what is only thought, without which all would be a dream'.[24]

Coleridge's readings in philosophy, literature, the life sciences and in theories of life readily complemented his interest in dreams and dreaming processes. When in Germany between March and June, 1799, he attended Blumenbach's 'delightful' lectures on physiology and natural history, and later his 1816 essay, 'Theory of Life', was a lengthy discussion of topical scientific and philosophical ideas on the subject.[25] The 'life science' debates that raged throughout the Romantic period encompassed argument about phrenology, mesmerism, physiogonomy and electrical experiments. Coleridge read influential works from Britain, Germany and France, by John Brown (1735–88), John Hunter, Albrecht von Haller (1708–77) and Marie François Bichat (1771–1802). These writers were at the frontier of new theories of physiology, anatomy, mind-body relations and life itself.

In both Germany and Britain, debates concerning the nature of life had immense impact across many intellectual debates and fields of enquiry. Studies of psychological and physiological life processes were eagerly pursued, and dreams were studied as instances of both psychological and physiological life processes. The theories expounded by the Scottish physician John Brown caused especially widespread and acrimonious debate in medical, theological and political arenas: argument became so intense in Germany in 1802 that riot almost ensued.[26] Brown had argued that life exists only as a response to external influences, and although initially (in the late 1790s) intrigued, Coleridge quickly became dissatisfied with this simplistic approach. He later spoke of the 'Brunonian' system as a 'false theory', and by 1807 had repudiated its 'tyranny of the mechanic system in physiology'.[27]

Brown argued that dreams were illustrations of involuntary excitability, certainly not instances of divine intervention nor of left-over thoughts from a tiring day. According to Coleridge, Brown and other supporters of the excitability theory treated dreams and dreaming slightly and superficially, explaining the process merely as illustrations of external sensory phenomena. Even Coleridge's friend, the respected Bristol physician and scientist Thomas Beddoes (1760–1808), whose ideas were well known to the poet, had stressed the role of excitement upon the nervous system during sleeping states.[28] Another prominent subscriber to materialist physiology, Albrecht von Haller, citing physiological principles, couched his explanation of the origin of dreams and sleep in terms of the sensitivity of organs and nerves to external events:

> dreams we judge to be rather referable to disease, or to some stimulating cause that interrupts the perfect rest of the sensorium. Hence we see, that intense cares of the mind, or the strong impression of some violent idea received in the memory, hard indigestible food, abounding, in its quantity, with any uneasy posture of the body, are the most usual causes that excite dreams.[29]

In this argument the entire human body was physiologically linked, even in sleep, and the actions of the digestive system could cause dreams. External sensations impinged upon the sleeping brain and caused dreams as well as disease. Dreams, then, according to von Haller, were involuntary productions of an unstimulated nervous system. Restful sleep was attained when there were no external sensations and consequently no dreams. Brown argued that sleep was the result of decreasing excitement upon the nervous system: sleep is the point where the 'degree of excitement, necessary to constitute the waking state, no longer exists'. Dreams were evidence that a small degree of excitement was reaching the nervous system.[30] These theories of dreams as dependent on excitement or stimulation of the nervous system aroused intense interest in medical circles, and were discussed in terms of other general questions surrounding the nature of life processes.[31] From such discussions and through his reading, Coleridge may have concluded that dreams were another illustration of the remarkably complex way in which the human body responds to stimulation or irritation.

While Coleridge was well aware of physiological approaches to dreams, his own particular bodily experiences added a complex dimension to his response to them. Throughout his lifetime he suffered from many different kinds of illnesses, often opium-related: resulting either from his continued use of the drug or his efforts to stop taking it. In May 1801, he complained of weeks of:

> blood-shot eyes & swoln Eyelids ... followed by large Boils in my neck & shoulders – these by Rheumatic Fever – this by a distressing & tedious Hydrocele – & since then by irregular Gout, which promises at this moment to ripen into a legitimate Fit.[32]

Thirty years later, he described the daily experience of his body as one of pain and discomfort:

> After a disturbed Doze was forced to get up, a little before 1, having retired in prayer for rather than in hope of Rest, a little after 10,

Monday Night – & soon after obliged to call up the servant – & from this time till near 9 this morning – O misery. [. . .] the sharp scream – [. . .] pain in the right-Shoulder, & so down to the knees had converted into pain and miserable sensation . . . looseness in the lower Bowels, aching across the umbilical region & distressful Sickness at the Stomach, and confusion in the Head.[33]

There was no possible refuge from the onslaught of these kinds of pain, and sleep itself became impossible. Dreams became manifestations of this painful body, a body that, for hour upon hour, ached across the stomach and had shooting pains in the shoulder. 'Damnable' dreams followed ingestions of 'mercurial purgatives', intended to relieve various sufferings, and those dreams were always characterized by a strong pressure and uncomfortable sensation around the umbilical region.[34]

What particularly perplexed Coleridge was that the sensation of pain in dreams seemed to be qualitatively different to the sensation of pain experienced while awake. The imposition of the body during dreaming states varied, depending on the state of consciousness:

This astonishing multiplication of Pain into itself, in dreams, – I do not understand it. This Evening sleeping I – for the first time I recollect, had a most intolerable sense of *Pain* as *Pain*, without affright or disgustful Ideas – a sense of an excruciating patience-mocking Rheumatism in my right arm . . . the astonishing difference in the degrees of the Pain felt or supposed when asleep & when awaked.[35]

Coleridge becomes even more aware of his body, because the pain experienced is multiplied, purified. His comment that there was an 'astonishing difference in the degrees of the Pain felt or supposed when asleep & when awaked' helps to explain why sleeping and dreaming became such terrifying experiences, psychologically as well as physically. In particular, nightmares had the potential to become physical realities. Pain seemed to be even more intense because experienced without 'affright or disgustful Ideas'. It was a purified pain, a pain so different to anything previously experienced that the language employed to express it must also be purified: 'pain as pain', not pain which is 'like' a hot burn or 'like' a dull ache. He remarked to friends in numerous letters that he feared sleep. To Thomas Wedgwood, for instance, in September 1803, he wrote, that he struggled to remain awake;[36] and to Sir George and Lady Beaumont he wrote of staying up late, reading, 'from the *dread* of falling asleep . . . from being literally afraid to trust myself again out of the leading-strings of my Will & Reason'.[37]

It was no wonder that he dreaded falling asleep: the pains of sleep were often worse than the pains of waking life:

> ... when the dream of night
> Renews the phantom to my sight,
> Cold sweat-drops gather on my limbs;
>   My ears throb with horrid tumult swims;
>   Wild is the tempest of my heart
> And my thick and struggling breath
> Imitates the toil of death.[38]

The constrained breathing and throbbing ears were characteristic of the nightmare. Sleep became a physical catalogue of discomfort and terror: the extremely accessible image of the 'cold sweat-drops' provides a contrasted physical immediacy to the potential quietude and rest of sleep. The nature of the somnial disease was perceived as both moral and physical, so that Coleridge felt himself 'afflicted' in every possible way.[39]

Coleridge drew strong connections between his dream life and his (diseased) bodily life. The gastric system in dreams was 'especially' singled out, and the ganglionic system seen as attaining 'paramouncy' over the brain (the 'cerebral') while he was sleeping. He also noted that certain feelings in dreams, such as guilt and falsehood, could be 'traced to the Gastric Life'. Referring to his own 'Pains of Sleep', he offered further proof of the important influence of his body in his dreams. The liver '&c' were the organic source of the 'life-stifling fear, soul-stifling shame' of the 'Pains of Sleep'.

The figuring of his body in dreams, especially of particular organs such as the liver or the nervous ganglionic system, is one of the most unusual and complex features of Coleridge's investigation into the nature of his dreaming life. While he certainly was not original in noticing the role of the body in dreams – many contemporaries had also done so – his particular bodily experiences and his wide readings in medical and scientific areas convinced him that dynamic and interactive physiological processes occurred during sleeping states. He readily discerned that his dreams were caused by some form of bodily (dys)function or that sometimes the mere awareness of bodily parts was sufficient to cause a particular type of dream: the effect of posture,[40] or of the digestive system and rectum. In a letter of June 1809, to Daniel Stuart, he observed the role of the digestive system in the formation of certain types of dreams, referring to the frightening prospect of a 'desperate experiment of abandoning all at once' his opium usage. While recognizing that opium had contributed to his suffering, he added: 'Sleep or even a supine Posture does not fail to remind me that something is organically amiss in some one or other of the Contents of the Abdomen'.[41] This offers convincing proof that the mind is 'never perhaps wholly uninformed of the circumstantia in Sleep'.[42] The posture of the body was not the sole determining factor in the formation of dream characters and events: pressing the thigh, or any slight alteration in body position or feeling could also cause a change in the dream's character, irrespective of whether it was day-dream or nightmare.[43] One of the earliest mentions of the possibility of dreams being caused by the body is in a May 1804 notebook entry:

> A really important Hint suggested itself to me, as I was falling into my first Sleep – the effect of the posture of the Body, *open mouth* for instance, on first Dreams – & perhaps on all. White Teeth in behind a dim open mouth of a dim face – /My Mind is not vigorous enough to pursue it –[44]

Coleridge implies here that we dream many times every night, and that each occurrence will be influenced in a slightly different manner by the body, depending on when the dream occurs. The face is of primary importance in this entry. Coleridge had complained of being 'desperately sick, ill, abed', possibly as a result of taking rhubarb. If it is assumed that the rhubarb was taken orally, then the open mouth in this entry had its origin in a physical activity prior to falling asleep, and led into the dream of 'white teeth in behind . . . open mouth of a dim face'. Admitting that his mind was 'not vigorous enough' to pursue the effects of the body's posture on dreams, Coleridge allowed his supposedly inadequate intellect to prevent him pursuing such associations – or to provide a convenient excuse to opt out of a complex problem.

Nevertheless, Coleridge was deeply concerned with the problem of how an awareness of the body could enter into the imaginative activity of his dreams. The body is said to 'act sometimes' in an imaginative realm, powerfully 'suggesting' how objects are positioned. Body and dream object are both said to be postured such that what is experienced in the dream and what the body is aware of are one and the same.

Coleridge's notion of self was closely connected and combined with 'bodily sensations' [45] He believed that his entire health was 'so intimately connected' with the state of his spirits, and these again 'so dependent' on his thoughts, that it was impossible at times to distinguish between a bodily pain originating in an organic disturbance, and a bodily pain originating in an emotional response.[46] All that is subjective and defines the self – 'myself', Coleridge believed, 'connect[s] & combine[s] with . . . bodily sensations'. He may well be using 'sensations' in at least two different yet related applications: as both a mental feeling and also the physical faculty of perceiving by means of the senses – through touch, hearing, sight, and so on.

It is not merely that the feelings both connected and combined with the bodily sensations, but also that they appeared to be distinct from the self: 'Certain Trains of Feeling acted, *on me*, underneath my own *Consciousness*'.[47] Coleridge became a passive instrument, as was often the case in his dreams. In dreams, both body and mind are seen as acting 'underneath' consciousness. The particular processes by which the feelings and the body connect and combine convinced Coleridge that both body and sensibility are diseased. It was the diseasing of both sensibility and body that he perceived to be the cause of many dreams.

Coleridge partly explained his own passivity in his dreams through what he termed the spirit theory.[48] In 'The Pains of Sleep', lamenting why such horrid visions and creatures 'fall' on him,[49] he is unable to determine if he acts or is acted upon. Much of the terror of his nightly pains of sleep lies in his inability to determine why the visions are experienced by a man who has not a nature 'deepliest stained with sin'. To understand why Coleridge's confusion and perceived passivity were so great, we must turn to one of the writers on dreams most widely read and debated in Coleridge's lifetime, Andrew Baxter (1686–1750). His particular influence has been clearly traced in Coleridge's poetry and other writings.[50] In his *Enquiry into the Nature of the Human Soul* (1737), Baxter argued that dreams were not the product of the mind or of the soul. Scenes and visions experienced in a dream were offered to the soul by external spiritual beings who had gained access to the dreamer's sleeping consciousness. Because the body was resting, these spirits were able to enter the soul with relative ease, and had substantial, if not complete, control over the senses. Part of the mystery of dreams has always been their novelty: how is it that one can dream of things never before seen, or people never before encountered? Baxter's concept of dream-spirits explained this. Dreams presented to the soul during sleep were both strange and new, sometimes disturbing and frightening. The soul could never be without consciousness of acting or creating, neither could it willingly frighten itself. The dream visions must, therefore, originate from outside the soul: 'there must be living Beings existing separate from matter . . . they act in that state, that they act upon the matter of our bodies, and prompt our sleeping visions'.[51]

In a letter dated December 1803, Coleridge lamented:

> the Horrors of my Sleep, and Night-screams (so loud & so frequent as to make me almost a Nuisance in my own house [)] seemed to carry beyond mere Body – counterfeiting . . . the Tortures of Guilt, and what we are told of the Punishments of a spiritual World – I am at length a Convalescent – but dreading such another Bout as much as I dare dread a Thing which has no immediate connection with my Conscience.[52]

Coleridge indicates here the disconnection between what was dreamt and what was apparent to the waking self. Indeed, dreams created the potential for the acute fragmentation of the self and revealed how the mind could be divided into entirely separate regions with utterly different moralities. A confusion as to who or what was responsible for the frightening dreams is part of the agonizing dilemma of 'The Pains of Sleep':

> . . . yester-night I pray'd aloud
> In anguish and in agony

Up-starting from the fiendish crowd
Of shapes and thoughts that tortured me:
A lurid light, a trampling throng
Sense of intolerable wrong
. . . Desire with loathing strangely mixed
On wild or hateful objects fixed.
Fantastic passions! maddening brawl!
And shame and terror over all!
Deeds to be hid which were not hid,
Which all confused I could not know
Whether I suffered, or I did:
For all seemed guilt, remorse or woe,
My own or others still the same,
Life-stifling fear, soul-stifling shame!
So two nights passed: the night's dismay
Saddened and stunned the coming day[53]

The intensity of the nightmarish visions are so powerfully conveyed in this poem that one of Coleridge's contemporaries exclaimed that it was a 'magnificent poetical description of disturbed sleep'.[54] The 'shame' that so strongly colours the whole dreaming experience is paradoxically diffuse and uncertain. Coleridge's questions as to who is the criminal and who should feel remorse, who is innocent and who is guilty, cannot be answered. What is particularly interesting is that this poem, so rich in images of painful sleep, was conceived at a time when Coleridge was suffering from stomach disorders and probable exhaustion as he walked across Scotland in September 1803. The imposition of a diseased physical self is perceived to create nightly experiences that are deeply bound up in issues of morality and ethics.

The confusion as to who or what is guilty or innocent in dreams is also seen in the poem 'Christabel'. All characters in this intriguing poem are powerful dreamers and the effects of dreaming linger longer into waking life. In the 1816 version of the poem, the narrator states that the very reason why Christabel is in the dark wood, 'a furlong from the castle gate', is because she had

dreams all yesternight
Of her bethrothed knight;
Dreams, that made her moan and leap,
As on her bed she lay in sleep.[55]

But Christabel's dreams are even more troublesome when the mysterious Geraldine sleeps beside her. Whereas Geraldine awakes the following morning and 'rises lightly from the bed', Christabel has again had an uneasy rest:

And Christabel awoke and spied
The same who lay down by her side
... Nay, fairer yet! and yet more fair!
For she belike hath drunken deep
Of all the blessedness of sleep! ...
'Sure I have sinn'd!' said Christabel,
'Now heaven be praised if all be well!'
And in low faltering tones, yet sweet,
Did she the lofty lady greet
With such perplexity of mind
As dreams too lively leave behind.[56]

This poetic portrayal of a dreamer's complete 'perplexity of mind' surely results from Coleridge's recognition of a deep, ontological confusion as to the power and the origin of dreams. Coleridge often awoke from terrifying nightmares with complete bewilderment as to where and who he was. If, as Andrew Baxter argued, the soul was possessed during sleep, then such ineluctable confusions upon waking might be partially explained. The confusions of identity need not always occur during moments of deep sleep: for Coleridge believed that there were hundreds of differing states of consciousness that could be classed as 'species' of dreaming. These perplexities and confusions might also occur during mesmeric sessions, religious trances or moments of somnambulism, which all, according to Coleridge, shared characteristics with night-time dreams.[57]

The external stakes for Coleridge were high: the possibility that, somehow, the 'blessed' state of sleep could be contaminated by an evil, unwholesome force was at times unbearable. The possibility rocked his conception of a Christian soul and of the nature of evil and goodness. After Christabel has slowly awakened, the narrator of *Christabel* recounts,

So quickly she rose, and quickly arrayed
Her maiden limbs, and having prayed
That He, who on the cross did groan,
Might wash away her sins unknown.[58]

The 'unknown' sins are so strong a force that they cannot be denied, but it is also impossible to fathom where such sins originated. Christabel is 'devoid of guile and sin': she is the apple of her father's eye, a lovely and mild child whose innocence is undeniable. And yet, after she has slept by the side of Geraldine, 'sins unknown' appear.[59] The mysterious processes of dreaming seem more likely to produce anxiety and evil than blessedness or peace. This view of dreams as containing the potential for evil was central for Coleridge's approach, but despite years of observing the strange incursion of evil into dreaming states, he was unable to explain how or why it happened.

Although he frequently found inadequacies in an account such as Baxter's, which claimed that spirits possessed the soul during sleeping states, it was also a comforting theory. And, ultimately, it was this comfort that Coleridge needed as he tried to comprehend the mysterious somnial visitations that so often tormented him.

The unspeakable evil that seems to lurk in the castle after Geraldine's arrival is confirmed by a dream and a vision. The bard Bracy begs Sir Leoline not to undertake a journey to Geraldine's father, intended to reunite father and daughter as well as Sir Leoline and her father. Bracy cries:

> 'This day my journey should not be,
> So strange a dream hath come to me,
> That I had vowed with music loud
> To clear yon wood from thing unblest,
> Warned by a vision in my rest!
> For in my sleep I saw that dove,
> That gentle bird, whom thou dost love,
> And call'st by thy own daughter's name
>   . . . I saw the same
> Fluttering, and uttering fearful moan
> Among the green herbs in the forest alone . . .
> I saw a bright green snake
> Coiled around its wings and neck
> Green as the herbs on which it couched,
> Close by the dove's its head it crouched
>   . . . I woke; it was the midnight hour,
>   . . . But though my slumber was gone by,
> This dream it would not pass away-
> It seems to live upon my eye!'[60]

Sir Leoline interprets that the dream indicates Geraldine is the dove; he vows to protect her from the snake and keep her in his house. At that same moment, Geraldine 'looked askance at Christabel', her eyes 'shrunk up to a serpent's eyes' and with a 'snake's small eye', she caused Christabel to collapse in a trance. Oblivious, Sir Leoline takes Geraldine by the arm and turns his back on his daughter. Bracy's dream, Christabel's terror and her father's cruel treatment seem to be linked to Geraldine's strange, somnial presence. As she fixes her snakey gaze upon the hapless Christabel, Geraldine is described as 'a thing': there is something alien about her, a suggestion that she is a creature of supernatural powers and unspeakably evil, emerging in moments of sleep and dream-like visions: she is a 'sight to dream of, not to tell'.[61]

That Coleridge was seduced by the spirit theory is also clear from his famous Preface to 'Kubla Khan'. This Preface exquisitely articulated the connections between dreams and poetry, and the ways in which both could be created by spirits external to the poet or dreamer. Coleridge claimed that he agreed to the publication of the fragment 'Kubla Khan' at the request of Lord Byron but also because of its elements of 'psychological curiosity'. The whole poem, Coleridge claimed after he wrote it, was composed in a somnial state:

> In consequence of a slight indisposition, an anodyne had been pre-scribed, from the effects of which [the author] fell asleep in his chair at the moment that he was reading the following sentence . . . 'Here the Khan Kubla commanded a palace to be built, and a stately garden thereunto . . .' The Author continued for about three hours in a pro-found sleep, at least of the external senses, during which time he has the most vivid confidence, that he could not have composed less than from two to three hundred lines; if that indeed can be called composi-tion in which all the images rose up before him as *things*, with a parallel production of the correspondent expressions, without any sensation or consciousness of effort.[62]

This claim is as interesting for the poet's defence of what he perceived to be inadequate and unfinished poetry as it is for the notion that in his dream, all the images rose up as 'things' that seemed to have no connection with consciousness but which produced 'correspondent expressions'. How very similar this is to Coleridge's claims in 'The Pains of Sleep' of a 'fiendish crowd' of 'shapes and thoughts that tortured' him but from whence or why he did not know. Only the expressions and emotions, the 'sufferings strange and wild', are remembered in 'The Pains of Sleep', in much the same way that the images of pleasure domes are remembered in 'Kubla Khan'. One is a sensual dream vision; the other a vision of 'unfathomable hell within'.

That Coleridge could hold such diverse views of dreams, maintaining that they could be caused either by physiological factors or by spirits, reflected the intellectual contexts of the eighteenth century. Dreams were often treated as specific diseases. In spite of medical and physiological discoveries many ailments and diseases, including nightmares and other nightly disturbances, were often still approached and treated according to superstitious beliefs.[63] Disease was still frequently thought to be a divine punishment for an immoral action, or an immoral agency within a community, the result of *maleficium* (spells cast by witches), or of demonic possession.[64] Nightmares especially were held to be the result of a temporary demonic possession, and were sometimes believed to be a prelude to epilepsy, insanity or apoplexy.[65] At the same time, dreams and diseases could be explained in terms of a 'spirit theory' such as Baxter's. A dream is sent to the dreamer from a divine or sometimes evil supernatural force; a disease or ache is forced upon the body as the result of an external cause – a cough was 'caught' from someone else, colic or toothache caused by creatures assaulting the body. This shared characteristic of dreams and disease was one means by which Coleridge was able to perceive similarities between his dreams and his bodily illnesses and infirmities. It also enabled him to try to distance himself from both the delightful and the terrifying aspects of his dreams: he could claim that the lush visions of poetry such as the pleasure domes of Kubla Khan were somehow unrelated to his consciousness – the images rose up 'as things' – or that the terrible throng of hideous shapes in the 'Pains of Sleep' fell upon him from anywhere else other than his own psyche. In the Preface to 'Kubla Khan', Coleridge interestingly claimed that the vision of Kubla Khan and the 'Pains of Sleep' were both fragments. In spite of, or perhaps because of, their fragmentary nature, they described 'with equal fidelity' the dream of 'pain and disease'. Where Coleridge differed from his contemporaries was in his insistence that there were complex processes involved between psyche and soma during sleeping states: processes that were more tortuous than in waking hours. A dream emotion or a dream character could be both caused by and cause a physiological state in the dreamer's body.

Coleridge coined the word 'psychosomatic' in 1828 to describe complex interactions between body and mind in his classification of passions.[66] The pains of sleep may have been dismissed by many of Coleridge's contemporaries as solely the result of poor digestion, but Coleridge had moments of being aware that his somnial experiences were also somehow connected to his psyche and self:

> ... the night's dismay
> Saddened and stunned the coming day.
> Sleep, the wide blessing, seemed to me
> Distemper's worst calamity.

The pains of sleep were precisely more painful because they were not only physical torments but also moral and ethical torments. It is this uneasy wavering between trying to discern the origin of dreams and recognizing the meaning of dreams that imbues Coleridge's poems in the 1816 Christabel collection with much of their psychological tension and depth.

NOTES AND REFERENCES

1 S. T. Coleridge, Poetical Works (ed. E. H. Coleridge), Oxford, 1988, 'The pains of sleep', p. 390. Further references to PW. The themes of this chapter are further explored in my book, Coleridge on Dreaming; Romanticism, Dreams and the Medical Imagination, Cambridge, 1998.

2 In this chapter I am more concerned with the historical contexts of his ideas than with the relation of his ideas to dream theories of the twentieth century, such as Freudian theories or depth analysis. For a discussion of the differences and similarities between Coleridge and Freud, see N. Halmi, 'Why Coleridge was not a Freudian', Dreaming 7, March 1997, pp. 13–28. Kathryn Kimball has argued that Coleridge did have a 'purposeful' theory of

dreams; see her essay 'Coleridge's Dream Theory and the Dual Imagination', *The Coleridge Bulletin*, 16, 2000, pp. 80–86.

3 Coleridge wrote in great detail on the language of dreams, believing that there were 'various dialects': *Notebooks of S. T. Coleridge* (ed. K. Coburn), 4 vols, London, 1957–, Vol. 3, entry 4,409. (Further references to *CN*.) For his dream languages, see Ford, *Coleridge on Dreaming*.

4 Coleridge to J. Blanco White, November 1827, *Collected Letters of Samuel Taylor Coleridge* (ed. E. L. Griggs), 6 vols, Oxford and New York, 1956–71, vol. 6, p. 715. Further references to *CL*.

5 Coleridge's notebooks contain many entries other than dream ones: he jots down recipes, drafts of poems or lectures, descriptions of travel journeys, translations from German philosophy, indulgent fantasies, mundane events, lists of bills to be paid and daily anecdotes of friends and family. For a discussion of Coleridge's style and preoccupations in the notebooks, see J. Dixon, 'The Notebooks' in *The Cambridge Companion to Coleridge* (ed. L. Newton), Cambridge, 2002.

6 For instance, see A. Hayter, *Opium and the Romantic Imagination*, London, 1968, pp. 67–83; and J. R. Watson, *English Poetry of the Romantic Period 1789–1830* (2nd ed.), London and New York, 1992, pp. 64–76.

7 There are numerous works on dreams in medieval poetry, see K. L. Lynch, *The High Medieval Dream Vision; Poetry, Philosophy and Literary Form*, Stanford, CT, 1988; S. Kruger, *Dreaming in the Middle Ages*, Cambridge, 1992. Of related interest is N. Armstrong and L. Tennenhouse, 'The interior difference: A brief genealogy of dreams, 1650–1717', *Eighteenth Century Studies* 23, 1990, pp. 458–478. Most of the Romantic writers included dreams in their works: for instance, John Keats, Percy Bysshe Shelley, Mary Shelley, Lord Byron, William Wordsworth and William Blake.

8 From the memoirs of Philarète Chasles, as quoted in *Coleridge the Talker; A Series of Contemporary Descriptions and Comments* (ed. and intro. R. W. Armour and R. F. Howes, reprint), New York and London, 1969, p. 129.

9 Leigh Hunt, *Lord Byron and Some of his Contemporaries*, London, 1828, p. 301.

10 *A Diary of Thomas De Quincey, 1803* (ed. H. A. Eaton), Noel Douglas, London, entry for Wednesday 1 June 1803.

11 With a little irony and envy Coleridge's great friend, Charles Lamb (1775–1834), once wrote that the 'poverty' of his own dreams mortified him; they were 'tame and prosaic' in comparison to Coleridge's, who 'at his will can conjure up icy domes, and pleasure-houses for Kubla Khan, and Abyssinian maids, and songs of Abara . . . when I cannot muster a fiddle': see Lamb's essay, 'Witches and other night-fears', *The Works of Charles and Mary Lamb* (ed. E. V. Lucas), 6 vols, London, 1903, vol. 2, p. 69.

12 For instance, Aubrey's popular *Miscellanies* contained dreams ascribed to English archbishops, Christopher Wren, and ancient notables such as Julius Caesar. J. Aubrey, *Miscellanies Upon Various Subjects*, London, 1721.

13 Many critics have also commented on the connections between dreaming and poetic creativity in the Romantic period: see F. Coyne, *Nightmare and Escape: Changing Conceptions of the Imagination in Romantic and Victorian Dream Visions*, Ann Arbor, MI, 1984; N. MacKenzie, *Dreams and Dreaming*, London, 1965, pp. 83–97; and C. la Cassagnère, 'Dreams', in *A Handbook to English Romanticism* (ed. J. Raimond and J. R. Watson), New York, 1992, pp. 97–102.

14 As in Reverend Saalfeld, *A Philosophical Discourse on the Nature of Dreams*, London, 1764.

15 R. Gray, *The Theory of Dreams: in which an inquiry is made into the powers and faculties of the human mind, as they are illustrated in the most remarkable dreams recorded in sacred and profane history*, 2 vols, London, 1808, vol. 2, pp. 26–28, 50.

16 J. Bond, *Essay on the Incubus*, London, 1753, p. 4. Another early work on the nightmare that Coleridge would have known was John Waller's *Treatise on the Incubus, or Night-mare, Disturbed Sleep, Terrific Dreams, and Nocturnal Visions: with the means of removing these distressing complaints*, London, 1815; CN 4, entry 4,514.

17 H. F. Ellenberger, *The Discovery of the Unconscious; the History and Evolution of Dynamic Psychiatry*, London, 1970, pp. 168–170.

18 M. V. DePorte, *Nightmares and Hobby Horses: Swift, Sterne and Augustan Ideas of Madness*, San Marino, 1974, p. ix.

19 Of many, see W. Buchan, *Domestic Medicine; Or, the Family Physician* (21st edn), London, 1813; J. Hunter, *The Works of John Hunter* (ed. J. F. Palmer), 4 vols, London, 1835–7; E. Darwin, *Zoonomia, or the Laws of Organic Life* (2nd edn), 4 vols, London, 1794–96; and A. Haller, *Physiology; Being a Course of Lectures Upon the Visceral Anatomy and Vital Oeconomy of Human Bodies: Including the Latest and Most Considerable DISCOVERIES and IMPROVEMENTS, Which Have Been Made by the Most Eminent Professors, through all parts of EUROPE, down to the present year*, 2 vols, London, 1754.

20 Buchan, *Domestic Medicine*, p. 78.

21 *The English Works of Thomas Hobbes*, ed. Sir William Molesworth, 11 vols, London, 1839–45, vol. 1, p. 401.

22 David Hartley, *Observations on Man, His Frame, Duty, and Expectations* (3rd edn), 2 vols, London, 1749, vol. 1, pp. 384–386.

23 Darwin, *Zoonomia*, p. 209.

24 Hunter, *Works*, vol. 1, p. 334.

25 German visit: *CL* 1, p. 494; 'Theory of life', *Collected Works of S. T. Coleridge: Shorter Works and Fragments* (ed. H. J. Jackson and J. R. de J. Jackson), 2 vols, Princeton, NJ, 1995, vol. 1, pp. 482–483. It was originally part of an essay on scrofula that Coleridge wrote in 1816. Never published in his lifetime, the essay on life is Coleridge's exposition of German philosophy as expounded by Kant, Schelling and Heinrich Steffens, and his contribution to the Hunterian debate on the nature of life that emerged in England in 1815. Johann Friedrich Blumenbach lived from 1752 to 1840.

26 On the controversy surrounding Brown's ideas and the near riots in Göttingen in 1802, see *CN* 3, 4,269n and T. Levere, *Poetry Realized in Nature*, Cambridge, 1981, p. 203. Also D. C. Macarthur, 'The first forty years of the Royal Medical Society and the part William Cullen played in it', in *William Cullen and the Eighteenth Century Medical World; A bicentenary exhibition and symposium arranged by the Royal College of Physicians of Edinburgh in 1990* (ed. A. Doig, J. P. S. Ferguson, I. A. Milne and R. Passmore), Edinburgh, 1993, pp. 247–251.

27 Coleridge, *Collected Works of S. T. Coleridge: Biographia Literaria*, ed. J. Engell and W. Jackson Bate, 2 vols, Princeton, NJ, 1993, vol. 1, p. 163. See also N. Leask, *British Romantic Writers and the East; Anxieties of Empire*, Cambridge, 1992, pp. 183–184.

28 From Beddoes's essay, *Observation in Calculus*, as quoted in Darwin, *Zoonomia*, vol. 4, pp. 206–209.

29 Haller, *Physiology*, vol. 2, p. 117.

30 J. Brown, *Elements of Medicine*, London, 2 vols, 1788, vol. 1, pp. 262–266. See also N. Vickers, 'Coleridge, Thomas Beddoes and Brunonian medicine', *European Romantic Review* 8, Winter 1997, pp. 47–94.

31 Questions concerning life processes were particularly relevant in the very public debate between the two surgeons John Abernethy (1764–1831) and William Lawrence (1783–1867): see A. Snyder, *Coleridge on Logic and Learning*, New Haven, CT, and London, 1929, pp. 16–25, and O. Temkin, 'Basic science, medicine, and the Romantic era', *Bulletin of the History of Medicine* 38, 1963, pp. 97–129. This debate was also an influential factor in the genesis of M. Shelley's *Frankenstein*: see M. Butler's Introduction to *Frankenstein; or the Modern Prometheus; the 1818 Text*, Oxford, 1994, pp. xv–xxxiii and Appendix C, pp. 229–251.

32 Letter to Thomas Poole, *CL* 2, pp. 730–731. A hydrocele is a tumour with a collection of serous fluid, most usually in the testis.

33 Unpublished notebook of Coleridge, held in the British Library, Add. MS 47, 536, Notebook 41, fo. 53v.

34 Unpublished notebook of Coleridge, held in the British Library, Add. MS 47, 534, Note-
    book 37, fo. 85v.
35 *CN* 2, 2,838.
36 *CL* 2, p. 991.
37 *CL* 2, p. 999.
38 'Ode to the Departing Year', lines 103–112.
39 *CN* 4, 5,360.
40 *CN* 2, 2,064.
41 *CL* 3, p. 212. The effects of opium account for Coleridge's singling out of the digestive
    system as possible cause for his dreams. Opium decreases the activity of the gastrointestinal
    tract, and can lead to constipation if taken in excess. As symptoms of opiate-withdrawal
    include abdominal cramps, diarrhoea and nausea, Coleridge's efforts to stop taking opium
    would have enhanced and aggravated his digestive symptoms. The focus on this part of his
    body is not surprising. But what is even more interesting is the ways in which this physical
    condition led Coleridge to explore in more detail the relationship between his dreaming
    mind and body.
42 *CN* 3, 4,396.
43 *CN* 1, 1,765.
44 *CN* 2, 2,064.
45 *CL* 2, pp. 1,045–1,046.
46 *CL* 5, p. 25.
47 *CL* 2, p. 1,046. See also D. Vallins, *Coleridge and the Psychology of Romanticism, Feeling
    and Thought*, London, 2000, pp. 42–48.
48 *CN* 4, 5,360.
49 *PW*, p. 391, line 50.
50 See J. Beer, 'Coleridge and Andrew Baxter on dreaming', *Journal of the Association for the
    Study of Dreams* 7, June 1997, pp. 157–161; D. Miall, 'The meaning of dreams: Coleridge's
    ambivalence', *Studies in Romanticism* 21, 1982, pp. 51–71; and E. Schneider, *Coleridge,
    Opium and Kubla Khan*, New York, 1953 [reprint 1975]. A. Baxter's *Enquiry into the Nature
    of the Human Soul* was published anonymously in 1733; a second edition followed in 1737.
    The third edition of the *Encyclopaedia Britannica* in 1803 cites both Darwin and Baxter as
    key sources of information on dreams, and Baxter's ideas remained well known for over a
    hundred years. Coleridge often maintained that the terrible nightmares he endured could
    never originate from his own consciousness. It followed that such nightly experiences must
    be caused by some external form(s).
51 A. Baxter, *An Enquiry into the Nature of the Human Soul* (2nd edn), 2 vols, London, 1737,
    vol. 2, p. 14.
52 *CL* 2, pp. 1,020–1,021.
53 *PW*, 'The pains of sleep', p. 389, lines 14–34.
54 The comment was made by Coleridge's friend, Thomas Poole. 'The correspondence of
    Poole 1765–1837', held in the British Library, Add. MS 35, 343, fo. 332.
55 The references to Christabel's moaning and leaping were removed from later versions of the
    poem. I quote from the 1816 edition, *Christabel; Kubla Khan, A Vision; The Pains of Sleep*,
    London, 1816 (ed. J. Wordsworth, Oxford and New York, 1991), p. 5.
56 *PW*, p. 228, lines 370–386. See also P. Cardinale, 'Noises in a Suround', *The Coleridge
    Bulletin*, 17, 2001, pp. 27–38.
57 The term 'species' of dreams is taken from a letter by the poet John Keats to his brother
    after meeting Coleridge in 1819. Keats wrote: 'I walked with him a[t] his alderman-after
    dinner pace for near two miles ... In those two Miles [Coleridge] broached a thousand
    things ... Nightingales, Poetry – on Poetical sensation – Metaphysics – Different genera
    and species of Dreams – Nightmares ...': *The Letters of John Keats 1814–1818* (ed. H. E.
    Rollins), 2 vols, 1958, vol. 2, pp. 88–89. Coleridge also considered as other types of dreams
    such topical events as mesmeric trances, animal magnetism, ghost-sightings and visionary

dreams, and wrote on the similarities between Luther's religious visions and Swedenborg's writings as instances of a special species of dream.

58 *PW*, p. 228, lines 387–390.

59 Another text extremely influential on Coleridge's thinking was John Milton's *Paradise Lost*: before Eve is tempted by Satan, she dreams that she will sin. Upon awakening from this horrid dream, she describes her dream to Adam who, ineffectually, tries to explain how she, being pure, has dreamt of an evil act. Adam is forced to conclude that he hopes that 'what in sleep thou didst abhor to dream,/Waking thou never wilt consent to do'. On Coleridge's use of Milton's poem in his dream cogitations, see Ford, *Coleridge on Dreaming*, pp. 151–155.

60 *PW*, p. 232, lines 526–559.

61 *PW*, line 253.

62 *PW*, p. 296.

63 R. French, 'Sickness and the soul: Stahl, Hoffman and Sauvages on pathology', in *The Medical Enlightenment of the Eighteenth Century* (eds A. Cunningham and R. French), Cambridge, 1990, pp. 88–110. David Morris remarks that nineteenth-century artists such as Honoré Daumier and George Cruikshank popularized the view that almost any affliction from headaches to insanity might be 'attributed to an influx of demons sent by an enemy': see his *Culture of Pain*, Berkeley and Los Angeles, 1993, pp. 45–46.

64 R. Porter, *Disease, Medicine and Society in England 1550–1860*, London, 1987, p. 26. See also H. Haggard, *Devils, Drugs, and Doctors*, London, 1929, pp. 3–49.

65 From Caelius Aurelianus, *De Morbis Acutis et Chronicis*, as cited in S. Jarcho, 'Some lost, obsolete, or discontinued diseases: Serous apoplexy, incubus, and retrocedent ailments', *Transactions and Studies of the College of Physicians of Philadelphia*, 1980, Part 2, Series 5, p. 253.

66 'Essay on the passions', *Shorter Works and Fragments* (ed. Jackson and Jackson), vol. 2, pp. 1,444–1,445.

Figure 7.1 *The Fortune Teller*, London, 1890. Courtesy of the Trustees of the British Library.

Chapter 7

The meaning of dream books

Maureen Perkins

> Whatever women may be, I thought that men, in the nineteenth century, were above superstition.
>
> Wilkie Collins, *The Woman in White*, 1860.

The title of Freud's magnum opus echoes a well-known, perhaps even notorious, form of street literature.[1] Dream books were as old as publishing itself, and for a short while towards the end of the nineteenth century became, in Britain at least, the dominant form of chapbook.[2] They were particularly aimed at women readers, forming an important part of women's popular culture. In using the same title, Freud was linking his own 'interpretation of dreams' to the many widespread interpretations that circulated in popular 'dreamers', and it is reasonable to assume that he expected some comparison to be made. Not only was he aware of the genre, but he seemed to acknowledge a debt of inspiration to it: 'One day I discovered to my great astonishment that the view of dreams which came nearest to the truth was not the medical but the popular one, half involved though it still was in superstition'.[3] He rejected the scientific opinion advanced by writers such as Carl Binz, that dreams were froth (*'Träume sind Schäume'*), and was drawn, instead, to the popular view that dreams have a meaning, 'which can be discovered by some process of interpretation of a content which is often confused and puzzling'. Distancing himself from those who smiled at attempts to find a significance in dreams, Freud set out, with what we now know to be revolutionary consequences, to replace the ancient, traditional code of meanings that came in every street pedlar's stock of dream books with his own collection of symbols – a new lexicography of dreaming. By developing the role of dreams as fragments of suppressed wishes he appropriated the common dream book's emphasis on fear, hope and desire; but by tracing those fragments back to childhood and repression, he transformed a significant aspect of nineteenth-century women's culture, moving the focus of dreams from the future to the past. The time-hallowed nature of dreams in chapbook literature, as oracles of the future consulted chiefly by women, was superseded.

Dream books, or dreamers, provided an A to Z of meanings; for example, the appearance of comets in a dream 'is ominous of war, plague, famine, and death', to dream of a cat signifies that you will soon catch a thief, beer is a portent of an accident, and crows flying in cloudy weather show coming loss and misery.[4] Although some writers expressed the belief that these meanings were derived from Artemidorus of Ephesus, whose work on dreams in the second century was thought to be the earliest surviving example of the genre,[5] dream books no doubt fed off one another, just as all street literature did. It was possible for the same material to be recycled in several different forms. First, there was the dream book itself, with little apart from its alphabetical list and perhaps a section on physiognomy. Then there were books of fate, which included several different ways of reading the future, from signs in the natural world to the casting of dice, as well as lists of fortunate and unfortunate days of the year. Finally, there were fortune-telling books, much more concerned with remedies and courses of action, guides to influencing the future: these might include what they called 'recipes', that is, forms of ritual to ensure dreaming about a particular subject.

In the middle of the nineteenth century, James Guest described how street pedlars sold this wide array of different types of fortune-telling books. Hawkers, he wrote, would sell

> at what they could get, at prices varying from 2d to 6d, sometimes a good supper and leave to sleep in the barn or outhouse, often when they could get the blind side of the old dame or the young one with their Pamphlets, Books of Dreams, fortune telling, Nixon's prophecies, books of fate, ballads, etc.[6]

The appearance on this list of the name of Robert Nixon, Cheshire prophet of the seventeenth century, is further indication of the belief that these chapbooks tapped into an old tradition. Any form of predicting the future, whether it was prophecy or fortune-telling, claimed to carry the authority of long-established lineage. The astrologer Raphael, otherwise known as Robert Cross Smith, claimed that the dream book he published (*The Royal Book of Dreams*, 1830) was derived from an ancient manuscript that he had simply stumbled across while out on a country walk. In the summer of 182- [*sic*] he had come across a broken-down Somersetshire court-house, and was there shown a 'curious manuscript, which was buried in the earth for several centuries, containing one thousand and twenty-four oracles or answers to dreams . . . whereby any person of ordinary capacity may discover these secrets of fate, which the universal fiat of all nations . . . has acknowledged to be portended by dreams and nocturnal visions'. Similarly, in 1850 the publisher of *The Dreamer's Oracle* claimed to have found the original of his dream book 'in the Ark of a Late Celebrated Wizard'. Throughout the nineteenth century repeated issues of *Napoleon's Book of Fate*, perhaps the most popular fortune-telling book of all, claimed to be a translation of a book 'written in German nearly 500 years ago', 'a cabinet of curiosities, and valuable secrets', which had been seized, so it was claimed, from the belongings of Napoleon Bonaparte after his defeat at the Battle of Leipzig.

These hoary pedigrees clearly conferred some kind of authority, but they also served to distance the publishers who reproduced them, as demonstrated by *The True Fortune Teller* of 1850, printed in Edinburgh, which issued the following disclaimer:

TO THE READER
The foregoing pages are published principally to show the superstitions which engrossed the mind of the population of Scotland during a past age, and which are happily disappearing before the progress of an enlightened civilisation. It is hoped, therefore, that the reader will not attach the slightest importance to the solutions of the dreams as rendered above, as dreams are generally the result of a disordered stomach, or an excited imagination.[7]

Other compilers achieved a similar distancing effect by publishing titles that claimed to come from abroad. Some noted that they were translated from the original Greek, while the *High German Fortune-Teller* was a frequent title, and the ubiquitous *Napoleon's Book of Fate* was said to be translated from the German.

Many dream books demonstrated a familiarity with the burgeoning discussion of dreams from a physiological standpoint. As Tony James has demonstrated so well for France, 'dreams and associated phenomena . . . preoccupied writers, philosophers, and psychiatrists [as a] key theme of nineteenth-century European thought'.[8] Those chapbook writers who aspired to respectability made sure, if only through a preface, that readers knew they were familiar with current discussion. Despite nods in the direction of scientific opinion, however, they proceeded to give all the usual interpretations. The compiler of the 1850 *True Fortune Teller* just quoted, for example, despite invoking 'a disordered stomach', published a traditional alphabetical list, though he also added that he could not be held responsible for such nonsense since he had found all this material in a cave in which a 'gypsey', old Mrs Bridget, or Mother Bridget, made her home.

The role of women in this genre was crucial. Mother Bridget was one attributed source, Mother Bunch another, and Mother Shipton a third. These apocryphal designations were doubtless intended to attract readers by assuring them that the compilers understood their needs and interests, and they point to a largely female readership. James Guest's comment above depicts the street trader as selling to 'the old dame or the young one'. As late as 1899 one London bookseller commented:

> I sell a most surprising number of publications of the prophetic alma- nac and dream book class . . . The greater number of my customers in this way are workgirls and domestic servants, or young married women of the 'small villa' class.[9]

In 1807, when Joseph Powell was arrested and tried for fortune-telling, amongst the papers seized from his house were 'numerous memorandums' recording the dreams of clients who had consulted him about their 'destiny and future events'.[10] Most of these clients were women, and many of their questions related to love, marriage, and children. There was indeed a com- mon belief that the use of dreams as oracles of the future was very much a part of women's culture. When Mr Blair, a member of the Society for the Suppression of Vice, set out to entrap Powell, he sent a letter claiming to ask questions put by a young maidservant. When would she marry? Would she have children? Such questions, and from such an innocent source, were, we are led to believe, commonly put to Powell. In an 1865 study, *The Literature and Curiosities of Dreams*, Frank Seafield wrote that dream inter- pretation 'is now an instrument by which a chap-book pedlar may best ascertain what is the smallest number of lies which Cinderella will insist on in return for her penny, without considering herself cheated'.[11]

The contents of the dream books themselves confirm that women were the most likely readers. The 1750 *Dreams and Moles* contains advice on 'How to restore a lost Maidenhead, or solder a crackt one' (a recipe using myrtle berries).[12] 'Charms for Dreaming' advised readers how to obtain a dream that would contain an image of their future marriage partner. In *Mother Shipton's Fortune Teller* of 1861, for example, there is 'A Charm for Dreaming', which advises the reader how to be sure to dream of the future by appealing to 'Luna every womans' [sic] friend'. *The Dreamer's True Friend* of 1861 includes 'how to choose a husband by the colour of his hair'. In *The Dreamer's Sure Guide; or the interpretation of dreams faithfully revealed* of 1830 a pull-out illustration shows a woman lying on a couch dreaming, with pictorial representations of her dreams all around her. *The Dreamer's Oracle* also has a large illustration showing a woman dreaming of a hand- some man.[13] The seeds of a wish-fulfilment interpretation of dreams are clearly here, with the difference lying in what these images actually represent. Are they visions of the future, appearing in dream as prophetic insights? Or are they spectral imaginings, lurking in the unconscious?[14]

Marriage and children are by far the most common subjects. 'A virgin dreaming she has put on new garments, shews an alteration in her condition by way of marriage'. 'If a woman dreams she is with child, it shews sorrow and sadness'. In *Small Books and Pleasant Histories* Margaret Spufford has related the popularity of courtship books in the early modern period to the late age of marriages, and in *Women in Early Modern England* Sara Mendelson and Patricia Crawford write that courtship 'comprised a major life-stage for the majority of the female populace, as women were left to their own resources [meaning outside the family home in which they grew up] for a lengthy period between puberty and marriage at about age 25 or 26'.[15] In the nineteenth century fears of spinsterhood continued to be an issue for many women. The 1851 census showed that women outnumbered men, and this contributed to widespread discussion about the problem of 'surplus' women.[16] There were certainly plenty of reasons for young women to want to read about the subject of marriage, but why should this be approached through dreaming?

Dreaming and day-dreaming, its related activity, were on the very borders of respectability. Seafield included a chapter entitled 'Analogies of Dreaming and Insanity', and Freud devoted the final section of the first chapter of *The Interpretation of Dreams* to 'The Relations between Dreams and Mental Diseases'. The dominant scientific opinion at the end of the nineteenth century was that dreams were an indication of disturbance, and that they did not occur in the deep, normal sleep of a healthy person. *Chambers's Journal* stated categorically: 'No one dreams when he is sound asleep. Dreams take place only during an imperfect or perturbed sleep'.[17] Carl Binz described dreams as 'somatic processes which are in every case useless and in many cases positively pathological'.[18] Certainly there had been great men in the past who had experienced prophetic dreaming, but just as prophecy was an activity that became relegated to history, so prophetic dreaming's greatest days were clearly over. When a contributor to *Blackwood's* in August 1840 discussed the topic under the heading 'A few passages concerning omens, dreams, etc.', he related stories of men who had premonitory dreams, while addressing his thoughts to an imaginary Eusebius, relegating the subject to a classical past.[19] Seafield wrote: 'Oneirocriticism is at present in the sere and yellow leaf of its fortunes. It sprang up to meet us like a god; it retires from us with the hang-dog expression of a rebuked costermonger'. In the nineteenth century, men who would admit to premonitory dreams were challenging the norms of middle-class masculinity of their day.[20] Dreaming was predominantly associated with mental or physical disturbance. In the latter half of the century, women's association with hysteria and altered states of consciousness was depicted by medical opinion as connected with menstruation and physiological weakness, and disturbed sleep was part of this pattern of neurotic disorder. Even in those instances when some approval was expressed of prophetic dreaming, women were most frequently the dreamers. In 1833, in just one example of many in the periodical press, *Chambers's Journal* carried a story of a young man's life being saved by the dreams of his aunt, who saw the fishing boat he was due to go out in sinking. She had this dream three times in one night, and in the morning entreated him not to go. He followed her advice, and learned later that the boat had sunk, and all in it drowned.[21]

Even if visionary dreams sometimes met with disapproval, why did dream books, with their largely conservative content, arouse condemnation? Wilkie Collins wrote of 'the helpless discomfort familiar to us all in sleep, when we recognize yet cannot reconcile the anomalies and contradictions of a dream', but dream books offered the calming reassurance that there was order and meaning in the apparent confusion.[22] They could help to pacify unruly imaginations even when dreams made the fixed nature of gender seem questionable. *Dreams and Moles*, for example, describes what it would mean if a woman dreamt that she was a man:

> When a woman dreams she is a man, and is not married, she will have a husband; or if she's without children she'll have a son, . . . and to a maid-servant, much incumberance; 'tis verre fortunate to a harlot, because she will forsake her evil ways.[23]

A woman's dreams of manhood, then, signify coming fulfilment. To a prostitute this is a good sign – the man, no doubt, will rescue her. The maidservant, it is suggested, might have cause to regret her dream, since it heralds an unwanted pregnancy. However, even more potentially threatening than such gender-subversive dreaming was the question of sexuality. *Dreams and Moles* relates what it means for 'a barren woman' to dream that 'she prostitutes herself with her own sex'. In this case, the interpretation is again decidedly conservative: it simply shows that she will have a child. However, a 'fruitful' woman having the same dream would have 'much pain in bearing her children'. In an example typical of the way in which chapbook material was repeated across titles and across many years, this same interpretation occurs in the *New Infallible Fortune Teller* of 1818, but with slightly less confronting language: 'For a barren woman to dream she embraces one of her own sex, denotes that in time she will have children; but to a fruitful woman it denotes pain and sorrow in child bearing'.[24] Such interpretations position the meaning of dreams outside the workings of the mind, implying an external set of forces that will decide destiny. Yet in many nineteenth-century dream interpetations, messages of individual responsibility and the benefits of hard work can also be found, alongside reassurances about external determination. Here the role of the dream book is ambiguous, like much popular culture, seeming both to challenge and validate the existing order. Several 'dreamers' signal on their title pages that they contain the interpretation of dreams 'by the most ancient as well as the most modern Rules of Philosophy'. Popular literature was, after all, a commodity, and as such it was profitable to leave it open to as many interpretations as possible.

In the case of dream books, ambivalence was almost certainly connected with the conflict between predominantly middle-class disapproval of prediction and plebeian fascination with it. As I have argued elsewhere, nineteenth-century reformers, of both Whig and radical persuasion, disapproved of attempts by those at the meanest levels of society to foretell the future.[25] For a middle-class Whig such a belief was an offence to rationality, flying in the face of all that was known about the steady progression of time. For a radical such as Henry Hetherington or Richard Carlile such a belief locked its victim into the hopelessness of a predetermined future, negating any effort to create social and political change. For the evangelical Hannah More it was also against religion. In one of her popular tracts, *Tawny Rachel*, she warned 'all you young men and maidens' against: '*cheats, impostors, cunning women, fortune-tellers, conjurers*, and *interpreters of dreams*', because 'God never reveals to weak and wicked women the secret designs of his providence', so 'to consult these false oracles is not only foolish but sinful'.[26] Dream books and fortune-telling books, then, were disapproved of by all those who sought to bring education and improvement to the labouring classes.

There is more to the unrespectability of dream books, however, than disapproval of superstitious beliefs or of fatalism. Dreaming is a notoriously atemporal activity, and any belief in the predictive capacity of dreams is a challenge to the fixed regularity of time. Many fortune-telling books, 'dreamers' amongst them, included lists of fortunate and unfortunate days in the year to come, implying that the passage of time was not equal: the quality of days differed, even if the number of hours did not. As many studies of popular belief have shown, certain days, especially those connected with the ecclesiastical year, were imbued with special significance.[27] These were given similar importance in dream books. *The Golden Cabinet or the Compleat Fortune-Teller* of 1795 instructed the hopeful dreamer:

> On St. Valentine's Day, take two bay leaves, sprinkle them with rose water, the evening of this day lay them across your pillow. When you go to bed, putting on a clean shift turned wrong side outwards, and laying down, say these words softly to yourself.
> Good Valentine be kind to me,
> In dreams let me my true Love see.
> So crossing your legs, go to sleep as fast as you can, and you will see in your dream the party you are to wed come to your bedside, and offer you all the modest kindness imaginable.

This charm depended for its efficacy on being carried out on a particular day of the year. Many other magical 'recipes' suggested the potentially irrational nature of time. Rules were published by which interpretation of the character of children might be made according to what days of the calendar they were born on, referring to the age of the moon. Certain days were good for travelling on, others not. These chapbooks were still appearing and still a highly popular form of street literature, when standardized 'universal time' was being promoted at government and international level (in conferences like the 1884 Prime Meridian Conference and the 1912 International Conference on Time), and when a uniform method for determining accurate time signals and transmitting them around the world was being established.[28] This is a very different economic context from that of chapbooks. In the modern world, setting out on a journey could not wait for lunar aspects or a propitious date.

Although women's association with dreaming was linked to medical constructions of physiological disturbance, the widely-accepted connection between women and 'superstitious' belief generally was more complex. As scorn became the dominant way in which the educated elite regarded beliefs about prediction, a link was forged between superstition and lack of education. Contemporaries regarded fortune-telling as something resorted to by the lower orders. *Dreams and Moles*, its title page proclaimed, was designed to appeal to 'the very meanest Capacities'. As literacy and education advanced throughout the eighteenth and nineteenth centuries, the nature of chapbooks did not greatly change (with the exception of almanacs). Content was still about courtship, marriage and the chances of good fortune. However, whereas the earlier versions had occasionally addressed a male reader, men as potential readers seem to have disappeared by the end of the century, and the genre was targeted entirely at women. One assumption demonstrated by compilers was that the least educated, the least literate, and therefore the least discriminating were most likely to be women. When reformers campaigned against superstition, they frequently referred to the need to protect women from their own gullibility. It was part of this scenario to present those most likely to suffer as being amongst the poorest in society. In Wilkie Collins's bestseller, *The Woman in White*, it is the low-born Anne Catherick, illegitimate child of a maidservant, who tries to warn Laura Fairlie by relating a prophetic dream: 'Do you believe in dreams? I hope, for your own sake, that you do'.

It may be that some women's lack of education predisposed them to irrational belief, although the existence of highly educated readers of dream books problematizes such a simple explanation. Hesba Stretton (1832–1911), later chief writer of tract fiction for the Religious Tract Society, slept with a dream-book under her pillow at the age of twenty-eight.[29] And whereas the thrust of the legislation against fortune-telling was against vagrants, implying that perpetrators would probably be vagabonds like Hannah More's Tawny Rachel, 'a famous interpreter of dreams', records suggest that prosecutions were brought largely against settled, even respectable practitioners. It is impossible, of course, to evaluate to what extent the purchasers of these little books believed or acted on their contents, and some may even have bought them simply for a laugh, as some present-day purchasers of *Old Moore's Almanac* no doubt do. Amongst Pepys's collection of chapbooks is

Mother Bunch's Closet,[30] which claims its author as 'your loving friend, poor Tom', one of that large family of 'poor' authors who signalled, for those who understood, that here was a work of satire.[31]

One very practical reason for women's interest in books of fate may have been a cultural role as guardians of the calendar. Women were the most likely purchasers of almanacs, for reasons that we can only guess, perhaps to do in part with the timing of menstrual cycles and pregnancy. The lists of lucky and unlucky days in fortune-telling books may well have fallen into this role of forward planning in the home, and point to an area of influence in the private sphere over the timing of journeys. As with so much about popular culture and popular literature, the questions raised by these books far exceed our capacity to answer them. Why was their content so little concerned with friendship, or health? Why are the fortune-tellers consulted in their illustrations and anecdotes nearly always women, when most prosecutions seem to have been of men? However, one thing is certain. Women's readership of books of fate and dream books was not only a demonstration of gullibility. Those areas of life where some women, perhaps chiefly young women, experienced the most anxiety are clearly signalled, as well as ways in which they tried to exercise some control over implementing their dearest wishes.

Freud's revolutionary achievement was to take a widely known feature of popular culture and to turn it around, so that by the early years of the twentieth century most educated people believed that dreams referred not to the future but to the past. The final paragraph of *The Interpretation of Dreams* refers again to popular belief:

> And the value of dreams for giving us knowledge of the future? There is of course no question of that. It would be truer to say instead that they give us knowledge of the past. For dreams are derived from the past in every sense. Nevertheless the ancient belief that dreams foretell the future is not wholly devoid of truth. But his future, which the dreamer pictures as the present, has been moulded by his . . . wish into a perfect likeness of the past.

In Freud's summary, the representative dreamer has been transformed from the woman for whom dream-book compilers wrote, to a universal man. Yet in clinical practice Freud's emphasis on women perpetuated the common belief that women were a fertile source of repressed wishes. Freud's relationship to popular belief was one of both continuity and rupture: his insights into dreams built on centuries of belief that dreaming was connected with the innermost desires and fears, not solely with the discomforts of the body; but he broke with tradition in removing the interpretation of dreams from its important place in the private culture of women. In appropriating it for psychoanalytical investigation, he conferred important rational status, but he removed an area of agency that generations of women had claimed as their own.

NOTES AND REFERENCES

The author would like to thank the Centre for the Book at the British Library, where she held a Visiting Fellowship in 1996 that made this research possible. She would also like to thank Pluto Press for permission to re-use some of this material, which appears in *The Reform of Time*, London, 2001.

1 H. Bloom (ed.), *Sigmund Freud's 'The Interpretation of Dreams'*, Chelsea House, New York, 1987, p. 1. Bloom here chooses to interpret *Traumdeutung* as dream book, presumably in allusion to the chapbook genre, rather than using the more familiar translation, 'the interpretation of dreams'. The implication is that Freud's choice of word referred to the older tradition.

2 To judge from references in the nineteenth-century British periodical press, French and German dream books were well known; but there do not appear to be any modern studies of their content or readership. Sales of dream books in Britain were closely linked with almanacs and broadsheets in the early nineteenth century, but these were replaced by calendars and newspapers in the second half of the century. See M. Perkins, *Visions of the Future: Almanacs, Time, and Cultural Change 1775–1870*, Oxford, 1996.

3 Freud, 'On dreams' (1901), in *The Essentials of Psycho-Analysis* (trans. J. Strachey, selected and introduced by A. Freud), London, 1986, p. 83.

4 *The Golden Dreamer, or Dreamer's Interpreter, clearly showing how all things Past, Present and to come may be ascertained by means of Dreams*, Newcastle upon Tyne, no date (British Library catalogue suggests 1850).

5 S. R. F. Price, 'The future of dreams: From Freud to Artemidorus', *Past and Present* 113, November 1986, pp. 3–37.

6 J. Guest, 'A free press, and how it became free', in W. Hutton, *The History of Birmingham*, Birmingham, 1861, quoted in J. H. Wiener, *The War of the Unstamped: The Movement to Repeal the British Newspaper Tax, 1830–1836*, Ithaca, NY, 1969, p. 17.

7 *The True Fortune Teller*, Edinburgh, 1850, p. 24.

8 T. James, *Dream, Creativity, and Madness in Nineteenth-Century France*, Oxford, 1995.

9 *Smithson's Northallerton Almanack*, March 1899.

10 *The Trial of Joseph Powell*, London, 1808.

11 F. Seafield, *The Literature and Curiosities of Dreams: A Commonplace Book or Speculations Concerning the Mystery of Dreams and Visions*, 2 vols, London, 1865, vol. 1, p. 134.

12 *Dreams and Moles. A collection of choice . . . receipts concerning love and marriage. First compiled in Greek, and now rendered into English by a Fellow of the Royal Society*, London, 1750, p. 23.

13 *The Dreamer's Oracle, being a faithful interpretation of two hundred dreams*, Derby, 1830.

14 T. Castle, *The Female Thermometer: Eighteenth-century Culture and the Invention of the Uncanny*, New York, 1995, p. 175.

15 M. Spufford, *Small Books and Pleasant Histories: Popular Fiction and its Readership in Seventeenth-Century England*, Methuen, London, 1981, chap. 7; S. Mendelson and P. Crawford, *Women in Early Modern England 1550–1720*, Oxford, 1998, p. 111.

16 A. Owen, *The Darkened Room: Women, Power, and Spiritualism in Late Victorian England*, Philadelphia, 1990, p. 2.

17 *Chambers's Journal* 53: 630 (4th series), 22 Jan. 1876, pp. 56–59.

18 C. Binz, *Über den Traum*, Bonn, 1878, p. 35, cited in Freud, *The Essentials of Psycho-Analysis*, p. 82.

19 *Blackwood's Magazine* 48, August, 1840, pp. 194–204.

20 Although most of the enormous literature on dreams was written by men, even those who acknowledged that prophecy might play a part in some dreams were usually ambivalent. For an excellent overview of nineteenth-century opinions about dreams, see M. Curti, 'The American exploration of dreams and dreamers', *Journal of the History of Ideas* 27, 1966, pp. 391–416 (of interest not only in an American context). Curti concludes from a survey of eighteenth-century American colonists' diaries that: '[T]he best known diarists merely report dreams [and] reflect on the rising fashion in Europe to discount their importance' (p. 393).

21 *Chambers's Journal* 2: 62, 6 April 1833, entry on 'Dreams', pp. 77–78.

22 W. Collins, *The Woman in White* (1860), Oxford, 1949, p. 27.

23 *Dreams and Moles*, 1750, p. 11.

24 *The New Infallible Fortune Teller, or a just interpretation of Dreams and Moles, to which are added, rules to foretell the Weather; drawn up from the strict observance of nearly half a century*, Edinburgh, 1818, pp. 12–13.

25 Perkins, *Visions of the Future*, pp. 61, 65.

26 'Z' [Hannah More], *Tawny Rachel, or the Fortune Teller; with some account of dreams, omens and conjurers*, Cheap Repository for Religious and Moral Tracts, no. 17, London, no date (British Library catalogue suggests 1797), p. 15.

27 K. Thomas, *Religion and the Decline of Magic: Studies in Popular Beliefs in Sixteenth and Seventeenth Century England*, London, 1971; J. Obelkevich, *Religion and Rural Society: South Lindsey, 1825–1875*, Oxford, 1976; R. Hutton, *The Stations of the Sun: A History of the Ritual Year in Britain*, Oxford and New York, 1997.

28 Stephen Kern has tracked the process by which 'universal time' was promoted: *The Culture of Time and Space 1880–1918*, Cambridge, MA, 1983, pp. 12–13.

29 N. M. Cutts, *Ministering Angels: A Study of Nineteenth-Century Evangelicals Writing for Children*, Herts, 1979, p. 117. My thanks to Dr Sue Rickard for this reference.

30 Spufford, *Small Books*, p. 61.

31 See Perkins, *Visions of the Future*, chap. 4.

Chapter 8

Artists and the dream in nineteenth-century Paris: Towards a prehistory of surrealism

Stefanie Heraeus
(Translated by Deborah Laurie Cohen)

Figure 8.1 Jean-Jacques Grandville, 'First Dream: Crime and Atonement', 1847. Archive of the author.

In 1847, shortly after the artist's death, the *Magasin Pittoresque* published two wood-engravings by the French caricaturist and illustrator Jean-Jacques Grandville (1803–47). What is most striking about both are the eccentric metamorphoses that objects undergo: eyes turn into fish, eyebrows into birds, a mushroom becomes an umbrella and then a bat. The prints are known as 'First Dream: Crime and Atonement' (Fig. 8.1) and 'Second Dream: A Stroll in the Sky' (Fig. 8.2).[1] These titles, which were added by Edouard Charton, the publisher of the *Magasin Pittoresque*, distracted both readers of the journal and art historians from Grandville's real concern in that they direct the viewer's gaze to the pictures' narrative content. In two letters to

Figure 8.2 Jean-Jacques Grandville, 'Second Dream: A Stroll in the Sky', 1847. Archive of the author.

Charton, Grandville had specifically reflected on the titles. In contrast to Charton's titles, he had attempted in his suggestions to focus attention on the mechanisms of dreaming: 'What will our title be? Metamorphoses in Sleep? Transformations, Deformations, Reformations of Dreams? Chain of Thought in Dreams?'[2]

Grandville was obviously less concerned with telling a story in pictures than with developing a specific language with which to convey the ways in which dreams manifest themselves. He wrote to Charton of the 'novelty and difficulty' of this venture – and not without a certain pride in his innovative achievement: 'Until now, to my knowledge, no work of art has understood and expressed the dream in this way'. Grandville's search for a new pictorial language focused on the dream. He claimed to have discovered a new understanding and artistic expression of dreams.

From the perspective of the early twenty-first century, this sounds curious. Instinctively, we associate a new understanding of dreams with Sigmund Freud's epoch-making work, *The Interpretation of Dreams*, and the artistic expression of this new understanding with the surrealists. This fixation seems to obscure recognition that in France, a paradigm shift in the pictorial as well as theoretical understanding of dreams was already taking place in the middle of the nineteenth century. In order to understand this shift, two developments must be viewed in relation to one another: on the one hand,

Figure 8.3 Francisco José de Goya y Lucientes (Spanish, 1746–1828), 'The Sleep of Reason Produces Monsters' (Caprichos, no. 43), 1796–1797. Etching and aquatint; first edition, 1799. Archive of the author. Copyright © Davison Art Centre, Wesleyan University, CT.

the conception that was gaining acceptance around the middle of the century of the radically subjective reality of dreams; and on the other, the artistic appropriation of this conception.[3]

Until then, works of visual art, when they concerned themselves with dreams, employed a visual language based on motifs derived from a familiar dream iconography: with the type 'dreamer/dream', with sleeping figures, owls, Jacob's ladders or spiral staircases. Such motifs are still present in Fuseli's 1781 'The Nightmare' and Goya's 'Capricho 43' of 1796–1797 (Fig. 8.3), the two great models for representing dreams at the beginning of the nineteenth century.[4] Grandville's work provides an ideal-typical example of how the borrowing of motifs from Fuseli and Goya gradually disappears in favour of a contemporary view of the dream.

Grandville's prints are, however, only one example of the new artistic treatment of dreams. In French graphic arts – the great field of experimentation in the visual arts in the nineteenth century – several artists can be found for whom engaging with the subject of the dream inspired them to try out new media and techniques. Victor Hugo (1802–85), Charles Meryon (1821–68) and Odilon Redon (1840–1916) all experimented, albeit in very different ways, with unusual pictorial strategies. To a greater extent than canvas, paper offered possibilities for experimentation.

While it is true that these four artists are not infrequently associated with dreams and the fantastical in the current scholarly literature, scarcely any attempt has been made to locate the term 'dream' historically. Thus it has been impossible to determine more precisely that which is 'dreamlike' in their works. An historical anchoring of these works in the then contemporary conception of dreams, on the other hand, can achieve two things: first it can reconstruct their conditions of creation; moreover, and more particularly, it can explain that which is specific in this form of artistic expression.

Naturally, 'dream' is a commonplace term, above all in the context of a time when it had not yet become a scientific one. One said 'dream' (*rêve* or *songe*) and meant – besides nocturnal dreams – day-dreaming, fantasies or visions, nightmares, hallucinations or madness, but also opium or hashish-induced dreams or somnambulism. Initially as a kind of unstructured 'knowledge', broad discourses on the dream began to take shape in Paris in the 1840s, a process in which writers, visual artists and men of letters were as involved as medical doctors, astronomers and practising 'dream interpreters'. Despite their official prohibition, premises existed in Paris (*cabinets*) where, in exchange for money, a middle-class, largely female clientele could have their dreams interpreted and the future predicted.[5] One cannot for this time yet speak of a specialized psychological discipline, as the 'field' as such did not exist. Psychological questions were dealt with within a medical or anthropological framework.[6] As with the fields of sociology, history and geography, the disciplinary institutionalization of psychology did not take place until the 1880s.[7]

EMPIRICAL DREAM RESEARCH AND THE EXAMINATION OF THE MECHANISMS OF DREAMING

The nascent empirical study of dreams elevated the 'course and material' (Maury) of dreams, their incoherent manifestations and mechanisms, to the status of an object worthy of observation. At the centre of the investigations stood questions regarding the rules of dreams, perception, memory, intelligence and the capacity for judgement and free will.[8] Precisely here a direct connection can be perceived between artistic strategies and ideas about dreams. The words into which the key concepts of the new dream research were condensed – 'association', 'automatism', 'combination', 'assemblage' and 'superimposition' – can just as easily be applied in a description of the aesthetic principles underlying the efforts of a Grandville, a Hugo, a Meryon or a Redon to appropriate the dream artistically.

Within the framework of the expanding study of mental alienation since the mid-1840s, many articles and monographs on the dream appeared.[9] The dream, as well as the so-called hashish dream – a 'dream without sleep' –

offered the possibility, as Jacques-Joseph Moreau de Tours emphasized in his much-discussed study 'Du hachisch et de l'aliénation mentale' (1845), that everyone could study these conditions, not from outside but from inside, through self-experimentation.[10] This introverted perspective also characterized the works of Grandville, Hugo, Meryon and Redon. Unlike almost the whole tradition, they were not interested in representing sleeping persons with their dreams, but exclusively in the interior dream images.

One of the most influential investigations, and one that was known far outside of a medically or psychologically specialized readership, was the empirical study *Le sommeil et les rêves* by Alfred Maury, first published in 1861 and reprinted numerous times. Maury, Librarian and, after 1857, Professor of 'History and Morals' at the Institut de France, had already published large sections of the text, both as separate pamphlets and in three articles for the *Annales médico-psychologiques* in 1848, 1853 and 1857.[11] Maury was concerned with the way in which, in dreams, one leaves the real world with its specific laws, its feeling for space and time and its social conventions. New laws, strange kinds of combinations and coincidental relations develop between persons, objects and words, whose contradiction with external reality does not surprise the dreaming subject.[12] There, 'everything is new, strange, outside of our habitual conceptions'.[13] A multitude of images is created, according to Maury, through a *combination* of sensory stimuli that at some point had impressed themselves upon the sleeper during wakefulness and were often subsequently forgotten.[14] The strange and new in dream images, he claims, results from the way in which they are assembled and grouped.[15] This insistence upon memory as a decisive motor of dream production is a significant feature of the contemporary discourse. In this connection, one can easily mention the names of Baudelaire or Grandville.[16] In the letter to Charton quoted at the outset, Grandville attributes a constitutive role to memory and describes the dream as a composite of fragments of the past:

> In my opinion, one never dreams of any object that one has not seen or thought about while one was awake, and it is the amalgamation of these various objects glimpsed or thought about, often at a considerable distance in time, which creates such strange, such incongruous unities in dreams.[17]

One occasionally finds such statements translated into sociological language, as for example in an article by the medical doctor Antonin Macario. He explains that the 'forms of dreams' not only reflect personal experiences but also 'the general ideas that mark every century'.[18]

A brief glance at the eighteenth century quickly reveals that such interpretations were not entirely new. As far back as the *Encyclopédie* of d'Alembert and Diderot (1751–72), an 'immeasurably large assemblage of all our ideas' was named as the cause of the peculiarity and weirdness of dreams. The article 'Songe', which is a slightly shortened version of the 'Essai sur les songes' (1746) by Samuel Formey, makes it clear that the groundwork for the new way of looking at the dream had long been in place.[19] Eighteenth-century philosophers such as David Hartley and Denis Diderot described the odd, incoherent manifestations of nocturnal dream images and the speed with which these unfold.[20] Formey, who expressly wanted to follow the 'path of experience' (*route de l'expérience*), described the lack of control in dreams and the influence of external and internal bodily sensations.[21] Indeed, he declared the appearance of particularly alien things, which stand 'in contradiction to all the laws and order of nature', to be a 'criterion' by which the dream state could be distinguished from that of wakefulness.[22]

However, in the eighteenth century, the discussions on dreams revolved above all around the role of the psyche in sleep, and dream images were generally understood as products of an 'objective' reality.[23] Formey had alleged that dreams were connected to the universe: nocturnal dreams, he argued, were a succession of images (*représentations*) that unceasingly unfolded in the mind and represented the universe but which were only visible to human beings in sleep in the form of dreams.[24] Although the subjective element in dreams was occasionally described, the notion that dreams allowed one to participate in an objective reality had not yet been discarded.[25] Even among the learned, such opinions would endure for generations: According to a few brief sentences that Baudelaire added to his *Paradis artificiels* (1860) concerning the 'hieroglyphic' nature of certain dreams, there were still people who attributed prognostic qualities to them:

> As it cannot be explained in terms of natural causes, they have attributed to it a cause external to human beings; and even today – not even speaking of oneiromancers – there exists a philosophical school that sees in dreams of this kind at times a reproach, at times a counsel; in sum, a symbolic and moral picture, engendered in the very spirit of the sleeping man.[26]

As Maurice Halbwachs had already observed, the notion that a dream has its own *logic* (Halbwachs), its own *law* (Maury), only first began to spread with Maury (and some of his contemporaries). This view – that thinking in dreams and in the state of wakefulness has a different 'frame of reference' (Halbwachs) – became widely disseminated only in the nineteenth century with the institutionalization of scientific journals and the establishment of an experimental approach to dreams.[27] Thus, although the key words in this discourse not infrequently resembled those of the eighteenth century, they were used in the context of a different interpretation of reality and perception: the dream now no longer made participation in an *objective* reality possible, as Formey could still argue in the *Encyclopédie* article. Rather it opened up a highly subjective reality, 'a world where there is no reality other than the beings created by our memories and our imagination', as Moreau de Tours put it, referring to the hashish dream.[28]

Such ideas about dreams being subject to their own laws and about the reality of dreams being subjective posed a particular challenge to artists and provided a decisive intellectual precondition for the production of new media and techniques. Interest in dreams seems above all to have meant interest in an area of experience where everyday laws do not apply, which is governed instead by other laws that one can attempt to grasp in treatises, poetic texts or with a pen, paintbrush or etching needle. Various motivations can be distinguished: while the dream researcher, but also Grandville, wanted to get hold of the tangible laws of dreams, some artists, such as Hugo and ultimately and especially Redon, were trying to approach the ephemeral.

GRANDVILLE'S CHAINS OF MOTIFS AND THE SCIENTIFIC DISCOURSE ON DREAMS

The principle of 'associative logic' was already apparent in both of Grandville's 'Dreams' of 1847. These prints from the end of his life do not stand alone in his work. In Grandville's *oeuvre*, an interest in associative logic is combined with the eye of the caricaturist, which perhaps made him more sensitive to such mechanisms. Already in 1844 he published the wood-engraving 'The Metamorphoses of Sleep' (Fig. 8.4) in the series 'Another World'.[29] Here two chains of associations interconnect after several stages into a vase with a flower, which in turn is transformed into a female figure, only to dissolve into the mist. The disparate objects are linked only through similarity of form. What is special in Grandville's metamorphoses is that the mutations do not follow a linear progression, but are continually being joined by new objects that cannot be deduced from the preceding stage. This is what constitutes their surreal character.

Grandville's 1840s prints contain obvious parallels to the observations of contemporary dream researchers. Here there are direct overlaps between the artistic and scientific discourses on dreams. This has not yet been noted because the start of empirical dream research is generally dated to the 1860s. Alfred Maury's monograph, published in 1861, and the 1867 study *Les rêves et les moyens de les diriger* by d'Hervey de Saint-Denys are held to be the pioneering works of dream research.[30] In fact, however, the journal *Annales médico-psychologiques*, which was founded in 1843, was already publishing numerous articles on observations of dreams, including some by Maury, in the 1840s. The founding of this journal and the holding of an open competition on 'Sleep from a psychological point of view' by the Institut de France in 1853 already marked the institutionalization of the empirical perspective on dreams. This earlier dating leads us back to

Figure 8.4 Jean-Jacques Grandville, 'The Metamorphoses of Sleep', 1844. Archive of the
author.

precisely the time in which Grandville, Hugo and Meryon were experiment-
ing in their graphic works. One must keep in mind that Grandville developed his 'new' manner of representing dreams at a time when such empirical
research was in its infancy. Nevertheless, Grandville's prints are particularly
instructive for having preceded the larger wave of publications on empirical
dream research.

The associative interconnection of objects related to one another only in
their external form was stressed as a peculiarity of dreams by many authors
in the *Annales médico-psychologiques*, including Maury with the example of
associative word chains in sleep. D'Hervey de Saint-Denys could think of
no better way to describe this than to refer to Grandville's 'capricious mutations'. In order to make his own observations comprehensible, he invoked
the example of Grandville's 'Revelation of the Ballet', a coloured wood-
engraving from the series 'Another World' of 1844.[31]

Marie-Jean-Leon d'Hervey de Saint-Denys, an orientalist and sinologist
at the Collège de France, also attempted to categorize the logic of dreams
pictorially by means of a coloured diagram on the frontispiece of his treatise
Les rêves et les moyens de les diriger (Fig. 8.5). These plates call attention to
the differing interests between the scientific and artistic approaches to dreams.
The upper part of the image, in which a man appears at a dinner party in
the company of a naked woman, seems like an illustration of the often-

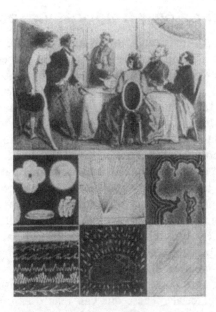

Figure 8.5 d'Hervey de Saint-Denys, *'Les rêves et les moyens de les diriger'*, Paris, 1867, Courtesy of Bibliotheque Nationale de France.

described sexual fantasies in dreams. More significant for the new perspective on dreams, however, are the abstract, coloured drawings in the lower six diagrams. Here we find organic forms and crystalline structures captured, mostly against a black background. The motifs recall flames or wheels of fire, graphic symbols or temperature curves, magnetic fields or cell structures. It seems as if the division of the frontispiece argues in the same manner as the illustrations of workshops in the *Encyclopédie* of Diderot and d'Alembert do.[32] These illustrations always show in the upper third a total view of the manufactury and in the lower part the different tools that are necessary for the craft in question. From this evidence, d'Hervey de Saint-Denys used a well-established academic style to depict a workshop of dream and its tools.

What is striking is the apparently scientific precision with which d'Hervey de Saint-Denys attempted to break down the phenomenon of dreaming into structures. The dream researcher, as it appears here, represents his way of seeing with positivist certainty. His schemata attempt to grasp the logic of dreams just as is promised in the title of his study: 'Dreams and the Means of Steering Them'. Artists, on the other hand, while also grappling in their works with the notion of dreams following laws of their own, were primarily concerned with the intangible, the ephemeral, the incoherent.

THE CREATION OF DREAM MOODS: VICTOR HUGO

One artist who dealt extensively with his 'nocturnal life' was Victor Hugo. This is apparent in a number of ink drawings and numerous recordings of dreams in his personal diary, as well as a few collections of poems (such as 'Les contemplations', 1856) and novels (Les travailleurs de la mer, 1866, and L'homme qui rit, 1869), and particularly the dream-text 'Promontorium somnii' – the Foothills of Sleep – from the year 1863. In the first years of his exile on the island of Jersey, between 1853 and 1855, Hugo also held seances, the protocols of which have survived.[33]

The combination of romantic motifs and unfamiliar media and techniques is the determining characteristic of Hugo's ink and wash drawings, which, in the words of Eugène de Mirecourt, 'transport [the viewer] into the regions of dreams'. Indeed, Hugo, whose works on paper fall into the so-called 'second Romantic' era, still relied in certain works on the traditional iconographic repertoire of medieval castles and ruins, sinking ships and lonely lighthouses for the creation of uncanny moods.

More interesting here, however, are those works that are dominated by experiments with materials. These one can regard as a calculated playing with chance, an artistic appropriation of automatic processes. Hugo developed procedures that attributed an important role during artistic work to free association and which went far beyond contemporary conventions of conceiving of pictures. He splashed ink on paper, strewed salt on fresh paint, made impressions or folded the sheets while they were still wet. In addition, he dipped objects like lace made of fabric or metal, ferns or his finger in ink or gouache and pressed them onto paper. Occasionally, he would lay the lace under the paper and make rubbings of its structure. Usually he did not leave the forms thus created unaltered on the paper, but rather used them as a source of inspiration.

In a lace print which Hugo entitled 'Laces and Spectres' (Fig. 8.6),[34] one can see how he discerned fantastical spectres in the printed structures: by adding a few lines, he formed two grotesque faces out of the openwork pattern, one of which appears in a frontal view and the other in profile. It was above all on the basis of these technical experiments that André Breton later declared Hugo one of the forerunners of surrealism.

Against the background of Hugo's intensive involvement with dreams and his interest in seances, it seems reasonable to interpret his controlled dialogue with chance as a pictorial strategy intended to evoke unseen forces. A good many prints bear a close resemblance to the symmetrical ink-blot pictures that Justinus Kerner was then making in Germany. A follower of mesmerism, Kerner interpreted these blots as expressions of a supersensory spirit world.[35] Even though Hugo was probably unaware of the existence of these images, the reference to Kerner may support this interpretation of Hugo's folded and ink-blot pictures.

Figure 8.6 Victor Hugo, 'Dentelles et Spectres', undated (exile period). Courtesy of Maison de Victor Hugo, Paris. Copyright © Photothèque des Musées de la ville de Paris/Joffre.

In the case of Hugo, however, one should never lose sight of the pathos with which he displayed his visionary powers and his apparently intuitive approach. Hugo created a veritable myth surrounding his own person and his entire artistic *oeuvre*. In his much-cited letter to Baudelaire, he spoke mystifyingly of his 'strange mixtures' and explained these in terms of the search for a language for the pictures in his mind, which he hoped to find not in motifs but rather in media and techniques: 'By the end, I was mixing pencil, charcoal pencil, sepia, coal and soot and all sorts of bizarre mixtures which managed to render a little more closely that which my eye and above all mind's eye sees'.[36] Probably it was he himself who gave birth to the widespread but spurious legend that he used coffee in his works on paper.

A MEETING OF ESSENTIALLY DISSIMILAR REALITIES: CHARLES MERYON

The etchings of Charles Meryon are also recognizable in the context of the nascent and directly popular dream research as an expression of a new aesthetic. This aesthetic is closely related to the later surrealist conceptions of collage, just as, not many years after Meryon's death, it found its poetic expression in the 'Chants de Maldoror' by Lautréamont.

'The Vampire' (Fig. 8.7) is a print from the series 'Etchings on Paris' in which Meryon invoked the old Paris, threatened with demolition in the

Figure 8.7 Charles Meryon, 'The Vampire' (Le Strye de Notre Dame), 1853, Frankfurt/Main. Courtesy of Städtische Galerie of the Staedelsches Kunstintitut, Frankfurt/Main.

framework of Haussmann's redevelopment programme.[37] His head resting on his hands, the winged monster from the Grand Galerie of Notre Dame looks down upon Paris. The meditative gaze and the iconographic gesture of the propped-up head is not only the most obvious reference to the 'infinite domain of dreams and of meditation',[38] as Meryon put it in an unpublished letter to his first biographer Philippe Burty. Furthermore, the foreshortenings and condensations of the architecture as well as the focus on individual details without regard to real proportions express precisely that conception of space which is described in detail in theoretical texts on dreams.

Meryon removed objects from their accustomed locations and tailored the view to his own purposes. He shortened the distances between the Vampire and the Tour St Jacques, compressed the houses in their vicinity and shifted the stone monster to the edge of the picture's front margin. Nor did he pay heed to real proportions: the church tower and the surrounding buildings appear too large for the cityscape behind. Meryon intensified the impression of unreality even more by means of the black birds, whose wings partly extend out of the space of illusion and into that of the viewer.

The montage character, demonstrated in other prints in Meryon's predilection for extreme pictorial details, is particularly apparent in the process through which this etching was created. Probably using photographic models, Meryon took individual objects out of their context and worked them out precisely. Only in the second, etched proof did he combine them

Figure 8.8 Charles Meryon, 'Collège Henri IV', 1864. Copyright © The British Museum, London.

into a single image. In one drawing and in the first proof of the etching, he dealt only with the surrounding house fronts and the large birds; the Vampire and the Tour St Jacques are merely contoured in faint outlines. In another drawing, he represented these in isolation, sketching but shadowy outlines of the surrounding buildings.[39]

Meryon's collage-like method is clearly visible in those etchings in which fantastic phenomena populate the otherwise dreary, stony cityscape. A particularly vivid example is the fourth proof of 'Collège Henri IV' (Fig. 8.8) from 1864.[40] The authentic appearance of the print's topography is marred by steep, towering cliffs and the presence of the sea in the upper region of the picture. A flotilla of sailing-ships and whales, accompanied by two over-sized sea gods and a flock of birds, is heading directly towards the closely packed houses. A confusing effect is created by the disproportionately large schoolboys standing under the imposing school complex, a few of whom have gathered around a female, apparently allegorical, figure. In the picture, a seamless interweaving of highly divergent levels of reality is achieved: details of a seemingly topographical view of nineteenth-century Paris, echoes of a Renaissance landscape, allegorical and ancient mythological figures as well as exotic native ships all encounter one another directly.

To be sure, in interpreting this picture one might consider the possible influence of Meryon's mental disturbance (this has repeatedly been done, particularly in the case of his later etchings). Nevertheless 'mental disturbance' itself is not an objective diagnosis but rather a social construct. Meryon's combination of different objects and levels of reality leads to an – according to mid-nineteenth-century standards – unusual organization of the pictorial field. It serves as evidence of that new, artistic treatment of reality that asserted itself in the second half of the century: objects became freely available, interchangeable and, as incoherent separate components, could be recombined to form something new.

ISOLATION AND SUPERIMPOSITION: ODILON REDON, THE 'PRINCE DU RÊVE'

The montage character of Odilon Redon's 'Noirs' is much more striking. Redon, whom his contemporaries dubbed the 'prince of mysterious dreams', was of a generation already familiar with the empirical discoveries of the middle of the century. He could play with the notion that dreams are a combination of familiar images that one has perceived while awake and which the powers of the imagination in sleep can recombine into new, often incoherent formations. By the 1880s, when a fourth, revised edition of his monograph appeared, the observations of an Alfred Maury fitted in with popular and much-cited views. This is made clear, for example, by Paul-Max Simon's 1882 publication, *Le monde des rêves*, which often makes reference to the authors of the mid-century.[41]

In the charcoal drawing 'Guardian Spirit of the Waters' from 1878, unconnected elements come together:[42] A gigantic head with a small wing hovers over a body of water on which a boat is sailing and over which a couple of birds are winging. In relation to the colossal head, the space with its low horizon appears endlessly wide and the sailboat tiny. With its black hair and partially darkened face, the head appears cut out against the light background. Only the shadows of the head, which are visible on the water, create a formal connection among the various elements in the picture. The modernity of Redon's approach lies in the conception of the picture plane as a field of experimentation for 'autonomous' collage ciphers.

In other prints, the combination of unrelated pictorial elements leads to the condensation of a new object. In the lithograph 'There was perhaps a first vision attempted in the flower' (Fig. 8.9), from the series 'The Origins' from 1883, a plant figure with an oversized, upward-looking eye is superimposed upon strata of other objects.[43] To the right of the plant, a flower can be seen under greyish-black crosshatching; to the left, the flesh-coloured detail of a face and the sketchy beginnings of a very dark black cap can just barely be made out. The individual regions of objects can only be interpreted in relation to their surroundings and only ever make parts of the print coherent.

Of the artists discussed here, Redon is the one whose oeuvre has received the most scholarly attention in the past few years. Particularly in the context of the Redon retrospective mounted in Chicago in 1994, possible connections to contemporary dream research have been suggested. The title of his first

Figure 8.9 Odilon Redon, 'There was perhaps a first vision attempted in the flower', 1883. Archive of the author.

album of lithographs, *Dans le rêve* (In Dreams), published in 1879, could have its source in Alfred Maury's famous treatise, *Le sommeil et les rêves*, reprinted the previous year. An unpublished short story by Redon is supposed to be structurally and compositionally analogous to Eduard von Hartmann's *Philosophie des Unbewußten* (Philosophy of the Unconscious). The motif of the winged heads of many creatures suggests an allusion to Hypnos, the ancient Greek god of sleep.[44]

Redon's 'Noirs' contain very different pictorial qualities. Some prints present dream-images, elements of nocturnal nightmares, in a very concrete and traditional manner featuring grotesque forms, skeletons, skulls and monsters. Others, more instructive here, deal with the concept of dreaming beyond the level of motifs and place media and techniques at the centre of attention. In 'The Polyp of the Dream', a charcoal drawing from 1885, a crude blackening around the edges intensifies into a deep black at the centre of the picture, out of which a half-darkened, three-quarters profile of a child emerges.[45] This is partly encircled by a snake-like creature, the polyp of the dream. In its intensity, the black counteracts any notion of a spatial continuum. Nothing is tangible, nothing can be visibly placed. Only in the lower third of the picture can a body of water and a column be made out.

With his use of the colour black – which for centuries, through the work of Rembrandt, Piranesi, Goya and Delacroix, had been associated with the uncanny, with night and death – Redon did indeed take up its traditional connotations. Yet the black in his prints is no longer an atmospheric darkness that bathes events in an uncanny ambience. In several prints, the black detaches itself from the objects it surrounds and becomes its own, independent bearer of meaning, an abstract expression of subjectivity and an inner world.

In the process, the black becomes a vehicle for a new, positively charged notion of melancholy and the dream. In the 1883 charcoal drawing 'The Sphinx', the dream is depicted not as a threat, as was still the case in Goya's 'Caprichos', but rather as a second reality interwoven with the external one.[46] Instead of juxtaposing two realities, the incoherence of the dream reality in Redon's works is integrated into a flowing black-to-white continuum with soft transitions and fine shading.

The image is dominated by the profile of a gigantic head wearing a diadem. Vegetal forms and horizontal hatching on the picture's lower margin suggest an overgrown bank and a body of water. In connection with this landscape and the dark clouds in the upper region of the picture, the head and shoulders of the 'Sphinx' can also be read as steeply rising cliff formations. Unlike the manner in which multiple meanings are played with in a traditional picture puzzle, a complete synthesis of face and landscape is not achieved here. Rather, the overlapping planes penetrate one another. Thus, although the eyes, nose and mouth of the sphinx can clearly be recognized, the skin on the face appears angular, stony. It is the simultaneity of several layers of meaning that provides space for the different associations.

With the superimposition of pictorial layers and the overdetermination of individual objects, Redon's prints not infrequently give the impression that he was searching for a pictorial language, the scientific conceptualization of which was to come only at the turn of the twentieth century with Sigmund Freud's *Interpretation of Dreams*. Freud, who like Redon spent some time in Paris at the end of the century, would later, in his reflections on dreamwork, declare the overdetermination of individual pictorial elements to be a central distinguishing characteristic of dreams. Such analogies make clear that the caesura of 'Freud' at the end of the century was not as radical as the myth of the *Interpretation of Dreams* might suggest.

In 1901, Henri Bergson gave a lecture on dreams at the Institut Psychologique in which he identified the mechanisms and role of memory in dreams as the central fields of dream research in the century that had just ended. He concluded this stocktaking with the prediction that 'psychical research' on the unconscious would be among the central tasks of the twentieth century.[47] Even though Freud, to whom Bergson at one point referred, blazed a trail with his *Interpretation of Dreams*, the French were slow to recognize this fact; the book was not even translated into French until 1926.[48] What had to be grasped, according to Bergson, was, as Starobinski later put it, that Freud 'in a manner of speaking put an end to the monopoly of organic life and instead bestowed the monopoly position on the psychical apparatus'.[49] Many an artist in the half-century before Freud had already granted a very dominating position to the 'psychical apparatus' in their works. For Redon, above all, the mechanisms of dreaming were of interest only insofar as such knowledge could serve in the search for the psychical dimensions of dreams, the moments of fear or of being lost. With Redon – as, at a more rudimentary stage, already with Grandville, Hugo and Meryon – that productive connection between dream conceptions and pictorial strategies, the legacy of which extends far into the twentieth century, was already bearing fruit.

NOTES AND REFERENCES

1 'Premier rêve, Crime et expiation', wood-engraving; 'Second rêve, Une promenade dans le ciel' wood-engraving: from *Magasin Pittoresque* 15: 27, 1847, pp. 212, 213. See A. Renonciat, *La vie et l'oeuvre de J. J. Grandville*, Paris, 1985, p. 283.

2 'Et d'abord, quel sera notre titre? Métamorphoses dans le sommeil? Transformations, déformations, réformations des songes? Chaînes des idées dans les songes, cauchemars, rêves, extases, etc.?': first letter, in *Magasin Pittoresque* 15: 27, 1847, p. 210, col. 2. Compare the original letter: 'Voyons d'abord quelques titres métamorphoses du sommeil? Transformations déformations reformations et du sommeil des songes. – Chaîne des idées dans les songes, les cauchemars, rêves extases etc. –': Grandville, 26 Feb. 1847, lines 12–18, Paris, Archives Nationales, Papiers Charton, 281 AP[1-2].

3 This article draws on my book: S. Heraeus, *Traumvorstellung und Bildidee–Surreale Strategien in der französischen Graphik des 19. Jahrhunderts*, Berlin, 1998.

4 Johann Heinrich Fuseli, 'The Nightmare', 1781, Oil on canvas, 1.01: 1.27 m, Detroit, The Detroit Institute of Art; see G. Schiff, *Johann Heinrich Füssli (1741–1825), Text und Oeuvrekatalog*, Zürich/München, 1973, p. 496, no. 757. Goya, 'El sueño de la razón produce monstruos', 1797/98, etching, aquatint, 216: 152 mm. Also see the two pen sketches for 'Capricho 43' in P. Gassier and J. Wilson, *Goya – Leben und Werk*, Fribourg, 1971, p. 181, nos 536–538.

5 Y. Ripa, *Histoire du rêve, Regards sur l'imaginaire des français au XIXe siècle*, Paris, 1988; on 'Clefs des songes', see pp. 18–28; on the dream *cabinets*, pp. 43–45, 56–58, 73–75.

6 A development which had already begun in the eighteenth century with the establishment of the psychological discipline '*psychologica rationalis*' and its complementary science '*psychologica empirica*'. See the overview provided by W. Riedel in 'Anthropologie und Literatur in der deutschen Spätaufklärung Skizze einer Forschungslandschaft' in *Internationales Archiv für Sozialgeschichte der deutschen Literatur* 6, special issue, 1994, pp. 105–110, although the focus here is on the German late Enlightenment. For the French late Enlightenment, see the study by S. Moravia, *Beobachtende Vernunft, Philosophie und Anthropologie in der Aufklärung*, 1970. It deals extensively with the anthropologically oriented Société des Observateurs de l'homme, which was founded in 1799.

7 On the formation of psychology as a distinct academic and professional discipline, see J. Carroy, *Hypnose, suggestion et psychologie, L'invention des sujets*, Paris, 1991.

8 See the bibliographies in *Proceedings of the Society for Psychical Research* 5, London, 1887, pp. 581–585, and Ripa, *Histoire du rêve*, pp. 259–71. The fundamental work is A. Maury's *Le sommeil et les rêves*, Paris, 1861, especially the third chapter, 'Des rêves et la manière dont fonctionne l'intelligence pendant le sommeil' (pp. 35–40).

9 The interest in dreams was directly related to the discussions between the opposing parties of the so-called 'physiologists' and 'spiritualists'; as the latter came out on top, greater importance was attributed to psychological aspects and the inner life, including dreams, became a central object of study. On this, see J. Goldstein, *Console and Classify, The French*

Psychiatric Profession in the Nineteenth Century, Cambridge, MA, New York and Port Chester, 1990, pp. 242–245.

10 See M. de Tours, *Du Hachisch et de l'aliénation mentale, Etudes psychologiques*, Paris, 1845, p. 37 ('un véritable *état de rêve*, mais de rêve *sans sommeil*'), pp. 29–32, 34, 146. In comparison with mental disturbance and the hashish dream, he described the dream state as 'l'expression la plus complète; on pourrait dire qu'il en est le type normal ou physiologique' (p. 350). See also C. Lévêque, 'Du sommeil et du somnabulisme, au point de vue psychologique', in *Revue des deux mondes* 14, 1858, p. 928.

11 A. Maury, 'Des hallucinations hypnagogiques', *Annales médico-psychologiques* 11, 1848, pp. 26–40; 'Nouvelles observations sur les analogies des phénomènes du rêve et de l'aliénation mentale', in vol. 5, 1853, pp. 404–421; 'De certains faits observés dans les rêves et dans l'état intermédiaire entre le sommeil et la veille', in vol. 3, 1857, pp. 157–176.

12 See Maury, *Le sommeil*, esp. pp. 36, 86, 100, 135 and 138; M. de Tours, *Du Hachisch*, pp. 38–39, 226, 350–352.

13 M. de Tours, *Du Hachisch*, p. 226: 'Et là, tout est nouveau, étrange, en dehors de nos conceptions habituelles: c'est le rêve avec toutes ses bizarreries, ses caprices, ses monstruosités, ses impossibilités de toute espèce'.

14 See L.-F. Lélut, 'Mémoire sur le sommeil, les songes et le somnambulisme', *Annales médico-psychologiques* 4, 1852, p. 332 and Maury, 'Des hallucinations', p. 39; 'Nouvelles observations', p. 406; 'De certains faits', p. 175. For more detail see Maury, *Le sommeil*, pp. 92–94, 102, 119, 135–137 (identical in places with the texts of earlier articles). Maury, *Le sommeil*, p. 135: 'Le rêve n'est le plus souvent, comme je l'ai dit plus haut, qu'un rappel d'images déjà perçues, d'idées déjà formulées par l'esprit, mais que l'imagination combine dans un nouvel ordre'. See also M. de Tours, *Du Hachisch*, p. 178.

15 See Maury, 'Nouvelles observations', p. 406, and *Le sommeil*, pp. 102 and 135.

16 In the *Paradis artificiels* (1860) Baudelaire distinguishes between two types of dreams and mentions the appearance of everyday memories as a characteristic of 'natural dreams': 'Les rêves de l'homme sont de deux classes. Les uns, pleins de sa vie ordinaire, de ses préoccupations, de ses désirs, de ses vices, se combinent d'une façon plus ou moins bizarre avec les objets entrevus dans la journée, qui se sont indiscrètement fixés sur la vaste toile de sa mémoire.' *Oeuvres complets* (ed. Claude Pichois), vol. 1, Paris, Pléiade, 1975, p. 408.

17 'A mon avis, on ne rêve aucun objet dont l'on n'ait eu la vue ou la pensée lorsque l'on était éveillé, et c'est l'amalgame de ces objets divers entrevus ou pensés, à des distances de temps souvent considérables, qui forme ces ensembles si étranges, si hétéroclites des songes. . . .': Grandville, *Magasin Pittoresque* 15: 27, 1847, p. 211, col. 2. Compare the original letter, lines 38–46: '. . . car à mon avis: l'on ne rêve rien que l'on n'en ait eu la vue ou la pensée etant eveillé, et ce dont ses amalgames, ces combinaisons d'objets divers entrevus ou pensés, à des distances de tems [sic] souvent assez considérables qui forment les assemblages si hétéroclytes et étranges des songes. . . .'

18 'Les formes des rêves reflètent les idées générales qui dominent dans chaque siècle. . . .': Macario, 'Des rêves considérés sous le rapport physiologique et pathologique', *Annales médico-psychologiques* 8, 1846, pp. 172, 179. One of the best-known examples of this was a dream of Maury's that was inspired by a falling headboard. It was set at the time of the French Revolution and involved Maury being beheaded. See Maury, 'Nouvelles observations', p. 418. The identical text appears in Maury, *Le sommeil*, pp. 133–134, and was later quoted in Freud's *Interpretation of Dreams*.

19 See the article 'Songe', in *Encyclopédie*, vol. 15, pp. 354–357 (reprint Stuttgart, 1967), which speaks of 'l'immense assemblage de toutes nos idées' (p. 355, col. 1). J. H. S. Formey, 'Essai sur les songes' (Berlin, 1746), in Formey, *Mêlanges philosophiques*, Leiden, 1754, pp. 174–204.

20 I base my remarks in what follows on L. G. Crocker, 'L'analyse des rêves au XVIIIᵉ siècle', in T. Besterman (ed.), *Studies on Voltaire and the Eighteenth Century*, Geneva, 1963

(pp. 271–310; pp. 284–295 on Diderot), which deals mainly with France. For Hartley's observations on dreams, see the short section in his *Observations on Man* (1749), London, 1769, pp. 383–389.

21 Formey did not use the term 'automatisme' but sought to grasp the conglomerate of nocturnal dream images and the state of absent reason with the metaphor of 'anarchy', an exclusively negative state: 'L'imagination de la veille est une République policée, où la voix du Magistrat remet tout en ordre; l'imagination des songes est la même République dans l'état d'Anarchie.' Formey, *Mélanges*, p. 180 (in *Encyclopédie*, vol. 15, p. 355, cols. 1–2).

22 Formey, *Mélanges*, p. 203 (*Encyclopédie*, vol. 15, p. 356, col. 1): '. . . tandis que tout cela, & des choses encore plus étranges, contraires à toutes les loix de l'ordre & de la nature, se produisent dans les songes. C'est donc là le *Criterium* que nous avons pour distinguer ces deux états'.

23 See Crocker, 'L'analyse', pp. 278 and 301–303. He notes that the belief in the forward-looking, at times even prophetic nature of dreams was also widespread among the *philosophes*. Formey's remarks appear in the *Encyclopédie* (vol. 15, p. 354, col. 2) under the rubric 'Songe (Métaphysique & Physiologie)'.

24 See Formey, *Mélanges*, pp. 183–184 (*Encyclopédie*, vol. 31, p. 400, col. 2): '. . . dès que le sommeil s'est emparé de la machine, l'âme a sans interruption une suite des représentations. . . . Depuis le moment que l'âme a été créée, & jointe à un corps, ou même à un corpuscule organisé, elle n'a cessé de faire les fonctions essentielles à une âme, c'est-à-dire, d'avoir une suite non interrompue d'idées qui lui représentent l'univers. . . .' On this see also the views of Louis de Beausobre in Crocker, 'L'analyse', pp. 276–277.

25 See Crocker, 'L'analyse', pp. 308–310.

26 '. . . et encore aujourd'hui, sans parler de oneiromanciens, il existe une école philosophique qui voit dans les rêves de ce genre tantôt un reproche, tantôt un conseil; en somme, un tableau symbolique et moral, engendré dans l'esprit même de l'homme qui sommeille', Baudelaire, *Paradis artificiels* (1860), in *Oeuvres complets*, vol. 1, p. 409.

27 See M. Halbwachs, *Das Gedächtnis und seine sozialen Beziehungen* (1925), Frankfurt am Main, 1985, pp. 44–46 and 81. In this context, Halbwachs draws attention to the basic agreement between Maury's observations and Freud's reflections on dreams as systems of signs. See Maury, *Le sommeil*, p. 38, 'suivant une certaine loi'.

28 '. . . un monde où il n'y a de réel que les êtres crées par nos souvenirs et notre imagination . . . ,' M. de Tours, *Du Haschisch*, p. 147. See also (p. 150): 'Les créations de notre imagination ont pris la place de la réalité. . . .'

29 'Les métamorphoses du sommeil', from *Un autre monde*, 1844, p. 243, wood-engraving, 127: 150 mm. See Renonciat, *Grandville*, p. 249.

30 Tony James has recently revised this view, at least implicitly. In his study *Dreams, Creativity and Madness in Nineteenth-century France* (Oxford, 1995), the first extensive cultural history of dreams in France in the nineteenth century, he portrays the years around 1855 as the time when ideas about dreams changed significantly. James does address the question of the potential for artistic creativity in dreams and other phenomena of sleep, but he refers only to literature, neglecting the visual arts. See my review of his book in *Kritische Berichte* 4, 1997.

31 'Parfois enfin, l'évocation successive des réminiscences s'enchaîne uniquement par des similitudes de formes sensibles, ce qui est d'ailleurs une sorte d'abstraction capable d'enfanter les composés les plus étranges. Sans l'appliquer aux songes, Granville [*sic*] avait eu le sentiment de ces mutations capricieuses, quand son crayon nous montrait une série graduée de silhouettes commençant par celle d'une danseuse et finissant par celle d'une bobine aux mouvements furieux': M.-J.-L. d'Hervey de Saint-Denys, *Les rêves et les moyens de les diriger*, Paris, 1867, p. 43, see also p. 411.

32 This argument was made in a review of my book by H. Ritter, 'Werkstatt des Wahns. Neue Traumvorstellungen im Frankreich des 19. Jahrhunderts', in *Frankfurter Allgemeine Zeitung*, 3 Feb. 1999, p. N5.

33 The records of the seances are printed in J. Massin (ed.), Victor Hugo, *Oeuvres complets*, vol. 9, Paris, Le club français du livre, 1967, pp. 1170–1182.

34 On the lower edge of the print 'Dentelles et spectres', undated (exile period), pen-and-wash drawing, brown ink, charcoal, impression of laces on paper, 72: 61 mm. Compare *Catalogue Maison de Victor Hugo*, Paris, 1985, no. 878, colour reproduction in exhibition catalogue, *Victor Hugo peintre*, Venice, 1993, no. 27.

35 See Karl-Ludwig Hofmann and Christmut Praeger in A. Berger-Fix (ed.), *Justinus Kerner. Nur wenn man von Geistern spricht, Briefe und Klecksographien*, Stuttgart, 1986, pp. 125–152.

36 'J'ai fini par y mêler du crayon, du fusain, de la sépia, du charbon, de la suie et toutes sortes de mixtures bizarres qui arrivent à rendre à peu près ce que j'ai dan l'oeil et surtout dans l'esprit': Hugo, 29 April 1860, in *Oeuvres complets* (ed. J. Massin), vol. 12, pp. 1,097–1,098.

37 'Le Stryge', 1853, etching, pl. 155: 116 mm, Frankfurt/Main, Städelsches Kunstinstitut, inv. no. SG 4174. See L. Delteil and H. J. L. Wright, *Catalogue raisonné of the Etchings of Charles Meryon*, New York, 1924, no. 23.

38 '. . . tout çela, dis-je, jette l'esprit, sans qu'on puisse se défendre, dans le domaine infini des rêves et de la méditation': Meryon, 13 January 1863, lines 48–51, Toledo, Ohio, Museum of Art, inv. no. 19.81 d.

39 See Delteil and Wright, *Etchings of Charles Meryon*, no. 23; and Burke in the exhibition catalogue *Charles Meryon: Prints & Drawings* (ed. J. D. Burke), Toledo Museum of Art, Toledo, Ohio, 1974, pp. 35–9, nos. 8–13.

40 'Collège Henri IV', 1864, etching, 4th proof, pl. 220: 410 mm, London, British Museum, inv. no. 1865-1-14–143. See Delteil and Wright, *Etchings of Charles Meryon*, no. 43.

41 See M. P. Simon, *Le monde des rêves. Le rêve, l'hallucination, le somnambulisme et l'hypnotisme, l'illusion, les paradis artificiels, le ragle, le cerveau et le rêve*, Paris, 1882.

42 'Guardian Spirit of the Waters', 1878, various charcoals, black and white chalk, 466: 376 mm, Art Institute of Chicago, David Adler Collection 1950.1420. See 1994 exhibition catalogue, *Odilon Redon: Prince of Dreams, 1840–1916*, Art Institute of Chicago, p. 438, no. 50.

43 'There was perhaps a first vision attempted in the flower', 1883, from 'The Origins', no. 2, 223: 172 mm. See A. Mellerio, *Odilon Redon, Peintre, Dessinateur et Graveur*, Paris, 1923, no. 46.

44 See Druick and Zegers in the 1994 Chicago exhibition catalogue (as note 42), pp. 93 and 103–105 (on Eduard von Hartmann), pp. 110 and 125–127 (on empirical research on dreams). The short story, 'Le récit de Marthe folle', previously unknown, was discovered in the 'Mellerio Redon Papers' (A 14, pp. 1–11). Discussion of Redon until now has focused mainly on his relationship to occult and esoteric theories. See Gott, in the exhibition catalogue *The Enchanted Stone: The Graphic Works of Odilon Redon*, National Gallery of Victoria, Melbourne, 1990, pp. 98ff; Leeman in the 1994 Chicago exhibition catalogue, pp. 215–236; and R. J. Mesley, 'Odilon Redon: Vision and visionaries', *Art Magazine* 2: 45, Sept./Oct. 1979, pp. 62–68.

45 'The Polyp of the Dream', 1885, charcoal, charcoal pencil, black chalk, 484: 357 mm, New York, Museum of Modern Art, Mr and Mrs Donald Strauss, inv. no. 279.73. See A. Wildenstein, Odilon Redon, Catalogue raisonné, Paris 1994, vol. 2, p. 249, no. 1,217.

46 'The Sphinx', 1883, various charcoals, black chalk, 526: 377 mm, Art Institute of Chicago, David Adler Collection 1950.1415. See exhibition catalogue, Odilon Redon, p. 442, no. 87.

47 See H. Bergson, 'Le Rêve', in *L'Energie spirituelle* (1901), Paris, 1982, p. 108: 'Sur ce sommeil profond la psychologie devra diriger son effort, non seulement pour y étudier la structure et la fonctionnement de la mémoire inconsciente, mais encore pour scruter les phénomènes plus mystérieux qui relèvent de la "recherche psychique". . . . Explorer l'inconscient, travailler dans le sousol de l'esprit avec des méthodes spécialement appropriées, telle sera la tâche principale de la psychologie dans le siècle qui s'ouvre.' He refers to Freud on p. 107.

48 Freud, *La science des rêves* (trans. I. Meyerson), Paris, 1926. For a list of French translations of parts of Freud's works and of reviews in journals up until 1926, see M. Bonnet, *André Breton, Naissance de l'aventure surréaliste*, Paris, 1975, pp. 102–103.

49 See J. Starobinski, 'Brève histoire de la conscience du corps', in R. Ellrodt (ed.), *Genèse de la conscience moderne, Etudes sur le développement de la conscience de soi dans les littératures du monde occidental*, Paris, 1983, p. 224.

Chapter 9

Policing dreams: History and the moral uses of the unconscious

Rhodri Hayward

In the spring of 1893, Herman Hilprecht thought his dreams had been invaded by spirits. As Professor of Assyrian at the University of Pennsylvania, he had been studying drawings of various inscribed fragments recovered from the Temple of Bel at Nippur.[1] Although for the most part their classification was easy, two of the sketches caused him particular trouble. These sketches appeared to be of agate finger rings, one bearing the letters KU whilst the other remained indecipherable. Tired of his work, Hilprecht hesitantly ascribed the fragments to the reign of King Kurigalzu, before retiring, exhausted, into a deep sleep.[2]

During the night, Hilprecht dreamt that he had been transported to the temple at Nippur. There he met one of the ancient Babylonian priests, who led him into the treasure chamber of the building. In this room, the priest revealed that the fragments that had so confounded Hilprecht were once part of the same votive cylinder. This cylinder, the dream priest told Hilprecht, had been sent by King Kurigalzu to the temple but was subsequently cut into three parts when the king ordered a pair of agate ear-rings for the statue of the god Ninib.[3]

When he awoke, Hilprecht recorded the dream and then rushed to compare the fragments' sketches. They did indeed join as the dream priest had predicted, revealing in their wholeness the original inscription of the votive cylinder – 'To the god Ninib, son of Bel, his lord, has Kurigalzu, pontifex of Bel, presented this'.[4]

For Hilprecht, the dream appeared to be a graphic and deeply romantic example of spirit inspiration. He had been presented with six pieces of novel information: the correspondence of the fragments; their existence as a votive cylinder; its presentation by King Kurigalzu; its dedication to Ninib; its transformation into earrings; and the location of a treasure chamber on the south-east side of the temple. Each of these conjectures was further confirmed when Hilprecht visited the Imperial Museum at Constantinople and inspected the agate pieces in person. The fragments confirmed the dream priest's proclamation, joining neatly to form part of the inscribed cylinder.

Like the agate pieces, the fragments of Hilprecht's dream could also be rearranged into a novel and constructive pattern – although in this case the design they revealed had a far more mundane implication. It was possible to read the dream as an entirely secular narrative. As the American psychologist William Romaine Newbold explained to Hilprecht, each one of the inspired pieces of information could be produced through the same process of association and analysis that the archaeologist employed every day.[5]

The common elements of the agate fragments, Newbold argued, would have brought them together in a subconscious association, from which their origin and inscription could have been deduced.[6] The origin of the final piece of information, the location of the treasure house, seemed more mysterious until it transpired that Hilprecht had been given an oral description of the treasure chamber by the archaeologist John P. Peters some five years previously.[7] What had appeared in the dream as an occult source of information was revealed as nothing darker than the lacuna produced by the individual's own forgetting.

Hilprecht's story immediately appears as an argument for the integration of psychology and history. Through an engagement with his own dreams and the assistance of experts, he recovers levels of lost order and meaning – both in his own life and in the Babylonian past. The thread of the unconscious draws together both the mysterious agate pieces and the fragments of Hilprecht's memory. Yet the easy recognition and acceptance that we accord to such arguments disguises the contingency of these interpretations. That we so readily accept them is more revealing of the moral operations at work within our own writing of history.[8]

The supernatural inspiration and psychological disenchantment experienced by Herman Hilprecht can be read as an allegory for the progress of dreams throughout the nineteenth century. A whole series of political and cultural assumptions were implicit within the final and secular interpretation of the dream. First, there was the insistence that the dream's origins must be located within the interior life of the individual rather than the external interventions of spirit guides. Second, there is the idea that the unconscious mind could reveal a level of association and connection where waking consciousness could perceive only confusion and fragmentation. Third, there is a belief in the mythopoeic ability of the unconscious, that it could be capable of correctly arranging the fragments and associating them with other distant memories, such as the oral testimony of John Peters. Last, Hilprecht's mistaken inferences as to the nature of his dream demonstrated the inadequacy of amateur attempts at oneirocriticism and the need for professional assistance in the correct explication of dreams. To the modern reader these assumptions may seem quite commonplace or unremarkable, yet their mundane nature obscures a whole series of political struggles that surrounded the Victorian interpretation of dreams.

* * *

Some of the certainty surrounding the psychological interpretation of Hilprecht's dream disappears when it is set against the religious culture of nineteenth-century Britain. For many Christians, mystics and Swedenborgians there was no easy connection between dreams and the memory of the individual. Rather the dream emerged at the point where memory and personal history disappeared. It was pictured as a liminal phenomenon, not simply as an event outside the boundaries of consciousness or the waking life, but as an experience that transcended the carnal limits of the personality and the possibilities of historical representation.

In the Christian models of personality developed from the writings of St Paul, a clear distinction had been drawn between the finite and representable self and the ineffable and sublime soul.[9] The finite self, as Paul had argued in his letters to Romans and Corinthians, was simply a confusion of inherited sins and desires, originating from the fall of Adam. In contrast the transcendent soul emerged through man's true relationship of dependence upon God.[10] Within Pauline anthropology, man's true soul thus stood beyond the compass of historical representation, being located within the immortal relationship between the individual and the Divine.

The psychological schemas of Pauline theology combined with the Biblical equation of sleep and death to promote a dynamic model of dreaming.[11] The dream was seen as a movement away from the fleshbound history of the individual man into a generalized communion between the soul and the spirit.[12] Philosophers, theologians and visionaries celebrated the dream as a form of minor ascension, a moment in which the spirit escaped the constraints of the material world. Writing in 1855, the theologian Franz Delitzsch pictured the process as one in which 'the spirit of the sleeper sinks not into the flesh, but into God, from whom it originated: it communes with God and finds itself with its senses in God, as in falling asleep, so also still in awakening'.[13]

Sleep thus mirrored the Christian ideas of death and resurrection.[14] It involved a transition from a finite self rooted in the world to a transcendent soul caught up within the universal Spirit. As the utopian socialist Robert Owen noted:

> Every night if blessed with health and tranquillity, we pass, in an unconscious moment, the threshold of material existence entering another world . . . our judgement is usually obscured, and our reasoning faculties are commonly at fault; yet the soul, as if in anticipation of the powers which the last sleep may confer upon it, seems emancipated from earthly trammels.[15]

In this moment of dreamy communion, the sleeper achieved an angelic detachment from the constraints of history and geography. In her popular work, *The Night-Side of Nature* (1848), the novelist Catherine Crowe explained how 'relations of time and space form no obstruction to the dreamer; things, near and far, are alike seen in the mirror of the soul'.[16] This sense of the soul's transcendence was reported by many Victorian dreamers. Frank Seafield, the editor of *Arena*, claimed that his unfettered dreaming soul achieved a god-like apprehension of the contingency of space and time:

> Distance is annihilated; our own planet is a sand grain and the entire universe is an hour-glass. The equator becomes the girdle of the pole; ice-bergs build up their towers in red-sea; the diameter of a planetary orbit is a hop, skip and jump, and the sun is brought near enough to be serviceable as a toaster of cheese. Time is no more. We give our right hand to Adam and our left to Campbell's last man . . .[17]

By the late nineteenth century these ephemeral glimpses of the soul's transcendence seemed to have received miraculous confirmation. The reports of 'travelling clairvoyance' and Highland second sight, which formed a staple of popular literature, provided experimental evidence of the soul's ability to travel during trance and sleep and return with convincing testimony of its adventures.[18]

This idea of sleep as a reflection of the carnal self's dissolution at death undid the idea of the individual's life as a discrete or bounded narrative.[19] At one level, as we have already seen, this dissolution allowed sleepers to enter into a realm of knowledge and experience beyond the compass of their own lives. At a second and parallel level, this breakdown rendered the dreamer vulnerable to the entry of alien desires and ideas. In many Victorian communities the sleeping mind was held up as an arena in which demons, angels, night hags, fairies and the ghosts of dead and dying friends acted out their nocturnal adventures.[20]

These episodes of spectral trespass provided graphic confirmation of the theory of inspired dreaming. The supernatural intruders tutored their sleeping hosts in a prophetic philosophy that stressed the authority of experience over consensually established descriptions of reality. The dangers of such dream-time insights were widely commented upon by Victorian philosophers and anthropologists. Herbert Spencer and E. B. Tylor complained that the primitive belief in ghosts and demons had been sustained through the corrosive presence of dreams.[21] Spencer pictured the theory of dream inspiration as a kind of intellectual saboteur, undermining the bases of truth and reason. As he argued:

> the acceptance of dream activities as real, strengthens allied misconceptions not otherwise generated. It strengthens them both negatively and

positively. It discredits those waking experiences from which right beliefs are drawn and it shields support to those waking experiences which accept wrong belief.[22]

Likewise Tylor insisted that modernity could never be achieved until individuals moved from a belief in the external origins of dreams to an acceptance of their internal generation within the psyche.[23]

These disruptive survivals in demon and fairy belief were reinvigorated in the nineteenth century through the rise of experiential religions, particularly spiritualism and Swedenborgianism.[24] Organized in Britain through the Academy of the New Church, this latter faith had drawn its theology from the inspired instructions and mystical visions of the spirit seer, Emmanuel Swedenborg. Theorizing from his own nocturnal experiences, Swedenborg had argued that the dream was a contested zone in which angels, demons and sirens or interior witches fought for the sleeper's attention and infested his memory.[25] He stressed the alien character of dream information, endorsing an angel's description of the dream as a merchant ship that docked and unloaded a strange cargo into the sleeping mind.[26]

Many spiritualists followed Swedenborg in this model of the dream as a form of nocturnal communion.[27] Although some professional mediums may have resisted the idea of the general possibility of dream inspiration, the main spiritualist periodicals maintained a steady stream of reports on prophetic and extraordinary dreams.[28] Andrew Jackson Davis, 'the Poughkeepsie Seer' whose inspired writings were foundational to much of the theology and cosmology of spiritualism, supported the idea of inspired dreaming.[29] Combining Swedenborgian doctrine with contemporary neurology, Davis claimed that the sleeper's passive brain could be played upon by superintendent spirits producing dreams as a musical instrument produced its tune.[30]

This model achieved widespread acceptance in the British Isles. In 1894, the Tory journalist, Frederick Greenwood, argued that the 'physiologist from his scalpel and knife knowledge' was bound to support the idea of spirit intervention in dreams.[31] Like Davis, he believed that spirits could play upon the nerves like harp strings in order to direct and control the substance of a dream. As with the folk belief in dream-time possession, such arguments were reinforced by the testimony of the senses. Greenwood's political antagonist, the republican spiritualist Roden Noel, insisted upon the independent reality of characters in dreams.[32] As Noel noted in *The Philosophy of Immortality*, the sense of presence achieved in dreams equalled that experienced in daily life. Such apprehensions suggested that the actors and events witnessed in dreams were at least as objective as those encountered in our waking lives.[33]

Spiritualists, Swedenborgians and superstitious Christians thus cherished the knowledge that dreams imparted. It was argued that the spirit visitors, freed from the constraints of space and time, granted the dreamer a privileged insight into their current or future life. These insights could be explicit, with scenes and glimpses from a future life or possible death imparted in the sleeping mind. For the most part, however, the message was allegorical, appearing either as the contrary of a future event or symbolized through a common stock of images contained within the many dream-books that flourished throughout the nineteenth century.[34] The transparency of these allegories precluded the need for reference to professional or expert diviners. Instead they supported a form of auto-interpretation in which friends and family gathered together to divine the meanings of their dreams.[35]

At one level this shared culture of dreams could strengthen the social fabric. Like the moralizing spectres identified by Keith Thomas in *Religion and the Decline of Magic*, the dream could work as a detective, revealing hidden crimes or attacking the criminal conscience.[36] Newspapers frequently told of corpses located in dreams and thieves and murderers revealed to distant inspired witnesses.[37] Such stories were immortalized in popular melodrama, most notably in the tale of Maria Marten and the murder in the Red Barn.[38] Within such stories, dreams and clairvoyance operated as supernatural sources of surveillance, disciplining the tempted and punishing transgressors by revealing the hidden contents of the criminal mind.[39]

Alongside this moralizing imperative, the prophetic dream could also carry a more subversive and radical implication. The Scripture promise given in Numbers xii 6, that the Lord would make himself known to his prophets in dreams, had long authorized a series of visionary attacks against the state.[40] Although such visions had been in rapid decline since the days of Richard Brothers and Joanna Southcott, there still persisted a whole host of small-town millenarians.[41] In the early 1850s Frank Starr, a Norfolk salesman anointed by angels in a Greenwich pub, pioneered a mystical critique of Owenism and capitalism. Likewise, by the end of that decade, J. G. H. Brown, a Nottinghamshire jeweller, had been inspired by the spirit of Swedenborg to launch a defence of the local poor.[42] Although the political effect of these inspired missions may have been minimal, their example popularized a more subtle radicalism that contested dominant notions of selfhood, responsibility and academic authority.[43]

The popular hermeneutic deployed in both the revolutionary and the moralizing approaches to dreams stood at odds with the mode of interpretation used in forensic detection or the historical project. Against the modern abductive operation that reads the dream for signs and clues leading back into the subject's past, the belief in the revelatory or prophetic power of dreams encouraged a typological interpretation in which the dream, like the Bible, was read for indications and anticipations of a future state.[44] Detached from the sleeper's past and imbued with a supermundane knowledge, the dream was seen as a form of *kledon* or oracle – 'a pronouncement of which the meaning (though it may make sense in its own time) can be determined only much later, and by illumination from a context unpredicted and remote from that of the original utterance'.[45]

The prophetic theory did not simply offer a new mode of interpretation for the dream experience, rather the idea of inspiration undid the possible connection between dreams and history. The idea of nocturnal communion opened up a universe of possible origins for the dream memory. In so doing, it provided a point of critique against the dominant notions of history, biography and the politics of personal identity. In their demonstration of the contingency and fluidity of selfhood and their importation of the sublime and inexplicable into the subject's personality, dreams frustrated one of the great disciplinary shifts that modern authors have identified in the nineteenth century. It could be seen as a counterpoint to the philosophy of *Bildungsroman* – the romantic ideal of a life determined by youth and childhood – which permeated nineteenth-century literature.[46] Against the literary insistence that growth and experience were dictated by the individual's personal history, religious dreams suggested that the actor was formed through a whole series of occult interventions, which could neither be contained in the individual's biography nor attributed to their environment.

The threat that the religious theory of dreams posed to the notion of individual biography had far wider implications. In its connection of distant and demonic memories and appetites to the sleeping body, the theory subverted contemporary notions of responsibility and agency. The sleeping mind did not produce its dreams, rather it was dreamt through by invading spirits. Moreover the disturbing desires and beliefs inculcated by these nocturnal visitors could not be traced back to any explicit source. Instead the theory of Divine connection suggested that their origins lay beyond knowledge and language in the mind of God, whilst the theories of angelic guidance and demon obsession surrendered the dream to a great cast of fleeting spirits, whose continued movements left ideas and images orphaned and untraceable within the sleeping mind.[47]

The inspired dream thus stood as a direct challenge to a Victorian culture that had stressed the integrity of the individual and the presence of the past. The boundary of sleep did not simply divide the conscious life of the individual, it demarcated rival moralities.[48] The waking world of continence and self-control stood in direct contrast to the wild abandon of dreams. A culture in which individuals strove to maintain control over their actions and desires was confronted with a dream world in which the self was surrendered to fickle forces beyond the compass of language, reason or history.

* * *

It was in the elite and conservative responses to the political threat of dreams and inspiration that the notion of the subconscious was first articulated. Before Freud had begun his researches into hysteria and dreams, British investigators based around the Society for Psychical Research (SPR) had pioneered ideas of the subliminal or subconscious mind in an attempt to police the visions and inspirations produced in the mystical contestation of personal identity.[49] Although the members of the SPR are now seen as genteel apologists for the spiritualist movement, this was a later innovation.[50] Before the society started trying to prove the existence of life after death, it had been concerned with a more mundane form of survival: demonstrating the continuation of personal identity between the minor fractures of biography produced in dreams, trance, automatism and possession. This conservative agenda, which aimed to re-establish the integrity of the forensic individual, was led by three members of Trinity College, Cambridge: Henry Sidgwick, Edmund Gurney and Frederic Myers.[51]

The hostility that the leading members of the SPR exhibited towards popular inspiration could be attributed to two sources. At one level, there was a fairly straightforward resistance to the carnivalesque implications of clairvoyance and dream-time possession.[52] Myers, in particular, disliked the spiritual enfranchisement that possession and inspired dreaming brought about. He complained that the spiritualists ascribed their inspired insights to authors such as 'Abraham or Abraham Lincoln or Isaac or Isaac Newton . . . as readily as a street seller labels his ices pineapple or vanilla' and he mocked the automatic writers' claim that they channelled true texts from Shakespeare when their 'content and grammar fell far below the level expected'.[53]

The assumption of inspired authority also raised a far deeper political question. Like Spencer and Tylor, the SPR was aware that the concept of inspiration provided a dangerous counterpoint to consensual society. They argued that once man began to believe in 'phantasms' there could be no basis for shared agreement or co-ordinated action.[54] Instead an anarchic ignorance prevailed in which each believed and acted according to their own mistaken whim. Myers was quick to identify the dangers of such ignorance and the wilfulness of irrational belief.[55] In 1886, he introduced the SPR's first collaborative volume, on the origins of dreams and visions, with a warning of the political dangers that arose when individuals made false inferences from apparently supernatural experiences:

> The men who claim to have experienced them have not been content to dismiss them as unreasonable or unimportant. They have not relegated them to the background of their lives as readily as the physiologist has relegated them to a few paragraphs at the end of a chapter. On the contrary they have brooded over them, distorted them, misinterpreted them. Where the savants have minimised, they have magnified and the perplexing modes of marvel which textbooks ignore, have become as it were the ganglia from which all kinds of strange opinions ramify and spread![56]

In order to counter the dangers of prophetic interpretation, the SPR developed a threefold strategy that aimed at the reintegration of the inspired dream and the life history of the individual. This strategy consisted of statistical, historical and psychological approaches, intended to demonstrate the continuity of the dream inspiration and the subject's waking life.

The statistical method functioned as a mechanism for transforming dreams into objects of scientific enquiry. This was achieved by detaching the phenomena from their local context of popular wonder and spiritual significance, relocating them instead within a common class of dreams that gradated from the familiar to the apparently inexplicable.[57] The technique emphasized the relative frequency of such experiences, suggesting that the possibility of inspiration should be measured against the probability of chance and coincidence.[58] Between 1882 and the publication of *Phantasms of the Living* in 1886, the Literary Committee of the SPR devoted itself to the collection and collation of thousands of anecdotes and experiences relating to possibly inspired dreams.

This statistical analysis was accompanied by a historical method in which dreams, visions, and inspired speeches were examined for evidence that would connect them to the waking life of the individual. As Gurney wrote:

> If the superiority of men to brutes depends on personality, and if personality depends essentially upon memory, then those who desire that man's dignity should be maintained, and that personality should be continuous can hardly afford to despise the smallest fact of memory which exhibits the possibilities of union and comprehension as triumphing over those of disruption and dispersion.[59]

This strategy was demonstrated in a whole series of articles that appeared in the *Proceedings* of the SPR between 1882 and 1900. Their general form was epitomized in the mundane analysis of Hilprecht's dream, as described at the beginning of this chapter. The waking lives of individuals were combed for images and incidents that could serve as profane sources for the inspired messages received in trances and dreams.

Typical examples included a trance writer whose graphic automatisms were traced back to a forgotten reading of Spinoza, and a crystal gazer whose prophetic visions of blood and dead friends led back to half-remembered images of spilt paint and newspaper obituaries.[60] This historicizing strategy relied upon a narrative process in which the individual's biography was reconstructed in a form that could account for the anomalous information given in the inspired dream or vision.[61]

The third investigative strategy relied upon the use of hypnosis. Hypnosis and its precursor, mesmerism, had long been used to imitate and hence discredit apparently supernatural phenomena.[62] From the earliest days of mesmeric performances, audiences had long recognized the homology between trance and possession behaviour. The examples of ecstasy, catalepsy and apparent exorcism produced by itinerant showmen challenged the hegemony of religious interpretations. Celebrated examples of inspired action or trance speech could now be attributed to a more prosaic process, to the actions of fragmentary ideas originating in the subject's everyday life and subsequently forgotten.

For Gurney and Myers, hypnosis thus presented itself as both an experimental technique and a rhetorical resource. At an experimental level, it allowed the researcher to recreate the experience of sleep whilst maintaining communications with the somnolent body. It was, according to Myers, a form of 'psychical vivisection' permitting an exploration of the unconscious mind.[63]

Such explorations allowed the psychical researchers to demonstrate the persistence of memory, and hence identity, beyond the apparent boundaries of ecstasy and forgetting. In a series of experiments, Gurney hypnotized subjects and presented them with information, which he would ask them to repeat upon waking. This information could not be retrieved until Gurney issued a pre-agreed hypnotic command or engaged the subject in some semi-hypnotic activity such as automatic writing.[64] These demonstrations suggested that hypnotic memories persisted within the individual, existing as concurrent streams of thought alongside the ordinary consciousness of waking life.[65]

Hypnotism in its experimental form and its demonstration of the persistence of trance memory provided the basis for a cogent and sustained critique of the religious theory of dreams. Whereas the mystical interpretations had suggested that the inspired dream involved the passage of information from beyond the history and personality of the individual, the hypnotic theory implied that such information came from an internal but forgotten source. It was a source that lay beyond the boundaries of waking consciousness but within the history of the individual as a whole.

The theory of the subconscious or the subliminal mind thus militated against the mystical politics associated with religious ideas of dreaming. At a micropolitical level it restored the integrity and forensic responsibility of the agent, suggesting that the dream-time inspiration lay in the forgotten memories of the subconscious mind. Moreover the theory suggested that there could be no movement beyond the personality and no escape from personal history, rather every event and idea lay recorded in the hidden layers of the subliminal self. As Max Dessoir, a German colleague of Gurney and Myers, wrote:

> Every thought that ever traversed our brain, every emotion that has ever thrilled our heart, every wish that has ever been animated for a fleeting moment in our breast – has all been entered in ineffaceable characters in the day book of our earthly existence. Would that this knowledge could strengthen our feeling of moral responsibility.[66]

This attack on the micropolitics of inspired dreaming likewise destroyed the mystical rhetoric that had supported the prophetic critique of society and the state. The nocturnal enfranchisement that divine dreams imparted was replaced by a more mundane realization that such visions probably originated in the half-forgotten desires of the discontented. As Myers noted in his mocking attack on the plebeian recourse to inspired authority, the spiritualists' ascription of their 'strings of sermonising platitudes' to authors such as 'Abraham or Abraham Lincoln', suggested that beneath 'there may lurk nothing worse nor better than our own small selves'.[67]

The rhetoric of the subliminal mind did not simply operate as a strategy for policing action and inspiration in public society. Rather, as Myers made clear, it also operated as a mechanism for understanding and controlling the anarchy of the interior life. Drawing upon the familiar metaphor of the body politic, Myers argued that the dreaming state, epitomized in the hypnagogic period between sleeping and waking, could be seen as a suspension of the controlling or dominant consciousness. Such a state allowed ordinary men and women 'to realise the incipient disintegration of the personality; the anarchy of competing groups in the absence of a ruler'.[68]

This metaphor was taken up by a close colleague of Myers, the post-office clerk Frank Podmore.[69] Podmore believed that the disconnected ideas and beliefs recovered in the memory of dreams could eventually threaten the integrity of the waking consciousness. There was a danger that these orphaned memories and desires, freed from the jurisdiction of the controlling self, would develop independently as automatic or hysterical routines.

> For the beginnings of such automatism are like the beginnings of disaffection in the State. Alike in the corporeal and in the political hierarchy certain anarchic elements may free themselves from constitutional control and work out their own ends within limits, with impunity. In a fairly stable constitution these limits are soon reached and the rebellious elements are suppressed ... When however from stress of external circumstances or inherent defect the forces of control are enfeebled, the contagion of disorder may stem further, and a permanent centre of rebellion may be formed – *imperium in imperio* – which may grow strong enough to rival and ultimately overthrow even the central Government.[70]

Psychical research was a tool that allowed for both the diagnosis and the eradication of this political danger. Its policing of dreams in the wider world of Victorian society was accompanied by a similar regulation of dream ideas in the inner environment of the psyche. Myers boasted of the new forms of government that could be achieved through the practice of psychical research:

> *Inward* the course of empire takes its way ... All these hypnotic experiments, for all their strangeness and grotesqueness, are following in the same sure track; their lesson also is of a concealed dominion; they too teach that by 'self reverence, self knowledge, self control' man may become the ruler of his own spirit and the fashioner of his own fate.[71]

Across society and through the psyche, the elite factions of the SPR pursued a general strategy: collapsing the discordant and anomalous knowledge of dreams into the sanctioned narratives of the individual life history. The policy, as we have seen, robbed dreams of their radical implications. In its place it left new forms of power. As many spiritualists and visionaries noted, the notion of the subliminal implied a necessary hierarchy between the deluded visionary, who misinterpreted their own experience, and the psychologist or 'psychic vivisectionist', who with the tools of hypnotism and a historicist hermeneutic achieved a global view of dreams.[72] This global view did not simply demonstrate the integration of dreams and history, it produced a narrative fashioned around the agenda of elite investigation.[73] The inner truth of the individual no longer lay in the divine communion of dreams, rather it was located in a subconscious mind, recovered and refashioned through the practice of psychical research.

* * *

The idea of the subconscious or unconscious mind thus emerged in the nineteenth century as part of a general strategy for containing the power of dreams. It was a rhetorical mechanism for returning the free-floating inspiration of the spiritual vision into the fleshbound history of the individual. In its insistence that the discordant fragments of the supernatural must be surrendered to a single personal narrative, it matched a transformation that characterized the nineteenth century as a whole. As authors such as Hayden White and Stephen Bann have argued, the Victorian belief in universal history, with its concomitant faith in the narrative representation of reality, rested upon a similar series of exclusions.[74] Irrational desires, religious events and subaltern actors all disappeared from the historical stage. As White writes:

> The subordination of historical narrative to the deliberative mode of the middle style entails stylistic exclusions and this has implications for the kinds of events that can be represented in a narrative. Excluded are the kinds of events traditionally conceived to be the stuff of religious belief and ritual (miracles, magical events, godly events), on the one side, and the kind of 'grotesque' events that are the stuff of farce, satire and calumny on the other. Above all these two orders of exclusion, consign to historical thinking the kinds of events that lend themselves to the understanding of whatever currently passes for educated common sense. They effect a disciplining of the imagination, in this case the historical imagination, and they set limits on what constitutes a specifically historical event.[75]

At one level, White's argument would seem to be borne out by a cursory survey of the dream stories and evidence presented in the opening sections of this chapter. Tales of prophecy, possession, dreams fulfilled and nocturnal inspiration have dropped from the mainstream of academic history into the popular but disparaged literature on the paranormal and the arcane. In their eagerness to demonstrate an inexplicable distance between the dreamer's history and the dream, such supernatural stories have fallen outside the canon as a whole.[76]

At another level, however, this disciplining of the historical imagination has been challenged in recent years. Many feminist writers have contested the canonical exclusion of fantasy and the psyche as causal agents in history. This exclusion, they argue, has had a twofold effect. At one level, it has rendered many religious episodes mysterious, leaving no line of possible connection between social processes and religious events. At a secondary level, it has limited the scope of history, reifying commonsense concepts such as 'selfhood' or 'desire' into transhistorical categories.[77]

Yet attempts to represent this supernatural dimension within narrative create a whole series of further exclusions. The leading figures in the SPR, Edmund Gurney and Frederic Myers, had been keen to include the sub-conscious in historiography, arguing that it would fill in the lacunae surrounding supernatural events such as witchcraft or revivals of religion, just as the subliminal self filled in the gaps in personal history created through moments of ecstasy or demonic possession.[78] Combined with the rhetoric of the subliminal, such supernatural episodes took on a very different meaning. Instead of demonstrating the limits or failure of the historical project, they reinforced the claims of both history and psychology. At a historical level, such manifestations could be seen as demonstrations of the power and persistence of the past. At the level of psychology, such episodes could be fielded as demonstrations of the universal basis of the mental processes and structures posited in psychical research.

As we have seen, the SPR strategy repressed the religious dimension of dreams and thus destroyed a form of popular enfranchisement. Similarly, modern attempts at the historical representation of the supernatural through psychoanalytic arguments have led to a comparable series of denials and exclusions. Histories of spiritualism or revivalism, which have explained the irrational or the magical through reference to unconscious desire, psychic fantasy or mimetic identification, domesticate its threat, precluding the possibility of divine or daimonic intervention.[79]

This exclusion of divine or magical agency exposes the politics inherent in our current attempts to historicize or psychoanalyse the inspired experience. Such attempts perpetuate a form of argument that itself had been forged in the Victorian struggles over plebeian and ecstatic identity.[80] In their connection of the fragmentary and the mysterious, and their recovery of pattern and order from the confusion of the past, the historical and the psychological projects complete the task of Victorian psychical research. Our attempts to write the history of inspiration mark new advances in an ongoing policing of dreams.

NOTES AND REFERENCES

Versions of this chapter were read at the Psy Studies Seminar, Department of History and Philosophy of Science, University of Cambridge and the Centre for Social History Seminar Series at the University of Warwick. I am grateful to the ESRC for funding the original research and to Matthew Hilton, Justine McCarthy, Francis Neary, Michael Neve, Carol Osborne, Roger Smith and Helen Ward, who alongside the editors of *History Workshop Journal*, where this essay first appeared, made many useful comments and suggestions.

1 On Hilprecht (1859–1925), see *American Dictionary of Biography* 9, pp. 58–59.
2 Hilprecht's dream has near-canonical status within the literature on psychical research: W. R. Newbold, 'Subconscious reasoning', *Proceedings Society for Psychic Research (SPR)* 12, 1896, pp. 11–20; T. Flournoy, *Spiritualism and Psychology*, New York, 1911, p. 131; A. Lang, *The Book of Dreams and Ghosts*, London, 1897, pp. 19–23; F. Podmore, *Studies in Psychical Research*, London, 1897, pp. 382–384; F. Myers, *Human Personality and its Survival of Bodily Death*, vol. 1, London, 1903, pp. 375–379. It has recently reappeared in a popular work by B. Inglis, *The Power of Dreams*, London, 1988, pp. 36–37, 60–61.
3 Newbold, 'Subconscious reasoning', pp. 14–15.
4 Ibid., p. 15. The dream-inspired realization of the fragments' common origin occurred too late for any revision of the plates prepared for the expedition catalogue. However, Hilprecht added brief notes to each engraving and also to the table of contents, see H. V. Hilprecht (ed.), *The Babylonian Expedition of the University of Pennsylvania*, Philadephia, 1893, pp. 50, 52.
5 Ibid., p. 17. For Newbold (1865–1926), see *American DNB* 7, pp. 448–449.
6 On the association of ideas, see K. Danziger, 'Generative metaphor and the history of psychological discourse', in D. E. Leary (ed.), *Metaphors in the History of Psychology*, Cambridge, 1994, pp. 331–356, esp. 339–348.
7 For Peters (1852–1921), clergyman archaeologist, see *American DNB* 14, pp. 506–507.
8 H. White, 'The value of narrativity in the representation of reality', *Critical Inquiry* 7, 1980, p. 26.
9 For the separation of the 'worldly self' and the 'divine soul' in Protestant Christianity, see L. Dumont, 'A modified view of our origins: The Christian beginnings of modern individualism', in M. Carrithers, S. Collins and S. Lukes (eds.), *The Category of Person*, Cambridge, 1985, pp. 93–123.
10 Romans 5:12–14, 7:7ff; 1 Corinthians 15:21–23, 15:45–49. For nineteenth-century commentaries on this division, see D. Somerville, *St Paul's Conception of Christ*, Edinburgh, 1897; R. L. Ottley, *The Doctrine of the Incarnation* (1896), London, 1902, pp. 113–117; W. Sanday and A. C. Headlam, *The Epistle to the Romans* (1895), Edinburgh, 1911, pp. 131–147; G. B. Stevens, *The Theology of the New Testament* (1901), Edinburgh, 1911, pp. 349–362; H. R. Mackintosh, *The Doctrine of the Person of Christ* (1912), Edinburgh, 1914, chap. 3.
11 Psalms 76:5; Jeremiah 51:39; Daniel 12:2; John 11:13; 1 Thessalonians 4:13–14. For commentaries on the Biblical equation of sleep and death, see J. Bigelow, *The Mystery of Sleep* (1897), London, 1904, pp. 155f; C. Greene, *Death and Sleep, the idea of their analogy*, London, 1904.
12 See also Isaiah 26:9; Psalms 139:18. Many unorthodox Christians, particularly Swedenborgians and spiritualists, argued that the Spirit permanently coexisted alongside the soul and the self in man. For spiritualist statements of the tripartite model, see A. J. Davis, 'The Poughkeepsie seer', 'Death and the after life' (1868), section 1 in *The Harmonial Philosophy, a compendium and digest of the work of Andrew Jackson Davis*, London, 1917, pp. 130–131; T. Grant, *A Scientific View of Modern Spiritualism, read before the Mid-Kent Natural History and Philosophic Society* (1872), London, 1873, pp. 3f. For less partisan accounts, C. Crowe,

The Night-side of Nature (1848) (reprint intro. Colin Wilson), Wellingborough, 1986, pp. 131f; C. C. Massey, 'Concerning geists', *The Spiritualist*, 20 Aug. 1880, pp. 85–87; T. J. Hudson, *The Law of Psychic Phenomena*, London, 1893, pp. 27–28.

13 F. Delitzsch (Professor of Theology at Leipzig) whose *System der Biblischen Psychologie* (1855) appeared in translation by R. E. Wallis as *A System of Biblical Psychology*, Edinburgh, 1867, pp. 332–333; H. Christmas, *On the Cradle of Twin Giants: Science and History*, London, 1849, p. 190; [Anon], 'Dreams, dreamers and dreamland', *Borderland* 3, 1896, p. 471. On the generality of the view, see H. Spencer, *Principles of Sociology* (3rd edn), London, 1885, pp. 136f.

14 For nineteenth-century models, see A. Chambers, *Our Life after Death, or the teaching of the Bible concerning the Unseen World*, London, 1894; J. W. Reynolds, *The Natural History of Immortality*, London, 1891. For an overview: M. Wheeler, *Death and the Future Life in Victorian Literature*, Cambridge, 1992.

15 R. D. Owen, *Footfalls on the Boundary of Another World*, London, 1860, pp. 79–80; F. Greenwood, *Imagination in Dreams and their Study*, London, 1894, pp. 52–53.

16 C. Crowe, *The Night-side of Nature*, p. 49. See also J. Ennermoser, *The History of Magic* (transl. W. Howitt), London, 1854, vol. 1, p. 49; Truthseeker, 'On the origin of dreams', *Light*, 22 Dec. 1885, pp. 621–622. On Crowe (1800–1876), see *DNB* 13, p. 237.

17 F. Seafield, *The Literature and Curiosities of Dreams* (2nd edn), London, 1869, p. 49. Seafield was the pseudonym of Alexander Henley Grant, see *British Biographical Archives* fiche #1229, no. 446. On the relativity of time and space perception in dreams, see E. Cox, 'On some phenomena of sleep and dreams' (1875), in *Proceedings of the Psychological Society of Great Britain*, London, 1880, pp. 54–55.

18 For Victorian reports of travelling clairvoyance, see: J. Darby, *Day Visions and Clairvoyant Night Dreams with facts on Somnambulism and Prevision*, London, 1892; A. Gauld, *A History of Hypnotism*, Cambridge, 1992, pp. 234–239; E. Dingwall, *Abnormal Hypnotic Phenomena*, London, 1967. For the dream mechanisms involved in Highland second sight, see J. G. Campbell, *Witchcraft and Second Sight in Highlands and Islands of Scotland*, Glasgow, 1902, pp. 124f, 179–180.

19 On the idea of death as a rhetorical device for defining a life narrative, see W. Benjamin, 'The storyteller', in *Illuminations* (1955), London, 1992, p. 93; P. Brooks, *Reading for the Plot*, Oxford, 1984, pp. 22ff.

20 On angelic supervision and intervention: J. B. Leslie, *The Angels of God*, London, T. Woolmer, 1885, pp. 23f; for general spirit invasion of dreams, see R. Noel, 'Hallucination, memory and the unconscious self', *Journal Society for Psychic Research* (SPR), Jan. 1886, pp. 158–170. For a massive collection of testimonies on visions of dying friends, see E. Gurney, F. Myers and F. Podmore, *Phantasms of the Living*, 2 vols, London, 1886. For late theories of succubi and incubi attacks, see E. Roberts and J. P. Lewis, *War on the Saints*, Leicester, 1912; M. Conway, *Demonology and Devil-lore*, London, 1879, p. 236. On demonic intervention in dreams, see J. L. Nevius, *Demon Possession and Allied Themes*, Chicago, 1894, pp. 85–88, 282; G. H. Pember, *The Earth's Earliest Ages*, London, 1883, p. 251; B. Warfield, 'Dreams and the moral life', *Homiletic Review* new series 20, Sept. 1890, p. 216. For the appearance of fairies in dreams, W. Y. Evans Wentz, *The Fairy Faith in Celtic Countries*, London, 1911, pp. 41, 51, 55, 58.

21 Spencer, *Sociology*, pp. 132–142; E. B. Tylor, *Primitive Culture* (1871), London, 1903, pp. 121, 439–445.

22 Spencer, *Sociology*, p. 140.

23 Tylor, *Primitive Culture*, p. 445. See also E. Clodd, *Myths and Dreams*, London, 1885, pp. 242–243.

24 The history of these religions has been repeated many times. For a comprehensive analysis, see J. Oppenheim, *The Other World: Spiritualism and Psychical Research in England, 1850–1914*, Cambridge, 1985, pp. 101–103, and the slightly less detailed work of A. Gauld, *The*

Founders of Psychical Research, London, 1968. For the relationship of spiritualism to plebeian culture, see L. Barrow, *Independent Spirits: Spiritualism and English Plebeians, 1850–1910*, London, 1986. For the feminist implications of the spiritualist project, see A. Owen, *The Darkened Room: Women, Power and Spiritualism in Late Victorian England*, London, 1990. On the growth of Swedenborgianism, see E. J. Brock (ed.), *Swedenborg and his Influence*, Bryn Aethyn, 1988.

25 E. Swedenborg, *Arcana Coelestia: The Heavenly Mysteries etc.* (1749–56), London, 1878, vol. 2, paras 1,975 ff. esp. 1,983. For an exposition of Swedenborg's philosophy, see T. Parsons, *Outlines of the Religion and Philosophy of Swedenborg*, London, 1876. Victorian psychiatric assessments of Swedenborg were remarkably sympathetic; see W. W. Ireland, *Through the Ivory Gate: Studies in History and Psychology*, Edinburgh, 1888, pp. 1–113; H. Maudsley, 'Emmanuel Swedenborg', *Journal of Mental Science* 15, 1869, pp. 170–196.

26 *Arcana Coelestia*, vol. 2, para 1,977. For further information on Swedenborg and dreams, see W. Van Dusen's introduction to *Swedenborg's Journal of Dreams* (2nd edn), London, 1989.

27 For the influence of Swedenborgianism on spiritualism, see Barrow, *Independent Spirits*, chap. 1; M. Davies, *Heterodox London*, London, 1874, pp. 90–115.

28 For the professional medium's reluctance to endorse dream inspiration, see J. Morse, 'Significant dreams', *Light*, 15 Dec. 1894, p. 604. For reports of prophetic dreams in the spiritualist press, see 'Dreams', *Spiritual Magazine*, 4 April 1879; 'Dream warnings', *Spiritualist* 13, 1878, pp. 172, 194; 'Symbolic dreams', *Spiritualist* 14, 1878, pp. 140, 239; 'Dreams', *Spiritualist* 16, 1880, p. 257; 'Dreamy shades', *Spiritualist* 17, 1880, p. 97; 'Fulfilled dream', *Spiritualist* 18, 1881, p. 237; 'A remarkable dream', *Light*, 28 Aug. 1894; 'A dream which came true', *Light*, 1 Dec. 1894; 'A useful dream', *Light*, 2 Jan. 1895; 'Dreams, dreamers and dreaming', *Borderland* 3, 1896, pp. 470–475; 'Dreams and dreaming', *Borderland* 4, 1897, pp. 301–302.

29 On Davis, see Podmore, *Modern Spiritualism*, London, 1902, vol. 1, pp. 158–176. Davis was a fundamental influence on British spiritualism, with his doctrines taught throughout the movement's Lyceum schools, see Oppenheim, *Other World*, pp. 101–103.

30 A. J. Davis, *The Great Harmonia*, vol. 3, Boston, 1858, pp. 316f.

31 Greenwood, *Imagination in Dreams*, pp. 70–71. On Greenwood (1830–1909), *DNB* 2nd Supp., vol. 2, pp. 157–159.

32 Roden Noel (1834–94) had served as Groom of the Privy Chamber but resigned his commission because of his growing republican sympathies, see A. W. Brown, *The Metaphysical Society: Victorian Minds in Crisis*, New York, 1947, pp. 154–155; *DNB* vol. 41, p. 92.

33 R. Noel, *The Philosophy of Immortality*, London, 1882, pp. 63, 123.

34 C. Mackay, *Extraordinary Popular Delusions and the Madness of Crowds*, London, 1852, estimated that each dream-book title still sold around 11,000 copies a year (pp. 294–295). The most popular titles included: *The Dreamers Sure Guide*, London, 1876; *The Universal Dreambook or Ladies Interpreter*, London, 1876. On the persistence of popular dream interpretation: J. Brand, *Observations on Popular Antiquities*, London, 1900, p. 657; Tylor, *Primitive Culture*, pp. 439–440. And see M. Perkins, 'The meaning of dream books', in this volume.

35 For dream interpretation as a family or household activity, see R. Bland, 'Dreams and their interpretation', *Borderland* 3, 1896, pp. 474–475; J. M. Dixon, 'Dreams', *Spiritualist*, 19 Sept. 1879, pp. 141–142.

36 K. Thomas, *Religion and the Decline of Magic*, London, 1971, pp. 595–601.

37 On dream evidence in Scottish trials, see J. H. Burton, *Narratives from Criminal Trials in Scotland*, London, 1852; for corpse-location evidence at Littleport coroners court, see C. H. Cooper, 'Dream testimony', *Notes and Queries* 8, 24 Sept. 1853, p. 287; in the Rose Foster inquest, Spring Hill, Birmingham, see 'A dream verified', *Light*, 4 May 1895. For dream revelations of an Ashford suicide and a Glasgow murder, see *Kentish Express*, 2 June 1894; *Glasgow Herald*, 3 Jan. 1895, abstracted in *Borderland* 2, 1895, p. 2.

38 This play had appeared in various forms from 1828 onwards with the first script being published in 1877, see M. Kilgarrif, *Golden Age of English Melodrama*, London, 1974, pp. 204–235. See also F. C. H., 'Dream testimony', *Notes and Queries* 2nd series, 2, 27 Dec. 1856, p. 515; and 3, 24 May 1857, p. 333.

39 Darby, *Day Visions*, p. 115.

40 For a good overview, see the introduction and bibliographic essay by B. Taithe and T. Thornton (eds.), *Prophecy: The Power of Inspired Language in History, 1300–2000*, Stroud, 1997.

41 For Brothers (1757–1824), see J. Barrell, 'Imagining the King's death: The arrest of Richard Brothers', *History Workshop Journal* 37, 1994, pp. 1–32. For Joanna Southcott (1750–1814), see J. F. C. Harrison, *The Second Coming: Popular Millenarianism*, London, 1979, chap. 5; B. Taylor, *Eve and the New Jerusalem*, London, 1983, pp. 163–171.

42 For Francis Starr, see *Mid-summer's Morning Dream*, London, 1852; *Twenty Years of a Traveller's Life*, Norwich, n.d. For J. G. H. Brown's prophecies, see *Revelations for the Late War*, London, 1846; *Message from the Spirits*, London, 1857. For their context, see Barrow, *Independent Spirits*, London, 1986, chap. 2.

43 On the radical implications of inspired authority, see I. M. Lewis, *Ecstatic Religion*, Harmondsworth, 1970; E. Bourguignon (ed.), *Religion, Altered States of Consciousness and Social Change*, Columbus, 1973.

44 On typology, see G. Landow, *Victorian Lights, Victorian Shadows: Biblical Typology in Victorian Literature, Art and Thought*, London, 1980.

45 F. Kermode, *Genesis of Secrecy: On the Interpretation of Narrative*, Cambridge, MA, 1979, p. 106. See also R. Caillois, *Logical and Philosophical Problems of the Dream*, Berkeley, 1966, p. 31.

46 F. Moretti, *The Way of the World: The Bildungsroman in European Culture*, London, 1987, p. 16, also chap. 1 throughout; C. Steedman, *Strange Dislocations: Childhood and the Idea of Human Interiority, 1780–1930*, London, 1995.

47 On the mystical failure of language and representation, see M. de Certeau, *The Mystic Fable* (transl. Michael B. Smith), Chicago, 1992, pp. 108–126. For the challenge inherent in the mobile identity of the possessed, see his essay: 'Discourse disturbed: The sorcerer's speech', in *The Writing of History* (1975) (transl. Tom Conley), New York, 1988, p. 258.

48 R. W. Emerson, 'Demonology', *North American Review* 74, March, 1877, p. 179; B. Warfield, 'Dreams and the moral life', *Homiletic Review* 20, 1890, p. 216.

49 The best accounts of the society's formation can be found in Gauld, *Founders*; and Oppenheim, *Other World*.

50 J. Cerullo, *The Secularization of the Soul*, Philadephia, 1982, chap. 3.

51 On Henry Sidgwick, Knightsbridge Professor of Moral Philosophy at the University of Cambridge, see D. G. James, *Henry Sidgwick, Science and Faith in Victorian England*, Oxford, 1970. On Gurney, see T. Hall, *The Strange Case of Edmund Gurney*, London, 1964. On Myers, see F. M. Turner, *Between Science and Religion*, New Haven, CT, 1974, chap. 5.

52 On carnival and transgression, see P. Stallybrass and A. White, *The Politics and Poetics of Transgression*, London, 1986.

53 'Further notes on the unconscious self, part 2', *Journal SPR*, March 1886, p. 225; 'Automatic writing or the rationale of planchette', *Contemporary Review* 47, 1885, pp. 235, 248; see also E. Gurney, 'Problems of hypnotism', *Proceedings SPR* 2, 1883–4, pp. 270–277.

54 For a discussion of this critique, see J. Glass, *Delusions: Internal Dimensions of Political Life*, Chicago, 1985, chap. 6 esp. pp. 133–138.

55 Alongside the examples cited below, see 'Automatic writing II', *Proceedings SPR* 3, 1885, pp. 1–64, esp. 3, 33, 62; 'Automatic writing III – physiological and pathological analogies', *Proceedings SPR* 4, 1885–7, p. 212; 'Automatic writing IV – the daemon of Socrates', *Proceedings SPR* 5, 1888–9, p. 525.

56 Gurney, Myers and Podmore, *Phantasms*, p. lviii. On the writing of *Phantasms*, see Gauld, *Founders*, pp. 160ff; Cerullo, *Secularisation*, pp. 92–93.

57 A. Lang, *The Making of Religion*, London, 1894, chap. 6.

58 F. Podmore, *Apparitions and Thought-Transference*, London, chap. 8.

59 'Stages of hypnotic memory', *Proceedings SPR* 4, 1886–7, p. 531. See also C. du Prel, *The Philosophy of Mysticism* (1885), London, 1889, vol. 1, p. 201. On the role of statistics in psychical research, see I. Hacking, 'Telepathy: Origins of randomization in experimental design', *Isis* 79 (Sept. 1988), pp. 427–451.

60 On the graphic automatisms: F. W. H. Myers 'On a telepathic explanation of some so-called spiritualistic phenomena', *Proceedings SPR* 2, 1884, pp. 226–237; the same material was covered in Myers, 'Automatic writing II', *Proceedings SPR* 3, 1885, pp. 24f; 'Automatic writing or the rationale of planchette', *Contemporary Review* 47, 1885, pp. 240–243. On the visions of blood, Miss X [Ada Goodrich Freer], 'On the apparent sources of subliminal messages', *Proceedings SPR* 5, 1888–9, pp. 486–501; 'Experiments in crystal vision', *Proceedings SPR* 11, 1895, pp. 114–144.

61 The most famous example of this process appears in T. Flournoy, *From India to the Planet Mars: A Case of Multiple Personality with Imaginary Languages* (1901) (transl. Daniel B. Dermilye and ed. Sonu Shamdasani), Princeton, NJ, 1994.

62 A. Moll, *Hypnotism* (1889) (3rd edn), London, 1899, pp. 291–292; J. Lapponi, *Hypnotism and Spiritualism*, London, 1906, chap. 1; H. Ellenberger, *The Discovery of the Unconscious* (1970), London, 1994, pp. 53–57; N. Spanos and J. Gottlieb, 'Demon possession, mesmerism and hysteria', *Journal of Abnormal Psychology* 88, 1979, pp. 538–539.

63 'Human personality in the light of hypnotic suggestion', *Proceedings SPR* 4, 1886–7, pp. 1–24, repr. *Nineteenth Century* 20, 1886; *Phantasms*, pp. xlii–iii; 'On telepathic hypnotism and its relation to other forms of hypnotic suggestion', *Proceedings SPR* 4, 1886–7, p. 185; 'Multiplex personality', *Proceedings SPR* 4, 1886–7, pp. 496–514, repr. *Nineteenth Century* 20, 1886. Myers's view was shared by continental researchers such as Beaunis, Forel and Krafft-Ebing: Moll, *Hypnotism*, p. 333.

64 'Peculiarities of certain post-hypnotic states', *Proceedings SPR* 4, 1886–7, pp. 268–323; 'Recent experiments in hypnotism', *Proceedings SPR* 5, 1888–9, pp. 3–17. For discussions of Gurney's experiments in hypnosis, see Gauld, *Hypnotism*, pp. 389–393; T. W. Mitchell, 'The contribution of psychical research to psychotherapeutics', *Proceedings SPR* 45, 1938–9, pp. 175–186; F. Myers, 'The work of Edmund Gurney in experimental psychology', *Proceedings SPR* 5, 1888–9, pp. 359–373; Williams, *Victorian Psychical Research*, chap. 7, section 2. Hall (*Edmund Gurney*) has suggested that Gurney's experimental results were produced through his subject's deliberate deceit.

65 I have omitted from this brief discussion Gurney's attempt to demonstrate the operation of a mesmeric influence in the trance state: see Gurney and Myers, 'Some higher aspects of mesmerism', *National Review* 5, 1885, pp. 581–703; Gauld, *Founders*, Appendix A.

66 M. Dessoir, 'The magic mirror', *Monist* 1, 1890–1, pp. 116–117.

67 'Further notes on the unconscious self, part 2', *Journal SPR*, March 1886, p. 225; see also E. Gurney, 'Problems of hypnotism', *Proceedings SPR* 2, 1883–4, pp. 270–277.

68 'Further notes on the unconscious self, part 3', *Journal SPR*, April 1886, p. 241.

69 On Podmore, post-office clerk and Fabian socialist, see Hall, *Edmund Gurney*, Appendix A.

70 Podmore, *Modern Spiritualism*, vol. 2, p. 328. For the classic statement on automatism, see P. Janet, *The Mental State of Hystericals* (1894) (transl. C. R. Corson, 1901), Washington, 1977, p. 243.

71 'The subliminal consciousness: Chap. 2, The mechanism of suggestion', *Proceedings SPR* 7, 1892, p. 355.

72 For example, Sarah Underwood channelled the spirit of Robert Chambers, who denounced the subliminal, *Borderland* 3, 1896, p. 84; 'The Psychical Research Society and its negative

record', *Borderland* 2, 1895, pp. 346–348; J. Farmer, 'Spiritualism, spiritualists and the SPR', *Light*, 19 Sept. 1885, pp. 447–449.
73 As Raphael Samuel wrote of contemporary psychohistorical investigations:

> the 'logic' which they discover in fantasy, the 'hidden order' which they explicate in a text, the parallelisms which they point out in developments between the moral and psychic economy, so far from being indwelling properties of the documents or symptomatic absences, are ones which they have put there themselves.

'Reading the signs II: Fact grubbers and mind readers', *History Workshop Journal* 33, Spring 1992, p. 242.
74 S. Bann, 'Analysing the discourse of history', in *The Inventions of History: Essays on the Representation of the Past*, Manchester, pp. 33–63; H. White, 'The value of narrativity in the representation of reality', *Critical Inquiry* 17, 1980, pp. 5–27. For an overview of White's argument, see W. Kansteiner, 'Hayden White's critique of the writing of history', *History and Theory*, 1992, pp. 272–295.
75 H. White, 'The politics of historical interpretation: Discipline and desublimination', in *The Content of the Form*, Baltimore, MD, 1987, p. 66.
76 For contemporary accounts of prophetic dreams, see D. Zohar, *Through the Time Barrier*, London 1982; Inglis, *Power of Dreams*.
77 S. Alexander, 'Women, class and sexual difference in the 1830's and 40's: Some reflections on the writing of a feminist history', *History Workshop Journal* 17, Spring 1984, pp. 134f. On the possibility that psychoanalysis could uncover a missing dimension of fantastic experience in history: L. Roper, 'Witchcraft and fantasy in early modern Germany', *History Workshop Journal* 32, Autumn 1991, pp. 37–38.
78 *Phantasms*, p. xlvi; Podmore, *Apparitions*, p. 373; A. Lang, 'Comparative psychical research', *Contemporary Review*, Sept. 1893, pp. 372–387. Spiritualists could also field similar arguments – C. C. Massey argued that mediumistic ability was an inherited trait that had been largely wiped out in the witch hunts: 'The influence of psychical research on the dominant culture', *Light*, Suppl. 24, Oct. 1885, pp. 519–522.
79 For a Lacanian model of spirit possession, see Owen, *The Darkened Room*, chap. 8. On the tensions between historical narrative and revivalist rhetoric, see R. Hayward, 'From the millennial future to the unconscious past', in Taithe and Thornton, *Prophecy*, pp. 161–180.
80 This argument has been made by the Jesuit historiographer, Michel de Certeau. In his essay 'Psychoanalysis and its history', 1978, in *Heterologies: Discourses on the Other* (transl. Brian Massumi), Minneapolis, MN 1986, p. 10, De Certeau criticizes the modern hypostatization of the practice:

> When psychoanalysis forgets its own historicity, that is its internal relation to conflicts of power and position, it becomes either a mechanism of drives, a dogmatism of discourse or a gnosis of symbols.

Figure 10.1 The Interpretation of Dreams of Martyn Zadeka, Moscow, 1885, front cover. By permission of The British Library. Shelfmark/manuscript number 8632cc26(I).

Chapter 10

The dreambook in Russia

Faith Wigzell

A visitor to Moscow at the close of the twentieth century, had he or she a smattering of Russian, might well have been forgiven for thinking that a number of different small books containing the words 'the interpretation of dreams' in their title indicated the belated promotion of Freud in Russia.[1] Judging by the huge print runs, these books were among the most popular on sale.[2] But though they had shared, along with Freud, the honour of being banned during the Soviet period, they owed nothing to modern psychoanalysis, belonging instead to a much older tradition of dream interpretation with its roots in antiquity. This tradition, which views dreams as a means of elucidating the future rather than as a key to the dreamer's unconscious, to his or her emotional state, present or past, survives still in all European countries, though it no longer enjoys prestige or, in Britain at any rate, widespread support. The view that dreams can hold a key to the dreamer's future is a commonly held assumption in Russia at all levels of society, though especially among women.

In this chapter my aim is to examine the distinctive history and character of the Russian guide to dream interpretation, and to attempt to explain its extraordinary persistence and popularity. Despite the identical or near-identical book titles both today and in pre-Revolutionary Russia, however, there is little uniformity of content. 'Interpretation of dreams', like the generic term 'dreambook', in the majority of titles simply conveys the function of these books as manuals for life. As the ethnographer Tereshchenko remarked disapprovingly in 1848, many believed in dreambooks absolutely, and were:

> guided in any undertaking by these meaningless interpretations, preserving and guarding the book of dreams as though salvation of the soul lay within.[3]

In those few modern dreambooks where contents as well as titles are identical, parallel editions or simple piracy provide the explanation. Since the same situation obtained in the popular commercial market for books in nineteenth-century Russia (as in popular publishing elsewhere), contemporary marketing ploys are simply a reversion, albeit unwitting, to past practice.

Although dream interpretation flourished in the ancient Near East and classical Greece, it was not until the second century AD that a physician, Artemidorus, first systematized the approaches in his *Oneirocritica*. His work, whether complete or variously abridged, continued to enjoy popularity and prestige in Byzantium. Versions were transmitted to Western Europe in Latin translation along with similar collections by authorities such as Astrampsychus and Achmet ben Sirin. There they continued to be copied in Latin, and over time were translated into many languages. The arrival of printing further assisted their popularity: the twenty-fourth English edition of Artemidorus, for example, came out in 1740. Even more popular in Europe, however, was the text spuriously attributed to the Prophet Daniel and based on late Byzantine dreambooks (themselves dependent on Artemidorus and Achmet). Attested from the tenth century in Europe and found in numerous Latin manuscripts and incunabula, by the fifteenth century it circulated in at least four redactions as well as in several vernacular renderings. The *Somniale Danielis* owed its popularity to its simplicity; objects were grouped alphabetically or semi-alphabetically, and followed by the briefest of interpretations.[4] Ultimately, the overwhelming majority of European dreambooks descend from this persistent tradition, though popular Freudian or Jungian concepts have made their way into some recent West European dreambooks.[5] Apart from the isolated instance of translations into Russian of such modern works, Russian dreambooks almost without exception stem wholly or partly from this older European tradition.[6] The occcasional use of selected excerpts from the writings of Jung in prefaces to predictive dreambooks is merely an attempt to confer authority on the contents, and indeed in the eighteenth and nineteenth centuries inclusion of excerpts from the writings of authorities on dreams was common practice in dreambooks other than the simplest, shortest kind.[7]

Recognition that dreambooks were originally imports into Russia should not mask the importance of a flourishing Russian folk tradition of dream divination. Similarities between written and oral traditions are strong. For example, both assign a meaning to an object seen in the dream and then weave these symbols into an overall interpretation. Second, both use some of the same principles for assigning meaning to dream objects, notably the principle of opposites (for instance, dreaming of excrement means money), the use of metonymy (dreaming of a saddle means a journey or ink a letter), interpretations based on perceived qualities or appearances (hares mean fear, a pancake a letter), and, much more uncommon, the direct interpretation of a symbol (dead relatives beckoning means imminent death, going to the tavern means poverty). In some instances interpretations are identical in written and oral sources, as with excrement meaning money.[8] Acceptance of dreambooks by the gentry who were losing touch with traditional oral culture was greatly facilitated by these parallels. The first dreambook, *The Interpretation of Dreams, According to Astronomy* (1768), appeared only a few years after the commencement of publishing activities by institutions other than the State, Church and Academy.[9]

From the first the popularity of dreamboooks was assured. *The Interpretation of Dreams* was reprinted in 1772 and 1788, and rivalled by others with almost identical titles.[10] Approximately a hundred fortune-telling volumes reached the public between 1765 and 1830, with the majority after 1800 published in omnibus editions and comprising instructions for a variety of skills in divination.[11] Nearly forty per cent were either dreambooks, or contained a guide to interpreting dreams; as such, they were the second most popular kind of divinatory text after the Russian versions of the Wheel of Fortune.[12] It might seem that thirty-eight texts over a period of sixty-five years hardly indicates success, but in fact fortune-telling books as a whole were outstripped in popularity only by songbooks and popular fiction.[13] It should be remembered that private presses were not licensed in Russia till 1783, and were occasionally banned thereafter, and that, as Max Okenfuss observes, 'in the last quarter of the [eighteenth] century, in any three-year period, as many titles appeared in Germany as in Russia in the entire century'.[14] In this context, nearly forty dreambook texts and editions demonstrates considerable demand from what was a tiny reading and book-buying public.

Taking the period 1765–1917 as a whole, the typical dreambook was sixty-four pages long (two signatures or printers' sheets), though they could range from eight to nearly 300 pages. The very first omnibus fortune-telling books came without a dreambook text, but by 1800 this had changed, and over the next thirty years nearly three-quarters included dream divination. During this period at least, these substantial tomes virtually excluded the simple dreambook. Some, like the three-volume *A Secret Microscope, or The Mirror of Magical Secrets . . .* (St Petersburg, 1817), proffered two different types of texts, astrological and alphabetical. Both reduced the dream to separate symbols (dream objects), but they organized the material differently. In the astrological type it was the zodiac sign that lent a given meaning to a particular dream object, which consequently varied in meaning depending on when the dream occurred. The alphabetical type, as the name suggests, simply listed dream objects with a single, brief interpretation. Longer dreambooks added detailed explanations, more variants of the given dream object (for example, instead of simply dreaming of a diamond, dreaming of finding or losing a diamond) or, particularly from the late nineteenth century, new dream objects. Long or short, dreambooks were marked by extreme conservatism of content. Dream objects often reflected their ancient origins, regardless of the likelihood of Russians dreaming of, say, eating lizard or camel meat (drawn ultimately from Artemidorus or Achmet). Most texts came with attachments, commonly essays on the significance of dreams by, amongst others, the medieval philosopher Michael Scot, and a table of lucky and unlucky days ascribed to the sixteenth-century Danish astronomer, Tycho Brahe. Though perhaps eighty or ninety per cent of dreambooks conformed to the alphabetical type, attempts were made to establish different kinds, mainly in the early years of their history in Russia and later, between 1890 and 1917 and since 1987.

The first Russian dreambook, *The Interpretation of Dreams, According to Astronomy* (1768), was one such. It was a neat little volume in album format with thirteen columns on each of seven pages, one for each day of the week. Each page contained a list of people or objects seen in the dreams along with columns containing the various meanings according to the zodiac sign under which the dream had occurred. Despite reprints and variants, it failed to catch on permanently.[15] The same may be said for *A Morning Pastime over Tea, Or a New, Complete and as Far as Possible Accurate Interpretation of Dreams According to Astronomy and in Verse*,[16] a translation of a West European rhyming dreambook. Zodiac signs are listed down the left-hand side of the page, and the dream objects along the top. The reader is then guided to interpretations in couplet form. Dreaming of crawfish, for example, means that:

Of this you may be truly sure
Your lover now will step through the door

Unlike the first dreambook, it does not differentiate between dreams on different nights of the week, and thus offers fewer interpretations.

The disadvantage with the type of dreambook that listed dreams under tables was that relatively few dream objects could be squeezed into the column of dreams and fitted on to one page. If the reader's dream did not embrace objects from this short list, then the book was useless. Furthermore, it demanded a minimal knowledge of astrology, which would have diminished its appeal to the backward country gentry, let alone the miniscule number of plebeian readers. By contrast with much of Western Europe, where astrology had left a longstanding cultural residue in all levels of society,[17] in Russia cultural isolation and low levels of literacy had for centuries restricted knowledge of the subject to a tiny circle. Nor did Russian folk belief derive significance from the relative position of the planets, though due weight was given to the time of night in which dreams occurred.[18] All these factors led to the demise of the astrological dreambook after a few appearances in fortune-telling handbooks along with an alphabetical version between the 1790s and 1830 as well as two reprints of *The Dreambook telling Mother Truth* in the 1830s.[19] Not surprisingly, the combination of two kinds of dreambook produced, in some instances, rival interpretations for the same object, but such concerns seemed almost never to have bothered compilers or publishers, either then or at any time before the Revolution.

Figure 10.2 A Million Dreams. A New and Complete Dreambook, Moscow, 1901, reprinted Moscow, 1990.

The alphabetical type of dreambook that prevailed in Russia was a version of *Somniale Danielis*. Though it had reached Russia in manuscript form translated from Polish in the mid-eighteenth century, the version chosen for translation for the first printed edition seems not to have had the name of Daniel attached.[20] As a consequence, the Prophet Daniel failed to acquire the reputation of sage he enjoyed elsewhere in Europe. Apart from *Somniale Danielis*, in the period before 1830 there was a market for the longer dreambook with detailed explanations: thus, the *New, Complete and Detailed*

Dreambook, Signifying the Amplified Interpretation and Elucidation of Every Dream . . . (editions in 1802, 1811, 1818) drew on an abbreviated version of Artemidorus's *Oneirocritica*, which was nonetheless much fuller than pseudo-Daniel.

In the period before 1780 the readership for dreambooks was almost entirely restricted to the urban gentry – a natural consequence of the high price of books, serious distribution problems for publishers and widespread illiteracy.[21] After 1780, as the less sophisticated rural gentry discovered the advantages of literacy, the book market, including that for dreambooks, expanded. Nonetheless, in spite of a gradual rise in the number of non-aristocratic urban readers, books still remained largely an upper-class preserve and the position did not change until at least the 1830s.[22] Thus the frequency with which dreambooks appeared before then rested upon their popularity with the élite classes, if not the most sophisticated among them.[23] Both from what we know of the book-buying and reading public and from the often elegant format of Russian dreambooks, we may conclude that they circulated almost exclusively in aristocratic and gentry households. The extent to which this situation contrasts with Britain and elsewhere in Western Europe is hard to determine, but the simpler format and style of, for example, British and American dreambooks of the period suggests that these were popular chapbooks or books for the reader of modest means.[24]

Despite the apparent naivety of these new readers and their desire for books that offered 'concrete examples or guides to personal behaviour and fulfillment',[25] dreambooks faced problems in gaining credibility. Books were presented as vehicles of enlightenment, leading the literate away from a pre-modern world view with its attachment to irrational superstition, of which oral dream divination formed a part. In fact, rejection of an outdated past seems to have been the more significant factor here, since interest in the irrational continued to flourish in the late eighteenth and early nineteenth centuries amongst the élite involved in Masonry and Rosicrucianism, or fascinated by pseudosciences such as physiognomy and, by extension, chiromancy.[26] In the case of dream divination, only the dream that was deemed to possess political significance gained a degree of acceptance in these circles.[27] Most fortune-telling books got around the problem by pre-senting themselves as harmless entertainment, either through titles such as *A Diversion in Times of Tedium, or A New Entertaining Method of Reading the Cards* (Moscow, 1788 and 1791), or through forewords that attempted to appease those who viewed them as mere superstition.[28]

Dreambooks had a more serious problem in that, since memorable dreams are often disturbing, few would volunteer to expose them to drawing-room banter. In any case, dream divination in Russia, as in Scandinavia, was traditionally a breakfast-time activity, and consequently an intimate largely family affair.[29] As a result fewer dreambooks than other types of fortune-telling books claimed to be entertainment, publishers generally paying only lip-service to rational dismissal of superstition. In his introduction to the first dreambook the editor declares firmly that 'without doubt to believe in its predictions is a sign of utter superstitiousness'. However, a little further on he assures readers that, judging by his own experience, the book 'rarely makes an error in its predictions'. Such assertions, combined with titles like *The Dreambook, Telling Mother Truth* vaunting the supposed accuracy of the book, suggest that dream divination avoided promoting sales through the trivializing strategy employed with drawing-room fortune-telling, preferring to rely on the perennial human desire to know the meaning of vivid or disturbing dreams. Fortune-telling titles such as *The Newly Appeared Wizard Recounting the Divination of the Spirits. An Innocent Distraction in Hours of Boredom for Those Not Wishing to Engage upon Anything Better* ... (St Petersburg, 1795) have no parallel in dreambooks. It may be surmised that élite male readers regarded dream divination with less scepticism than other types of fortune-telling, much of which concerned matters of the heart and was thus deemed to fall primarily into women's sphere.

Nonetheless, dreambooks failed to escape mockery as their readership shifted from the urban élite towards the less-educated rural gentry. Evidence comes from two gently satirical fictional portraits, referring to the first years of the nineteenth century, one by A. E. Izmailov and one by Ivan Goncharov, which mock the reading tastes of the backward rural gentry. Both Oblomov's father in Goncharov's novel *Oblomov* and Izmailov's Nevezhin (Mr Ignoramus) possess a dreambook and little else.[30] However, judging by the elegant editions on sale up to 1830, plenty of purchasers of dreambooks did come from circles with pretensions to sophistication. By the beginning of the nineteenth century it is likely that many of these were women, who became literate later than men and whose sphere was home and drawing room. Breakfast was normally presided over by an older woman. Expensive editions were designed for women users, as may be inferred from titles such as *A Morning Pastime over Tea*. Indeed, fortune-telling books generally were clearly very highly valued by some users, as the copy of *A Lady's Album, or a Fortune-Telling Book for Entertainment and Pleasure* (Moscow, 1816) in the Russian State Library shows. From 1824 to 1856, its owner used the blank pages to record major family events.

Perhaps the educated élite would have ceased to take any interest in divinatory books by the 1820s had it not been for the influence of Romanticism, with its fascination for the irrational. The Romantics' sympathy was primarily directed towards folk belief because it embodied national character, or so it was thought,[31] but the differences between folk and literary traditions were perceived less clearly than they were later in the century. In 1827 a dreambook was seen on the poet Pushkin's desk at his country estate, Mikhailovskoe. Its presence could be explained simply by suggesting that it was research material for the fifth canto of *Eugene Onegin*, in which his heroine Tat'iana consults her beloved dreambook to explain her terrifying dream. Certainly, Pushkin's treatment of this episode suggests a highly ironic attitude. On the other hand, he himself was very superstitious, believing in folk omens of various kinds, and like many creative artists of his generation in Europe, he held that dreams might be prophetic.[32] What can be said with confidence is that, whether Pushkin trusted only in folk belief or was prepared to extend his belief to printed guides, his interest in the irrational ensured that references in his work to dreambooks are ambiguous or serve to characterize a milieu, rather than being condemnatory.

With the main types of dreambook (all variants of the alphabetical) fixed by 1830, the Russian dreambook tradition was to change little thereafter. Differences that occurred were less of content than of format, which was a function of readership. After 1830 dreambooks were increasingly produced for wider social groups. As the influence of Romanticism waned, and young educated men turned away from 'superstition', the climate for dreambooks worsened. Whereas Pushkin had smiled indulgently at his heroine Tat'iana's love for her dreambook, now writers and commentators viewed them as synonymous with irrationality and backwardness, whether in country bumpkins or women.[33] Despite this, dreambooks gradually became the second most popular type of fortune-telling text.[34] They appealed to better-off urban readers as well as, later in the century, to poor workers and peasants, with different books being produced for each type of reader. It seems likely that as dreambooks passed down the social scale, initially men bought them, while women stuck to oral dream divination, but that as such traditions grew weaker, usually as a consequence of relocation to towns, when the acquisition of literacy and the authority ascribed to books drew people away from oral tradition, women became the chief users. The descent of dreambooks down the social scale is reflected in various ways. Quality of printing declined, with illustrated and therefore pricey books becoming rarities.[35] Fortune-telling compendia also slowly disappeared until the 1890s.[36]

In the 1840s variants of the simple alphabetical dreambook began to gain a hold on a popular market much less interested in novelty and change than was drawing-room society. Since ordinary readers' interest was directed to the core element of the book, and books needed to be modestly priced, introductions and extracts from the works of the 'ancients' became redundant. After 1860 the established length for a cheap dreambook was thirty-two or sixty-four pages, and some even less; an eight-page *lubok* (woodcut or lithographed) version was on sale in the 1860s and 1870s.[37] By the 1880s these books were being republished almost annually by all the publishers operating at the bottom end of the market, and were certainly among the most popular books on sale.[38] One of them came to be regarded as the pre-eminent Russian dreambook. Taken from one of the texts first published in the late eighteenth century, and ultimately based on the *Somniale Danielis*, it was produced first in 1848 under the title of *Interpretation of Dreams by the*

Venerable 106-year-old Man, Martyn Zadeka. Not much bigger than a passport, it, like rival titles, was an ideal item for market stalls or pedlars' boxes. The contents of late nineteenth-century versions of this book differ remarkably little from those published in the late eighteenth and early nineteenth-centuries, as indicated by a comparison between the entries under the letter 'A' in Martyn Zadeka dreambooks of 1860 and 1885 and a dreambook of the same type published in 1784.[39] The sole novelty in 1860 is '*anushkiny glazki*' (pansies), while a Zadeka edition of 1885 put out by a different publisher adds only '*arshin*' (= 0.71 metres) and '*aspid*' (serpent). These additions were none of them unique, having featured already in other nineteenth-century Russian dreambooks, and may themselves have come ultimately from different variants of the *Somniale Danielis*. Clearly by the second half of the nineteenth century, short dreambooks had developed a traditional core, to which a few new interpretations were added, albeit gradually and inconsistently.

Though dreambooks had ceased to be currency among the educated and by the 1880s were widely available to workers and peasants, publishers did not neglect the rest of the market. Between the 1850s and early 1880s, some longer and more expensive dreambooks were produced for the socially fragmented urban market. These varied considerably, in recognition not only of social differences, but also the desire of readers with pretensions to possess something other than the ordinary dreambook, whether this meant expansion of the conventional type or the willingness to accept novelty. In the last half of the nineteenth and the early twentieth centuries attempts at real innovation were restricted to books for the more affluent reader.

The simplest form of innovation was in the number of dream objects. Lists could be expanded by fusing separate categories of dream object, often carelessly, that is without proper alphabetical sorting. There are even instances of dreambooks that are an imperfect amalgam of two other alphabetical dreambooks, with the result that the reader gets two conflicting interpretations for the same dream object, listed twice under the same letter of the alphabet.[40] Evidently, it was assumed that the purchaser would discover this only after buying the book, and that, in any case, he or more likely, she, would not mind, since it allowed for a choice of the more favourable explanation. Though the core dream objects persisted from edition to edition, there was a natural tendency to omit the most grotesquely inappropriate entries, such as dreaming of eating lizard-meat or wearing a white four-cornered hat, both of which featured in longer dreambooks of the first decades of the nineteenth century, and for others, such as '*apteka*' (pharmacy) or '*arshin*' to become established in their place.[41] By the late 1880s, this process accelerated in the lengthier dreambooks and fortune-telling compendia designed for the slightly more affluent; dream objects such as '*ananas*' (pineapple) or '*arap*' (Arab), which had appeared earlier were joined by others such as '*anis*' or '*algebra*'.[42]

Figure 10.3 The Dreambook. 215 Dreams or the Interpretation of Dreams by Various Egyptian and Indian Sages and Astronomers, Mtsera, 1883, front cover.

An obvious source of new objects was the folk tradition, but it took until the end of the century for items more obviously Russian such as snow, rye or mushrooms to find their way into dreambooks. At the same time, a few publishers began to advertise the oral origin of their wares through titles such as the *Folk Dreambook* (1883).[43] It is notable that such books were published by Petersburg publishers who catered almost exclusively for an urban market. It may be conjectured that they supposed some of their buyers to be sufficiently distanced from their rural origins to find homespun wisdom a plus. By contrast, Moscow publishers seem to have recognized that their main market, the peasants, knew their own oral interpretations and would not be interested in them in written form.

Attempts at more radical change generally failed. It might be assumed that the widespread presence of specialist dream interpreters in the country-side, and to a lesser extent in towns, might in some instances have led to native sages going into print, thereby entering the world of domestic dream divination. Gender appears to be one of the reasons for the failure of this to happen. In the countryside, women, who formed the majority of those specializing in dream interpretation, were rarely literate. Indeed in the area of fortune-telling and the practice of magic as a whole, the use of books or manuscripts seems to have been largely restricted to men.[44] Furthermore, although the thin evidence we possess suggests that dream interpreters in towns were generally female and almost certainly mainly illiterate, authorities and famous experts in all fields of fortune-telling from the ancients to the nineteenth century were predominantly male.

Thus it comes as no surprise to find that the sole purely Russian dreambook of the nineteenth century was authored by a man: *The Reference Guide and Encyclopedic Lexicon of Dreams. More than 3000 Explanations of the Phenomena of Sleep. Collected over 66 Years by the Kindly Old Man of Duck Street* . . . (St Petersburg, 1863). Though the Kindly Old Man was evidently literate, it was in fact his nephew who arranged posthumous publication of his uncle's collection.[45] The most distinctive feature of this book comprises the very large number of dream objects and explanations; for example, while the average dreambook contained anything from four to twelve items under the letter A, the Kindly Old Man came up with seventy-eight, approximately seventy-five per cent of which were his own. Although some of his interpretations followed conventional dreambooks, others are idiosyncratic; for example, dreaming of pineapples, which earlier meant tears, here meant joy, and eating them, profit of any kind. The book did not catch on and was reissued only once, this time without any mention of the Kindly Old Man.[46] Its fate suggests further reasons for the absence of books by or attributed to local sages; dreambooks with their largely stable contents had settled into a tradition and were by then (as now) regarded by users as quintessentially Russian. New versions did not enjoy confidence precisely because they did not conform to printed tradition. In this respect Russian dreambooks differ from their European and American counterparts. Although there, too, names like Artemidorus or Descartes often featured on the title pages, texts were frequently attributed entirely to local experts, whether learned gentlemen (for instance Dr Trotter) or wise women (Mother Shipton, Mrs Bridget). In

Russia, it seems, ancient authorities enjoyed respect while native prophets, even if male, were without honour.[47]

The Kindly Old Man's concern for comprehensiveness was picked up towards the end of the century. In the last three decades of the century, rival publishers tried to outdo each other, several producing dreambooks claiming to contain a million dreams, later *Over One Million . . .* , then 1,200,000 and finally one and a half million dreams. Commercial considerations outweighed truthfulness: in the case of the last, interpretations number well under a thousand, though most of the others were longer. In an alternative move, the omnibus fortune-telling book was relaunched in the 1890s. Imitating the format and contents of its early nineteenth-century predecessors, it might even include historical curiosities such as the prophecy of Martyn Zadeka, predicting the future of Europe from the perspective of 1769. Judging by the multiple editions these underwent, the pre-Revolutionary buyer was undeterred.

The revival of compendia further exemplifies the trend at the end of the nineteenth century towards renovation of the dreambook tradition. One may suppose that well over a century of continuous publication had had two contrasting effects. On the one hand, readers' confidence in dreambooks was reinforced by their traditional contents; for many urban readers this literary tradition replaced or became intermingled with the folk interpretations. On the other hand, publishers in the cut-throat world of popular books may have felt that the old texts were losing their appeal for better-off buyers. Given the huge number of dreambooks regularly appearing in the three decades before the Revolution, saturation of the market was not the problem. The attempt to introduce innovations may simply have been a commercial move on the part of publishers to steal a march on competitors.

Apart from the reintroduction of omnibus editions, the period from 1880 is marked by attempts to launch new types of dreambook, of which the most successful was one where dream objects were organized under categories such as 'birds and insects', 'the moon', 'teeth' and so on. Though new to Russia, the principle derives from Western Europe. Judging by the references to Artemidorus, who also sometimes groups dreams thematically, the text is translated, though it hid its origins by appearing as *One Million 500,000 Dreams . . .* (Moscow, 1896), while being organizationally quite distinct from similarly named dreambooks. Others attempted to attract purchasers with pretensions, who might sneer at the basic dreambook. *Sleep and Dreams, a Scientifically Based Interpretation of Dreams, Compiled by the Famous Medium Miss Hussey* (Warsaw, 1912), for example, sought to appeal to fashion (the use of the vocabulary of spiritualism), and with an article by a psychophrenologist laid claim to be scientific. Attempts were also made to foster a scholarly interest in exotic dream traditions through the publication of non-European dreambooks such as a *Turco-Tatar Dreambook*, published by V. Kondaraki in Moscow in 1884 as a supplement to an ethnographic description of the Crimea. Whereas the thematic type of dreambook enjoyed some success, in particular in the post-Soviet revival, these other 'scientific' or scholarly books were not republished.

To sum up: by 1917, Russian dreambooks had settled into the steady pattern of an alphabetical text, based on European originals, but open to variation and expansion. A major enabling factor in their evolution was the lack of any understanding of copyright, which ensured that innovations were rapidly copied, to pass then into the accepted canon of dream objects. Though essentially conservative, these books did evolve, mainly through the accretion of new dream objects. Some of these reflect social or technological change. Among the additions to dreambooks were objects reflecting an urban readership and technological advance. Initially, these were few and came from a foreign original: pineapples, for example, appear in a dreambook translated from French in 1839, but reappear many times afterwards. By the last years of the nineteenth century, objects such as oranges, Americans, waltzing, watching the ballet, artichokes, planes or chocolate became increasingly common. Compilers did, however, sometimes react to the contemporary Russian scene. In the early years of the century, some began including an interpretation for 'agitator'. By 1915, this had changed to 'Bolshevik agitator'.[48] The conservative inclinations of publishers and purchasers alike are revealed in the meaning given to dreaming of agitators (loss of honour, deception or unhappiness). Those who found themselves dreaming of following Bolshevik agitators were promised the same miserable future, while merely catching sight of them in a dream meant something unpleasant would happen shortly. Many Russians would now argue that this is evidence of genuine prescience, though equally one might add that it places a new gloss on the reasons for the banning of dreambooks after 1917!

The process of adaptation would surely have continued had official pressure not put paid to their publication. One may assume that Russian dreambooks would otherwise have followed their European counterparts in expanding the list of dream objects and adapting them to modern life, but probably also with some input, however distorted, from Freud's and Jung's writings. The demise of dreambooks after 1917 was only a matter of time: a temporary ban in Moscow on the distribution of cheap books in December 1917 turned into a permanent national one in April 1919, and publishing was gradually nationalized.[49] The attitude of the Bolsheviks towards all popular literature was an extension of the dearest wish of many educated Russians in the pre-Revolutionary period, that the peasants and other humble members of society might share in a common culture, based on their own. In this context, dreambooks represented the worst of both worlds, pandering to primitive superstitiousness, and doing so through the medium of enlightenment – print. With their commitment to reason and their hostility to bourgeois and popular commercial culture, the Bolshevik government could not allow dreambooks to survive. Even the status of oral dream divination, higher because it was perceived as ancient and 'of the folk', failed to provide any support. In the 1920s and 1930s folk dream interpretation fell victim to the rush to turn peasants away from age-old practices and harness them to socialist ideals that perceived the future in social not individual terms. Folklorists ceased collecting dream beliefs since these had been vanquished by socialism and hence were deemed not to exist any longer. In one instance in 1926, however, dream beliefs were harnessed to the cause of advancing socialism, by their parodic adaptation as agitprop in wall newspapers (*stengazeta*) from the far north and the Urals. For example, dreaming of a policeman meant shortfalls in consumer goods (magicked away, presumably).[50] The production of these mock dreambooks relied upon the complete familiarity of the target audience with the originals.

And naturally, what went on in private was a different matter. In the pre-Revolutionary period fortune-telling books as a whole attracted hostility in varying degrees, being viewed as indicators either of ignorance or of feminine irrationality, depending on period. In such a situation one natural reaction is to restrict discussion of such topics to sympathetic groups, in particular other women. After 1917, as attachment to dream interpretation became an indicator of an unreconstructed mind, this strategy became essential: books would be concealed or relevant parts committed to memory, and dreams interpreted with like-minded people. In 1989–90 I conducted a survey with 130 Russians (eighty-four women and forty-six men from different parts of the Russian Federation) about the vitality of dream interpretation. Seventy per cent of the women questioned believed in predictive dreams but only thirty-five per cent of the men. Many knew the meaning of one or more dream symbol, usually acquired from mother or grandmother rather than directly from a book. Though traditionalist families, especially in the countryside, still interpret dreams over breakfast, the survey also revealed that many people now turn to friends, a reflection both of the loosening of family bonds and of the need to find a sympathetic milieu, something that could not be guaranteed in the Soviet family. At the same time the other common strategy adopted by fortune-tellers in eighteenth- and nineteenth-century Russia, trivialization, has now been applied to dream divination. Judging by the survey, many Russians, in particular men, regard it now as a fun social activity. Of course, the survey may have underplayed the level of belief in dream interpretation in contemporary Russia, since in 1989–90 there was probably some nervousness at being interviewed by a foreigner about such a dubious activity, but a rise in the numbers of sceptics at the end of a period dominated by socialist ideas would seem natural. Nonetheless, despite seventy years of official disdain, this and other evidence, together with the huge sales of recent dreambooks, furnish evidence of the durability and vigour of dream interpretation, especially in the countryside and among women over fifty.[51]

Some of the impulse towards the purchase of dreambooks must stem from nostalgia, since these are now seen as archetypically Russian, whatever their origin. Furthermore, in a country where the promise of a shining future along with stable prices and the social certainties of life have collapsed, there is every reason to seek to look into the future. If life is a nightmare, perhaps dreams can offer hope.

Yet such time-specific reasons fail to explain the enduring popularity of dream divination. Speaking generally, it may be seen, like fortune-telling as a whole, as a manifestation of the natural desire to exert more control over life by learning what may happen. Looking more specifically at the setting in which it was conventionally conducted, there seems little doubt that the primary reason was therapeutic. As already mentioned, powerful or enigmatic dreams were discussed in the family, mainly at breakfast. Breakfast dream-telling, a formalized procedure in many societies, performed functions beyond interpretation. It was not simply a request for information, but an expression of the individual's need to tell her or his dream – in effect, a form of purification, the discharging of the dream's power over the dreamer. It helped the individual understand his or her own desires and impulses. The implication is that discussion of the dream with others was a valued activity, whether the aim was to rid oneself of the lingering spell of a disturbing dream, legitimately gain the attention of others, join in a family activity or any combination of these. That dream interpretation was part of women's culture is indicated by my survey (in which none of the respondents had learnt dream beliefs from a man), by the titles of some dreambooks, by the confirmation of informants and by pre-Revolutionary ethnographic and literary references. Writing in the 1830s I. P. Sakharov noted that it was impossible to find a woman or girl who did not believe in dreams, a view echoed at the end of the century in a pamphlet put out by the Church, which regretted that 'many people, especially women, firmly believe that every dream must mean something'.[52] The leading role in dream interpretation played by the older woman (whether grandmother, mother or aunt) conferred a degree of authority upon her, even if it was an authority disputed by doubters. At the same time, interpreting the dreams of the younger generation gave her some control over them. For example, dreams that could be interpreted as being about a girl's future husband gave the interpreter a chance to present a reading that was in tune with parents' and society's norms and expectations, important at a time when parents conventionally chose, or at least approved, a suitable spouse for their children. Dream telling and interpretation may further be seen as a form of social bonding within families and more particularly among women of different generations. Even today, when activity has shifted more to interpretation in peer groups, many grandmothers, mothers and daughters in traditionalist families share and value the experience. It remains to be seen whether, as popular Freudianism finally becomes part of the Russian consciousness, women will be persuaded to abandon belief in the predictive power of dreams, leaving the dreambook to become a key to knowledge for just a dedicated minority.

NOTES AND REFERENCES

1 For example: *Dreambook (The Interpretation of Dreams)*, comp. E. Tsvetkov, Moscow, 1990; same title, comp. A. A. Stirbu and R. G. Polenova, Tiraspol', 1991; *Sleep and Dreams. A Scientifically Based Interpretation of Dreams*, comp. Miss Hussey, Moscow, 1990; two editions of a volume with a slightly different title: *Dreambook or the Interpretation of Dreams*, comp. G. H. Miller, St Petersburg, 1995, and Moscow, 1995; *The Interpretation of Dreams: A Dreambook*, Saratov, 1990; *Dreambook: The Interpretation of Dreams*, Almaty, 1990. By the late 1990s their popularity had declined.

2 In order: Tsvetkov's dreambook, 200,000; Stirbu and Polenova, 70,000; Miss Hussey, 500,000; the Petersburg Miller, 100,000, and the Moscow edition, 35,000; the Saratov book, 40,000. Information about print-runs is normally provided in Russian books.

3 A. V. Tereshchenko, *Byt russkogo naroda*, St Petersburg, 1848, pt 7, p. 275.

4 M. Hélin, *La clef des songes*, Paris, 1925, pp. 65 ff.; S. R. Fischer, 'The dream in Middle High German epic', *Australian and New Zealand Studies in German Language and Literature* 10, 1978, p. 28; H. Kapełuś, 'Senniki staropolskie. Z dziejów literatury popularniej XVI–XVII wieku', *Studii z dawniej literatury czeskiej, słowackiej i polskiej*, Warsaw-Prague, 1963, pp. 296–297.

5 This is evident in forewords, and the body of some, but by no means all texts; T. Crisp's volume as well as those of N. Dee (for example, *Your Dreams and What They Mean*, Wellingborough, 1984) combine analysis of the dreamer's character with prediction, but others stick to tradition: see, for example, G. H. Miller, *The Dictionary of Dreams. 10,000 Dreams Explained*, Ashburton, 1983, or *Dreams. Hidden Meanings and Secrets*, London, 1987.

6 The volumes on sale in the first half of the 1990s were either reprints from pre-Revolutionary times or translations of twentieth-century West-European works. Thus, books attributed to G. H. Miller and T. Crisp are recent translations, whereas Miss Hussey's *Sleep and Dreams. A Scientifically Based Interpretation of Dreams* had first appeared in Russian translation in 1912. But whereas this book clearly advertises its foreign origins, the many reprints of nineteenth-century texts, such as *A Million Dreams. A New and Complete Dreambook* (Moscow, two editions 1990, from the edition published regularly by Sytin and Co., 1890–1918), do not. They too are translations, stemming ultimately from the same Greek tradition by way of Western Europe.

7 On the use of famous names in Russian fortune-telling books generally, see F. Wigzell, *Reading Russian Fortunes: Print Culture, Gender and Divination in Russia from 1765*, Cambridge, 1998, pp. 145–164.

8 Contamination of the Russian folk tradition by imported manuscript dreambooks must be excluded. Similarities must be attributed, therefore, to common human psychological processes. For a discussion of the role played by folk oneirocritical traditions, see Wigzell, *Reading Russian Fortunes*, pp. 55, 57–61; on folk and printed dreambooks in Poland, see Stanisława Niebrzegowska, *Polski sennik ludowy*, Lublin, 1996.

9 On the spread of printing in the period after 1755, see Gary Marker, *Publishing, Printing and the Origins of Intellectual Life in Russia, 1700–1800*, Princeton, NJ, 1985, pp. 70–89.

10 For example, *Svodnyi katalog russkoi knigi grazhdanskoi pechati XVIII veka, 1725–1800* (ed. I. P. Kondakov and others), Moscow 1962–75 (henceforth *Union catalogue*), nos 6700–01, no. 198 in the addenda, and no. 775 in the list of books no longer extant.

11 Since no catalogue yet exists for Russian printed books published 1800–1830, I have had to rely on my own extensive bibliographical searches. Figures should therefore be regarded with caution. For more information on the history of fortune-telling in Russia, see Wigzell, *Reading Russian Fortunes*.

12 Numerous variants of what was a type of geomancy existed. It is probably best known in Britain as *Napoleon's Book of Fate*.

13 Witnessed by the indexes to the *Union Catalogue*.

14 M. J. Okenfuss, *The Rise and Fall of Latin Humanism in Early-Modern Russia: Pagan Authors, Ukrainians and the Resilience of Muscovy* (Brill's Studies on Intellectual History 64), Leiden – New York – Cologne, 1995, p. 142.

15 It was reprinted (or possibly retranslated) in 1799 in the guise of the engagingly entitled *The Dreambook, Telling Mother Truth* (*Union Catalogue*, no. 6702). The 1829 variant pretended to be an update: *The Newest Dream Interpreter, Telling Mother Truth*.

16 *Union Catalogue*, no. 7626.

17 See K. Thomas, *Religion and the Decline of Magic: Studies in Popular Belief in Sixteenth- and Seventeenth-Century England*, London, 1971, chaps 10–12; P. Curry, *Prophecy and Power: Astrology in Early Modern England*, Cambridge, 1989; and *A Confusion of Prophets: Victorian and Edwardian Astrology*, London, 1992, pp. 9–13.

18 Tereshchenko, *Byt russkogo naroda*, pt 7, p. 274.

19 For example, *Soothsay, Do not Jest* . . . 3 pts, Moscow, 1808 (vols 1 and 2) and 1827 (vol. 3); *The Ancient Astrologer or Oracle of Those Most Skilled in Divination* . . . , Moscow, 1814, and 1824–5.

20 The alternative explanation, that the Russian translator ignored Daniel's name, is much less likely. Names of foreign luminaries in the titles of Russian dreambooks are so numerous and frequent that it is clear that generally they were held to confer authority. Some Western texts of Daniel did not give his name.

21 For the fullest discussion of the problems faced by the book trade, see Marker, *Publishing, Printing and the Origins of Intellectual Life*, especially chaps 6 and 7.

22 Evidence for a wider social readership is given in V. Shklovskii, *Chulkov i Levshin*, Leningrad, 1933, pp. 32–43; T. Grits, V. Trenin, and M. Nikitin, *Slovesnost' i kommertsiia (knizhnaia lavka A. F. Smirdina)* (ed. V. B. Shklovskii and B. M. Eikhenbaum), Moscow, 1929, pp. 87–9. Semi-literate inscriptions in dreambooks of the period by a clerk in one instance and a merchant's son in another confirm the existence of lower-class readers (*The Prediction Worthy of Note of the Renowned Martyn Zadek . . . With the Addition to that Interpretation of the Interpretation of Dreams* . . . (1807, inscription dated 1818) and *A Secret Microscope* (1817), both in the Russian State Library in Moscow).

23 Though evidence is very thin, it may be deduced that the few highly educated and cosmopolitan Russians rapidly learned to disdain them. First, library holdings in this period seldom include fortune-telling books: I. P. Annenkov, a rarity in being a well-read provincial landowner, purchased one in the mid-1760s but no more, suggesting either that he bought out of curiosity or was misled by the title (he almost certainly ordered from a list) (P. I. Khoteev, *Kniga v Rossii v seredine XVIII veka. Chastnye knizhnye sobraniia*, Leningrad, 1989, p. 33). Second, statements asserting the harmless nature of the contents conventionally prefaced fortune-telling books at this period.

24 Though this does not mean that others did not buy them, even if surreptitiously. Very little has been written on the readership for dreambooks in Western Europe and America. On dreambooks in America, with some material on pre-1800 British texts, see H. B. Weiss, *Oneirocritica Americana. The Story of American Dreambooks*, New York, 1944, esp. p. 9; on Polish dreambooks, see Kapełus, 'Senniki staropolskie', pp. 295–306.

25 Marker, *Printing and Publishing*, p. 210. A century later, attitudes of dreambook buyers had not changed. Referring to the publishers of cheap commercial books, sold to the peasants and urban dwellers, A. V. Blium remarks that 'every cheap publisher, along with literature and books of spiritual guidance, considered it his duty to publish a variety of guides and manuals, essential in everyday life', of which the most important were fortune-telling books ('Russkaia lubochnaia kniga vtoroi poloviny xix veka', *Kniga. Issledovaniia i materialy* 42, Moscow, 1981, pp. 94–114, 109).

26 F. Wigzell, 'Preemstvennost' i peremeny v russkoi kul'ture: fiziognomiia i khiromantiia', *Germenetika drevnerusskoi literatury* 10, 1999; or more concisely, in *Reading Russian Fortunes*, pp. 68–69.

27 In Russia this applied particularly to a little-known, and perhaps fictitious, Swiss sage Martin Zadeck, whose prophecy underwent frequent publication and led to a lengthy career as Russian dream interpreter par excellence, his name somewhat russified to Martyn Zadeka (see Wigzell, *Reading Russian Fortunes*, pp. 150–157).

28 For example, I. Kurbatov in the foreword to *Soothsay, do not Jest . . .*, pt 1, Moscow, 1808.

29 Sergei Aksakov, in the first 'fragment' of his family history published 1846, describes the old-style life of his grandparents. Every morning his grandmother asks her husband whether he had any dreams. See *A Russian Gentleman* (transl. J. D. Duff), Oxford, 1982, p. 21. On Scandinavian traditions, see L. Virtanen, 'Dream-telling today', in A.-L. Siikala (ed.) *Studies in Oral Narrative* (Studia Fennica 33), 1990, pp. 137–145.

30 *Oblomov* was published in 1859; the childhood passages refer to the second decade of the century. For Nevezhin, see V. Shlovskii, *Matvei Komarov, zhitel' goroda Moskvy*, Leningrad, 1929, p. 14.

31 For example, the treatment of Yuletide divination in Zhukovskii's *Svetlana* and Pushkin's *Eugene Onegin*. See W. Ryan and F. Wigzell, 'Gullible girls and dreadful dreams (Zhukovskii's *Svetlana* and Pushkin's *Evgenii Onegin*)', *Slavonic and East European Review* 70, 1992, pp. 647–669.

32 M. O. Gershenzon, 'Sny Pushkina', *Stat'i o Pushkine*, Moscow, 1926, pp. 96–110. On the general interest in dreams, see D. A. Nechaenko, *Son zavetnykh ispolnennyi znakov*, Moscow, 1991, pp. 104–161.

33 For instance, the memoirs of the writer N. S. Sokhanskaia, referring to the late 1830s or early 1840s, record her horror at discovering that her family's neighbours in the country owned only two books, of which one was an oracle (probably a fortune-telling compendium). Fictional references support this: Lavretskii's deceased aunt in Turgenev's *House of the Gentry* (1859) owned only calendars and dreambooks, while Gogol''s hero in 'Ivan Fedorovich Shpon′ka and his auntie' (1832) only reads his dreambook, a clear indication of his hopeless 'feminised' behaviour.

34 The most popular was a Wheel of Fortune style text known as *King Solomon's Divinatory Circle*, which possessed enormous authority with the peasantry thanks to its archaic Church Slavonic language and easy availability, first in cheap woodcut form and later printed on a single sheet.

35 For instance, the attractive *Newest Dream Interpreter compiled from the Manuals of Foreign Men Skilled in the Art of Dream Divination . . .* (Moscow, 1829) became scarce, whilst lengthy books like the long dreambook of 1802, 1811 and 1818 (*New, Complete and Detailed Dreambook*) appeared only in truncated versions: *The New Dreambook or The Interpretation of Dreams in Alphabetical Order*, Moscow, 1831; *The Sibyl, or Morning Teller of Dreams . . .*, Moscow, 1839. The variations in title suggest that they are independent adaptations.

36 A mere couple of titles, of which only *The Shop of All Delights* ran to several editions 1830–50.

37 *The Dreambook of 215 Dreams, or the Interpretation of Dreams by Various Egyptian and Indian Sages and Astronomers*, Mstera, 1865, 1867, 1868, 1871, 1874, 1879, 1883 (and certainly other years besides, but popular commercial publishers frequently failed to lodge copies with deposit libraries, rendering full publication history extremely difficult).

38 Religious literature and cheap fiction were the main draws for the rapidly growing peasant market (see Blium, 'Russkaia lubochnaia kniga', p. 102; J. Brooks, *When Russia Learned to Read. Literacy and Popular Literature, 1861–1917*, Princeton, NJ, 1985, esp. pp. 360–364). The survey by the Moscow Literacy Committee of cheap books on the market in 1893 indicate that there were seven different dreambooks on the market plus several compendia containing dream texts (*Ezhegodnik. Obzor knig dlia narodnogo chteniia v 1893*, Moscow, 1894). Print runs were generally around 10,000, sizeable for the period (see V. I. Mezhov, *Piatoe pribavlenie k sistematicheskoi rospisi knigam, prodaiushchimsia v knizhnykh lavkakh Ivana Il′icha Glazunova. Sostavleno za 1883–87 vkl.*, St Petersburg, 1889).

39 *Union Catalogue*, no. 6700. The 1860 dreambook was published by Smirnov, the 1885 version by Presnov, both in Moscow.

40 For example, in *The Interpreter of Dreams by the Well-Known French Dream Interpreter, Mlle Lenormand* . . . , St Petersburg, 1862.

41 Ancient dream categories took a long time to disappear entirely: the purchaser of a short dreambook of 1865 was still able to discover that dreaming of eating camel-meat meant a long illness, and in *One Million, 500,000 Dreams* . . . (Moscow, 1896) dreaming of eating lions was said to bring honour and riches.

42 '*Azbuka*' is commonly found in dreambooks from 1802, while '*ananas*' was apparently first included in 1839, and '*arab*' or '*arap*' in 1859.

43 No. 2062 in Mezhov, *Piatoe pribavlenie*. Judging by the free use of the term 'folk' in titles of fortune-telling books as a whole, there is no guarantee that this or others contained genuine folk beliefs (see Wigzell, *Reading Russian Fortunes*, p. 55).

44 There was a special word for the sorcerer who possessed a book of black magic (which did not have to be much more than a manuscript containing harmful charms). For a discussion of the gender roles played by the various types of magic practitioner and divinatory specialist in the countryside, see Wigzell, *Reading Russian Fortunes*, pp. 48–50.

45 A survey carried out in 1894 in Petersburg suggests very low educational levels among fortune-tellers, and confirms that most humble fortune-tellers were women (Otshel'nik, *Peterburgskie gadalki, znakhari, iurodivye i pr. (Ocherki peterburgskoi zhizni)*, St Petersburg, 1894. On professional urban fortune-tellers, see Wigzell, *Reading Russian Fortunes*, pp. 127–144.

46 *3000 Dreams. A Detailed Explanation of All Manner of Dreams, in All Their Manifestations. Presented in Alphabetical Order*, St Petersburg, 1870.

47 On the attribution of dreambooks to famous sages, see Wigzell, *Reading Russian Fortunes*, pp. 144–164.

48 *The Popular Dreambook for 1915*, Petrograd, 1915, quoted by Nechaenko, *Son zavetnykh ispolnennyi znakov*, p. 4.

49 C. A. Ruud, *Russian Entrepreneur. Publisher Ivan Sytin of Moscow 1851–1934*, Montreal and Kingston, 1990, pp. 174 ff.

50 Quoted by A. Nasimovich, 'Stengazetnyi iumor', in *Pechat' i revoliutsiia* 6, 1927, p. 23, from *Arkhangel'skaia pravda* 6, Jan. 1926 and *Vpered, derevnia* no. 7, 1926, publ. by the village reading room in Bolotovo, Ural region.

51 On other evidence for dream beliefs in contemporary Russia, see Wigzell, *Reading Russian Fortunes*, pp. 168 ff.

52 I. P. Sakharov, *Skazaniia russkogo naroda sobrannye I. P. Sakharovym*, republished Moscow, 1990, from the edition of 1885, p. 1.

Chapter 11

'A nice type of the English scientist': Tansley and Freud

Laura Cameron and John Forrester

> I dreamed that I was in a sub-tropical country, separated from my friends, standing alone in a small shack or shed which was open on one side so that I looked out on a wide open space surrounded by bush or scrub. In the edge of the bush I could see a number of savages armed with spears and the long pointed shields used by some South African native tribes. They occupied the whole extent of the bush-edge abutting on the open space, but they showed no sign of active hostility. I myself had a loaded rifle, but realized that I was quite unable to escape in face of the number of armed savages who blocked the way.
>
> Then my wife appeared in the open space, dressed entirely in white, and advanced towards me quite unhindered by the savages, of whom she seemed unaware. Before she reached me the dream, which up to then had been singularly clear and vivid, became confused, and though there was some suggestion that I fired the rifle, but with no knowledge of who or what I fired at, I awoke.
>
> Sir Arthur Tansley, FRS, *The Dream*

Arthur Tansley had this dream some time during the First World War, when he was working at the Ministry of Munitions in London.[1] It was, he later made very clear, one of the major turning points in his life. From this dream came his interest in psychoanalysis.

On 6 April 1922, Sigmund Freud wrote to Ernest Jones in London: 'Tansley has started analysis last Saturday. I find a charming man in him, a nice type of the English scientist. It might be a gain to win him over to our science at the loss of botany'.[2] Such information was the staple of the correspondence between Jones and Freud that comprised some 671 letters over a thirty-year period to Freud's death. Implicit in such exchanges was the sustaining of the joint project that kept these two men, never soul mates, bound together – the fate and future of psychoanalysis – as a theory, a therapy and an institutional movement.

By following the trail revealed by this little snippet about an analysis begun in Vienna in the spring of 1922, we will discover that the early history of psychoanalysis in England was by no means confined to the professional and institutional lines that Jones, and even Freud, had in mind. And then, by focusing on Tansley, we will gain a more balanced and more intriguing sense of the intellectual vitality and novelty of the set of ideas and practices spawned by Freud. In addition, we will be drawn into speculating about the historical significance of dreams and their interpretation, which, following Freud, many in the twentieth century have come to regard as 'the royal road to the unconscious'.[3]

* * *

It is the very implausibility of Tansley's involvement in psychoanalysis that, oddly enough, makes him so representative. He was, as Freud endearingly described him in his eccentric but precise English, 'a nice type of the English scientist' – and a distinguished one at that. Born in central London on 15 August 1871, Arthur George Tansley was the second child and only son of Amelia Lawrence and George Tansley – the 'exceptional people' to whom, at the end of his life, he would attribute the fact that his own Oedipus complex was 'almost negligible'.[4] George had a good business organizing society functions, and he also taught at the Working Man's College, where his real heart and enthusiasm lay. Arthur was educated at Highgate School; he went on to University College London, to study the sciences, and in 1890 entered Trinity College, Cambridge, where he obtained a double first in the Natural Sciences Tripos in 1893–4. During his final year at Trinity College, he assisted his first teacher, the botanist F. W. Oliver, in teaching and research at UCL. Oliver aroused Tansley's interest in fern-like plants and shared Tansley's interests in the new subject of ecology. Tansley taught and researched at UCL for the next twelve years with Oliver and other colleagues, such as F. F. Blackman and Marie Stopes, with whom he would form long-lived associations. While at UCL, Tansley taught himself German and thus could read the 1896 German translation of Warming's *Plantesamfund* and Schimper's 1898 *Pflanzen Geographie auf Physiologischer Grundlage*. Tansley felt these books laid the foundations for plant ecology as they developed concepts of plant communities and described the relations between plants, soils and climates. In 1903, he married his former student, Edith Chick, F. F. Blackman's sister-in-law, Stopes's classmate and daughter of a lace merchant, Samuel Chick. They were to have three daughters, who were to become a physiologist, an architect and an economist. In 1906, he returned to Cambridge on his appointment to a University Lectureship in Botany.

Tansley had by this time already demonstrated two of his most salient intellectual characteristics: his willingness to assist an admired intellectual figure in a seemingly subordinate position without loss of dignity or standing and his gift for organizing and leading scientific projects as one of a group of like-minded enthusiasts. An admirer of Herbert Spencer's scientific philosophy, Tansley had overseen the sections on plant morphology and physiology in the 1899 revised edition of his *The Principles of Biology*.

Already a Fellow of the Linnean Society, Tansley was pivotal in yoking the concerns of professional botanists to the activities of naturalist societies in the national survey projects of the British Vegetation Committee, which he co-founded in 1904. As the scope of these necessarily collaborative survey activities was broadened to include botanists from outside Britain, Tansley founded the International Phytogeographical Excursion (IPE), hosted first by the British botanists and subsequently by the Americans in 1913. To acquaint the non-British scientists with local vegetation, of which they knew virtually nothing, Tansley edited and wrote *Types of British Vegetation* (1911) for the IPE. This was the first systematic account of British vegetation, and immediately found a larger home market besides the foreign botanists. The IPE, an organization perhaps rather similar to the International Psycho-analytical Association in the latter's early years, became a permanent institution (still in existence), meeting every two or three years in a different country, with its headquarters at the Institut Rübel in Zurich.

In 1913, the British Vegetation Committee became the British Ecological Society, the world's first ecological organization. Tansley was its first president. Already editor of a botanical journal, *The New Phytologist*, begun in 1902, funded by his private income and (with shades of things to come) entirely independent of universities and the scholarly presses,[5] Tansley also acted as editor of the new Society's *Journal of Ecology* from 1917 to 1938. In 1915, he was elected Fellow of the Royal Society; in later years, affirming that this was the recognition that counted, he would always add the letters 'FRS' to his signature.

Concerned with effective teaching of the new ecology, Tansley used his editorial authority to advocate a new curriculum. The key term for early proponents of self-conscious ecology like Tansley and the American plant ecologist F. E. Clements was 'dynamic'.[6] This was a departure from static morphology and biogeography, the prevailing focus on structure over function, and what ecologists derided as mere 'descriptive' botany with its emphasis on species lists. The 1917 so-called 'encyclical' in *The New Phytologist* (signed by Tansley, Oliver, Blackman and two others) pleaded for a vitalized and practical curriculum, to be based on plant physiology and ecology alongside, rather than subordinate to, the currently dominant (and in their opinion, static and dull) morphology.[7] Tansley's ideas for reform were denounced as 'Botanical Bolshevism' by Frederick Bower, the Regius Professor of Botany at Glasgow, and received a similarly chilly response in the Cambridge Botany School. They may have been a significant factor in his not being elected to the Sherardian Chair of Botany at Oxford, for which he was a candidate in the autumn of 1918[8] – a professional setback that may have had profound inner consequences, with reverberations to which his conversation with Freud in 1928 (see below) may have been alluding. As he complained to Frederic Clements in 1918,

> I've been getting some experience in the 'Gentle art of making enemies' lately. . . . Reactionary forces are pretty strong here, and it will be a hard struggle to get anything progressive done. But I am going to have a good try.[9]

However, by 1918, Tansley was looking elsewhere than the Cambridge Botany School or even the international ecology movement for his intellectual direction forward. A key influence since the early years of the century was his own former student Bernard Hart. Hart, working as a doctor in asylums near London, would often entertain Tansley, who thus came to have an unbookish and hands-on experience of mental disturbances. Hart's interests were in the psychology of insanity – the title of his very influential short book published in 1912. Hart was eclectic – absorbed first by Janet's ideas, then by Freud's, and in turn by Jung's – and he impressed Freud as well as Tansley. Writing to Jones in 1910, Freud called Hart's essay on the subconscious 'the first clever word upon the matter'.[10] Jones, always alert to any danger to his position as first among English Freudians, replied:

> He was one of my best pupils in England, although I had at first some difficulty in getting him to take up your work. Ultimately he said 'Freudism is strictly speaking a religion; you can't *prove* it, but you have to accept it because "it works"', which was quite clever.[11]

Hart played a considerable role in the integration of Freudian and non-Freudian psychotherapeutic practitioners during the Second World War, when he was in charge of psychotherapy co-ordination for the Emergency Medical Services first in London, and then throughout Britain.

Tansley was clearly quite intrigued by the new theories in psychopathology before the war but, by his own account, his knowledge owed more to conversation than study or research. What then happened to him was curious and was, according to him, the reason why the second half of his professional life became intertwined with the early history of psychoanalysis in England. In 1916 or thereabouts, aged forty-five, married with three daughters, secure (though restless) in his profession and having recently attained the pinnacle of a scientist in early twentieth-century Britain and with further successes and achievements in his chosen field undoubtedly ahead of him, he had the dream quoted at the opening of this chapter. In 1953, when setting down for Kurt Eissler of the Sigmund Freud Archives, later sited at the Library of Congress, his memories of his involvement with Freud and psychoanalysis, he wrote:

[The dream and my analysis of it] impressed me very deeply and led to a resolve to read Freud's work. This I did in the months that followed, beginning with the *Traumdeutung*, and following with the *Drei Abhandlungen zur Sexual Theorie*, and some others. The latter – the *Sexualtheorie* – interested and excited me immensely. I felt that it was an extraordinarily able and illuminating work, and, after having read far more widely in Freud since then, I still think that in some respects it is his most outstanding contribution – a daring and successful synthesis clearly and admirably expounded. My interest in the whole subject was now thoroughly aroused, and after a good deal of thought I determined to write my own picture of it as it shaped itself in my mind.

This 'picture' was Tansley's book, *The New Psychology and its Relation to Life*, completed in January 1920 and published in June. Reprinted twice within eight months, ten times in four years, in the first three years it sold over 10,000 copies in the UK, over 4,000 in the same period in the USA,[12] and was translated into Swedish and German. Tansley had caught the post-war wave of enthusiasm and fascination with Freudianism and depth psychology (as it was often called) in general. The book was an attempt, he said, to capture for the general reader the 'biological' view of the mind with the concepts taken from the work of 'the great modern psychopathologists, Professor Freud and Dr. Jung'.[13] Modestly, Tansley assured his reader that it was neither a treatment of 'psychopathology proper' nor a comprehensive review of the literature – the book is simply 'an outline picture of the subject as it shapes itself in the mind of the author'. (This, we might note, is exactly how Tansley had allowed his own dream to 'interpret itself' – almost 'automatically', as he put it to Eissler.)

According to Tansley, he was disconcerted by the response to his book. Not only did he have a best-seller on his hands, but he received 'a good many letters from strangers asking all sorts of questions, many of which I did not feel I could answer adequately without a much more extensive knowledge of psycho-analysis'.[14] Like his old friend and colleague, Marie Stopes, whose *Married Love* (1918) was an even bigger seller than *The New Psychology*, and like both Krafft-Ebing and Havelock Ellis before them, whose writings on sexual idiosyncrasy expanded enormously in their later editions from the weight of private confession and testimony, Tansley clearly found himself addressed as an expert by numerous individuals in need.[15]

Accordingly in 1921 I asked Dr Ernest Jones to give me an introduction to Freud, to whom I then wrote asking if he could receive me for an analysis. On his consenting to do so I arranged to spend three months in Vienna, from March to June, 1922.[16]

This account of Tansley's journey to Freud's couch is, we will speculate later, not the whole story. What happened next surely makes us more certain of this: in the spring of 1923, Tansley resigned his position at Cambridge. Undoubtedly, from earlier on than this decisive step, Freud, Jones and others had begun to follow Tansley's psychoanalytic progress with some interest.[17] Freud found a place for Tansley on the last day of March 1922. Beginning his analysis in German, Tansley was soon obliged by the difficulties of communicating his innermost thoughts to switch to English.

From the beginning of the decade, Americans and English were making the pilgrimage to Vienna to be analysed by Freud. In the American cohort of – roughly – 1920–22 were Albert Polan, Clarence Oberndorf, Leonard Blumgart, Monroe Meyer and Abram Kardiner; the British contingent consisted of the two Stracheys and John Rickman, who were joined by Joan Riviere in early 1922.[18] John Rickman had been at King's College, Cambridge from 1910 to 1913, taking the Natural Sciences Tripos in which Tansley was lecturing, but his lasting interest in psychoanalysis was sparked by W. H. R. Rivers in 1919 when Rickman was working at Fulbourn Hospital near Cambridge after returning from wartime hospital work for the Quakers in Russia. At his request, the 'indefatigable' Rickman, as Freud called him,[19] found suitable – extremely suitable, given the symbolism – lodgings in Vienna for Tansley in the house of the recently deceased famous botanist, Wiesner (whose lectures on Plant Physiology Freud himself had attended as a student in 1876)[20]: Freud was pleased Tansley would be able to make use of Wiesner's library. Obviously well informed on Tansley's journey to Vienna, Jones enquired almost too eagerly the day after Tansley's analysis began: 'Has Tansley started yet? I think he is a very able and careful thinker, and shall be glad to hear your impressions of him'.[21] Freud's opinion of Tansley chimed with Jones's, and their joint effort to catch this big fish is palpable.

It is plausible that, with Tansley's resistances now mobilized, both Freud and Tansley agreed that the three-months' analysis that ended in June 1922 was woefully incomplete. Tansley was obviously intent on returning to Freud, but it is probable that his duties in Cambridge kept him from Vienna in the academic year 1922–3. But by the late spring of 1923, he had made his decision and resigned. However, his increasing involvement with psychology did not stop him from publishing substantial works in botany;[22] in addition, he was President of the Botanical Section, British Association for the Advancement of Science in 1923, and spent part of the summer months doing research at Wicken Fen near Cambridge, a site of special scientific interest for Tansley and his botanical co-workers.[23]

Nonetheless, his colleagues, particularly his American rival and friend, the plant ecologist F. E. Clements, expressed some consternation – and understanding – about his resignation and the career and intellectual crossroads it represented. They were obviously aware of the profound shift in Tansley's vision of his future. Clements even voiced an ambiguous fear: 'I am not at all sure that your new field may not have greater opportunities for distinct and distinguished services'.[24] Tansley's course now seemed set:

> Probably I shall cease to be a professional botanist after the [University] term, though for the present, at least, I shall continue to edit the two journals. . . . Adamson is going to the Cape and will be a terrible loss to me – I need a good 'florist' at my elbow. Together with the 'conservatives in authority' his departure will help make me spend more time at psychology and less at ecology. The last year or two I have been pursuing both, and though my power of work is much better than it was, largely I think to the release of powers through emotional clarification – the double pull is a considerable strain.[25]

In May, having resigned from Cambridge, he told Clements of his plan to have more months of analysis with Freud in October – 'but for the present, at least, I shall continue to edit the two journals. It is likely that I shall take my whole family with me to Vienna'.[26]

Move they did. But Freud was not ready to restart the analysis; he was undergoing the first of his many major operations for cancer in the autumn of 1923. Tansley waited in Vienna, and Freud was recovered sufficiently to start work again at the end of December. This second slice of analysis lasted a further six months.

Tansley having made his decision, Freud galvanized other analysts into welcoming him to his new profession. On 14 March 1924, he wrote to Karl Abraham, then Secretary of the International Psycho-Analytic Association and convenor of the Congress to be held at Salzburg in April 1924, describing Tansley's book as having

> done a great deal for the spread of psychoanalysis, although it shows him still in a phase of development before being completely an adherent. He is now in analysis with me for the second time, and I hope to make considerable progress with his convictions. He is a distinguished, correct person, a clear, critical mind, well-meaning and highly educated.[27]

Tansley was obviously welcomed with open arms by the analysts, just as Ernest Jones's somewhat diffident review of *The New Psychology* in late 1920 did not miss the opportunity to emphasize how distinguished Tansley was.[28] From Jones's point of view, Tansley appeared to be a godsend, who would help secure the biological flank of psychoanalysis and, if need be, stem the tide of biological speculation to which so many analysts, including Freud, were prone. Thus, on 19 October 1920, Jones announced in the Rundbrief to the Committee that:

A. G. Tansley, Professor [*sic*] of Botany at Cambridge University, who has just written a good book called *The New Psychology*, read a paper on Oct. 13th on Freud's Theory of Sex from a Biological Point of View, before the British Soc. for the Study of Sex Psychology. He regretted the Ablehnung of biology in the preface to the Drei Abhandlungen, and asked me the meaning of the passage, which I should be glad to hear from Professor himself. T. was enthusiastically in favour of the theory, which he declared to be throughout essentially sound from a biological point of view and supported by much evidence from that science.[29]

Tansley and Jones were referring to the following passage from the Preface to the 1915 edition of Freud's *Three Essays*:

[These essays are] deliberately independent of the findings of biology . . . my aim has rather been to discover how far psychological investigation can throw light upon the biology of the sexual life of man . . . there was no need for me to be diverted from my course if the psycho-analytic method led in a number of important respects to opinions and findings which differed largely from those based on biological considerations.[30]

To the 'modern, deterministic, empiric and dynamic' minds of Jones and Tansley, such a disdain for or even distancing from biology might not be the way in which to develop a truly scientific psychoanalysis. Two years later, there are hints in Jones's worrying to Freud about biology that he longs for Tansley to be able to take over the biological side completely, and to correct some of the errors to which Freud was inclined:

I am not happy about our recapitulation theory and wish we could enlist the services of a good modern biologist. If Tansley were more advanced or experienced I would discuss it with him, but he is not yet sure of the ontogenetic side of the Oedipus complex, let alone the phylogenetic or prehistoric.[31]

Jones's perception was correct: Tansley was to remain resolutely agnostic on the question of the universality of the Oedipus complex and to employ lofty irony for attempts to employ a theory of use-inheritance to underpin psycho-analytic findings.[32] But Jones continued to use Tansley as a secret weapon against the more speculative biological theorists, most prominently Ferenczi. Writing to Freud in September 1924, he adopted an almost threatening tone:

I do not trace any suspicion of anti-analytic tendency in [Ferenczi's] work, but cannot refrain from the diagnosis of narcissism combined with poor judgement. No doubt you saw Tansley's review of his work in the *British Journal of Medical Psychology*.[33]

Coinciding roughly with the end of Tansley's analysis, back in London on 22 May 1924 John Rickman nominated him as an Associate Member of the British Psycho-analytic Society, which approved the motion.[34] Freud had recommended that Tansley take on a psychoanalytic case, to acquaint himself fully with the technique and the findings of the discipline. At some point, probably starting in late 1924 or 1925, Tansley did so – 'an experimental analysis, lasting nearly two years, on an obsessional neurotic'.[35] On 7 October 1925, he was elected to full membership of the Society, and for a year, until 17 November 1926, attended meetings frequently.[36] Even before his membership, Tansley was sought out as a powerful ally for psychoanalysis. At the Salzburg IPA Congress in April 1924, which he attended, it was agreed to hold the next Congress in Cambridge, a decision possibly connected with the curious fact that, by 1924, the British Psychoanalytical Society had become the largest in the world, with 49 members (the Viennese Society had 42, the Swiss 40, the American 31, the Berlin 27 and 26 in the New York). It would have been very much in character for Jones to wish to carry on building his empire by holding the International Congress on British soil, in a city as welcoming of intellectual endeavour as was Cambridge, not to speak of the respectability that might as a result be conferred on psychoanalysis in English eyes. Once Tansley had become an Associate Member of the British Society and completed his nine months of analysis with Freud, he was the obvious person to turn to as organizer of some kind of the Cambridge Congress. This Jones certainly did. But in November he found himself obliged to write a letter to Abraham, the newly elected President of the IPA:

> Although Tansley promised me verbally to investigate the situation in Cambridge and I have written to him since reminding him, there is as yet no answer. I think that the delay is more likely to be due to personal inhibitions than to outward circumstances, but I will of course write to you the moment I hear anything.[37]

Newly freed from his teaching and academic responsibilities, Tansley may have felt somewhat uneasy about taking on similar responsibilities on behalf of his new psychoanalytic colleagues and institutions. Not being a Fellow of a Cambridge College – an increasingly common fate for practitioners of the burgeoning new disciplines, particularly in the sciences – he may not have had the base for organizing the beds, dinners and rooms that conferences require.[38] Or there may have been other, more personal inhibitions – his father, after all, had, although he despised them, spent his life organizing social functions for high society. Certainly Tansley seems to have been the only plausible Cambridge-based person for such organization – the two other British Society members resident in Cambridge were Susan Isaacs, newly arrived as head of the Maltings House nursery school (scurrilously known as the 'pre-genital brothel'[39]), and Dr. C. R. A. Thacker, physiologist and specialist on nervous diseases and shell shock, Fellow of Sidney Sussex College, by this time already suffering from the illness that was to kill him in 1929.

Whatever Tansley's ambivalences about specific involvement with the psychoanalytic movement, he was an intensely social being, a born scientific networker. Free of those commitments at Cambridge that had become a burden and an incessant source of unprofitable struggle, he made these links in at least two different directions: both informal, one within Cambridge and one within the field sciences milieu. We have sketched the network of Tansley's psychoanalytic colleagues and contacts elsewhere.[40] Some of these links acquired that characteristic of being in large part hidden from history that necessarily accompanies the duty of clinical confidentiality. But, interestingly enough, Tansley's work to galvanize support for psychoanalysis was not confined to informal and private contacts. Throughout the summer of 1925, Tansley was engaged in IPE ecological activities in Europe and at the same time in a public polemic defending psychoanalysis in the correspondence column of the *The Nation and The Athenæum*. Perhaps the quirky manner in which he rounded off his robust defence pointed to the next step in his career: 'may I beg your correspondents' attention to the fact that I am not, and never have been, a professor? Nor do I hold a doctor's degree'.[41] Plain Mr Tansley he certainly was at that time, neither academic nor doctor, whether of philosophy or medicine. But not for much longer.

At some point in 1926–7, Tansley's younger colleague Harry Godwin[42] did some behind-the-scenes work in the botany world. In Godwin's later judgement, the years 1923 to 1927 had been for Tansley years 'in the wilderness so far at least as his relations to botanical science were concerned and especially those with British botanists'.[43] Through his encouragement, Tansley accepted an invitation to apply for the Sherardian Chair of Botany at Oxford. In an authoritative tone that betrays familiarity with Tansley's relations with Freud and psychoanalysis, Godwin wrote:

> Not until the end of 1926 did he complete what Freud had forecast for him, 'the return to the mother subject', . . . He was elected in January 1927. Indecision was abandoned.[44]

He took up the post in October 1927, together with a Fellowship at Magdalen College. His lectures from then on were on more conventional botanical subjects; he obviously felt the need to devote himself to reforming teaching and research in botany at Oxford. Nor do we know if he included discussion of psychoanalysis in those lectures, as he had done in Cambridge where, as Joseph Needham, the Cambridge biochemist and sinologist later recalled, it had been Tansley who helped to generate an interest in Freud among students during the 1920s by mentioning him in his lectures.[45] But once at

Oxford, he did not leave psychoanalysis entirely behind him. In 1928, he himself initiated a further polemic in *The Nation and The Athenæum*, seemingly stung by Vera Brittain's charge – which he must have read as a covert attack on psychoanalysis – that 'certain men of science have bestowed upon sexual gluttony a blessing which they would withhold in horror from any other form of immoderation'. Having pointed out to Brittain that the views of such 'men of science' on sexuality involved recommending moderation instead of abstinence – quite the opposite of advocating licensed gluttony, as in her image of little boys let loose on an unlimited quantity of jam – he moved on to his psychoanalytic point when he declared that a statement such as Brittain's 'that there is a danger of "over-estimating the importance of the part which sex plays in life" is a contention only ever, in my experience, made by those who seriously under-estimate that importance.'[46]

Although he contemplated writing a history of the early development of Freudian psychology,[47] and drafted chapters for it, Tansley's main work of the 1930s was in the 'mother subject' of botany – and productive of a concept of great significance for the future development of the discipline: the 'ecosystem'.[48] In this and other projects, there is substantial evidence of his continued interest and commitment to 'psychology', in particular manuscript materials relating to the project Godwin mentioned, a history of the development of Freudian psychology. Towards the end of 1932, Tansley wrote at least two papers on the early development of Freud's theories, which he intended to submit to the *British Journal of Medical Psychology*, focusing on the relation between psychoanalysis and biology, and he left an incomplete manuscript entitled 'The Historical Foundations of Psychoanalysis', which may have incorporated those papers. Tansley was sufficiently immersed in this work to write asking Freud what became of the first patient of psychoanalysis, Anna O.[49] In addition, there is a manuscript preface to 'a series of essays on various topics that have interested me specially in what I call the New Psychology'; the book, obviously a follow-up to his 1920 best-seller, was never completed.

Thus, even though Tansley published little work in psychology after 1927 until his final book, *Mind and Life*, an overarching synthesis of the twin preoccupations of his professional career, his interest in psychoanalysis did not diminish, nor did he lose his contacts with the British Psychoanalytical Society.[50] In 1941, he provided the Royal Society with an obituary for Sigmund Freud.[51] Botany did, quite clearly, however, dominate his life. During the 1930s, he worked on his revision of his 1911 *Types*. Eventually completed after his retirement from Oxford in 1937, *The British Islands and their Vegetation* (1939), his magnum opus, was a vast survey of over 900 pages, the culmination of the phase of ecology that he had initiated. It was the first major book to employ the ecosystem concept: vegetational communities are shown to be the result of the interacting processes of plants, climates and soils in a dynamic landscape lively with human and animal activities. In 1931, he handed over ownership and editorship of *The New Phytologist*. In 1938, he finally gave up the editing of the *Journal of Ecology*. The fifteen years following his retirement were very productive of publications.[52] In 1941 he took a guiding role in the planning of government post-war nature conservation, which led to the foundation of the Nature Conservancy in 1949, of which he was the first Chairman, retiring in 1953.

He was also heavily involved (as President from 1947–53) in the Council for the Promotion of Field Studies (later the Field Studies Council), a voluntary organization that created and maintained resident field centres in various locations of ecological and geological interest (such as Flatford Mill in Suffolk) where students could explore natural history interests and painting. Such an interest in decentralized education and the nurturing of 'scientific curiosity'[53] resonated with his active joint leadership (with John Baker and Michael Polanyi) of the Society for Freedom in Science (SFS), an organization that, from 1940, fought strongly against the central planning of scientific research being introduced as orthodoxy with the new bureaucratic forms and quasi-socialist ideals of the post-war settlement. Perhaps in part due to Tansley's recruiting activities, ecologists made up more than a quarter of the SFS membership.[54] In this, yet another of the new and extra-academic institutions that he had helped to found over some fifty years, Tansley felt free to express his views on psychology in a pamphlet, 'The psychological connexion of two basic principles of the SFS'. And, being now a distinguished knight and longstanding member of the British Psychoanalytical Society, Tansley was one of the signatories for an Appeal for £100,000 for an Institute and Clinic of Psycho-analysis, along with Dr J. C. Flugel, Dr William Gillispie (its Chairman), Dr Ernest Jones, Professor L. S. Penrose, and Professor F. R. Winton.[55] Tansley died on the 25 November 1955, aged 84, in the house in Grantchester just outside Cambridge where he had lived since 1907.

TANSLEY'S DREAM

> But the dream itself, the patent, the obvious content of it, is entirely harmless. Nobody outside the psychoanalytically trained could possibly tell what it meant, that it meant hell, deep . . .
> Prof. Sir A. G. Tansley, FRS, 1953

Looking at Tansley's life from the outside, we have located him as an intriguing and symptomatic character in the development of psychoanalysis in England. Coming from the non-medical sciences, inspired by his friends and colleagues in psychiatry to immerse himself in Freud's work, he unexpectedly wrote a book – as much for his own satisfaction, it appears, as for any other reason – that caught the spirit of the times and led him, dissatisfied with his academic position and future, to engage seriously in psychoanalysis with Freud and other like-minded colleagues in Cambridge and within his informal scientific community. As he himself put it, writing in 1932, in 1926 'it was touch and go whether I became a professional psychoanalyst' or took the Chair in Botany in Oxford. Oxford won out and psychoanalysis suffered the loss of the 'nice type of an English scientist'. In reconstructing this story, we have been able to shift significantly the accepted view of how psychoanalysis was received in England: in particular, we have been forced to emphasize the extent to which elite cultural and, importantly, scientific circles could be drawn to psychoanalysis and on to the couch, could even pass without difficulty into the ranks of the practising analysts, without medical background, interests in academic psychology or formal training. Frank Ramsey, C. C. Fagg, Tansley, Sir Harold Jeffreys, Lionel Penrose – respectively a Cambridge prodigy in philosophy of mathematics, a Customs Officer who was a vigorous organizer of field sciences, a bastion of scientific ecology, a polymathic geophysicist and a geneticist turned psychologist and critic of eugenics – this is not the usual cast of characters found in histories of psychoanalysis, yet they are some of the actors in the network Tansley created in the 1910s and 1920s, based in Cambridge, who were committed to psychoanalysis.

However, we also have a number of pieces of evidence that make it possible to undertake a speculative reconstruction of Tansley's life from within. First and foremost, he himself transcribed a dream which he regarded as a crucial turning-point in his life. In addition, he left a number of autobiographical works in which he tried to explain how and why his life took the shape it did. So, with these materials, and with the benefit of hindsight, we might also venture a psychoanalytic reading in order to make clearer how his influential and, it would seem, fulfilling life came to have that shape rather than another.

Before attempting this, it is advisable to make some historiographical remarks about using dreams as historical sources. After all, on the face of it, a dream is a source unlike any other. By definition, it does not pertain to reality. What its dreamer or any other commentator says about it will be liable, more purely so than with any other 'event', to retrospective distortion and self-interested reinterpretation. One might argue that, at its most extreme, a dream (its textual rendition or its trace as memory) will function as a Rorschach ink-blot, ready for projection and elaboration according to the needs, desires and interests of the remembering or interpreting subject at the moment the dream is called upon to bear witness to or reveal a historical truth.

Similar sceptical remarks have informed much discussion concerning the topic of creativity and dreams in the history and sociology of science. An older tradition, attempting to analyse the sources of intellectual creativity, pointed to dreams as one such source among several others. More recent sociologically oriented accounts emphasize less the inner creativity, the 'frenzy' as Max Weber called it, of creative intellectual discovery or production than the community for which this act is a discovery, an achievement – something comprehensible to privileged others. Without wishing to decide one way or the other between these readings, we can note that the publication of *The Interpretation of Dreams* and the subsequent development of a Freudian-style discourse on dreams – on their meaning, their interpretability, their significance as giving access to the unconscious – complicate without under-cutting the contrast between the private inner psychical act and the publicly scrutinizable community of 'dream-discoursers'. What is certain – and is well illustrated by the case of Tansley – is that, after Freud, a dream could become a resource for inner knowledge and an acceptable code or key for self-description. It is this resource and code that Tansley drew upon, in different ways no doubt, at different points in his life.

The archival source of this dream is the Sigmund Freud Archives at the Library of Congress in Washington, DC.[56] In the summer of 1953, when interviewed by Dr Kurt Eissler, founder of the Sigmund Freud Archives, Tansley's account of why and how he became involved with psychoanalysis centred entirely around the dream. He found the interview procedure un-congenial for recalling the events that Eissler was interested in, and instead promised to send Eissler a written account, which he did. Eissler, for his part, sent a transcript of the interview to Tansley, who returned it together with two other documents he had prepared. Thus the complete holding of the Tansley Section of the Freud Archives in the Library of Congress con-sists of three documents: the first, a seven-page account prepared by Tansley and entitled by him: '(1) The impact of Freud's work and personality on a non-medical biologist'. The second is a two-page typewritten document he entitled 'THE DREAM'. The third is the Eissler transcript. Before returning the documents to Eissler, Tansley added in pen a new title to the package: 'Three Contributions by Sir Arthur Tansley, FRS'.

All three of these 'contributions' centre on Tansley's dream. In the first, his written account of Freud's impact, he notes:

> At that time [the first decade of the present century] I had read none of Freud's publications, and although I was intrigued by what I heard from Hart and his colleagues my interest was only vividly aroused as the result of a dream which I had some years later, after I had moved to Cambridge. This dream and my 'automatic' analysis of its content are described in another contribution to the Archives (Ref. 2). I was so deeply impressed by this experience that I began to read Freud's works, notably the *Drei Abhandlungen zur Sexualtheorie* and Brill's translation of *Die Traumdeutung*, as well as Jung's study of Dementia praecox and his *Wandlungen und Symbole der Libido*. The *Sexualtheorie* I found particularly impressive and illuminating. . . .

The third document, the transcribed interview, gives a similar, though less focused account of his initial serious interest in psychoanalysis as a result of the dream, which, as 'Ref. 2', thus forms the centrepiece of this triptych.

It is Tansley's whimsical afterthought for his submission that makes one pause, in Freudian style, for thought. To call these three documents, each centred primarily on Tansley's own dream, his 'Three contributions' is to allow them to mirror the work of Freud's that Tansley most admired, the *Drei Abhandlungen* – 'one of his most penetrating fundamental works, those *Three contributions*, as they have been called in translation'.[57] Yet the overall message of these three documents is: he learned little from Freud that he had not already discovered in this dream. To put it crudely: when Tansley was asked about Freud's influence upon him, he replied by saying that influence was minimal, and offered as proof the dream he had had long before meeting or even reading Freud.

We have already quoted in full the dream text he submitted to the Sigmund Freud Archives. Tansley also included the following comments, associations and a page he entitled 'Interpretation':

> The dream was so vivid and dramatic and had made such a strong impression on me that I recounted it at breakfast with no notion that it had a hidden meaning. I was aware at the time of Freud's work, which had been described to me by a friend who was a psychiatrist, so that I knew roughly the nature of the technique of free association in the interpretation of dreams. At that time, however, I had read none of Freud's writings.
>
> Very shortly afterwards (I think the day following the night of the dream) I began to analyze this dream by seeking associations to the general picture and to the various dream images and sensations. This I did without conscious intention – my mind wandered, as it were, without conscious volition, while I was riding a bicycle, around the dream images and sensations. Gradually, but surprisingly quickly, with no notable resistance, the interpretation took shape and gained my complete conviction of its correctness.
>
> These occurrences impressed me very deeply and led to a resolve to read Freud's work. This I did in the months that followed, beginning with the *Traumdeutung*, and following with the *Drei Abhandlungen zur Sexual Theorie*, and some others. The latter – the *Sexualtheorie* – interested and excited me immensely. I felt that it was an extraordinarily able and illuminating work, and, after having read far more widely in Freud since then, I still think that in some respects it is his most outstanding contribution – a daring and successful synthesis clearly and admirably expounded. My interest in the whole subject was now thoroughly aroused, and after a good deal of thought I determined to write my own picture of it as it shaped itself in my mind.

The New Psychology and its Relation to Life was published in 1920, and in 1922 I spent 3 months with Freud in Vienna, and in 1923–4 another six months.

Free associations to the setting, images and sensations of the dream

The sub-tropical scene – South Africa. Several of my old pupils had gone to that country, including a girl with whom I had fallen in love.
'Separated from my friends' – My old pupils, who were dispersed owing to the war of 1914–18, and especially the girl.
The savages. Pictures of Zulus on the warpath.
Their numbers and spears – my rifle – Overwhelming strength against me in spite of my superior weapon.
My wife's white clothing – 'Purity' in the sexual sense.

Interpretation

I was separated from my beloved and unable to take any active steps towards union with her because I was married and public opinion (of the 'herd'[58] in Wilfred Trotter's sense) symbolized by the savages would be unanimously against me. (Note that the 'herd' in this case was not of my own race and was regarded by me as intrinsically inferior.) Since I had a good reputation in 'my' world, this opposition was quiescent, only potential – there was no active hostility. I was in no danger where I was provided I remained there. But the barrier was impregnable, in spite of the fact that my mental equipment, symbolized by the rifle, was much superior to that of herd in quality, symbolized by the spears. The numbers and unanimity of the potential opposition made a successful escape impossible and my superior weapon useless. But the savages made no attempt to attack my wife or stop her coming to me – that she could legitimately be with me was a matter of course.

The end of the dream in confusion meant that my problem was insoluble. The suggestion of firing the rifle – quite vague and uncertain – I could not interpret. It occurred to me that the rifle might be thought to symbolize the male genital organ and the firing, orgasm. But this would not fit in with the rest, and I concluded that the only reason I thought of it was because any offensive weapon, especially an elongated one, is well known as a symbol of the penis, not because it had any such significance in the dream. A possible alternative is that I shot at my wife, but I cannot confirm this, perhaps because it was as impossible in the dream as it would be in real life.

This document highlights the principle of interpretative charity that historians will, when pushed, usually agree to: namely, that if an historical actor claims an event was important for them, unless there is substantial evidence to the contrary, the historian takes that actor at his or her word. We therefore should, whatever our inclinations when it comes to dreams and their meaning, accept in all seriousness Tansley's view. In particular, we should give great weight to that uncertainty or doubt or even blankness that surrounds the issue of the rifle and whether it fired; we should, thus, give considerable weight to our own misgivings concerning the temptation to offer 'symbolic' interpretations of Tansley's rifle.

What are the principal elements of Tansley's interpretation of his dream? He interpreted his dream as being a representation of an insoluble conflict between his desire to be with his 'beloved' and the overwhelming barrier of public opinion. It appears to be a dream in which the familiar themes of purity and pollution, the wife and the beloved other woman, are placed in the context of a struggle of conscience between 'civilized' sexual morality, as Freud called it, and the desires of the individual.

Yet, in a sense, the dream and Tansley's comments (written some forty years afterward) carry no sense of this struggle. Everything in the dream appears already decided: it is inconceivable for the dreamer to shoot his wife, in the dream as in real life; it is inconceivable for a single individual, no matter how gifted, to stand against public opinion, no matter how inferior. The game is lost before it has begun. There is an atmosphere of resignation to the inevitable in the dream. (It is possible that this atmosphere stems in part from the tragedy unfolding in France, the victory of the 'herd' of public opinion over the intelligence of superior men. Certainly at the time of his dream Tansley had a striking example of that defeat close to hand, in the destiny of his close Cambridge friend Bertrand Russell, deprived of his Trinity Fellowship and imprisoned in 1916 for his protests against the war. But we have no evidence that there is such a network of associations to the dream.) One doubt does remain: the question of the firing of the rifle. Tansley could not interpret this element, but asserted quite definitively that it had neither a sexual, phallic meaning nor a murderously aggressive one. This curious gesture, of leaving the rifle neither sexual nor aggressive, makes the dream more mysterious than it appears.

And without some mystery, we would not be able to sense the importance of this dream. After all, Tansley's life, and his account of the dream, lead us to believe that his life was transformed by the experience of this dream. We thus seek in the dream a mystery, a significance, which is worthy of such a thing as the transformation of a man's life. We must, therefore, go somewhat slowly in discussing it.

The first thing to note is that Tansley's discussion of his own dream is divided into four parts: the exposition of the dream, followed by a context for the dream – his prior knowledge of psychoanalysis, the circumstances surrounding the dream, including his initial complete lack of awareness of its meaning, the almost involuntary process of interpretation and its effect on him – his reading of Freud, his writing of *The New Psychology*, followed by his analysis with Freud. The third part is the set of associations, followed immediately by the fourth, the interpretation.[59] One would expect the content of the dream, and its interpretation, to throw some light on the connection between the preamble and the effect of the dream on his life. Yet we are immediately confronted with a mismatch. The centre of the dream appears to be about a moral conflict whose resolution is never in doubt, yet its effect on Tansley is in an entirely different sphere: in his relation to Freud and to the development of psychoanalytic ideas.

To put it crudely: where the dream appears to be about whether he should remain faithful to his sexually pure wife or disappear into the sub-tropical bush with his 'beloved', his account of its effect on him has him disappearing into the bush of the new psychology with another new beloved, Freud. The mapping of the interpretation of his dream concerning his 'beloved' on to his new absorption in and by psychoanalysis is very close. Yet this is clearly a retrospective analysis of the dream, because on his bike-ride when he interpreted the dream, Tansley could not know that Freud and psychoanalysis would become his new beloved, a new affront to public opinion. In other words, his interpretation is not an interpretation in a Freudian sense, which recognizes dream-wishes as moulded into a 'perfect likeness [*Ebenbild*] of the past',[60] but rather more akin to a perfect likeness of the future. In interpretative terms, we smell a rat.

But let us go over this ground again, more slowly. Tansley's narrative of the dream and its immediate after-effect tells us that he recounted the dream over breakfast 'with no notion that it had a hidden meaning'. That is, even though he knew through Bernard Hart of some of Freud's views on dreams, he obviously did not take them to heart. He includes this detail in order to demonstrate that he believed thoroughly, at that time, in the innocence of dreams. But in the course of the next day, he underwent a process of automatic interpretation – a vision on the road to Damascus, except in all probability his was a vision on a bike-ride to Grantchester.[61] The result of the epiphany was not a moral decision, but an intellectual certainty: 'my complete conviction' of the 'correctness' of this interpretation. This intellectual conviction then led to his absorption in Freud's work, principally the book on dreams and the essays on sexuality.

On the face of it, this is an odd response to a new intellectual enthusiasm. Tansley had few qualifications for this task – as he was to find out, after the event, when his readers wrote to him. Yet it repeats his own experience of his own dream: instead of resolving a moral dilemma, he emerged with an intellectual conviction of his own correct interpretation. In response to reading Freud, he did not engage in a moral or personal debate with Freud or any other worker in the field of psychoanalysis, but developed and then displayed his own intellectual convictions. In short, he responded pre-emptively with intellectual mastery, just as he had done with his dream. Faced by the confusion in his dream, which he knew signified an insoluble problem, he quickly arrived at 'complete conviction' of his own interpretation.

Tansley displayed his considerable intellectual virtues in this process: encountering an interesting problem, which led him to a profound conviction, he mastered the literature and provided a general, judicious and unbiased overview of a large and unstable field of antagonistic views. The very literary success of Tansley's book revealed something incongruous about his achievement: it was the first general account of the new findings in dreams, sexuality, psychopathology and the theory of the unconscious in English, when it came out in June 1920. Freud's most generally available book in English at that date was *The Interpretation of Dreams*, but in an American edition. Tansley had published the right book at the right time. Yet the response from readers and, we may speculate, residual doubts of his own, led him to view with some scepticism his right to stand before the English public as an authority in the field of psychology. Perhaps the problem that he regarded as insoluble in his dream still remained insoluble, despite his having successfully displaced it into the intellectual terms of the relations between biology and psychology.

One of the strangest effects, then, of his proclivity for intellectual mastery was him appearing as an authority on psychoanalysis. A self-taught authority, and therefore in danger of occupying Freud's position as authority. It is this independence that so clearly marks Tansley's relations with psychoanalysis from the start. He is astonished to make the independent discovery of the meaning of his dream; he acquires his authority on psychoanalysis entirely independently. He is, it would seem, rather like Freud.

The similarity between the two men should not be discounted. Tansley was older than most of those interested in psychoanalysis at this period. In 1920, he was 49. Born in 1871, he was four years older than Jung, eight years older than Jones, and fifteen years younger than Freud. More immediately relevant, perhaps, his scientific trajectory had two important similarities to that of Freud's: he was identified by others as the founder of a new scientific discipline – ecology for Tansley, psychoanalysis for Freud; and his appetite for the organization of colleagues into newly minted institutions was, if anything, even greater than Freud's. Tansley's journals and his societies were commercial in the same way as Freud's were, not primarily affiliated with university departments, again, like Freud's, and were astutely sensitive to a new wave of internationalism in the early years of the twentieth century. There is, then, a strange similarity between these two men, on the face of it so different. Tansley's tone in discussing Freud was predominantly that of an equal, discerning the grounds for his undoubted admiration of the founder of psychoanalysis. It was Tansley who wrote Freud's obituary for the Royal Society and, as Godwin astutely noted, nearly all of the gifts that Tansley described in Freud were ones that he 'unconsciously acknowledged' as being his own gifts – or were at least those they had in common.[62] The key difference between them, though, and it was one Tansley would have readily admitted, was Freud's striking originality. Nonetheless, in talking to Eissler, Tansley remembered that Rickman's 'impression was that Freud and I discussed analysis rather like two sovereigns when we conducted Analysis'.[63] Tansley had a right to be regarded as a sovereign in his own discipline, and may himself have viewed his analysis like that (from where else could Rickman have received his impression?). Nonetheless, it is a telling observation about how Tansley approached analysis with Freud.

What happened in Tansley's analysis? When recollecting it in 1953, he was evidently disappointed that he had made no great discoveries of forgotten scenes from his childhood, and he was disappointed that Freud spent more time discussing theoretical questions than Tansley's own unconscious. Yet who exactly was to blame for this disappointment is not clear. Tansley made it plain to Eissler that he was not neurotic and did not need analysis:

> We never seemed to penetrate at all deeply into my 'Unconscious', and I think the main cause of this failure was probably that I had no marked neurosis, but a fairly stable mental and emotional equilibrium which was difficult to upset or penetrate, so that there was little unconscious material which could be brought to the surface. The analysis was thus of the nature of a 'Lehranalyse', and could not closely resemble the analysis of a neurotic patient.[64]

Thus Tansley gives the impression that nothing much happened – and that it was a mixture of Freud's fault for being too interested in theory, and his own fault for not being neurotic enough.

> ... from a personal point of view, as I say, I don't think it was a really good analysis. I think he departed /laughs/ from his own technical procedure. Because of course he recognized that I was not an ordinary patient. /Laughs/ I wasn't, I wanted information to get to know more about the subject and so on, rather than concentrating on my unconscious, as I say.[65]

Tansley gives two different sorts of reason for this unsatisfactory state of affairs. First, Freud didn't focus on Tansley's own personal life, being too ready to discuss general questions. Second, Tansley implies that he was a special patient, who was in analysis to learn about the theory, not cure himself of a neurosis. The image of the two sovereigns discussing analysis obviously appealed to Tansley; he liked to think of himself as Freud's equal and hence independent of him. As he said to Eissler: 'The best dream that I ever had I analyzed myself. And I told Freud what my interpretation would be. And he said I was perfectly right'. The same held true for Tansley's overall view of Freudian theory. Enormous respect and agreement – but somehow he was a special case:

> I think in my own case, the Oedipus complex was almost negligible. Maybe, because my parents were exceptional people. But I, I could not trace by any means the sort of effect that the complex is supposed to have on one's life and emotions in my own case.[66]

Equally telling was Tansley's aside to Eissler about his dream: 'An excellent example, surely, of a frustrated, not a fulfilled, wish! But I did not say so to Freud.' Clearly, Tansley held himself back from the analysis, not willing to hurt Freud's feelings or provoke a conflict and thus preserving his independence from Freud. Despite his sovereign distance, though, he became and remained a great admirer of Freud's; perhaps even besotted with him. The most striking piece of evidence for Tansley's high regard for Freud comes from a story recounted by his close friend and colleague, Harry Godwin: when Tansley, while at an Oxford social function in the 1930s, was asked to name the most influential man since Christ, he answered, without hesitation, 'Freud'.[67]

Yet these accounts still leave a mystery, the question: why was Tansley there in the first place? Accepting for the moment that the reason he gave – that he needed to acquire more expertise about psychoanalysis in order to answer those of his readers who had approached him – is insufficient as a motive for starting analysis with Freud; the account he gave Eissler in 1953 made it transparently clear that he was there because of something in his dream, or as a result of his dream, which he analysed before he had read Freud and before his analysis: he was still seeking with Freud something that was 'left over' from his dream. Although his account of his analysis indicates his disappointment – he appears not to have found what he was in search of – the consequences of the dream constituted such an upheaval in his life that we should follow them all out before returning to the question of what, exactly, the dream changed in his life and what the dream signified that he changed his life in order to find.

The obvious question to ask is: what did Freud think of Tansley's dream? Tansley mentions this in his account of the dream to Eissler and in the written version of 1953: 'I recounted the dream and my interpretation to Freud in 1924, and he said the interpretation was undoubtedly correct'. Maybe this was what Tansley was in analysis for: Freud's approval of the interpretation of his dream? Certainly something to do with dreams took place early on in his meetings with Freud.

On Maundy Thursday, 1922 – the day when a sovereign reverses social roles, washes the feet of his or her subjects and gives out special gifts – Tansley presented Freud with a copy of *The New Psychology*, in which he inscribed the words: 'Prof. S. Freud, from the author, 13 April 1922'.[68] The next day, Good Friday, Freud returned the compliment – he gave Tansley a copy of the sixth edition of *Die Traumdeutung*, and signed it: '14.4.22 Herrn Prof. Tansley zur freundlichen Erinnerung an den Verf.' – 'To Prof. Tansley with friendly memories from the author'.[69] Two days later, on Easter Sunday, Freud reported to Jones on Tansley's analysis: 'Tansley is bringing up enormous resistance'.[70] To the commentator, it is no surprise that the giving of the gifts provoked something substantial in the way of analytic material. And it was, it appears, Tansley who began the cycle on the Thursday, only to be outmanoeuvred by Freud.

This was to be Freud's last communication to Jones concerning the analysis; as with other patients, once something 'analytic' started happening, his communications to those outside dried up.[71] We have no record of the next three months of Tansley's analysis; nor do any letters survive giving us a clue as to what happened in the second period of analysis in 1924. What we do have, again, are a record of the gifts Tansley presented to Freud and Freud's responses to them. In the first week of 1924 Tansley re-started analysis with Freud, which came to an end with the summer break, when Tansley and his family returned to England. Tansley later admitted he did not have an extensive correspondence with Freud, but he did continue to send him gifts. The first was at the end of the year: a copy of A. A. Milne's *When We Were Very Young*, with the dedication: 'To Prof. Freud, A.G.T., Christmas, 1924'.[72] With this gift (the knowing reader at the beginning of the twenty-first century imagines with a smile Sigmund Freud's reactions to James James Morrison Morrison Weatherby George Dupree taking great care of his mother, though he was only three), Tansley revealed yet another surprisingly astute intuition, this time in a very different field. This book was the first of Milne's (1882–1956) publications for children – the first addressed to his son Christopher Robin Milne. It was published on 6 November 1924, six weeks before it arrived on Freud's desk (although individual poems were published in *Punch* in the preceding years, with considerable immediate success, even provoking parodies, before the book was published).[73] The equally well-known *Winnie-the-Pooh* was first published in 1926, *Now We Are Six* in 1927 and *The House at Pooh Corner* in 1928. Milne's book must have been very little known in Vienna, when Tansley chose it as an 'end-of-analysis' gift. It is, of course, possible that Tansley was aware of Milne's work, may even have been a friend of Milne's, who studied mathematics at Trinity College, Cambridge, Tansley's own college, in the years 1900–03.[74] Nonetheless, the gift bears the hallmark that Tansley was to bring to further gifts to Freud: something quintessentially English, appropriate to Freud, given his tastes and interests, and yet in a mysterious sense inaccessible to him.[75]

Tansley's next contact with Freud came in 1928. Probably while attending the IPE meeting in July and August 1928 in Czechoslovakia and Poland, he paid Freud a visit in Vienna. Tansley remembered this as their last meeting.

[S]eeing on the card I had sent in to him that I was now a professor at Oxford he immediately enquired: 'Ordentlich?' 'Jawohl,' I
replied. 'Das ist gut,' he said. He had had enough experience of being
'ausserordentlich' himself to be acutely conscious of the difference, and
was unfeignedly glad of my new academic status, which he was sure
would be good for me psychologically. At the previous Christmas
I had sent him a reproduction of Leonardo's cartoon of the Virgin,
St. Anne and the infant Christ, and this he now showed me hung on
the door of his study where he could always see it as he sat at his
study table. I had known it was a gift he would appreciate because he
was of course a great admirer of Leonardo, and it was unlikely that
he had seen the original cartoon which hung in the Diploma Gallery
at Burlington House in London. I was proud that my present was
so much honoured, and flattered when he added, 'You do know how
to give presents!' ... I never saw him again and we exchanged very
few letters.[76]

What do we learn of Tansley's relationship to Freud from the four gifts he
made him: his own book, then A. A. Milne's book of children's verse,
followed at about the same time by Pepys's *Diary* and the London Leonardo
cartoon?[77] All four of them are very 'English' – the Leonardo because of
its physical location, the others, being books, in a cultural rather than
geographic sense. Tansley may have been careful only to send Freud things
'he would like and would be interested in', but he was also careful only
to send Freud things that he didn't 'possess' already – because they were
English. The Pepys *Diary* and the A. A. Milne verses are telling: the first
appears to contain a message that it was an Englishman, over two hundred
years before Freud, who first conceived of the unravelling of the daily and
inner life in a discipline of writing.

The Milne verses demonstrate an approach very different from Freud's
but equally honouring to the inner life of the child – as if Tansley's message
is that Freud may well be the great discoverer of the inner world of the child
but his English contemporaries are pursuing equally searching, if infinitely
more light-hearted and less scientifically pretentious, projects of understanding
the mind of the child. With hindsight, we can acknowledge how culturally
alert Tansley was with this gift – it is not clear whether Christopher Robin
or Little Hans should serve as the exemplary child of the early twentieth
century. With these truly excellently chosen gifts, Tansley thus conveyed
a curious message: a repeated attempt to reveal to Freud the autonomy of
English culture with respect to psychoanalysis – its autonomy in the quest
for self-revelation, its autonomy in the quest for knowledge of the inner
world of the child. Yet again, it is the 'sovereignty' question, with Tansley,
this 'nice type of the English scientist', implicitly cast as not required to
submit to Freud's sovereignty.

Interwoven with the account of Tansley's gifts is his account of Freud's response to the news of his Professorship at Oxford. 'Ordentlich?' is Freud's response – and Tansley then explains how Freud, knowing very well – too well, Tansley implies – the difference between 'Ordentlich' (or 'Ordinarius') and 'Extraordinarius'. Tansley cannot resist letting Eissler – his reader – know what Eissler already knew very well: that Freud was never an 'Ordinarius' Professor. But Tansley here distorts rather severely the more usual view of Freud's academic status: that he struggled mightily, as an outsider, and against considerable prejudice, to be appointed Professor Extraordinarius; then having achieved it (in 1902) appeared perfectly content with his position, satisfied that it guaranteed him a place from which to disseminate his teaching and the social recognition that went with the title of Professor.[78] In Tansley's implied version, Freud's position of Extraordinarius was the source of an acute sense of an inferior status, rather than the achievement of a long wished-for goal. Here the question of sovereignty is being harped on with a vengeance – and strictly to Tansley's advantage: he implies that he had now achieved something that Freud himself had long wished for and had never succeeded in (at the date of the conversation, Freud was 72, and thus beyond an age at which one could hope for such promotion). But it is clear that the person who cares about being Professor Ordinarius is not Freud but Tansley. Freud's question to Tansley – 'Ordentlich?' – may well have been one based on Freud's acute awareness of the relevant differences between ranks, but the question was addressed not from Freud's own preoccupation with this question but to Tansley's pride at having fulfilled what must have emerged in his analysis with Freud as a heartfelt ambition of his own.

Tansley's appointment to the Chair at Oxford does not only represent his assertion of independent, even higher, sovereignty in relation to Freud; he 'was unfeignedly glad of my new academic status, which he was sure would be good for me psychologically'. It is here that there is a sliding from the issue of sovereignty to an issue more closely tied to Tansley's analysis with Freud. It is not the fact that Tansley has become a Professor that is important to Freud, one might say; it is the fact that he has made what Godwin acutely called the 'return to the mother subject' of botany. What Tansley had done, in Freud's eyes, we speculate, was finally resolve the crisis in his life that had been initiated by his dream and the events it referred to. The intriguing – but not, finally, atypical – form of that life-crisis was Tansley's involvement with psychoanalysis and Freud. In this sense, we can stand back and see this psychoanalytic episode in Tansley's life as a protracted transference neurosis. To remind readers: the transference neurosis is that structure created during psychoanalytic treatment in its central phase, after the initial phase when the pre-existing symptoms have been interpreted and disappear – the expression of the subject's neurosis entirely in terms of his or her relation to the analyst, to psychoanalysis, and to 'Freud'. Tansley's dream undoubtedly precipitated him towards an intense relationship with Freud. Despite the fact that his account of the dream in his deposition to the Library of Congress affirms the *achievement* represented by the dream – an achievement of interpretative mastery – it is more than likely, given what happened in the next ten years of Tansley's life, that it initiated a period of great confusion rather than clarification. 'Nobody outside the psychoanalytically trained could possibly tell what it meant, that it meant hell, deep', Tansley told Eissler. His moment of psychoanalytic understanding had revealed to him how his life had become hell. Thus precipitated into a period of emotional upheaval by the dream, we can regard his writing of the book, his resignation from Cambridge, his analysis with the man himself as the unravelling of this transference neurosis. And, Tansley plausibly intimates, Freud regarded the appointment to the Chair in Botany at Oxford as its final resolution.

One piece of evidence indicates that, no matter how Tansley had resolved his vacillation in the 'displaced' professional domain, his inner erotic preoccupations had not been resolved. We saw how the normally efficient Tansley failed to organize the 1925 International Psycho-Analytic Congress in Cambridge; when the 1929 IPA Congress took place from 27–31 July at Queen's College in Oxford, Tansley, despite his being the sole member of the British Society who had a formal connection with the University, was at no point involved – the organizers were Joan Riviere and Sylvia Payne, and guided tours of the colleges were organized led by Ernest and Mrs Jones, Edward Glover, J. C. Flugel and the psychiatrist W. H. B. Stoddart. Tansley was absent from the Oxford Congress because he was on those days in South Africa – the scene of his dream – his first trip there in reality, attending the meeting of the British Association for the Advancement of Science in Cape Town and Johannesburg.[79] In a notebook from this period, there is the following undated paragraph:

> There is no 'armour' to protect one against such elemental hurts, I find. You must know this because the knowledge that we are sharing the pain may help. I am numb toward everything but these two days. But I cannot, cannot regret them, nor can I face absolute finality. . . . It eases the pain to write but it is an indulgence, and I have hurt you too much already, my very dear.[80]

While it is difficult to be certain to what this refers, it is probable that Tansley's trip to South Africa allowed him to meet up with his 'beloved', and this note stands as testimony to the continued strength of their mutual feelings. The conflict of his dream from more than ten years was still as alive as ever. What is more, this theme of 'South Africa' may have infiltrated his professional work: one of Tansley's major ecological arguments in the 1930s was with John Phillips, a botanist based in South Africa, whom Tansley charged with drinking 'the pure milk of the Clementsian word':[81] the 1935 paper in which he introduced the concept of the ecosystem was largely an attack on Phillips.[82] From the early 1910s on, South Africa was the scene of many important events and themes in Tansley's botanical work – and it probably continued to possess the secret emotional resonance stemming from his 'beloved's' presence there.

We are thus reconstructing Tansley's 'neurosis' as having as its principal content the dual vacillation or splitting: splitting of his interest or commitment between botany and psychoanalysis, a vacillation or splitting that duplicated the stark choice in his dream between his love for a woman who was not his wife and submitting to the inferior but stronger forces of 'public opinion'. He is married to botany, but his beloved is psychoanalysis. Tansley himself used the terms splitting to describe his situation in 1923: 'I am doing psychological work here now [in Vienna], having resigned my lectureship at Cambridge . . . I shall continue to edit the journals and also to work at ecology, but I do not know to what this splitting of interest will eventually lead'.[83] His resignation from Cambridge and his moves in the mid-1920s towards becoming a full-time psychoanalyst represent perhaps a more courageous defiance of 'public opinion'; yet it is recognizably a displacement of this defiance from one domain to another. And it is an interesting question whether the defiance of leaving botany for psychoanalysis was more or less stark than the alternative action of leaving his marriage for his 'beloved'.

It is natural, given this displacement, to seek understanding of his vacillation between botany and psychoanalysis in the more private vacillation of his familial and erotic life. But of this we know very little. His wife Edith figures as hardly a shadow in any account he or any others gave of his life. She was his student at UCL but, apart from acknowledgements of indebtedness to her in some early index work and two early collaborative articles they wrote together, she is remarkably absent from his professional life.[84] James Strachey's letters to Alix of 1925 include a portrait of Tansley family life, but it says as much about Strachey and his tastes as it does about his hosts:

> Give me a well-off middle class household. Blazing fire in the bedroom, perfect bed, five-course dinner, excellent cooking, claret and port at dinner, hock at lunch, good coffee – what more can one desire? But besides these essentials Tansley himself is very nice & quite intelligent, Mrs. T is not too tiresome, and the girls most inoffensive though unluckily far from beauties. – They were all most affable; and last night Tansley went rather further, I think, than he'd intended, and poured out a good deal of his troubles: his life's interest hopelessly divided between his old love, botany and his new one, psychoanalysis.[85]

The plain fact is that we lack sufficient information about Tansley's private life to hazard guesses at the domestic resonances of his crisis, his vacillations and his decisions in the ten years – roughly – from the dream to his accepting the Chair at Oxford. According to his eldest granddaughter, 'there was a frankness and openness with the family, quite unusual for the times'.[86] Subsequent evidence indicates only that he resolved the split in his professional life more successfully than that in his personal.

However, in Tansley's psychoanalytic writings, the theme of splitting is interestingly highlighted. We should not read too much into passages such as the following, from Tansley's *The New Psychology*, which, however apt they may or may not have been in Tansley's case, are not exceptional amongst those influenced by psychoanalysis:

> Thus a man may be deeply attached to his wife and children, but have a mistress who satisfies both his physical and his mental sexual desires, or he may even have two mistresses – a physical and a spiritual one.[87]

But a note from 1926 to the British Psychoanalytic Society indicates what 'clinical material' arrested Tansley's attention and stimulated his theoretical interest:

> March 3, 1926: Mr A. G. Tansley read a short note on a definite type of masturbation-phantasy, in which he described a variety of phantasy turning on the procuring of a virginal sexual object for the masturbator by an older woman, and suggested that the imagery was determined by the early splitting of the subject's libido between mother and sister.[88]

However Tansley might have made use of his own analysis in working with such material, it wasn't received entirely favourably by his psychoanalytic colleagues:

> Dr. James Glover and Dr. Ernest Jones, however, thought it more likely that the two female persons of the phantasy represented a splitting of the mother-imago.[89]

This rather peremptory correction of Tansley's clinical work may not have made him feel entirely accepted by his new scientific colleagues. But its content is of some interest: it indicates that where Tansley saw a split between two female persons in dream or phantasy that reflected two different persons in reality, a more sophisticated analytic reading attributed responsibility for the splitting entirely to the subject. Tansley's mother/sister interpretation allowed the subject too much of an alibi in disowning this responsibility – just as the subject-less 'procuring' evades the question of who is doing the procuring – and from whom (whose prior rights over the women are being ignored).

Such splitting of the mother into the figures of the affectionate and the sensual, the mother and the prostitute, was of course set out in Freud's paper of 1912 'On a special type of object-choice made by men'.[90] Whereas Freud had shown the origins of these two familiar cultural figures of women in defensive splitting in phantasy, in his *The New Psychology* Tansley had proposed a biologically grounded account of the two types of women necessary to civilization:

> the feminine mind has two paths open to it, either of which may lead to fairly complete satisfaction – the sexual sphere with its normal result, in the case of permanent mating, of the care of the family and the administration of the home; or the herd sphere, in which the affect of public service takes the place of the sex affect. . . . It has even been suggested to the writer by Mr. Trotter that we may see a psychical and functional differentiation among women analogous to that existing among the bees – a splitting into two distinct classes, the one of perfect females, the other of non-sexual workers in the service of the community, derived from potential females.
>
> It is certainly true that the type of woman most attractive to men – at least to what may be called the crude masculine sex instinct – is the type whose psychic energy is almost entirely concentrated in the sexual sphere, and when it is recognized that the other type is likely to play a more and more important part in the world, it is perhaps not unnatural that the masculine intelligence should tend to insist on the reality of such a segregation as has been indicated, so that the type attractive to the masculine sex instinct should not be destroyed or blurred . . .[91]

Tansley's account of the splitting of women into two types is very different from Freud's. It is true, just as in Freud, that one type of woman is desexualized; but this is the 'worker' female, leaving all sexual functions to the reproductive female. Freud's account has the wife and mother as desexualized, in contrast with the 'worker' female, the whore. Most crucially, the strict split between the two types is defensive for Freud, designed to de-sexualize the idealized wife/mother, whereas Tansley points to the needs of the male not to desexualize but to keep the functions divided – as if the category that is required by males is the 'purely sexual', where it is not clear if all the weight of the category derives from the 'purely' or from the 'sexual'. Thus, looked at more closely, we find in Tansley's account of the split functions of the female a more social, economic even, rather than psychic-sexual, analysis. Certainly this account of 1920 does not give us a clear idea of the sources of his conflict between the dream-figure of the wife dressed entirely in white and the 'beloved' who has gone away.

Thus, in attempting to understand the significance of Tansley's dream, we are left with fragments, rather than solutions. We have insufficient evidence to articulate Tansley's erotic and professional crises. We have been struck by the parallels between the figures of his wife and 'beloved', and his relationship to botany and psychoanalysis. In a moment of interpretative audacity, we might suggest that the core wish of the dream – the truly 'impossible' thing to contemplate, 'as impossible in the dream as it would be in real life' – was a desire to murder his wife (botany) in order to be with his new beloved, in which case, his ten-year dalliance with psychoanalysis was an 'acting out' of this core wish.

But when we look to Tansley's work in botany, one of its most striking and original features is the *lack* of 'splitting' – between Man and Nature, between Nature and Culture. Tansley's principal contributions were, in contradistinction to American ecology, to emphasize the systemic inter-relations of human activity and botanical phenomena – he sees no real difference between those ecosystems which are natural and those which are 'anthropogenic' (nature 'produced by man', as he glossed it in 1923). [92] The American and 'preservationist' theme of the 'wilderness', prior to and independent of human intervention, with its image of 'virginal nature' and its ethos of non-interference, was not Tansley's, in whose work there is very little talk of 'mother Nature'. What is ever-present there is the possibility of the human control or 'regulation' (Tansley's preferred term) of natural processes. We might say that his natural posture is that of a celebration of the mastery of knowledge, rather than the erotic power of the object. Reading this posture alongside the dream, we note how the rifle is what symbolizes Tansley's knowledge, his 'superior equipment'. And, in terms of his life-choices, Tansley's quest for psychoanalytic knowledge continues his over-estimation of the importance of this mastery embodied in knowledge, at the expense of the resolution of his conflict by an erotic choice. Here we recall how Tansley's principal responses to Freud are to emphasize his own mastery, his epistemic independence from his analyst. And it was this attitude that he reiterated in 1953 when interviewed by Eissler. More than that: this attitude helps us explain how Tansley felt it appropriate to submit his dream and its interpretation to the Freud Archives as the principal testimony concerning his place in the history of psychoanalysis. A strange decision: a dream that Freud never analysed, dreamt prior to any real knowledge of Freud or his writings. What Tansley's dream bears witness to is the superiority of psychoanalytic knowledge, and thus implicitly disdain for Freud himself. And, implicitly, also to the 'hell' of the erotic conflict in which he had found himself at this time. It is the mastery that always seems to win out over the recognition of the conflict.

Yet we should not underestimate how strong this conflict was for him; including the dream – anonymously – in *The New Psychology*, Tansley offers it as the clearest example of a dream in which symbolism expresses powerful emotions bound up with a deep conflict:

The more extreme forms of symbolism are met with in the dreams of adults when the affects are very deep and very strongly repressed as the result of conflict. Very many such dreams are concerned with sexual relations, and a great number are recorded in Freud's book, and in other works. A good example of such symbolism is contained in the dream of a man who dreamed that, armed with a rifle, he was alone in a sub-tropical country, separated from his friends and surrounded by a tribe of armed savages with spears and shields, who, however, remained quite passive. Psychoanalysis showed that he knew in the depths of his mind that he was in conflict with the public opinion of his fellows, which separated him from his beloved, and that while he thought much more highly of his own mental equipment (symbolized by the rifle) than of that of the 'herd man' (symbolized by the spears) who typifies public opinion, he was quite aware that he was powerless against them on account of their numbers and unanimity. The savages did not actively threaten him – they merely surrounded him: there was no overt conflict with public opinion – only a potential one. He was in no danger where he was, provided he remained there.[93]

In this censored version, the elements associated with place ('South Africa'), the figure of his wife dressed in white and the confusion about the rifle are omitted. Yet Tansley makes clear to the reader that the emotional significance of the dream is considerable: the affects are 'very deep', are 'very strongly repressed' and clearly associated with sexual relations. On the next page, he summarizes it as follows: 'The man with a rifle surrounded by savages and unable to break through them is a true poetic symbol of the man in conflict with the herd, which separates him from the object of desire'. Once again, we are tempted to see Tansley's involvement with psychoanalysis as an attempt to arm himself with a more powerful rifle so as to win out over 'the herd'. As he said to Eissler:

T: It was really this remarkable dream of mine that impressed me most deeply. I [was] sure that psychoanalysis is going to be a very important fundamental contribution to the general theory of psychology. And that was why I went to Freud, you see. But I have also been an amateur, I have never got a professional, I always have been an amateur if you like /laughs/

E: But you always were engaged in /unclear/ /laughs/ You wrote a book on the topic!

T: Oh yes, I wrote a book that's true! That book I wrote before I went to Freud. As a result of this stirring up of my interest and emotion about the thing. . . .[94]

In this version, Tansley makes it clear that the book he wrote was an result of emotion stirred up by his dream and its interpretation.[95] Quite clearly, the book was an attempt at mastering these emotions. It may be fair to say that this was a desire to win the battle, as if that was the only way to resolve the conflict, and in that quest he may have later used psychoanalysis against 'the herd', such as Vera Brittain, who equated sexual freedom with sexual gluttony; but a truer resolution would be less couched in terms of the superiority of psychoanalytic knowledge than in his eventual return to his first love, botany. Like other analysts, including Freud, writing before the full lessons of World War One were digested, Tansley may have underestimated the erotic conflicts associated with mastery, with aggression – the rifle. Virginia Woolf, however, certainly had a keen eye for such erotics in her portrayal of Tansley as the arrogantly superior academic setting himself against the herd:

> he was proud of it; that he was [Charles] Tansley – a fact that nobody there seemed to realise; but one of these days every single person would know it. He scowled ahead of him. He could almost pity these mild cultivated people, who would be blown sky high, like bales of wool and barrels of apples, one of these days by the gunpowder that was inside him.[96]

* * *

When Tansley died in 1955, his papers passed into the care of Harry Godwin, and these eventually were deposited in his old Department in Cambridge, now known as the Department of Plant Sciences. His wife Edith lived on to 1970, dying at the age of 101. As is well known, virtually nothing of Freud's presence in Vienna survived the Nazis. For years, the city of Vienna behaved as if it had successfully forgotten Freud. Early in the 1970s, Anna Freud was asked by the newly formed Sigmund Freud Gesellschaft in Vienna if she could help locate psychoanalytic books to furnish the beginnings of a Museum that was intended to occupy Freud's old apartment there. Some time after 1972, she made an appeal to members of the International Psycho-Analytical Association for contributions to the library.[97] Somehow, she located the psychoanalytic books of Professor Sir Arthur Tansley, FRS, which he had bequeathed to Harry Godwin, along with his other books, papers, pamphlets and copyrights.[98] As a result of Godwin's gift, the Freud Museum in Vienna acquired 47 books from his library, including fourteen books by Freud in German, some of them first editions. It is the books of this 'nice type of the English scientist' that make up a significant portion of the oldest of Freud's books to be found in Freud's old apartment that now houses the Freud Museum in Vienna, making reparations for the destruction of the Nazis.

One of the consequences of this scouring of the psychoanalytic community for early editions of Freud's work is that Tansley's own library contains no psychoanalytic books. The books on botany from his library were donated to the Department in Cambridge, where, for a time, they were housed separately from the main collection; more recently, they have been integrated with that collection, and have thus lost their unity as elements in a distinguished botanist's life-work.[99]

Even Tansley's edition of *Die Traumdeutung*, with Freud's own dedication to him, has completed the circuit it started out on a few days after his analysis began on 31 March 1922, from Freud's hands to Grantchester, and now back on the bookshelves of Berggasse 19. This journey of Freud's dream book is a fitting allegory of Tansley's own journey, driven by his own dream, which he interpreted himself, to Freud's books, then on to involvement with the psychoanalytic movement and the nine months he spent on Freud's couch, and back to his own field of ecology. Nonetheless, this circular journey of Freud's dream-book back to its point of departure was in danger of erasing its own history, the itinerary of its circuit as determined by Tansley's own history and analysis, which we have here attempted to retrace and reconstruct.[100]

NOTES AND REFERENCES

We thank Dr Anna Dickens and Mr Martin Tomlinson for permission to quote from the materials that their grandfather, Sir Arthur Tansley, submitted to the Sigmund Freud archives and we are very grateful to the late Dr Kurt Eissler and the Library of Congress for access to these 'Three Contributions'. We also thank Professor Roger Leigh of the Department of Plant Sciences, the Librarian, Dr David Briggs, and the Assistant Librarian, Mr Richard Savage, for their assistance with materials from the A. G. Tansley Collection.

1 Sir Harry Godwin, 'Sir Arthur Tansley: The man and the subject, The Tansley Lecture, 1976', *Journal of Ecology* 65, 1977, p. 13: 'Tansley undertook a more or less routine clerking post in one of the Ministries, where his powers were barely called upon'.

2 *The Complete Correspondence of Sigmund Freud and Ernest Jones, 1908–1939* (ed. R. Andrew Paskauskas, introduction by Riccardo Steiner), Cambridge, MA, & London, 1993 (hereafter abbreviated to FJ), Freud to Jones, 6 April 1922, p. 468.

3 Freud, *Five Lectures on Psycho-analysis*, SE 11, 33.

4 *Three Contributions by Sir Arthur Tansley, FRS*, The Sigmund Freud Archives, Manuscript Division, Library of Congress, Washington DC, USA (hereafter abbreviated to LoC), interview with Kurt Eissler, Summer 1953, p. 9. Quoting these words does not mean we endorse their accuracy – such is always the case, but particularly so when it comes to verdicts on a historical actor's inner mental states.

5 H. Godwin, 'Arthur George Tansley 1871–1955', *Biographical Memoirs of Fellows of The Royal Society* 3, November 1957, pp. 227–246, this from p. 232.

6 R. McIntosh, *The Background of Ecology: Concept and Theory*, Cambridge, 1985, p. 69.

7 'The reconstruction of elementary botanical teaching', *The New Phytologist* 16:10, December 1917, pp. 241–252. Psychological language infuses the piece.

8 F. E. Bower, 'Botanical Bolshevism', *The New Phytologist* 17:5, 6, May/June 1918, pp. 105–107; A. D. Boney, 'The "Tansley manifesto" affair', *The New Phytologist* 118:1, May 1991, pp. 3–21.

9 Letter dated 18 December 1918, Frederic Clements Collection, American Heritage Center, University of Wyoming, Laramie, cited in F. Golley, *A History of the Ecosytem Concept in Ecology*, New Haven, CT, 1993, p. 208. An additional source of frustration may have been

Tansley's ultimately unsuccessful attempt, beginning in late 1917, to create a Scientific Research Association for the promotion of pure research (an initiative supported by E. Jones, B. Hart, C. S. Myers, T. H. Pear, Capt McDougall, and W. H. R. Rivers amongst others): the SRA was dissolved in December 1919.

10 FJ, Freud to Jones, 10 March 1910, p. 48.

11 FJ, Jones to Freud, 30 March 1910, p. 49.

12 W. Cooper, 'Sir Arthur Tansley and the science of ecology', *Ecology*, 38:4, October, 1957, pp. 658–659, quoting a letter from Tansley dated November 1923. The book was widely reviewed, and favourably by such luminaries as Havelock Ellis in the *Daily Herald*, 22 December 1920.

13 A. G. Tansley, *The New Psychology in its Relation to Life*, London, 1920, p. 6.

14 Tansley, 'The impact of Freud's work and personality on a non-medical biologist', LoC, p. 2. Tansley's scrapbook of reviews and correspondence regarding *The New Psychology* is held in the A. G. Tansley Collection, Department of Plant Sciences, University of Cambridge.

15 See R. Hall, *Marie Stopes: A Biography*, London, 1977, and *Dear Dr Stopes: Sex in the 1920s*, London, 1978.

16 Tansley, 'The impact of Freud's work . . .', LoC p. 2. Jones mentioned to Freud that Tansley had approached him in a letter dated 6 May 1921 and Freud responded on the 19 May informing Jones that he had received Tansley's letter (see FJ, p. 424).

17 See FJ, Jones to Freud, 6 May 1921, p. 421, and Rundbrief by Jones, 19 Oct. 1920, Otto Rank Archives, Columbia University, New York, USA. We thank Ernst Falzeder for valuable assistance with unpublished Freud correspondence and the Rundbriefe.

18 Kardiner Oral History Interviews, interviews conducted by Bluma Swerdloff, 1963, Columbia University Oral History Project, New York, p. 102.

19 Freud to Anna Freud, 19 March 1922, Anna Freud Archives, Library of Congress, Washington DC, USA.

20 S. Bernfeld, 'Sigmund Freud, MD, 1882–1885', *International Journal of Psycho-Analysis 32*, 1951, p. 216.

21 FJ, Jones to Freud, 1 April 1922, p. 467.

22 Including *Elements of Plant Biology* in 1922 (based on the lecture course he gave to first-year medical students), *Practical Plant Ecology* in 1923, and a co-edited volume *Aims and Methods in the study of Vegetation* in 1926. See Godwin, 'Arthur George Tansley, 1871–1955', *Biographical Memoirs*, p. 232.

23 Wicken Fen, purchased in 1899 by the National Trust for Places of Historic Interest and Natural Beauty, is the oldest of Britain's nature reserves. See L. Cameron, 'Histories of disturbance', *Radical History Review* 74, 1999, pp. 4–24 for possible connections between Tansley's ecology and psychology in this place/period.

24 Letter from Clements to Tansley, 12 January 1923, Tansley Papers, Dept. of Plant Sciences, Cambridge, cited in Golley, *A History of the Ecosystem*, p. 209.

25 Letter from Tansley to Clements, 8 March 1923, Frederic Clements Collection, University of Wyoming, cited in Golley, *A History of the Ecosystem*, p. 209.

26 Letter from Tansley to Clements, 30 May 1923, Clements Collection, University of Wyoming: cited in Golley, *A History of the Ecosystem*, p. 209.

27 Freud to Abraham, 14 March 1924, Sigmund Freud Archives, Library of Congress, Washington DC, USA.

28 E. Jones, 'Review, *The New Psychology*', *International Journal of Psycho-analysis 1*, 1920, p. 480.

29 Rundbrief written by Jones, 19 October 1920, Otto Rank Archives.

30 *Three Essays on the Theory of Sexuality*, SE 7, 131.

31 FJ, Jones to Freud, [?] October 1922, p. 501.

32 Tansley, 'Review, C. J. Patten, *The Memory Factor in Biology*', *International Journal of Psycho-analysis 8*, 1927, p. 292.

33 A. G. Tansley, 'Critical notice *of Versuch einer Genitaltheorie* by Dr S. Ferenczi', *British Journal of Medical Psychology 4*, 1924, pp. 156–161.

34 Archives of British Psycho-Analytic Society, FAA/134 Committee Minutes.

35 'Autobiographical introduction', probably delivered to Magdalen Philosophy Club, 5 May 1932, Tansley Archives, Dept. of Plant Sciences, University of Cambridge.

36 Archives of British Psycho-Analytic Society, FAA/161 Committee Minutes.

37 Jones to Abraham, 12 November 1924, Sigmund Freud Archives, Library of Congress, Washington DC, USA.

38 Tansley was eventually elected an Honorary Fellow of Trinity College, but only in 1944, well after his retirement from the Chair at Oxford.

39 J. R. [John Rickman], 'Susan Sutherland Isaacs, CBE, MA, DSc (Vict), HonDSc (Adelaide)', *International Journal of Psycho-analysis* 31, 1950, p. 270. Susan Isaacs would 'read some notes upon Child Life' at a meeting hosted by Tansley at his Granchester home 13 or 14 June 1925; see P. Meisel and W. Kendrick, *Bloomsbury/Freud: The Letters of James and Alix Strachey 1924–1925*, London: Chatto & Windus, 1986, p. 281.

40 See Cameron and Forrester, 'Tansley's psychoanalytic network: An episode out of the early history of psychoanalysis in England', *Psychoanalysis and History* 2: 2, 2000, pp. 189–256.

41 A. G. Tansley, 'Freudian psycho-analysis', *The Nation & The Athenæum* 12, September 1925, p. 700.

42 In addition to pioneering Quaternary research in Britain with his wife, Margaret (who took up pollen analysis at Tansley's suggestion), Godwin (1901–1985, FRS. 1945) was, like Tansley, a leader in the Nature Conservancy. See R. G. West, 'Harry Godwin', *Biographical Memoirs of Fellows of the Royal Society* 34, 1988, pp. 261–292.

43 Godwin, 'Arthur George Tansley, 1871–1955', *Biographical Memoirs of Fellows of The Royal Society* 3, 1957, p. 236.

44 Ibid., p. 236.

45 The source for Needham's reminiscence is a personal communication from Edward Timms (to Cameron, 17 March 1997), who asked Needham about interest in Freud in Cambridge in the 1920s. Charles Raven, botanist, distinguished historian of natural history and biographer of John Ray, probably had the same teacher in mind when he noted that in the early years of this century ecology and psychology were being drawn together – a comment that, without the particular research interests of Tansley, would be somewhat mysterious. In a speech to the Cambridge Natural History Society in 1957, Charles Raven said 'at the beginning of the century, the tide had begun slowly but surely to turn and though the gulf betwen the men of museums and the men of the open-air was still wide, the liveliest minds in biology were already moving towards a denial of the antithesis, towards ecological and psychological problems and to that sense of wholeness which is now influencing every dept. from medicine to nuclear physics'. Cited in F. W. Dillistone, *Charles Raven: Naturalist, Historian, Theologian*, London, 1975, pp. 174–175.

46 *The Nation & Athenæum*, Brittain's letter is in the number dated 28 July 1928, p. 552; Tansley's first response, from Kielce in Poland, is in that for 11 August 1928, p. 618; Brittain's response is in the edition dated 18 August 1928, pp. 644–645; and Tansley's long and final rejoinder, from Saas Fee in Switzerland, is 15 September, 1928, p. 757.

47 Godwin, 'Arthur George Tansley, 1871–1955', *Biographical Memoirs of Fellows of The Royal Society* 3, 1957, p. 238.

48 See P. Anker, 'The Context of Ecosystem Theory', *Ecosystems* 5, pp. 611–613; A. G. Tansley (prepared by P. Anker), 'The Temporal Genetic Series As a Means of Approach to Philosophy', *Ecosystems* 5, 2002, pp. 614–624; and L. Cameron, 'Ecosystems' in S. Harrison, S. Pile and N. Thrift (eds.), *Patterned Ground: Ecologies of Nature and Culture* (forthcoming).

49 See J. Forrester and L. Cameron, ' "Cure with a defect": A previously unpublished letter by Freud concerning "Anna O." ', *International Journal of Psycho-Analysis* 80, Part 5, 1999, pp. 929–942.

50 For instance, he gave a confidential opinion on a Prize Essay submission on 'The sense of injustice and its relation to oral sadism' in a letter to Sylvia Payne, 18 June 1941, British Psychoanalytic Society Archives, G06/BA/F04/03.

51 A. G. Tansley, 'Sigmund Freud (1856–1939)', *Obituary Notices of Fellows of The Royal Society* 3, 1939–1941, pp. 247–275.

52 *The Values of Science to Humanity*, 1942; *Our Heritage of Wild Nature*, 1945; *Plant Ecology and the School* (with E. Price Evans) 1946; *Introduction to Plant Ecology*, 1946; *Britain's Green Mantle*, 1949; *Oaks and Oakwoods*, 1952.

53 A. G. Tansley, 'The psychological connexion of two basic principles of the SFS', *Society for Freedom in Science*, Occasional Pamphlet No. 12, March 1952.

54 The figure, seventeen ecologists out of sixty-one members, comes from S. Bocking, *Ecologists and Environmental Politics: A History of Contemporary Ecology*, New Haven, CT, 1997, p. 27.

55 F. R. Winton was also an early Associate Member of the British Psycho-Analytic Society, elected in the same year as the Stracheys, 1923, and remaining a member until his death in 1985. He was a physiologist who spent most of his working life, apart from the years 1927–37 when he was in Cambridge, at University College London.

56 The attempt to gain access to the Tansley file is detailed in Cameron, 'Oral history in the Freud archives: Incidents, ethics and relations', *Historical Geography* 29, 2001, pp. 38–44.

57 The *Drei Abhandlungen* were known in translation as either *Three Contributions to the Sexual Theory* in Brill's translation of 1910 or from later editions on as *Three Contributions to the Theory of Sex* (1916, 1918, 1930, 1938). The first English edition to use the title *Three Essays on the Theory of Sexuality* was that of James Strachey in 1949. The volume of the *Standard Edition* in which the *Three Essays* appeared, Vol. 7, was published in 1953.

58 The typescript has 'hero' here and in the next parenthetic phrase: apparently a typing error, either Tansley's or introduced by Tansley's assistant (if he had one) or by the Sigmund Freud Archives. The third possibility seems more probable as the typescript is in Pica 10 pt, unlike Tansley's first document, which is in Courier 12 pt. On the cover sheet for THE DREAM, a stamp specifies: 'THE SIGMUND FREUD ARCHIVES/*Recollections*/*Sir Arthur Tansley's*/self-interpretation of a dream./#832 (Copy).' Given the date, the word 'copy' probably refers to a typing-out, rather than to a photostat or other mechanical copying process.

59 In choosing this expository structure, Tansley used a method similar to Freud's own, as first set out in the analysis of his 'specimen dream', the 'dream of Irma's injection' – Preamble, Dream, Analysis. Whereas Freud fuses the associations and their interpretation, Tansley separates them, and inverts the order of Preamble and Dream.

60 Freud, *The Interpretation of Dreams*, SE 5, 621.

61 Another epiphanic bike-ride to Grantchester was made by Bertrand Russell in the spring of 1902, when 'suddenly, as I was riding along a country road, I realised that I no longer loved Alys': Bertrand Russell, *Autobiography*, London, 1963, pp. 147–148; also commentary in R. Monk, *Bertrand Russell. The Spirit of Solitude*, London, 1996, p. 145. Russell was, during their undergraduate years together at Trinity, as Tansley put it (writing in the third person): 'the most penetrating mind with which he came into contact, and who was his favourite companion in midnight talks' (Godwin, 'Arthur George Tansley, 1871–1955', *Biographical Memoirs*, pp. 227–246, this from p. 229); Russell's autobiography was published only after Tansley's death and we have no evidence if Russell – in Cambridge for most of the time till his dismissal by Trinity during the First World War in 1916 – and Tansley talked intimately at this time. There remains the faint possibility that either Tansley or Russell used each other's recounted story of an epiphanic bicycle ride for his own purposes.

62 Godwin, 'Arthur George Tansley, 1871–1955', *Biographical Memoirs*, pp. 227–246, this from p. 243; see A. G. Tansley, 'Sigmund Freud', *Obituary Notices of Fellows of The Royal Society* 3, 1939–1941, pp. 247–275.

63 Eissler interview, LoC, p. 4.

64 Tansley, 'The impact of Freud's work . . .', LoC, pp. 4–5.

65 Eissler interview, LoC, p. 3.

66 Eissler interview, LoC, p. 7.

67 H. Godwin, 'Sir Arthur Tansley: The man and the subject', *Journal of Ecology* 65, 1977, p. 25.

68 Copy in Freud's Library, Freud Museum, London. We thank Michael Molnar for information and assistance concerning the books held there, and also unpublished correspondences held by the Museum.

69 Copy in Library, Sigmund Freud Museum, Vienna. Special thanks to Lydia Marinelli, Curator, for her generous assistance concerning books held by the Museum that were once owned by Tansley.

70 Freud to Jones, 16 April 1922, p. 474.

71 For examples, see his analysis of Loe Kann and of Joan Riviere, discussed in Lisa Appignanesi and John Forrester, *Freud's Women*, London, 1992.

72 Inscription in Freud's copy in the Freud Museum, London.

73 Personal communication, Ian Patterson, 26 February 1999.

74 In *The New Psychology*, p. 197, Tansley referred to another children's author to illustrate his point that 'the moral law holds for animal communities just as it does for human societies' – 'Mr. Kipling, one of our greatest modern exponents of the glories of herd life and the herd instinct, has brought this out in his delightful stories of the wolf pack and the bee-hive'. He specifically recommended 'Mowgli's brothers' in *The Jungle Book* (1894), 'How fear came' in *The Second Jungle Book* (1895), and 'The mother hive' in *Actions and Reactions* (1909).

75 Freud did not make professional use of Milne's verses, but his daughter Anna did, quoting and interpreting a passage from *When We Were Very Young* in her *The Ego and the Mechanisms of Defence* (1936), London: Hogarth Press & Institute of Psycho-Analysis, 1968 (rev. edn.), p. 83, concerning 'Denial in word and act'.

76 Tansley, 'The impact of Freud's work and personality on a non-medical biologist', LoC. In the interview, Eissler asked Tansley if Freud ever gave him a gift and he replied: 'No, he . . . Yes, he gave me a portrait, a photograph, and a copy of the *Traumdeutung*'. The Leonardo figures in Engelmann's photographs of Freud's study, taken in 1938: visible from his desk, as Tansley noted, with evident pride, when he saw it on his 1928 visit to Freud. There is no record of the Pepys' *Diary* ever having been part of Freud's library, neither in the collection of books he took from Vienna to London, nor in the portion sold when Freud was forced to leave Vienna. See N. D. C. Lewis and C. Landis, 'Freud's library', *Psychoanalytic Review* 44, 1957, pp. 327–356 and D. Bakan's corrective 'The authenticity of the Freud Memorial Collection', *Journal of the History of the Behavioral Sciences* 11, 1975, pp. 365–367. Tansley's recollection that this was their last meeting may not have been accurate. Freud entered Tansley's name in his Diary for the date Sunday, 12 April 1931 (see Michael Molnar (trans., annot., and ed.), *The Diary of Sigmund Freud, 1929–1939, A Record of the Final Decade*. London, p. 96); such an entry nearly always meant a personal visit. The date of the hypothetical visit was in the middle of Oxford's Easter Vacation; but there is no extant evidence of Tansley's movements or attendance at conferences for this period. It is not so much the fact of their meeting that is of significance; perhaps equally so is the fact of their not meeting in 1938 or 1939, when Freud was living in North-West London, where Tansley had himself grown up and gone to school. Tansley certainly did not visit Freud then.

77 The Leonardo used to hang in the Burlington, and thus off the beaten track – as Tansley recognized. Its acquisition by the National Gallery, London, was the occasion for a very public and impassioned campaign in the 1960s.

78 Freud's desire to be a Professor is analysed in both Jones' and Gay's biographies of Freud and in the detailed studies of Joseph and Renée Gicklhorn and of K. R. Eissler. In 1924, Freud pedantically corrected Pfister on this biographical fact: 'Actually I was never a full professor of neurology and was never anything but a lecturer. I became a titular professor

in 1902 and a titular full professor in 1920, have never given up my academic post, but have continued with it for thirty-two years, and finally gave up my voluntary lectures in 1918' (Freud and O. Pfister, *Psycho-Analysis and Faith*, London, 1963, 9 June 1924, p. 95). 'Titular' here means something between 'Associate' and 'Honorary'.

79 We thank P. Anker, an historian of ecological science, for pointing out, when we noticed Tansley's absence from the IPA Oxford Congress, that he was probably attending the 1929 South African BAAS meeting (July 22–August 3).

80 Undated entry in notebook entitled 'Psychology', which contains notes for 1929–36, Department of Plant Sciences, University of Cambridge.

81 A. G. Tansley, 'The use and abuse of vegetational concepts and terms', *Ecology*, 16: 3, July 1935, p. 285.

82 Tansley argued that Phillips simply trotted out F. E. Clements's theory that vegetation constituted a 'complex organism', which could be studied in the manner that physiologists approached the individual organism. Although Tansley had initially adhered to this idea, he increasingly expressed dissatisfaction with Clements's organismal analogy as well as his 'monoclimax' – the theory that there was a single end point to vegetational succession in a given climatic area. In his 1935 paper, Tansley wrote that Phillips' three linked articles in Tansley's *Journal of Ecology* – 'Succession, development, the climax and the complex organism: An analysis of concepts I', *Journal of Ecology 22*, 1934, pp. 554–571 and '[Parts II, III]', *Journal of Ecology 23*, 1935, pp. 210–246, 488–508 – invited 'attack at almost every point'. See P. Anker, *Imperial Ecology: Environmental Order in the British Empire, 1895–1945*, New Haven, CT, 2001, pp. 118–156 for a fascinating analysis of the political dimensions of the ecological debate.

83 W. Cooper, 'Sir Arthur Tansley and the science of ecology', *Ecology* 38:4, October 1957, p. 659, citing letter dated November 1923.

84 'Notes on the conducting tissue-system in Bryophyta', *Annals of Botany* 15, 1901, p. 1 and 'On the structure of Schizaea malaccana', *Annals of Botany* 17, 1903, p. 493. Edith also created the index for *Types of British Vegetation*, Cambridge, 1911, for which Arthur thanked her in the Preface.

85 Meisel and Kendrick, *Bloomsbury/Freud*, p. 216, letter dated 23 February 1925. According to his granddaughter, Dr Anna Dickens, Tansley's daughters 'were well known for being attractive both in appearance and intellect'.

86 Personal communication, Dr Anna Dickens, Cambridge, 23 June 1999. Given the insufficient evidence as to the identity of Tansley's beloved, it is not appropriate to give extensive information concerning those whom we regard privately as candidates. If a cache of papers belonging to any of these candidates emerged and illuminated further aspects of this study, this might well change our view of what is appropriate to publish. Permission to publish from the close relatives or estate of the person would still be needed.

87 Tansley, *The New Psychology*, p. 223.

88 D. Bryan, 'Reports. British Psycho-Analytic Society', *Bulletin of the International Psycho-Analytical Association, International Journal of Psycho-analysis* 7, 1926, p. 533.

89 Bryan, 'Reports', *International Journal of Psycho-analysis* 7, 1926, pp. 533–534.

90 Freud, 'A special type of object-choice made by men', SE 11, 165–175.

91 Tansley, *The New Psychology*, pp. 236–237.

92 A. G. Tansley, *Practical Plant Ecology*, London, 1923, p. 48. For more detailed analysis, see Cameron, 'Histories of disturbance', *Radical History Review* 74, 1999, pp. 4–24 and 'Anthropogenic natures: Wicken Fen and histories of disturbance, 1923–1943', Ph.D. dissertation, University of Cambridge, 2001.

93 Tansley, *The New Psychology*, p. 130.

94 LoC interview, Kurt Eissler, p. 12.

95 A number of passages in *The New Psychology* single out a married man who conducts 'a serious illicit love-affair' (p. 103) as peculiarly subject to intense conflict; see also p. 111.

96 Virginia Woolf, *To the Lighthouse* (1927), London, 1992, p. 100.

97 Ms. letter, undated but clearly after 1972, addressed to Members of the International Psycho-Analytical Association, Anna Freud Archives, Library of Congress, Washington DC, USA.

98 Information received from Dr Richard West, Godwin's colleague and executor, who donated much of Godwin's estate, including Tansley's papers, to the Department of Plant Sciences, Cambridge, and informed us (14 May 1999) that it was Godwin who donated the books to the Freud Museum in Vienna. Tansley's will was probated 14 April 1956.

99 Professor Peter Grub of the Dept. of Plant Sciences in Cambridge has a small private collection of Tansley's botanical works, received from Sir Harry Godwin. Tansley's own edition of Freud's works in English, prepared by his long-standing friend James Strachey, found its way into a second-hand bookshop in Cambridge in the 1970s, where it was eagerly acquired by Edward Timms, now Professor of German at the University of Sussex and a distinguished commentator on psychoanalysis. He retained the original invoices that came with the set, from which the following information is derived: Tansley subscribed to the *Standard Edition* on 2 April 1953, ordering it through the London booksellers I. R. Maxwell of 4–5 Fitzroy Square. Before his death in 1955, Tansley certainly received two other volumes (Vol. 13, 1953, and Vol. 18, 1955, dispatched to him in May 1955). The final volume must have been delivered to Tansley's estate in 1974.

100 In a chance conversation with Lydia Marinelli, Archivist of the Freud Museum in Vienna, JF discovered the presence of Tansley's books on the bookshelves beside which he was sitting. As professional librarians and experts on the history of psychoanalysis, the Freud Museum staff had excellent records of the source of the books, but no knowledge of the identity of Sir Arthur Tansley, FRS.

Chapter 12

Psychoanalysis, dreams, history: An interview with Hanna Segal

Daniel Pick and Lyndal Roper

Figure 12.1 Hanna Segal, 1997. Copyright © 1997 Victoria Mihich.

INTRODUCTION

This brief, informal interview with the psychoanalyst Hanna Segal, who had recently celebrated her eightieth birthday, took place in London in April 1999. Hanna Segal is well known as the most prominent and lucid post-war interpreter of the work of Melanie Klein; she is the author, for instance, of the widely read Fontana 'Modern Master' on Klein. Over the last fifty years,[1] Segal's many papers, essays and books have explored the nature of her own psychoanalytic experience and made important conceptual contributions, for instance regarding the nature of unconscious phantasy, the clinical relevance of the death instinct, and the psychic consequences of the capacity (or lack of it) to use symbols. She has investigated the wider applications of psychoanalytic ideas in diverse fields, notably aesthetics, politics and literature.

Segal grew up in Poland; her family had cosmopolitan interests and her father was an able linguist. She has described her mother as a person of exceptional resourcefulness, who helped pull the family through during times of great upheaval. When Hanna was twelve, her family moved, under difficult personal circumstances, to Geneva, where her father took up a post as an editor of a journal. She returned for a time to Warsaw in order to complete her secondary education and to pursue medicine. She had an allegiance to socialism, but also encountered Freud's work at an early stage. Again under pressure, her family had to move once more, this time to Paris (her father's role as an anti-fascist had by then made it politically untenable for them to stay in Geneva). Hanna herself had continued to study medicine in Poland, but when she visited her family in Paris during the holidays in August 1939, she found she could not return. In 1940, in the face of the German occupation of France, the family fled to England, crossing the Channel on board a Polish ship. As she puts it, 'I arrived in time for the Blitz'. She pursued medical work in Britain but by this stage saw it as a staging post to a different end: psychoanalytic training. She had quickly come into contact with the pioneers of the 'object relations' tradition that had emerged in psychoanalysis in Britain. In what was to turn out to be a profoundly significant introduction, Ronald Fairbairn (in Edinburgh) put Segal in touch with Klein, with whom she had analysis and, later, supervision.

The period of Segal's arrival on the psychoanalytical scene, soon after Freud's own death in London, was marked by enormous ferment in the movement, with followers of Klein, of Anna Freud and of neither in intense and profound dispute over theoretical models, technique and much besides. This led to a series of formal debates in London, between 1941 and '45; contributions were detailed, sometimes intellectually brilliant and often deeply acrimonious. On occasion, these highly charged meetings were disturbed by the real air-war going on outside. (These illuminating 'Controversial Discussions' became readily accessible in published form in 1991.)[2] After the war, several followers of Klein, amongst whom were Herbert Rosenfeld and Hanna Segal, undertook clinical work with very severely disturbed patients. Writings of lasting import, for instance, on the nature of psychotic and non-psychotic functioning, were produced by these practitioners, as well as, notably, by Wilfred Bion (1897–1979), whose work has long been an important point of reference and dialogue for Segal herself, and who is directly mentioned in the interview below. In 1987 Segal was appointed to the newly established Freud professorship at University College London. Some of the ideas sketched in the discussion below are further elaborated in two collections: *Dream, Phantasy and Art* (1991) and *Psychoanalysis, Literature and War* (1997). A two-volume collection edited by David Bell, containing essays about or inspired by Hanna Segal's work, has recently been published: *Reason and Passion*, 1997, and *Psychoanalysis and Culture: A Kleinian Perspective*, 1999.[3]

Daniel Pick

INTERVIEW

DANIEL PICK: The first thing that we want to explore is the significance of Freud's *Interpretation of Dreams* for psychoanalysis today. As we reach its centenary, does its original interpretative model still provide 'the royal road' to a new understanding of dreams and of the unconscious in the way that Freud believed?

HANNA SEGAL: Yes and no. Freud is often misquoted; he never said that the dream is the royal road to the unconscious; but he did say that the interpretation of the dream is the royal road to the unconscious. In present-day analysis people vary greatly in how much attention they pay to the dream. I belong to those that like to work with dreams, but the whole attitude to the dream has changed. Freud's great discovery was that our repressed unconscious expresses itself in dreams and that this involves a lot of psychic work; a whole language has to be developed in order to have a dream; symbols have to be found and things have to be put together. It's really quite an effort; an unconscious psychic production of the dream which is a working through, a working out, of experiences which are not elaborated consciously. In Freud's time, this was a great discovery and it gave direct access, in a way, to expressions of unconscious phantasy. He would analyse dreams bit by bit and ask for associations and sometimes go on for days. That was at the time when he wasn't so aware of the importance of the transference so that he could continue the same dream because it was like a set task till the dream was analysed.

Nowadays, when we understand much more about the importance of the transference and the developing relationship between the patient and the analyst, we are also concerned with the function of the dream. Why does the patient have this dream and tell it to us in a particular way at a particular time? In that way the dream is treated like any other material. The other thing that has happened since Freud is that we differentiate much more between the time and type of dream, and we consider what dynamic psychic function it performs. Dreams can have very different functions. Earlier I spoke of the working through and the psychic work that comes into dreaming, but not all dreams are of that kind. Freud spoke of a dream as a night-time hallucination. But I think, in fact, that not all dreams are night-time hallucinations. Some are like that; they are felt as very concrete. They sort of stay in the mind. Their use (I'm generalizing here) is not to establish a communication – a dream as communication between the unconscious phantasy and our conscious mind – but on the contrary, to get rid of mental content. Bion speaks of patients who treat their dream with shame, as though they had defecated or urinated in their beds. And in those situations dreams are not used to elaborate symbolically and to communicate to oneself or the analyst. They're very close to hallucination. It's something used to get rid of our own experience, by putting it outside. I once had a patient who wrote down his dreams; he had notebooks and notebooks of them; he had an 'agenda' in the analysis to go through his dreams. We were always years behind his agenda. He would come and read the dream and tell it to me and in this way it was as though the dream had nothing to do with him. What was particularly striking was that he was very often getting rid of more positive parts of his psychic personality because those were the painful ones. For instance, he was extremely fixated on his mother; when she died, he had a lot of dreams which were extremely moving. He put them in his little diary. This was not a way of working through his mourning, but a means of getting rid of it. And it comes very close to hallucination because then dreams are used not to elaborate a psychic reality but to get rid of it by putting it in an image, telling it, invading the analyst's mind with the image, not really elaborating the problem. They are used for action – to seduce, to impress, to frighten. So we pay much more attention not only to the content, but also to what is the actual function that the dream performs. I won't add more on this now because I've written a great deal on this.

LYNDAL ROPER: We also wondered whether you felt that the question of how one should interpret dreams and what one should make of dreams, had been particularly contentious within psychoanalysis as you have experienced it. Or has it been just an organic change in the way people have approached dreams?

HANNA SEGAL: Well, technique has changed a great deal, at least in the Kleinian development, and other people have also changed very much. Freud used to give a sort of symbolic explanation; he would translate the symbol. We don't do that now; one might sometimes just use one fragment of the dream that the patient has brought. We don't interpret symbols in the same immediate automatic way. We don't have a dictionary of symbols. One has to wait to know what this symbol means to this patient. Also one has to be very watchful whether it really is a symbol or whether it's felt as a more concrete thing. Whether this is contentious is difficult to say. I may be wrong [in generalizing] about it because I speak from England, where there is so much interchange [between groups] that very few people today would analyse a dream like Freud does (asking the patient to associate to this and to that and to the other). Everybody is much more aware of the transference.

LYNDAL ROPER: Coming at this as a historian, from a rather different perspective, this raises for me the whole question of how one might think about symbols in dreams in the past. If a symbol and the way a symbol is used in a dream is very much part of an individual's working through, then how might that be true for dreams in the past? To what extent is a language of dreams something that's shaped not just by the individual but by a culture or a period?

HANNA SEGAL: I think everything is affected. Nowadays a certain type of phallic potency would often be represented by a motorcycle. Obviously there was a time when there were no motorcycles. New symbols are needed all the time; also symbols are very overdetermined. Some say that a thing can be represented by many symbols, but the symbol has only one meaning. That certainly isn't true and actually Freud spoke of overdetermination. But a symbolism evolves as the object relationships evolve. The same symbol can have very varied meanings and come up at different times. A snake may represent a penis at one level. It could be seen as the wise thing or the poisonous thing. But in another sense, it may be a poisonous breast. At still another, it may be the baby's poisonous mouth. So you sort of work through the symbols. Symbols carry a history with them. In fact I would say that the view that symbols have one meaning is the opposite of the case; probably there's nothing that represents just one thing.

LYNDAL ROPER: There's also the issue of the role of culture in dreaming and what role you think it does play. Is it just that the symbols changed depending on time?

HANNA SEGAL: No, all sorts of factors change. Situations change, anxieties change. Take dreams, let's say, in adolescents confronted with endless unemployment or confronted with a nuclear threat. We can see not only the alteration of symbols but that certain anxieties are more prominent in certain cultures. There's nothing that is not influenced by our environment.

DANIEL PICK: We've been asking question about dreams in history or dreams in culture. But how much can the question be put the other way round: how far do you see dreams as registering or featuring changes in personal history, relationships to the past?

HANNA SEGAL: Yes they do, and so does the culture. Whatever culture we have is an outcome of past culture. The past is always with us, that's clear, whether in dreams or in the culture. But I don't think, as Freud did, that we have got a sort of racial memory of things in the past. I think it's more that the current situation and environment carry the past to which we react.

DANIEL PICK: One of the points you suggested earlier is that without close analytic work on the dreamer as well as the dream, we know very little. This does raise a problem for historians who might for instance have a dream text that someone recorded in the past, like your patient's note-book writings. We may have an archive, even something akin to those notebooks, but no access psychoanalytically to the dreamer. I'm won-dering how much in your view that leads to the problem of what used to be called 'wild analysis'. Does it not suggest that one must be very cautious about what one could actually say if one were to take, say, the dreams of historical figures?

HANNA SEGAL: Speculation can be dangerous in analysis. About dreams in history, nobody who has any sense would say that that dream means this or that for sure. But one might still speculate – knowing something of an artist's history and his preoccupations. One can have some freedom of thought here; we can speculate, but we cannot say that because such and such symbols were there, it means anything for sure. That's the difference between you historians and me. For in relation to patients, one has to be very careful, because making mistakes costs lives as it were. On the other hand I think one should have more freedom in reconstructing imaginatively a biography of an artist, provided one doesn't become autocratic about it.

DANIEL PICK: There are at least two directions that one could imagine a critic taking in relation to this whole discussion. One might be the direction of a more historically sceptical commentator, who would want to chal-lenge some of the more universalizing claims that have been made by psychoanalysts about dreams, symbolism, phantasy and so forth. The other direction of critique might be from the natural sciences today. There has been so much work on dreams from a more empirical 'labor-atory' viewpoint. From either of these directions is there a real problem that actually needs to be addressed by analysts or are these simply different languages that have nothing to do with the psychoanalytic understanding?

HANNA SEGAL: I think criticism which is valid and well based has to be addressed – but by others. I do not personally go in for that kind of documentation or debate. Regarding the physical phenomena, as far as I know, there is nothing that really would contradict our view. I think at some point a much greater synthesis has to be made. But I think at the moment it's very premature. We have to know a lot more about those fields. And to my mind – I may be prejudiced – I think we know much more about the psychic functioning now than the neurophysiolo-gists and chemists know about the functioning of the brain. I think so.

DANIEL PICK: But I'm interested that, in a way, you share Freud's aspiration that one day natural science and psychoanalysis will meet.

HANNA SEGAL: I don't say will take over, but will come closer. I don't think that there is anything in analysis that contradicts natural physical laws. You know, if I smack you and you get a redness in your cheek it may mean an awful lot of things to you, but the fact remains the fact. But how can a historian criticize psychoanalysis? The historian's job, as it were, is to describe things as they have evolved in various areas, not to pass judgement. A historian can criticize me if I write a biography of Freud full of mistakes. Or if I said a certain idea appeared at a certain time and it didn't.

DANIEL PICK: During the half century in which you have been a member of the British Society, do you think there have been major changes in the understanding of dreams within the Kleinian tradition and in the evolution of your own thinking?

HANNA SEGAL: Oh yes, very much so. Here I have to take some personal credit. I mean that I identified the difference between concrete symbolism and symbolism of a more depressive kind, and I differentiated dreams in those terms. It was pushed much further by Bion who was dealing with even more primitive elements of concrete symbolism. So there has been a great shift in that way.

DANIEL PICK: Would you also say that close clinical attention to the psychic life of children has transformed the broader theory of dreams in psychoanalysis?

HANNA SEGAL: Yes. Working with children has taught us so much about the unconscious and the child's phantasy. We could recognize more in dreams of the child, and what the child felt, and what the kind of phantasies were. We have also changed our view on children's dreams. Freud said that children's dreams are wish fulfilments and without any conflict. I don't think now that analysis of children bears that out. We know that their dreams are as complicated and show the same mechanisms as adult ones.

DANIEL PICK: Perhaps we could also ask you more personally at this point about your own history in relation to psychoanalysis. You moved from Poland through France to England and Scotland. How did you first come to psychoanalysis?

HANNA SEGAL: From very early in adolescence I came to psychoanalysis through reading. I read pretty well everything available, translated into Polish or into French. Some people think that I was influenced by Madame Sokalnicka. She was Polish, a psychoanalyst, and a friend of my mother. But actually if anything I would have been put off by her. I thought she was rather neurotic! But mainly, it was through reading. I had many incompatible interests. I was interested in literature and art, but I was also a bit of a do-gooder. I wanted to be of social use in the world. It was difficult to find a profession. Analysis was an answer to my dreams, probably because my basic interest is in people and human minds. I went into medicine with the idea of becoming an analyst only I didn't know how to set about it. I went to Bychowski who later became quite well known in America. He was an analyst, one of only two in Poland. He told me I must go to Vienna. But I didn't want to go to Vienna, having no particular liking for Germanic countries at all, so that was that. Then when I was in Paris in 1939, I contacted an analyst, Laforgue, because I knew his book on Baudelaire. He told me he was skedaddling out of Paris which was very lucky for me because I subsequently came to the conclusion he was bad news in all sorts of ways.

During the first year and a half in London I was too busy surviving. But in Edinburgh, I met Fairbairn and he told me about the Institute, how to set about it. I am also very grateful to Fairbairn for alerting me to certain controversies and various other developments in the Society – up till then I had read Freud, but not heard of Anna Freud or of Melanie Klein. He gave me Anna Freud's *The Ego and the Mechanisms of Defence* which I found one of the most boring books I have ever read and Melanie Klein's *Psychoanalysis of Children*, which was like opening a world for me.

LYNDAL ROPER: But how old were you then?

HANNA SEGAL: I was born in 1918 and we're speaking of Edinburgh in 1941. I was in my early twenties.

DANIEL PICK: You mention Fairbairn saying to you that there were these controversies going on in London. That was something of an understatement for that period!

HANNA SEGAL: It was in the war. It was just before the 'Controversial Discussions'. Yes, I had no idea how acute it was and that there was such personal enmity. I just knew about it on the basis of the books. And it also rang bells for me immediately, I tell you what, when we were being evacuated from Paris, we walked out of Paris, but at some point we caught a train. And in that train a young adolescent girl had a schizophrenic breakdown and her parents didn't know what to do. I was a medical student, that was my only experience and they asked me to look after her, which I did – I also took her to hospital. She was talking non-stop and the thing that stuck in my mind was that she was screaming 'I've lost it, I shat out my lover in the lavatory. I shat out my lover in the loo!' And also when I was in Edinburgh I started working voluntarily in a very bad child-guidance clinic, but I listened to children talking. So when I read Klein, it was not only that it appealed to my imagination, but that the contact that I had with a schizophrenic absolutely corresponded with what she was talking about.

LYNDAL ROPER: Was it difficult to work with Klein? What was it like to work with her?

HANNA SEGAL: Well, analysis is never easy, but I never found her persecuting. On the whole it was a very good experience. And working with her, which I did later, was not difficult at all. She didn't have any side or pretentiousness. She was extremely open to new ideas. She would only get fierce if one undermined her basic concepts derived from her discoveries, then she got very fierce. But she was very open to criticism and to ideas, and she was very encouraging. I think she disagreed quite a lot with the things that Bion started developing but she never in any way blocked him or attacked him. She was a very good person to work with.

LYNDAL ROPER: I wondered if I could ask you about your own writing. Are your own creative processes puzzling to you?

HANNA SEGAL: I'm not an artist, but like all artists I don't want to inquire too much into the process. My first book took much too long, that was the *Introduction to the Work of Melanie Klein*. I feel a bit bad about it because she very much wanted this book. It didn't appear until after she died. But all the other books I wrote were always under contract and that went much faster.

LYNDAL ROPER: One of the things that we are looking at in this book is dreams and creativity, an area on which you have written a great deal.

HANNA SEGAL: Here I would mention the dreamer, the madman and the artist (I think it was a lover in Shakespeare). One could paraphrase and say that the madman, the dreamer and the artist have a lot in common. I think that the unconscious expresses itself all the time, in all sorts of ways. But it seems to me that there are more direct ways because they are less involved in dealing with reality. One is the dream; it happens in our mind. Even when it is influenced by happenings outside, it is a purely psychic production. There is a difference between a night dream and a daydream. A daydream is very defensive. In night dreams, there is a sort of psychic pressure to work out a problem. In daydreams, the problem is denied and one creates an ideal illusory world in which one lives. This is actually linked with madness in a way. You know a dream is a product of your mind. If you're in a daydream you tend to see it as a reality. If you do, that way lies madness.

DANIEL PICK: In your early work you were renowned for trying to work psychoanalytically with severely disturbed patients, sometimes with schizophrenic patients. I'm wondering how you would link that experience to the point you are making now about forms of dreaming and states of madness.

HANNA SEGAL: Yes. What could in one person be represented by a dream, in the psychotic becomes a reality – a hallucination; the external world is as it were wiped out or distorted. The psychotic's actual night dreams are felt to be like that very often. So that psychotics sometimes get this strange sense that the dream is the sanest part, in that they are capable of certain psychic work and feeling but that that is put in the dream and the dream is as it were put away while reality gets invaded by nightmare.

But I brought in the daydream because Freud makes this distinction between the daydreamer and the artist. He says the artist comes back to reality because he acquires a love of women and money and so on. I think the difference between the daydreamer and the artist is very much bigger than that. For one reason because the daydreamer denies problems and the artist deals with the same problems that the dream would deal with – deep unconscious anxieties; the artist differs from the daydreamer because to my mind the former is rooted in reality in two ways. We are aware that in his own area the artist is extremely perceptive – you know, a painter who looks at a landscape or a novelist, or a poet who describes something. He is also very close to psychic reality and in a way the more psychic reality there is in the work the more and the deeper it hits us. The artist must also have an extremely realistic perception of the tools of his trade and of his materials. So it seems to me that the artist is one who can, as it were, have a dream – let us say an unconscious phantasy – and can give it symbolic expression. After all the artist's work is making symbols. That's why it is so directly in contact with the unconscious. He has no other work. His work is to make symbols, in fact to make new symbols, and that is what comes into the culture. We use the symbols made by the artist who created them and he must have an acute awareness of the reality of his materials. He knows that the things he will make will not be really his dream and he has to recognize the limits of the reality of his material, of his technique, in order to actualize the dream. I don't like action painting and things like that. I think that the idea that you let your unconscious loose and splash paint, like in free association, doesn't appeal to me because it is the working through of the contradictions, of the pain, that actually give the aesthetic experience to which people respond.

One of the differences is also that dreams deal with our internal problems to our satisfaction, but may be completely meaningless to others. On the other hand, the artist does want to communicate his dream, make a reality in the external world which involves much more psychic work and involves a lot of real, conscious work, which of course a dreamer doesn't do. We can all dream and daydream – we can't all be artists.

NOTES AND REFERENCES

1 A half century of publications that began with 'Some aspects of the analysis of a schizophrenic', *International Journal of Psychoanalysis* 31, 1950, pp. 268–278.
2 R. Steiner and P. King (eds.), *The Freud-Klein Controversies 1941–45*, London, 1991.
3 This summary draws on Bell's account of Segal's background and intellectual contribution in his introduction to *Reason and Passion*, London 1997, which is vol. 1 of the *Festschrift*.

Chapter 13

A dream to dream

Edna O'Shaughnessy

A hundred years after Freud's great work *The Interpretation of Dreams*, we all recognize that various new dimensions have been added to what Sara Flanders, in her excellent collection of writings from various psycho-analytic schools, calls *The Dream Discourse Today*. I shall present a session in which a patient's dream poses a problem: how to consider the dream's important content, while at the same time giving analytic attention to the way in which the dream structures the relationship between patient and analyst? The way I approach my patient most of all reflects current Kleinian thinking as well as some other recent influences in the British psycho-analytical tradition.[1]

A SKETCH OF MY PATIENT

Mrs A has been in analysis for several years. She is much less anxious and less passive than she used to be. Relations with her colleagues and her standing in the office where she works have also improved though it sounds to me that she is still rather exploited, doing over-much without recognition. Currently, she is disappointed at not being offered a promotion she had expected – even though she had not contended for it. She and her husband seem much attached; he is in finance and she finds him intelligent and attractive though she describes him as doing nasty deals and complains about his unhelpfulness in family life – it is always she who does what needs to be done for their grown-up son and daughter. She believes she has bene-fited from the analysis and is grateful; yet, significant problems remain which come well into view in the session with the dream.

The session with the dream was on a Monday. On the preceding Friday Mrs A had been very disturbed about a lump she had detected while exam-ining her breasts the evening before.

THE SESSION

Mrs A started the Monday session by talking in a bright, lively way about her dreams. She had had two dreams. Now there was one. She had dreamt *she was in a beautiful palace. The queen, Queen Elizabeth, was there.* Mrs A laughed and commented 'I'm laughing at myself for dreaming about the Queen. I don't like her'. She continued: 'But in the dream, *there the Queen was, just like an ordinary person. The palace was beautiful, with many pictures and antiques, and there were lots of people there. The Queen came over to me and spoke to me. She said she would show me round the palace herself. She was friendly and intimate. The Queen took me about and pointed out things'.* My patient went on: 'In the dream of my dream, I mean' – she corrected her slip of the tongue – 'in the palace of my dream I did like her. *The Queen took me and showed me where she lived in a little cottage outside. I told the Queen I was amazed she was living there, but the Queen explained it. She said "What's the use of living in a palace? The Americans would come and bomb it"'.*

After telling her dream Mrs A fell silent. I waited for a while and then asked if she had any associations. She answered 'No!' as if I had asked a wrong and irritating question.

A long silence followed. I found myself remembering the lump in her breast that had worried her on the Friday, and thinking that what had happened about the lump, or indeed anything else on the weekend, was absent, and by contrast, how bright and present Mrs A's Dream Palace was, and also how it brought a coherent picture of important unconscious features in Mrs A's life.

She suddenly broke the silence to speak with resentment about her friend from Paris who is called Regine. She pointed out that 'Regine' also means 'Queen'. She said how annoyed she is with the way Regine lives in London – Regine's always visiting them, just arriving, and her (that is, Mrs A's) husband doesn't like Regine's husband, yet if they both come he understands he has to be there. Mrs A concluded: 'We feel really *put upon* by them. I can't just say "She's my friend, I'll see her whenever I like. I can't go there because my husband has nothing in common with Regine's husband"'.

I remarked on how she also couldn't see me whenever she liked and wondered whether especially this weekend with her worry about the breast lump on Friday it might have been especially hard for her. Mrs A ignored me. She continued talking about Regine and how annoyed she was that Regine keeps visiting them. She was silent for a while. Then speaking as if remote from her session, with no glimmer that her thoughts might also hold some immediate meaning related to her or me, she said that yesterday she had heard her husband make a telephone call about a sum of money. She could hear him behaving very badly on the phone, although he didn't have as much money as people thought.

Mrs A fell silent again. I felt all the work of thinking about what was happening in the session was being lodged in me, for instance the voicing of the fact that she'd felt put upon by my visiting her like an annoying Regine with uninvited remarks about her breast lump and waiting for me on the weekend, and then she behaved badly and ignored me. And furthermore, it was I who had to worry that, what with the long silences, time was going by and the potential of the insights expressed in her dream – there were certainly valuable pictures there – might be lost if the content of the dream was just ignored.

Suddenly from the street outside some voices and then a child crying could be heard. Mrs A remained silent after these intrusions, still passively waiting for me to speak. I remembered her slip of the tongue as she related her dream; how instead of saying 'in the Palace of my dream' she had said 'in the dream of my dream', and I thought she was dreaming her dream, and were I to act like the Queen of her dream, personally and intimately, instead of being the psychoanalyst she doesn't like, then she would feel as if she liked me.

So I spoke about how it disturbed her when she didn't like me and became resentful when I asked for associations or mentioned the breast lump and that she shouldn't come to me on the weekend, and she wanted to lose these feelings by dreaming her dream here with me. Suddenly, Mrs A was attentive. She nodded her head. I continued saying that if, however, I stop functioning like an analyst and become part of her dream, become a Queen who shows her around like an ordinary friendly person would, for example mentioning the voices and the crying child we'd just heard, then she likes me.

Mrs A listened, waiting for more from me. She stayed silent. I thought it was unclear by now who was the Queen – she or I? I said to her that during the session she herself seemed to have become more and more the same as her image of me as a Queen waiting to be served. And indeed Mrs A went on waiting.

I eventually said that although we might seem to be together and friendly here in a rich Dream Palace, each of us is diminished. I admit to abandoning my real place and evading our difference of status as patient and analyst to avoid rousing her dislike of me; she loses her energy and what she knows and really feels, and passively persuades herself she likes such a Queen, though enduring false intimacy and condescension from me. I concluded by saying something about how in her dream she had been able to reveal a painful truth – that she knows this bright dream palace is a false sort of place.

Mrs A responded with conviction: 'Yes.' 'I get your point', she said.

It was almost the end of the session. In its last moments, sarcastic and disparaging, Mrs A said: 'But are you not going to say anything at all about the *actual* events and people I mentioned?' Her sudden attack, a seeming incomprehension of the analytic enterprise the nature of which she in fact understands well, bombs away the bit of analytic work I thought we had done on the actual events and experiences of the session. Was it hatred and/or fear?

DISCUSSION

When the session begins Mrs A is active; she has had a dream, in fact she says two dreams, and as she reports her dream she is able to comment on and laugh at herself. You remember, she says: 'I'm laughing at myself for dreaming about the Queen. I don't like her'. We glimpse a lively self-reflective ego, which later goes passive. When I ask for associations she is irritated. Her refusal to associate is important – it is part of not wanting to be out of the dream, of wanting me also to be in her dream, and come at once to her as a Queen who points things out so that together we look at her dream picture in her Dream Palace.

She gets resentful when I wait and speaks of how she feels 'put upon' by an annoying little Regine who visits her whenever she chooses and whom she can't visit when she wants to. When I link this to my unavailability at the weekend, when she may have been worried about the breast lump, she does not take the interpretation. She continues talking resentfully about Regine. I think she finds these frustrating, unequal relations between us too disturbing, and she becomes passive, wanting to 'dream her dream' and I am put in the position of having to do all the work while she takes on the identity of a Queen. I point this out to her, but she doesn't want to know about this either and she still waits.

It is only when I interpret how she wishes her session to *be* the dream of her dream, that is to say, when I refer to how my role of analyst with her as my patient arouses such resentment of me, that she wants to lose these feelings by dreaming her dream with me, that Mrs A becomes attentive. It is then that I reach her. In my view, this is the key interpretation.

After this, though she is still in her dream, Mrs A is at the same time enough out of it to listen and to understand what I, as the active one, say. For her I am half defined by her dream as the Queen pointing out things to her, and I am also half her analyst interpreting to her. Mrs A met my last interpretation about the painful truth she had revealed in her dream about the Dream Palace being a false and impoverishing place by saying with conviction: 'Yes, I get your point'. This too is double. She got the point, in the sense of receiving it and actively acknowledging it – hence her bomb at me as the giver at the end. She also stayed inside her dream – passively having the point served up to her.

We could say that my patient brings her dream to me, primarily, though not exclusively, to be *lived*, so that the session becomes a setting where deeds and passive actions are more important than words. We see here a striking discrepancy between my patient's capacity to dream a dream rich in meaning, with valuable antique pictures of childhood feelings and primary relations that have lasted till the present day, and her incapacity to work with the analyst about it. Mrs A wants to dream her dream with me in the way she dreams her dream in her life, and there is the same loss of potential in analysis as in life. For some months she waited like a Queen to be offered a promotion, without actively contending for it, and she is currently very resentful, though she takes care not to show it at work, that another colleague whom she thinks is less able and less hardworking than she is (and I believe her) has obtained the higher post. In such ways she ends up, like the image she has unconsciously internalized of her analyst, overworking and under-valued. Her dream is thus an insight into a central unconscious defensive phantasy that structures her existence.

Is Mrs A's dream perhaps one of those that the Swiss psychoanalyst Quinodoz has recently described as 'dreams that turn over a page'? Quinodoz speaks of their 'clarity and coherence' and how 'such dreams often reveal more clearly than others the structure of the unconscious intrapsychic con-flicts'. He calls them 'integration dreams'.[2] Mrs A's dream is a pellucid picture in the terms of which and through which she seeks to construct her object relations and it is, potentially, an 'integration dream'. However, even though her dream pictured for the first time in a full and coherent manner this basic defensive phantasy, she is still too much in it – too fearful of her destructiveness and envy (which she keeps projected into her husband) for it to be part of the process of relinquishment and succeed as a dream that 'turns over a page'.

Of what type, then, is Mrs A's dream? It has some of Freud's benchmarks. It is a fulfilment of a wish, though not a simple libidinal wish, but a wish driven by a fusion of instincts in which the Death instinct predominates over the Life instinct, a dream wish that cuts the patient off from the pains of real life and finds an alternative form of living in a Dream Palace. And Mrs A's dream, while not a unique Royal Road (all her object relations especially those in the transference also lead there) is, I think, a special road to her unconscious. Its specialness lies in the fact that it is Mrs A's own insight expressed in her personal iconography. Mrs A's dream is of the type that has been called 'a predictive dream' or 'dream as a definitory hypothesis'. What we see lived out in the session is a range of phenomena consequent upon Mrs A's state of semi-projective identification with an object. In this defensive phantasy she is half in the rich palace she imagines the insides of her object to be, with the result that there is no clear separateness and a mix of symbolism and symbolic equations that make for concrete enactments.

Mrs A's silences and her passivity placed me in the dilemma of being either too talkative and obviously enacting her dream, or too silent and neglectful of its significant content and still enacting her dream, though less obviously, by being a Queen who isn't really personally interested in her subjects. I tried to reduce such inescapable enactments to a minimum while trying to understand my patient and interpret to her. I struggled all the way, not entirely successfully, but not I think failing altogether either. After all, Mrs A did get the point, which then roused the hatred which she had been afraid of and tried all the session to defend against, which finally came out in a bomb at the end.

POSTSCRIPT

There are always things the analyst never finds out. What happened to Mrs A's other dream? I cannot know whether it was just forgotten, or withheld, or indeed whether her words 'I had had two dreams. Now there is one' expressed something quite other, for instance to do with the two of us merging into one dream, as we seemed to do in the session. Also, Mrs A never spoke about her breast lump again and she stayed physically healthy. It therefore remained unclarified what the significance was of her fear of something deadly being in her breast.

NOTES AND REFERENCES

1 See, for instance, B. Joseph, *Psychic Equilibrium and Psychic Change: Selected Papers of Betty Joseph* (ed. Elizabeth Bott Spillius and Michael Feldman), London, 1989; H. Segal, *Dream, Phantasy and Art*, London, 1991; M. Masud R. Khan, 'The use and abuse of dream in psychic experience', in *The Dream Discourse Today* (ed. Sarah Flanders), London, 1993, ch. 4; H. Stewart, 'The experience of the dream and the transference' in Flanders, ch. 7; H. Rey, *Universals of Psychoanalysis in the Treatment of Psychotic and Borderline States*, London, 1994.
2 J.-M. Quinodoz, '"Dreams that turn over a page": Integration dreams with paradoxical regressive content', *International Journal of Psychoanalysis* 80, 1999, pp. 225–238.

Chapter 14

The shark behind the sofa: Recent developments in the theory of dreams

Susan Budd

Figure 14.1 Salvador Dali, 'The Accommodations of Desire', 1929. Copyright © Salvador Dali, Gala-Salvador Dali Foundation/Design and Artists Copyright Society, London, 2002.

In a sense, psychoanalysis began with dreams. *The Interpretation of Dreams* was first published in 1900, followed quickly by two books, on jokes and on the psychopathology of everyday life, in which Freud demonstrated how his new theory of the processes of the unconscious mind could be used to explain a great deal of everyone's everyday behaviour.

His stress throughout was on the normality and ubiquity of activities like dreaming, forgetting things, making mistakes, telling jokes and so on, which are rooted in the unconscious mind. We've all got one, and the way it makes us think and behave unites us with those outsiders, those others, young children, primitive peoples and the mentally ill, from whom we spend much of our lives trying to distance ourselves. I often think that much of the hostility to psychoanalysis expressed by academics and public figures stems from its anarchic, banana-skin effect on our wish to be seen as properly grown up, balanced, judicious, full of *gravitas*; our dreams especially can be wonderfully debunking productions. A patient comes in and tells us that they dreamt that we invited them to tea and then we hadn't got any to offer so they kindly cooked us a hamburger, or that they arrived in a consulting-room which was full of our badly behaved children and turned into a sandpit. We can enjoy these subversive images together, and also notice the relief that both analyst and patient feel in being liberated momentarily from our customary roles in the consulting-room.

It is strange, given the high value that Freud placed upon dreams – 'the royal highway to knowledge of the unconscious aspect of the mind', he called them – that a century later, many psychoanalysts take no special interest in dreams, and do not think that they offer us any special access to the inner world or demand any particular interpretative technique. This change is not particularly new – Freud himself was noticing and regretting it by the 1920s.

Vicky Hamilton's recent study[1] of how a group of English and American analysts of different theoretical persuasions actually put psychoanalytic theory into practice found that analysts differ widely in their attitudes to dreams. Some find them not particularly interesting, and hard to work with. Others find them enjoyable and fascinating. (Unsurprisingly, the second sort of analyst is told far more dreams.) But few contemporary psychoanalysts think that dreams are a uniquely valuable source of information about the patient's psyche. This is because of the overwhelming contemporary emphasis on the central role of the transference interpretation. Hamilton thinks that this is part of the contemporary restriction of psychoanalysis to a focus on the patient's present relationships, particularly that with the analyst, at the expense of the earlier aim to recreate the patient's psychic history, laid down in sedimentary layers that the dream, like a geological bore, brings up in condensed and scrambled images the forgotten and concealed psychic past.

> The focus on the here-and-now transference interpretation has changed analysts' use of dream material. When dreams are interpreted as manifestations of disguised thoughts and feelings about the present transference relationship, dreams are understood along a horizontal as opposed to a vertical dimension. Relational, present-time interpretations flatten and extend laterally the condensed and dispersed associations to dream content. The dream, like the mind, loses depth both historically and as an imaginative elaboration of everyday experience. And with this loss, the fragility, specificity, and complexity of dreams disperse into more

simple affective and relational transactions. . . . If analysts are no longer concerned with the detailed histories of their patients, the idiosyncratic imagery of dreams has less to reveal about the mind of one of the two participants in the analytic relationship. And perhaps that means that imagination is, after all, less central to the analyst's creativity than is his capacity for empathic or projective identification.[2]

Hamilton regrets this change, as I do. How has this situation come about? Let us begin at the beginning.

The Interpretation of Dreams is a stiff read. When teaching psychotherapy students, I try to console them with the thought that it is not only about dreams, it also contains Freud's theory of how the mind works, but they still find it tough going. Unlike Jung, Freud did not consider that dreams were in themselves sources of any unique wisdom or insight inaccessible by other means. He thought that dreams allow us to sleep by discharging in veiled form primitive impulses stirred up by the previous day; his attitude to dreams was more like that of Scrooge, telling Marley's ghost that he was really caused by a speck of indigestible mustard. But what fascinated Freud was the process of symbolic transformation by which an unconscious wish is translated into a conscious thought. The contents of the unconscious, being derived from infantile wishes and bodily drives, he did not think particularly remarkable. He saw the dreaming mind as continuous with and working in a very similar way to the waking mind. Most of our perceptions and mental activity are not accessible to consciousness whether we are asleep or awake. Dreams for the psychoanalyst are akin to daydreams, hallucinations, visions and jokes.

Theoretically speaking, Freud's views on dreams were based on the topographical model, and never clearly modified to fit in with the later structural model. His account of the formation of a dream was that of a lengthy system of transformations and translations undertaken by the dreaming mind to smuggle forbidden ideas past the censor. The forbidden wish can appear in consciousness or in the dream because it is heavily disguised. So the classical technique of dream interpretation involves putting the process of forming a dream into reverse.

Classically, the analyst works back from the manifest dream, or more accurately, the dream as it is remembered and reported in a session, by gathering the patient's associations to each element of the dream, putting them together with the events of the previous day and his knowledge of the patient's life, and decoding from its symbolic language the dream thoughts, the latent dream, which lead back to the particular infantile wish, generally sexual and often on one level about the relation with the analyst, which threatened to disturb sleep and so produced the dream in the first place. The metaphor that Freud used is that of the archaeologist deciphering hieroglyphics that refer to events long ago, buried in the mists of time. He saw the unconscious as striving to speak in a kind of visual language, full of puns and reversals.

Freud realized that people have generally been interested in dreams because they wonder if they are significant; in particular, if they predict the future. He made only one reference to this. The preconscious mind, he thought, recognizes things that the conscious mind denies. So if we dream that a friend is dead, and shortly afterwards discover that he is indeed fatally ill, this is because the preconscious knows more than we wish to know. We have pushed away from consciousness all the clues that tell us that there is something wrong. Since Freud, Jung certainly, and many other analysts implicitly, have seen the manifest as well as the latent content of the dream as informing us about the patient. The early analysts spent a good deal of time on dreams; the impression one gains from some accounts of sessions is that dreams provided the most important sort of material.[3]

The surrealist artists and poets who enthusiastically adopted psycho-analytic ideas in the 1920s and 30s saw the dream as a means of access to the irrational layers of the mind. They tried to represent dreams by means of automatic writing and pictorially. They followed Freud in seeing the dream as reflecting a crazy, unpredictable world, in which reality is discontinuous. But unlike him, they thought this world a valuable counterweight to rational thought. Dali explicitly used Freudian dream symbols in pictures in which he tried to explore his mental difficulties, and in the recent exhibition of Dali's work at the Tate in Liverpool, his homage to Freud was represented at the beginning of the exhibition by Freud's analytic couch.

In 'The Accommodations of Desire' of 1929 (Fig. 14.1), the thoughts appearing repeatedly on each of the discrete pebbles remind us of Freud's principle of over-determination in dreams – the same thought appears over and over again. It has a flat, pale-brown background, which many surreal-ists use to suggest dreams and which I will return to later. The picture is concerned with the horror of a woman's genital, which is either swarming with ants, or a lions' mouth. The lion is derived from Freud's view that wild beasts in dreams symbolize forbidden desires, and it reappears several times in various forms, illustrating the mechanisms of displacement and reversal, together with other vaginal images – the vase – and as part of the protective father whom the painter is seeking. Dali's paintings of this period often contain a protective male figure who is both his father and Sigmund Freud. In 1938, Dali had visited Freud, who wrote afterwards,

> until now, I have been inclined to regard the surrealists, who have apparently adopted me as their patron saint, as complete fools (let us say 95%, as with alcohol). That young Spaniard, with his candid, fanatical eyes and his undeniable technical mastery has changed my estimate. It would indeed be interesting to investigate analytically how he came to create that picture . . .'[4]

But although in the popular mind, psychoanalysts interpret dreams as one can the painting by playing a game of spot the symbol, in fact very few analysts now work in this classical way; it is rather stultifying, it tends to bracket off the dream from the rest of the analysis, and we often feel it is not the most important thing to focus on in a session.

Why is this? Why have we changed? Partly it is the impact of modern dream research, which has confirmed many of Freud's views, but not others; we now think the dream is not always based on a forbidden wish. Dreams stand on the frontier of the mind and the brain; they have both somatic and ideational roots. This has been known for a long time; Lucretius commented in *De Rerum Naturae* that children who wet their beds often dream of pissing into chamberpots; the dream protects our sleep from the need to get up and go and find one. The research undertaken in sleep laboratories on the relationship between dreams and various kinds of sleep shows the complexity, and the importance, of the dream in our psychic life.[5]

Partly, psychoanalysts have changed their attitude to dreams for the same reasons that have changed our technique in other areas. Patients and dreams seem to have changed; we focus now much more on the interaction between patient and analyst, and the dream, for bad or good, is the patient's possession. Many of us now see the manifest content of the dream as significant in its own right, and not just a clue to hidden wishes. I shall discuss these changes in turn, but I'd like to say from the outset that many of the changes that we have made in our ways of seeing and using dreams Freud had made as well. As so often, it is his early work that is taken as definitive, but he was to go on writing about dreams and changing his mind for another forty years.

CHANGES IN PATIENTS AND IN DREAMS

It has often been said that psychoanalysts don't see so many of the 'good neurotic' patients as Freud did – or do we analyse them differently? Certainly hysterics, of whom Freud saw so many in his early years, are on the whole good and vivid dreamers, and we now see more character disorders and schizoid personalities. Modern patients don't often produce the kinds of dreams that Freud had. Modern dreams mostly seem to be shorter and more fragmentary, and this is because the dream is undoubtedly a cultural as well as a neurobiological product. It is not just a kind of mental garbage. Dreams are very specific to each individual but they are also products of the social order; the visions of schizophrenic patients as recorded by asylum keepers had a predominantly religious quality until the mid-eighteenth century, when they began to be replaced by images of sexuality and of machines. But the modern world is both short of time, and pays no official attention to dreams; patients in treatment tend to find their dreams changing and becoming richer as someone else takes an interest in them. (It is comforting that Ella Sharpe (*Dream Analysis*, 1937) thought that the shortest, fragmentary dreams are often those which most repay attention.)

Dreams vary in the extent of their cunning disguise. Sandor Ferenczi was the first to remark on how the forbidden wish is often extraordinarily transparent in the dreams of the unsuspecting person who insists, on meeting us at a dinner-party or other social occasion, that we tell them what their recent dream means.[6] Freud thought that if an analysis is going well, patients can be increasingly left to interpret their own dreams. I remember a young woman, going through a negative patch in analysis, who dreamt of sitting in the Royal Free Hospital casualty department, and remembered hearing the previous day of a boy who had shot himself in the eye with an air-rifle. She then burst out, 'If I shot myself in the tongue, I wouldn't have to talk to you', and this account of her unconscious wish was entirely convincing to us both.

Freud took the ability to dream for granted. We now think that to be able to have a dream, tell it and think together with someone else about what it shows, is a considerable mental achievement. The most important thing that we have to be able to do to enable us to dream successfully is to know the difference between a dream and reality. This is similar to being able to be in and use an analytic session by keeping a frame round it. Some authorities believe that deeply psychotic patients do not dream, because their waking life is full of hallucinations and dream-like confusion. Young children confuse the contents of their minds with physical reality; they wake, and ask indignantly where the sweets are that you had put on the shelf, or think that the gorilla really is lurking behind the curtains. The mental world is not yet out there, or representational; the inner reality of dreams is also part of the external world. In the same way, very disturbed patients struggle to separate dreams from reality, and may feel that hallucinations and dreams are real, and they must act them out. If the analyst appears as hostile or friendly in the dream, they will find it difficult in the session not to react as if the analyst really were like that. Their dreams often seem to reflect their anxieties directly, without the elaborate symbolic disguise of the dreams of the more normal person.

The first challenge to Freud's theory that we dream to enable us to go on sleeping was the nightmare or anxiety-dream; the dream that wakes us so violently that we find it hard to sleep. The well-known painting of the Nightmare by Fuseli, painted around 1782, was one of the early icons of the romantic movement. It is said that Freud had an engraving hanging in his waiting-room. It depicts the ancient view that the choking anxiety of a nightmare is caused by a demon sitting on the chest, which will sexually invade the body of the dreamer and try to take over her mind. Ernest Jones thought that these sorts of dreams were caused by a specific kind of homosexual anxiety that was commoner in the sixteenth and seventeenth centuries,[7] but it seems more likely that here we seem to be looking at a physiological universal.

If we look at images of nightmares from other cultures we can see the same themes appearing; the pressure on the chest, the sense of there being other beings inside one's head, the animals who invade us. Presumably the similarity of these images across time and space stems from the universal human experiences of inhabiting the same bodies, having the same sorts of experiences in early childhood, experiencing the physiological states of fear in the same way and so on. Even in cultures where dreams are believed to predict the future rather than revive the past, patients vividly dream of past traumas as they do in the West. Such dreams are doubly frightening for them, since they fear that the trauma is not only past but will come again in the future. The dreams of borderline patients commonly depict the body or the inner self being invaded by a parasitic being, just as many horror films do. But to dream even this is an accomplishment; the worst nightmares are those with imageless sensations of terror; in them, we experience a horror without being able to symbolize it.

There was plenty of evidence for this among the shell-shock patients of the Great War, whose treatment gave such an impetus to psychoanalysis. Night after night, soldiers would experience again the horrifying events that had led to their breakdown. Modern research into traumatic dreams shows that as people begin to recover from horrifying experiences, images of the terror begin to appear in their dreams, and finally they begin to dream that they can master the horror – escape from the burning building, flee from the assailant – and then they can use the process of symbolization to begin to sleep. In Hanna Segal's terms, they are moving from a symbolic equation to a true symbol.[8]

In the same way, the drawings of sexually abused children will at first show broken fragments, or tearing and scratching of the paper, and then begin to show in symbolic form and increasingly directly what the bodily invasion felt like. Ferenczi, who worked with some very damaged patients, told of a woman who every night would experience imageless sensations related to her early traumas, wake, and then have a dream in which the sensations were represented in images, which would allow her a refreshing sleep.[9] Indeed, many of us have the sense that a good night's sleep involves satisfactory dreams, even if we do not particularly remember them.[10] We could say that the dream does indeed represent a wish; but it is a wish to dream, to represent our psychic life in image or narrative.

The evidence from dream research is equivocal about the merits of post-traumatic dreams as a method of mourning and coming to terms with the past. Some studies show that the best way of surviving horrifying experiences is to repress them so deeply that we never even dream of them. Others suggest that for the mildly depressed, dreaming is indeed a way of coming to terms with distressing events, and their dreams during a single night show progressively more pleasant themes, and a lighter mood on waking.

It was Jung who pointed out that dreams can be analysed in series; he believed that they show the unconscious mind returning over and over again to a central dilemma or theme in the life of the dreamer, and some dreams certainly are of this type. I shall return to this again when I talk about symbolism in dreams. Ronald Fairbairn, who produced a revised meta-psychology for psychoanalysis in a series of papers in the 1940s and 50s, saw dreams as being like cinema-shorts; they represent in condensed form our self-narrative.[11] His analogy is interesting; the cinema has drawn extensively on the psychoanalytic view of dreams, and perhaps is the medium most capable of representing the dreaming experience to us.

Freud always implicitly assumed that there is a distinction between reality-based thinking, located in the ego, and psychotic thinking, such as dreaming, which is dominated by unconscious processes. Melanie Klein was less interested in dreams as such because for her, all thinking was more permeated by unconscious elements. She thought that we cope with un-acceptable ideas less by repression than by splitting the ego, and in our dreams, our divided minds often appear, represented by different levels, or different rooms in a house.

We can see these two approaches reflected in visual representations of the mind. For example. Goya's familiar engraving of 'The Sleep of Reason Brings Forth Monsters', where the dreamer, slumped forward in sleep, is separate from the monsters that appear in the background, even though the advance made by the romantic movement was intermittently to realize that the monsters come from another part of oneself. But the dreamer will awake, and they will disappear into the underworld. Melanie Klein was working in a more modern idiom, in which there is no such reassuring division between the sane, waking world and the world of dreams; dream images are part of the divided inner self. Consider Figure 14.2, 'Cerebral Palsy', produced in

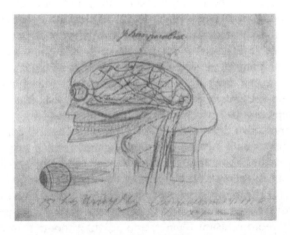

Figure 14.2 Louis Umgelter, 'Cerebral Palsy', 1906, Courtesy of Prinzhorn Collection, Heidelberg University and Hayward Gallery, London.

1906 by Louis Umgelter, a mental patient suffering from alcoholism and *dementia praecox*. (It forms part of the Prinzhorn collection, of art produced in European mental asylums between the start of the last century and the 1920s, which was on show at the Hayward Gallery as part of the exhibition of 'Art and Psychosis' December 1996–February 1997.) Like many of the other drawings in the exhibition, it showed the space inside the head as fragmented, muddled, divided. It is not an unsophisticated production; it reflects the medical diagrams that the patient must have seen of the inside of the head. It is rather reminiscent of the 'X-ray' images of Australian aboriginal art, produced by a culture in which all reality starts in dreams; we are literally dreamed into existence. These artists must be aware that kangaroos and men don't really look like this inside; these are pictures of psychic space.

Many modernist artists and thinkers in the twentieth century have been excited by the direct access that some mental patients and primitive peoples apparently have to the unconscious. The Nazis took the opposite point of view. They condemned modern art precisely because it resembled either primitive art or that of the insane. They exhibited some of the Prinzhorn paintings together with modern art as examples of the degenerate, primitive and savage developments in painting that they were trying to stamp out. Indeed, some of those artist/patients were to die in the camps.

DREAMS AND THE TRANSFERENCE

The second major shift in British psychoanalytic thinking that has affected our attitude to dreams has been the increasing focus from the 1950s onward on transference-countertransference issues. In its extreme form, the analyst focuses on the events of the session as it proceeds, scanning the material for the projections and introjections that both block and express the interaction between analyst and patient. Here, the dream is less important for its content than for its place in the session. Is it seen as a gift? Is it an escape? Is it a part of the self being evacuated? Is it a repository for things that cannot be talked about otherwise? Why is it being told at this moment, and in this way? Is the dream the patient's secret possession to which he alone has the key, or does he hand it over passively as something whose meaning belongs to the analyst? How does the relation between analyst and patient find reflection in the dream?

At the same time as this change was occurring, because of the influence of Melanie Klein, there was also an increasing focus in British psychoanalysis on the death instinct and on experience in very early childhood. This meant that the unconscious content of dreams came to be seen as very traumatic and overwhelming to the ego. The early unconscious fantasies that were uncovered were of being attacked by a cruel and archaic superego, which makes us feel terribly ashamed of memories of childhood experiences –

wetting the bed, for instance. I think that this situation is well represented in medieval paintings of hell – the doom paintings found in so many churches remind us of the archaic fantasies that Melanie Klein found to haunt young children. God is the superego dividing us into the good, who cannot do anything except stand around looking relieved, and the bad, who are punished by cruel demons, a fusion of the superego and the id. The demons in Bosch and other painters are the images of nightmares; their vividness derives from the energies of the id. Such nightmarish figures, part man and part animal, often seem to be devouring and shitting out figures through every orifice. The mouth and the anus are equated, as in the child's earliest oral fantasies about birth. The internal angry feelings have been externalized into a multitude of angry persecutors. The blessed, cut off from that 'seething cauldron of impulses', seem lifeless and monotonous by comparison.

Many analysts came to believe that these unconscious phantasies are ubiquitous; because they underlie all thought and feeling, therefore dreams are a less important and special means of communicating them. Also, if the analysis of the transference is seen as the most important thing, dreams, which take place outside the session, are less interesting in themselves than in the way they are used in the session. Vicky Hamilton, in the passage I cited earlier, thinks that in this way we flatten the dream out, and lose its capacity to surprise us, or make us see things anew.

Freud emphasized all his life that we do not really know what a dream means, any more than we can ever know the unconscious mind. The dream, he said, has a navel that joins it to the underworld; the most important part of the dream will always be too deep for us to capture it, because we can never know the unconscious. But if we focus on the transferential aspect of the dream, we tend to interpret from a position of the person who knows, rather than being able to hear about the dream from its author and be surprised by it. The modern tendency is to focus on the telling of the dream as part of the relationship between analyst and patient, and not systematically to ask for associations to the dream. This increases the likelihood that the analyst will be felt to know about the patient's mind through empathy rather than through listening to associations, which remind us that the connections the patient makes to the images in their dreams are to some extent unique to themselves.

I think that dreams, even fragments of dreams, are valuable in analysis precisely because they are produced outside the session. Not only can we notice how the analysis is progressing through changes in dreams, but also things come to light in dreams that have been unconsciously censored in the session. This can happen in surprising ways; I remember a patient who had been in analysis with me for some years, who had recently rather unsuccessfully sold a valuable family heirloom. His dream was apparently a simple wish-fulfilment; he dreamt that the sale had been successful instead. But in recounting it, he was struck by the light in the dream, which reminded him of the light, soft but brilliant, of the winters in Teheran when he was a child. As he went on reminiscing, most unexpectedly a girl appeared, with whom he used to play in an overgrown apricot orchard and enjoy exploring both sexual and aggressive feelings in a way that he had, until that moment, completely forgotten. And this led to recognition of another aspect of his transference to me. Would we ever have reached this material other than via a dream?

For normal and neurotic people, the dream has an imaginative, 'as if' sort of quality. By means of it, they can explore areas of themselves, or feelings about the analyst, which feel hard to acknowledge. 'It was only a dream', they say, just as people say 'it was just a joke'. I find myself reminding them that it was them, after all, who dreamt it, but the untraumatic dream seems a gentle and convincing way of showing them some of the unconscious aspects of their minds. Lewin wrote an influential paper in 1946[12] in which he compared the dream to the projection of an image on a neutral surface, a screen like a cinema screen, which was originally the mother's body. I think that the flat, pale-brown surface found in many surrealist paintings is alluding to this. If we can view the dream as something outside ourselves, as if it were happening on a screen we were watching, we do not feel that we are disrupted and invaded by it. It is when the image seems to fragment, or crumple, or become uncannily still, or when people dream of falling forever, or disintegrating, liquefying and pouring out of their skin, that the containment function of the analyst and the maternal presence seems to fail and the screen, or the skin-ego we imagine round ourselves, is pierced. Then the dream seems to be less separate from us, and becomes more frightening.

I have often been struck by the importance of the spatial dimension in the dream and in the unconscious. Patients seem strongly subliminally aware of the shape of the analyst's consulting-room and its relation to other spaces and, in their dreams, they seem very conscious of the analyst being behind them. Rear-view mirrors in dreams are one way of showing how they wish to check up on us; and seating-arrangements in dreams often show the associations created by the unusual situation in which one person lies down and looks at a blank wall, while the other sits out of sight and sees only the top of their head. One patient came in with a dream in which I appeared as the shark behind the sofa.

The final section of my account of how our views on dreams have changed is the interpretation of symbolism in dreams.

SYMBOLISM IN DREAMS

Freud sometimes interpreted as if there were a universal symbolism, and sometimes not. He starts out *The Interpretation of Dreams* by saying that he is not thinking in the eastern-European tradition of the Dream Book, i.e., the assumption that you can look up in a book what a particular dream means because there is a fixed and universal symbolic language. But in his interpretations of dreams, he sometimes asserts that a given image has a fixed meaning; boxes and hollow closed spaces standing for the vagina, etc. Jung thought that there was a universal language of mankind revealed in myths, visions and dreams because dreams were messages, not only from the self, but also from the collective unconscious. Freud, who was always anxious after his rift with Jung to dissociate himself from him, can be seen in the case-history of the Wolf Man veering back and forth as to whether there was indeed a phylogenetic inheritance of unconscious fantasy, or whether our dreams refer back to our specific histories.

In an influential paper, Ernest Jones[13] argued that the situations that are symbolized in dreams are quite limited; they refer to the universal human experiences of living in our bodies, birth, death and procreation, and our earliest family relationships. Energy flows from these ideas via the channel of symbolism to all other ideas. But symbolic systems themselves shift and change, moving in and out of consciousness. Even Victorian paintings can sometimes puzzle us with their imagery. 'The Daydream' is a beautiful water-colour of William Morris's wife Janey, painted in 1880 by Dante Gabriel Rossetti, by that stage using laudanum and much obsessed by her. The painting contains at least two symbolic orders, the first of which would be more apparent to the Victorians, the second to us. The first is the language of flowers, or perhaps the Pre-Raphaelite view of the medieval world, of why it is that the woman is holding honeysuckle, and what the particular species of bush is that surrounds her. This would have been in the conscious mind of the painter and his contemporaries, but these symbolisms are now largely forgotten. I can only speculate about why he chose these plants. We know that Rossetti dreamt all his life of a dark-haired beauty in whom he could bury himself: whose daydream is this? However our post-Freudian eyes register the sensuous dreaminess in the face – Victorian genre painters had an extraordinary capacity to render human expression – and notice the phallic quality of the stick she is caressing.

It is certainly true that many dreams seem to contain ideas of the human body. A patient troubled about his potency dreamt of driving through a dark threatening underground passage to a safe car-park. Another told her Kleinian analyst of a dream of marching soldiers; they were marching, she said, 'eight a-breast'. An analyst tells of his patient's dream of a multitude of red and white soldiers fighting; quite astonishing because the next day, the patient was diagnosed as suffering from leukaemia. Patients certainly seem to recover in analysis images of birth, and the sea does often seem to stand for the mother in whose amniotic fluid we all swim. These ideas of the body are subject to different kinds of symbolic disguise, showing and denying at the same time.

There is a famous painting by René Magritte, which exists in various versions, called 'The Treachery of Images'. On a flat, pale-brown dream-screen floats an image of a pipe, painted in the hyper-reality of an advertisement, or an illustration in a children's book. Underneath is written, 'This is not a pipe'. Magritte wanted to use his painting to challenge everyday notions of the solidity and familiarity of reality. He uses his skill, and every pictorial device, to make us believe that this is a pipe. But he writes underneath that it is not a pipe. And of course it isn't, but if it isn't, what is it? It illustrates Freud's idea of negation – the thing which is denied is the thing that is. And yet it is not. It reminds us of the oddity of dream images. Somebody comes in and says, 'last night I dreamt of a woman who looked like my mother, but it wasn't her – she was in this room, but it was also the garden shed at home', and we know what they mean.

Like other analysts, I have been struck by the importance of the animals who appear in dreams. People who dream of small smashed fragments of animals, multitudes of insects, invertebrates who have a hard shell and a soft inside like snails, seem to be telling us about their sense of a fragmented self, or one with a tough armour to protect its lack of internal structure. Wholer patients seem more likely to dream of vertebrates. I remember a most important, crucial dream of a patient who dreamt he was inside a gorilla-suit in which he could act in a freer, more spontaneous way, and this dream was a turning-point in his ability to come to terms with his animal nature.

Hanna Segal tells a story of a psychiatrist interviewing a mental patient who was a violinist, and asking him why he never played the violin any more. He replied that he didn't want to masturbate in public. That is, the analogy between a woman's body and a violin had become too concrete; he couldn't liberate himself from it. If we cannot know that a symbol is not what is symbolized, we cannot think.

Figures 14.3 and 14.4 are two levels of symbolism around the same idea. Figure 14.3 is a photograph by Man Ray from 1924 called 'Le Violon d'Ingres'. It alludes to the wonderful Ingres painting 'La Baigneuse', which beautifully conjures up a woman's passive flesh, and to the similarity between the shape of her back and of the violin, both of which can be brought to life by the fingers. The second image (Fig. 14.4) is another Magritte, 'Le Viol', painted in 1934. It is an image he drew many times slightly differently, and which other artists have used as well. It is a much more disturbing picture; we expect to see a face and see something different. It is even more perturbing to babies, whom we now know to be pre-wired, so to speak, to notice and read the human face. Like the medieval pictures of demons, this painting equates bodily orifices with each other. In this particular version though not in others, the woman's head and neck also resemble a penis. Magritte maintained he named his pictures at random, but 'Le Viol' not only sounds like Violin again, as if that association was in his mind, but it also means The Rape. It puts the spectator in the position of the rapist, who obliterates the woman's face beneath his perception of her body, and may

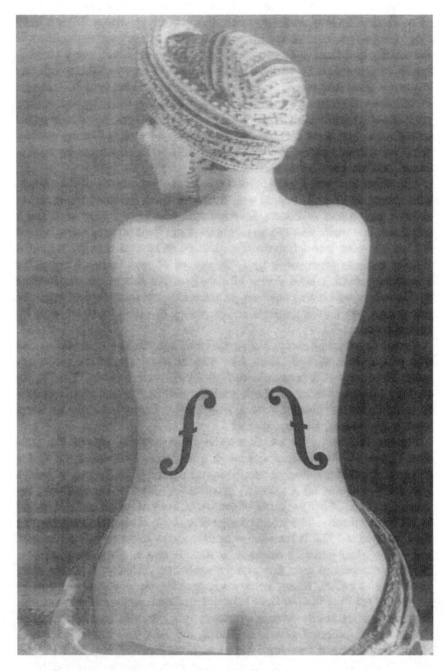

Figure 14.3 Man Ray, 'Le Violon d'Ingres', 1924, Man Ray Trust/ADAGP, Paris and DACS, London 1999.

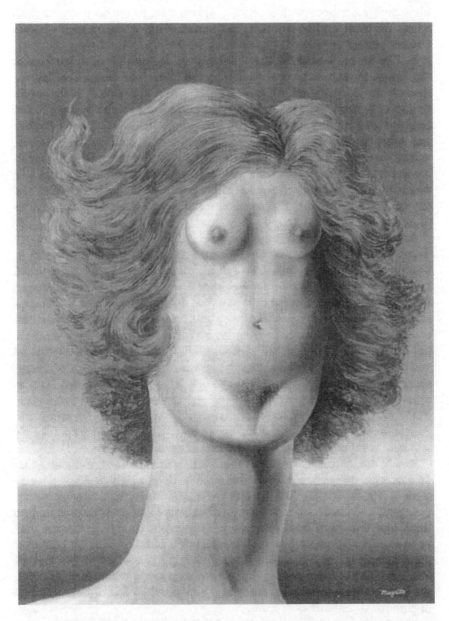

Figure 14.4 René Magritte, 'Le Viol', 1934. Copyright © ADAGP, Paris and DACS, London
1999.

also confuse her body with a penis. It also alludes to the deep unconscious where the sexes and bodily parts get muddled up, where women's bodies contain penises anyway.

In Ella Sharpe's book on dreams, based on lectures given to students at the British Psycho-Analytical Society in the 1930s, she points out that the mechanisms of transformation of dreams, which are related to the mechanisms of defence, are akin to literary ideas. Dreams exhibit synonyms and similes, they pun, they take the part for the whole and so on. Charles Rycroft and other authors in the Independent tradition, such as Marion Milner, valued the dream for its creativity, its capacity to turn thoughts into narrative and images. They equated the dream far more to creative play than to a disguised wish; and indeed Freud, in his paper on the creative writer and daydreams, speculated that the reason we are so fascinated by and envious of artists and writers is because they seem to us to play all day.

Analysts do not now always look behind the manifest content of the dream for the hidden symbolism. We now think that the dreamer may be directly representing his current, adult dilemmas in life. Freud came round to this view in 1920, when he distinguished dreams from above from dreams from below, perhaps recalling the classical distinction between the dreams that come through the gates of ivory and of horn. Indeed, the manifest content of his own dreams as recorded in *The Interpretation of Dreams* are full of his adult dilemmas; his responsibilities as a doctor, his intellectual and political ambitions. This change brings the psychoanalytic view of dreams nearer to the romantic view that they are worthwhile in their own right as a part of our creative imagination, our capacity to reflect and fictionalize. Many dreams seem semi-lucid, scarcely transformed by the dream-work. Patients report that they edit them; say to themselves in their sleep, it's only a dream, it should end this way, and dream again, and so on.

Recent dream research suggests that we should not abandon the idea that dreams refer to past memories saturated with powerful feeling. Dreams seem to appear for the first time in the higher mammals, together with a perceptual code and long-term memory the ability to store: memories, retrieve them, and thus learn from experience. Their evolutionary significance may be as a pre-verbal method of recalling past difficulties to us as we mull over present dangers. As Freud thought, a dream image is apparently a layered one, consisting of a day-residue superimposed on a stored long-term memory, the links between them being made at a pre-verbal level by auditory, visual or emotional similarities or puns.

Men and women have always known that there is something very important about dreams, and will doubtless go on wondering how to interpret them, inside psychoanalysis and out. There is something inexhaustible about them, just as Freud said; and doubtless as psychoanalytic theory and technique changes, the way that we are told dreams, and the way that we interpret them, will change as well. It is comforting to reflect that dreams themselves are not quite so plastic. I end with a typically caustic observation from Freud's 1923 remarks on dream interpretation: 'I think that in general it is a good plan occasionally to bear in mind the fact that people were in the habit of dreaming before there was such a thing as psychoanalysis'.[14]

NOTES AND REFERENCES

This chapter is the revised version of a lecture given in an introductory lecture series held annually at the Institute of Psychoanalysis, London. I am grateful to the then convenor of the series, Antonio Fazio, for giving me the opportunity and incentive to write it. I am also grateful to Philippa Lewis and Helen Scott Lidgett for having helped an amateur with the illustrations, and to the various copyright holders for permission to reproduce the images.

1 V. Hamilton, *The Analyst's Preconscious*, New York, 1996.
2 Ibid., p. 283.
3 E. Sharpe, *Dream Analysis*, London, 1937.
4 D. Ades, *Dali*, London, 1995, p. 82.
5 See, for example, the papers presented to the Ninth International Psychoanalytic Conference on Psychoanalytic Research, University College London, March 1999.
6 S. Ferenczi, 'Dreams of the unsuspecting', in *Further Contributions to the Theory and Technique of Psychoanalysis*, London, 1926. (First published 1916/17.)
7 E. Jones, *On the Nightmare*, London, 1931.
8 H. Segal, 'Notes on symbol formation', *Delusion and Artistic Creativity*, London, 1986.
9 S. Ferenczi, 'On the revision of The Interpretation of Dreams', Part 3 of Notes and Fragments in *Final Contributions to the Theory and Technique of Psychoanalysis*, London, 1931.
10 M. Parsons, 'Do we think our dreams? Do we dream our thinking?', 1997, unpublished public lecture.
11 R. Fairbairn, 'Endopsychic structure considered in terms of object relationships', *International Journal of the Psychoanalytic Association* 25, 1944, reprinted in *Psychoanalytic Studies of the Personality*, London, 1952.
12 B. Lewin, 'Sleep, the mouth and the dream screen', *Psychoanalytic Quarterly* 15, 1946.
13 E. Jones, 'The theory of symbolism', *Papers on Psychoanalysis*, London, 1916.
14 S. Freud, 'Remarks on the theory and practice of dream interpretation' (1923), SE 19.

Index

Lightning Source UK Ltd.
Milton Keynes UK
UKOW03f2255071013

218635UK00002B/21/P